RENT-A-GIRLFRIEND

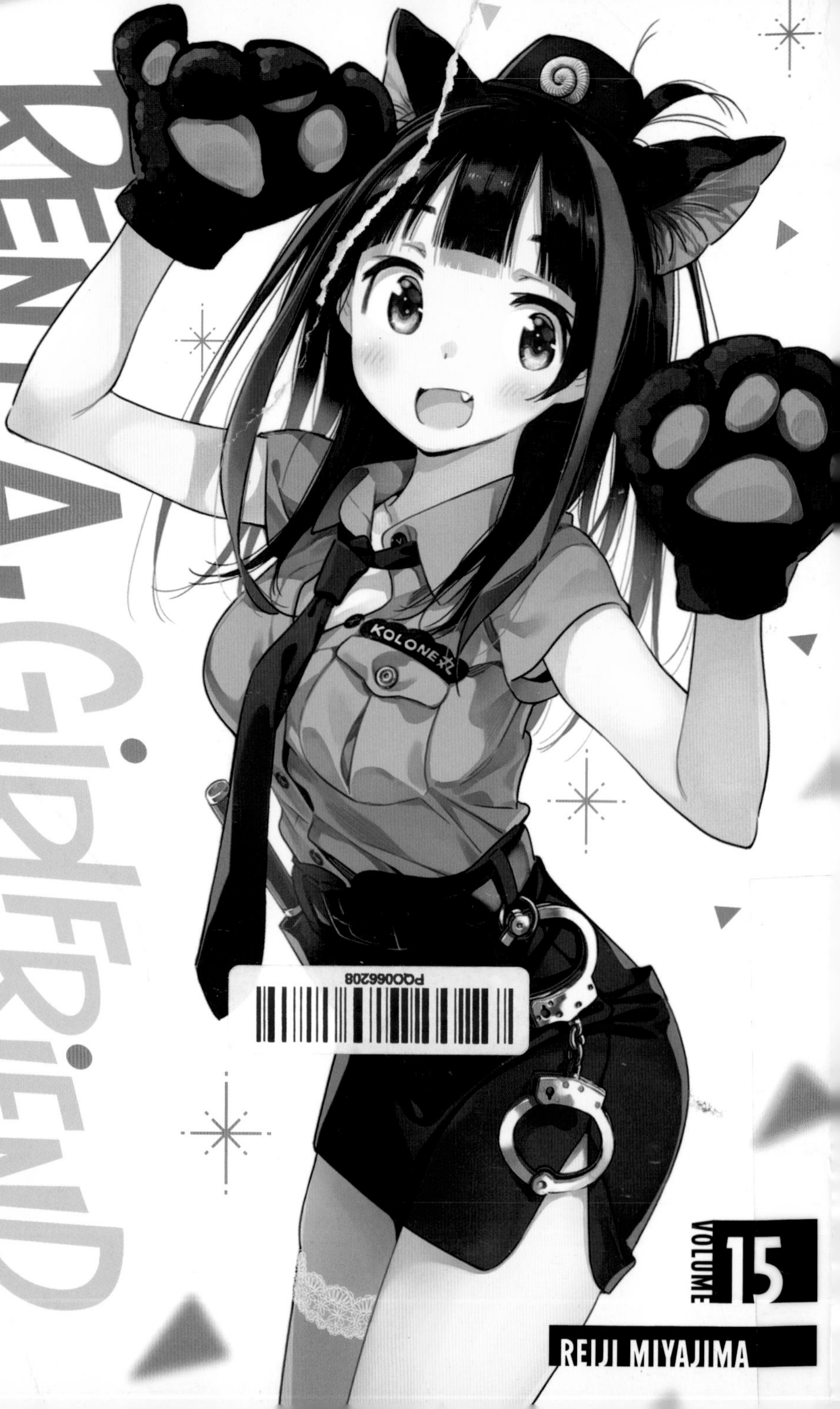
KOLONEX

VOLUME 15

REIJI MIYAJIMA

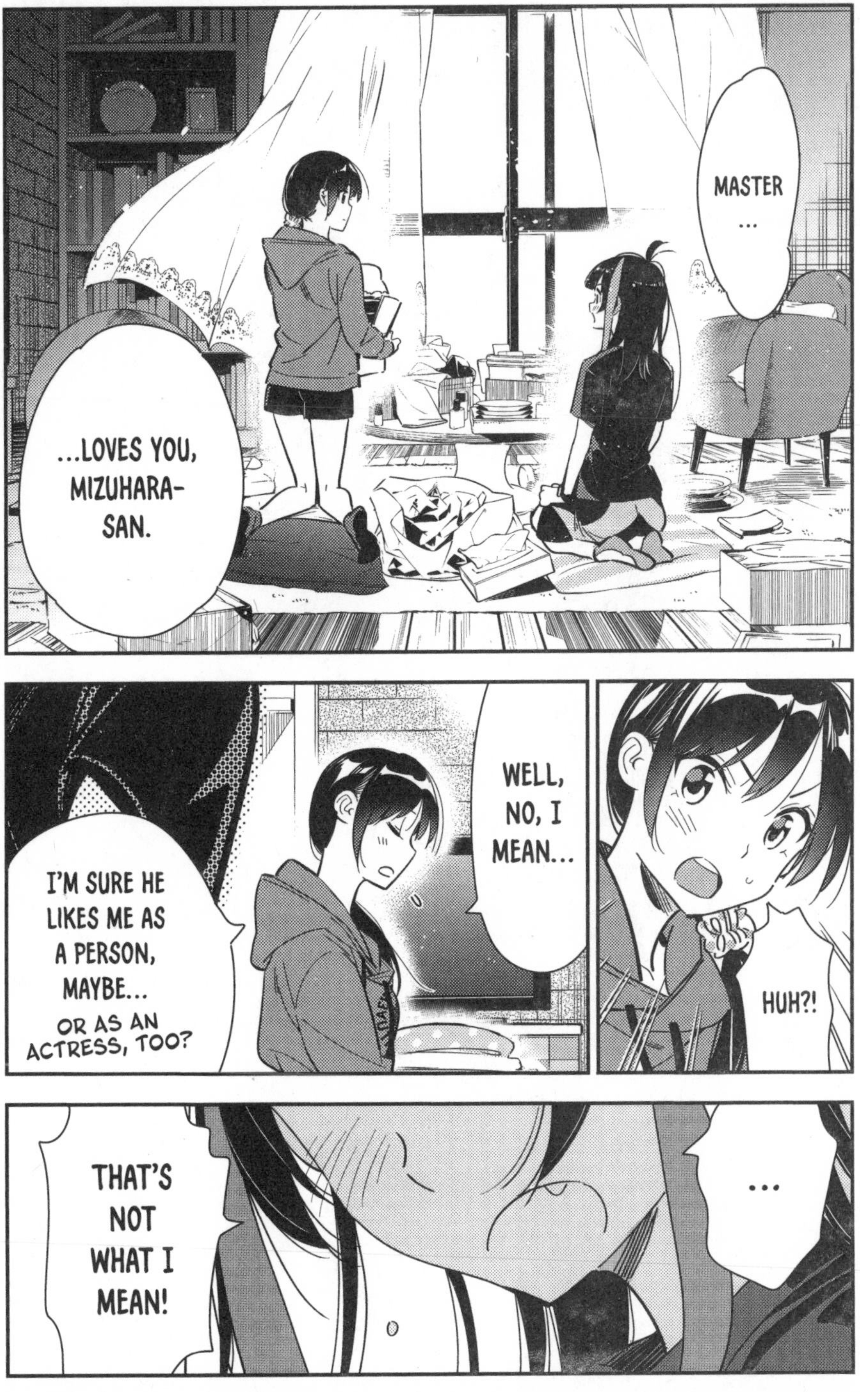
MASTER ...
...LOVES YOU, MIZUHARA-SAN.
HUH?!
WELL, NO, I MEAN...
I'M SURE HE LIKES ME AS A PERSON, MAYBE...
OR AS AN ACTRESS, TOO?
...
THAT'S NOT WHAT I MEAN!

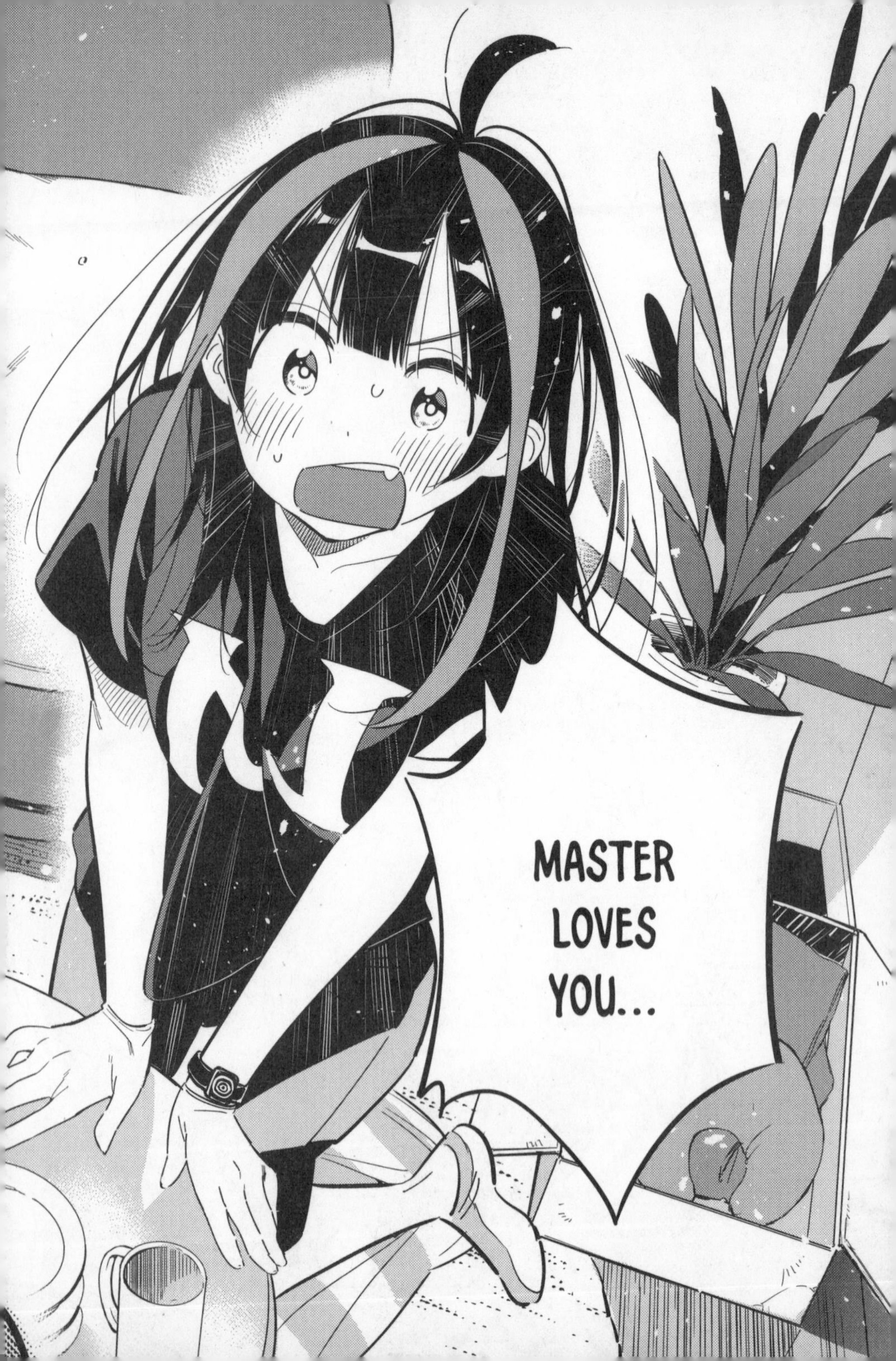
MASTER
LOVES
YOU...

RATING 122 MY GIRLFRIEND AND ROOM 204 2

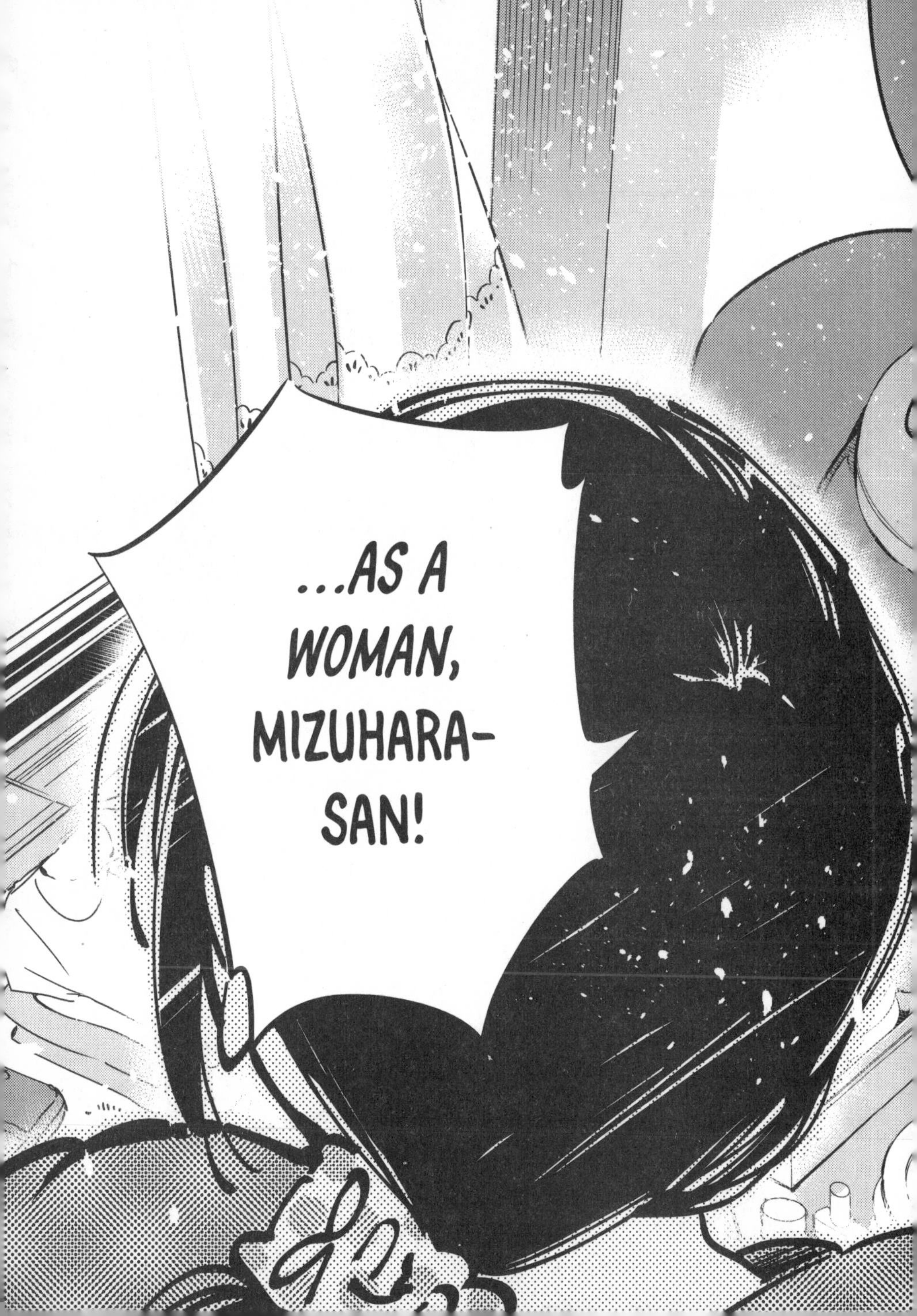
...AS A WOMAN, MIZUHARA-SAN!

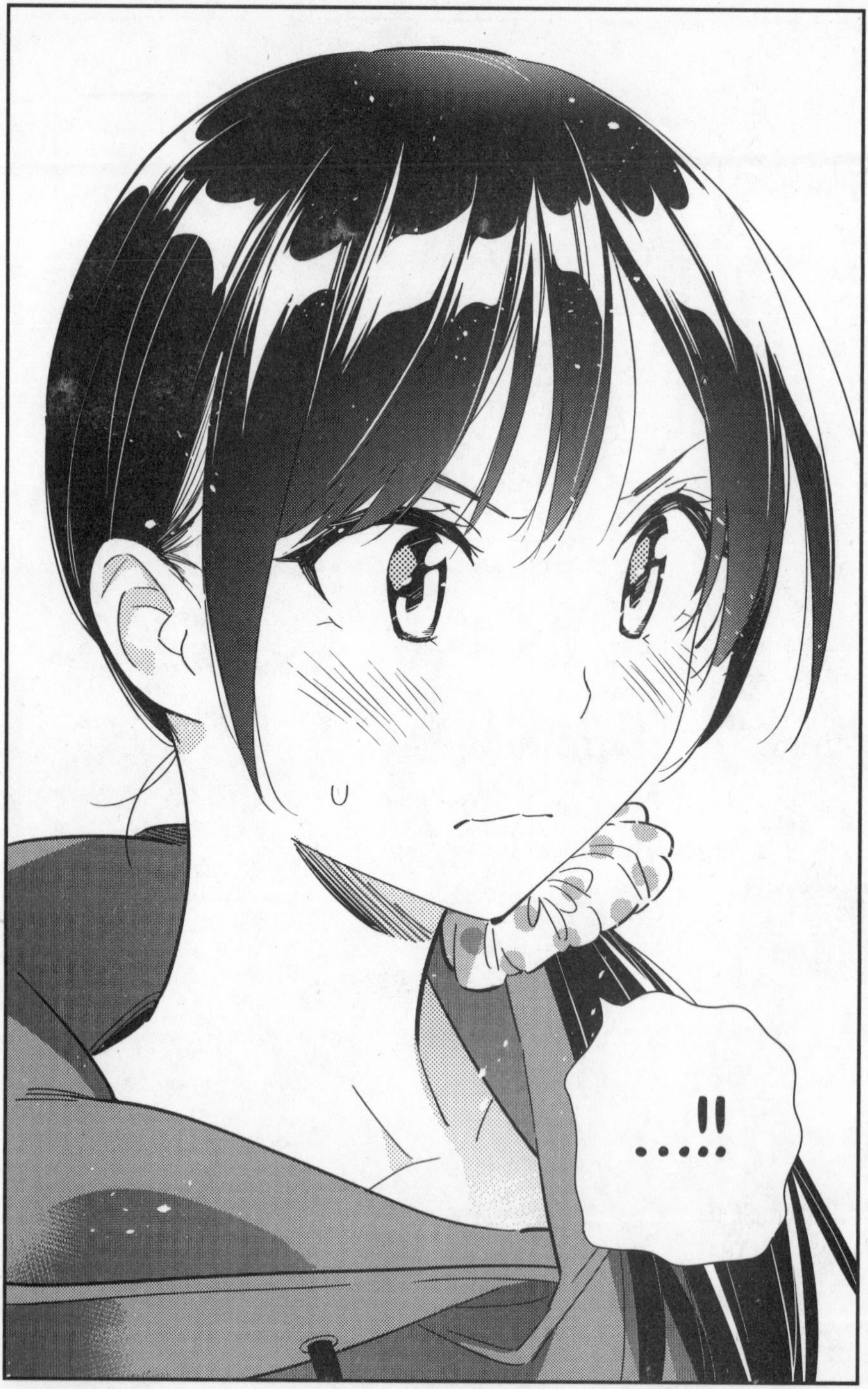
.....!!

HUH?

THAT'S NOT POSSIBLE.

I ASKED HIM THAT ONCE, YOU KNOW. WHETHER HE LOVED ME.

BECAUSE IF HE DID, THAT WOULD CHANGE THINGS...

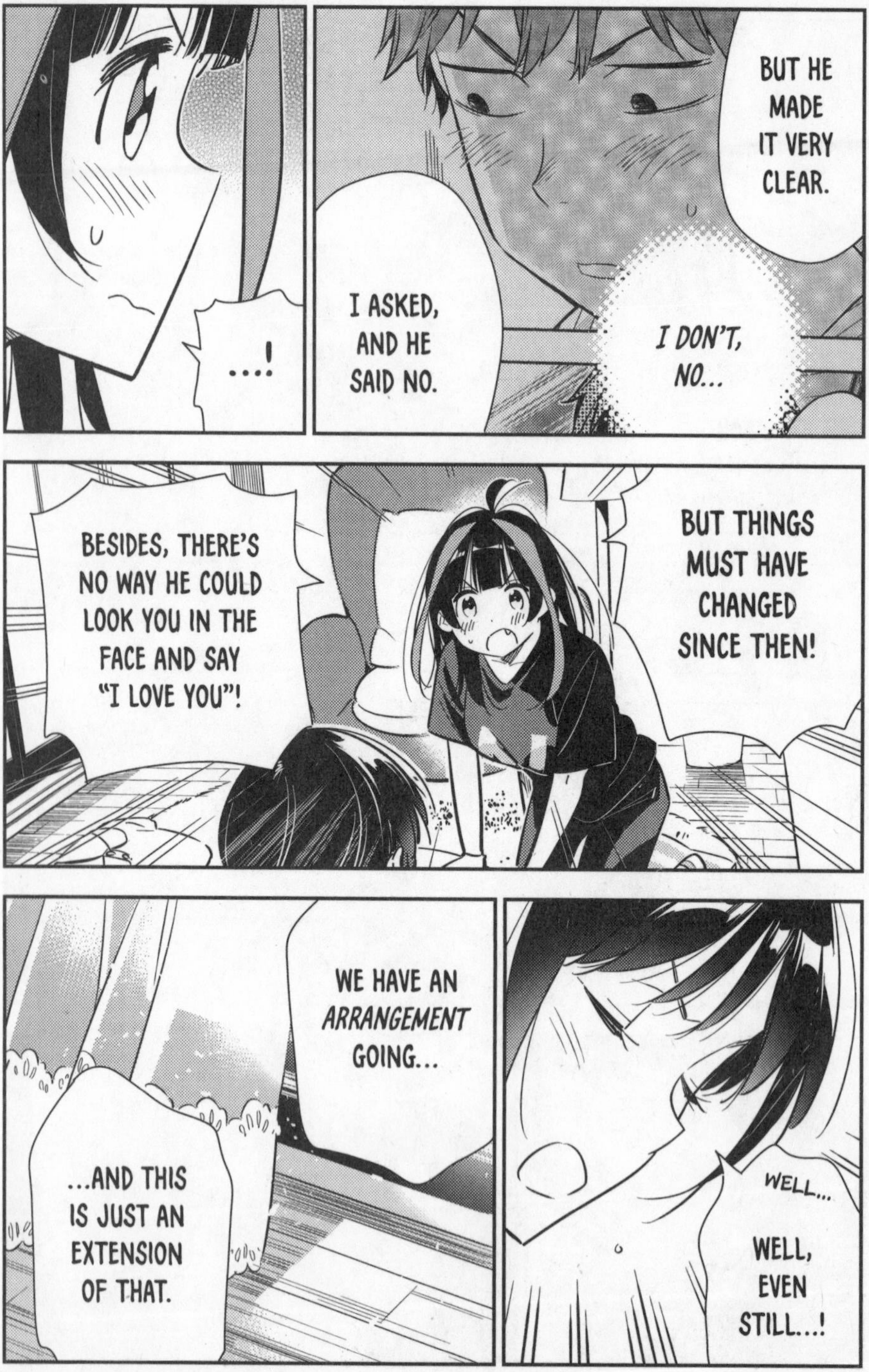
BUT HE MADE IT VERY CLEAR.
I DON'T, NO...
I ASKED, AND HE SAID NO.
...!
BUT THINGS MUST HAVE CHANGED SINCE THEN!
BESIDES, THERE'S NO WAY HE COULD LOOK YOU IN THE FACE AND SAY "I LOVE YOU"!
WELL...
WELL, EVEN STILL...!
WE HAVE AN *ARRANGEMENT* GOING...
...AND THIS IS JUST AN EXTENSION OF THAT.

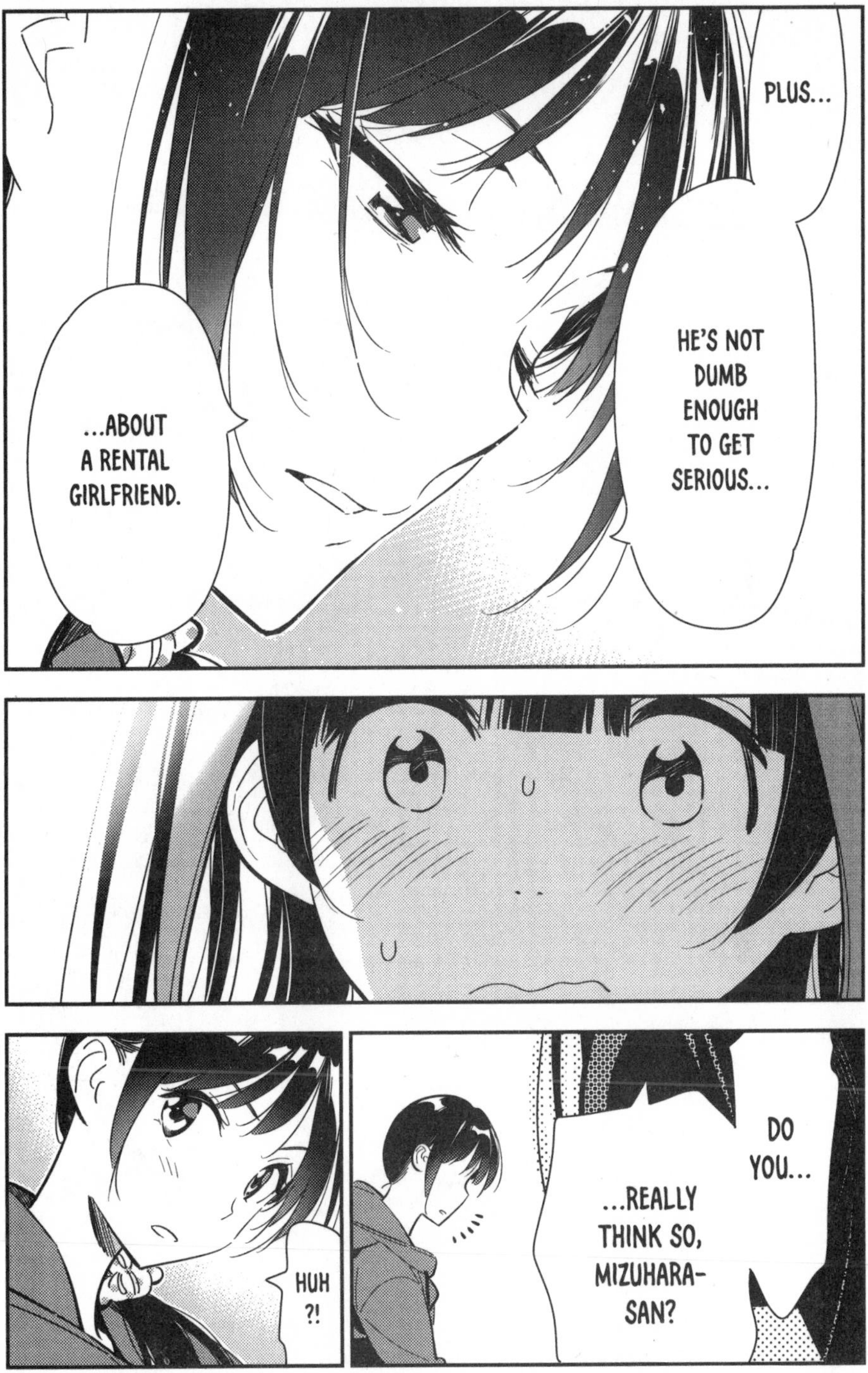
PLUS...
HE'S NOT DUMB ENOUGH TO GET SERIOUS...
...ABOUT A RENTAL GIRLFRIEND.
DO YOU...
...REALLY THINK SO, MIZUHARA-SAN?
HUH?!

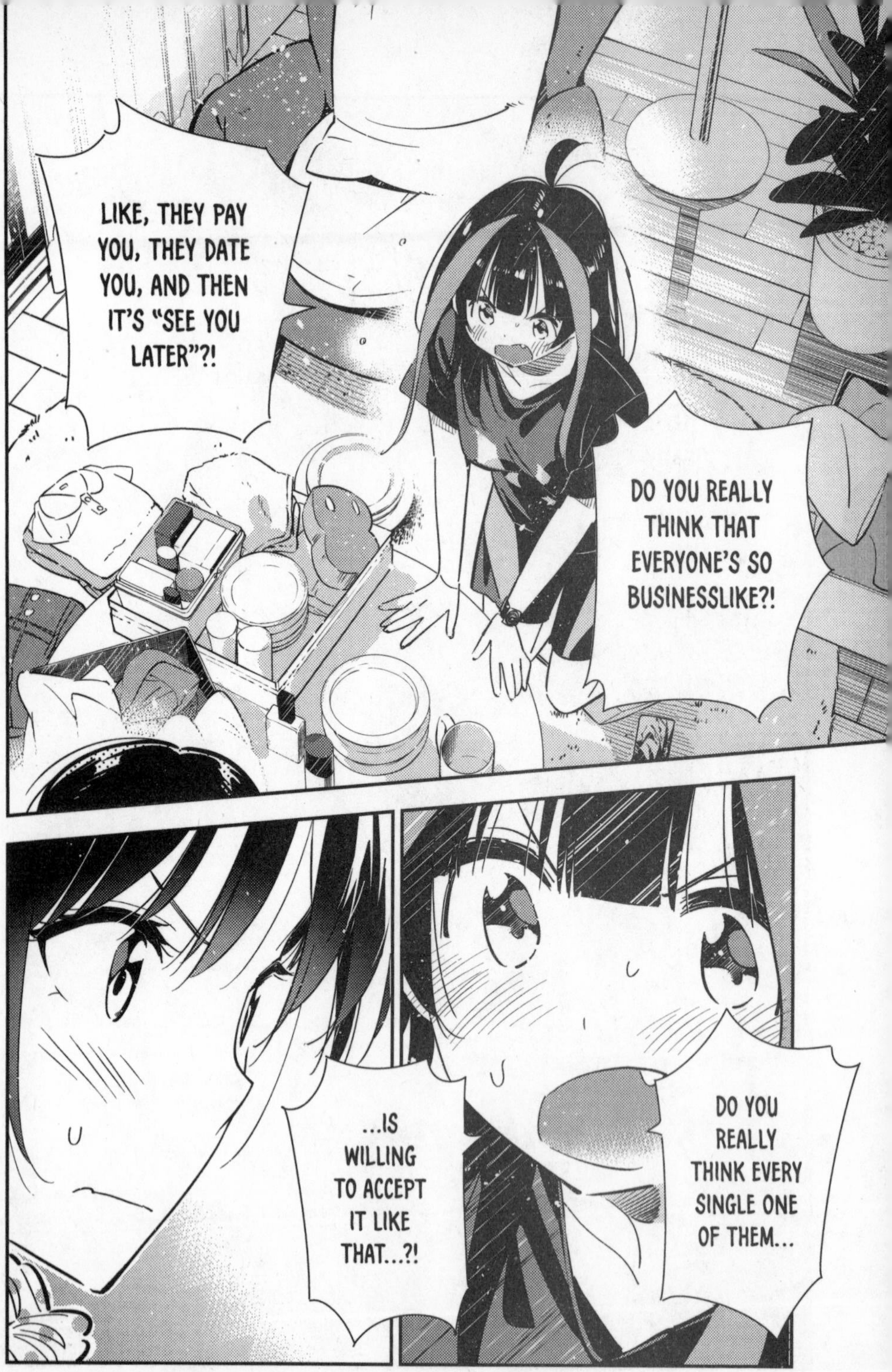
LIKE, THEY PAY YOU, THEY DATE YOU, AND THEN IT'S "SEE YOU LATER"?!
DO YOU REALLY THINK THAT EVERYONE'S SO BUSINESSLIKE?!
DO YOU REALLY THINK EVERY SINGLE ONE OF THEM...
...IS WILLING TO ACCEPT IT LIKE THAT...?!

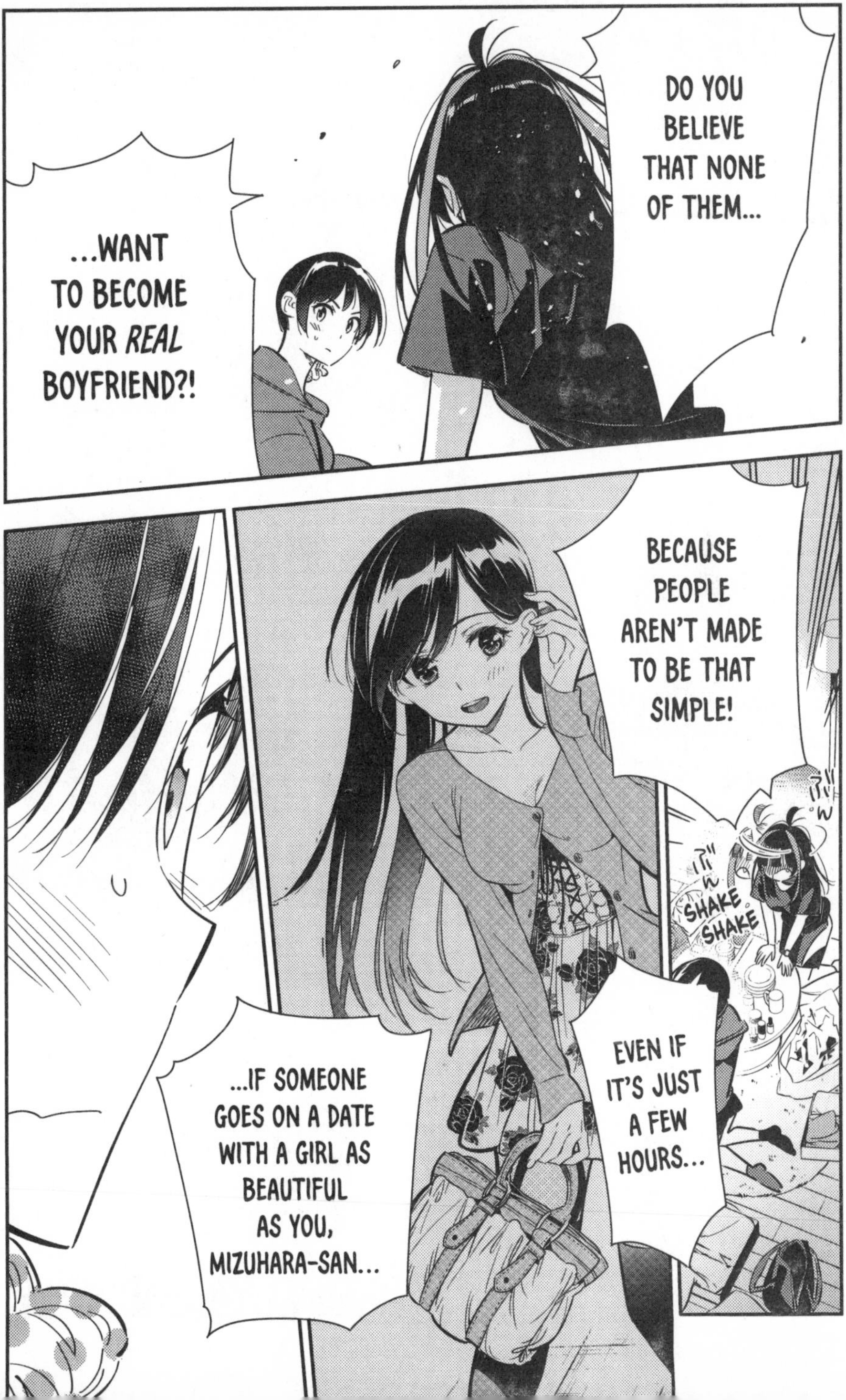
DO YOU BELIEVE THAT NONE OF THEM...
...WANT TO BECOME YOUR *REAL* BOYFRIEND?!
BECAUSE PEOPLE AREN'T MADE TO BE THAT SIMPLE!
SHAKE SHAKE
EVEN IF IT'S JUST A FEW HOURS...
...IF SOMEONE GOES ON A DATE WITH A GIRL AS BEAUTIFUL AS YOU, MIZUHARA-SAN...

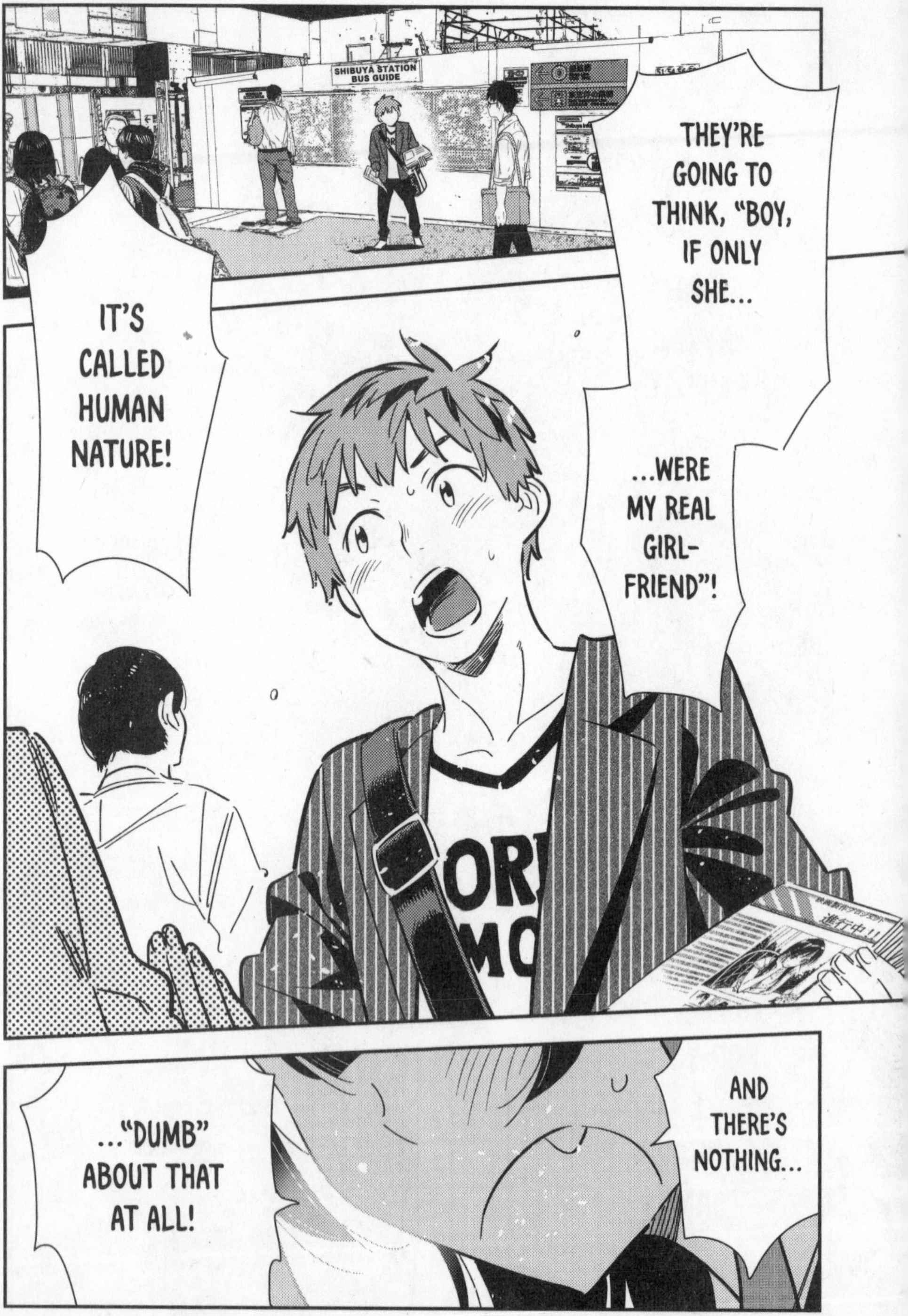
SHIBUYA STATION BUS GUIDE
THEY'RE GOING TO THINK, "BOY, IF ONLY SHE...
...WERE MY REAL GIRL-FRIEND"!
IT'S CALLED HUMAN NATURE!
AND THERE'S NOTHING...
..."DUMB" ABOUT THAT AT ALL!

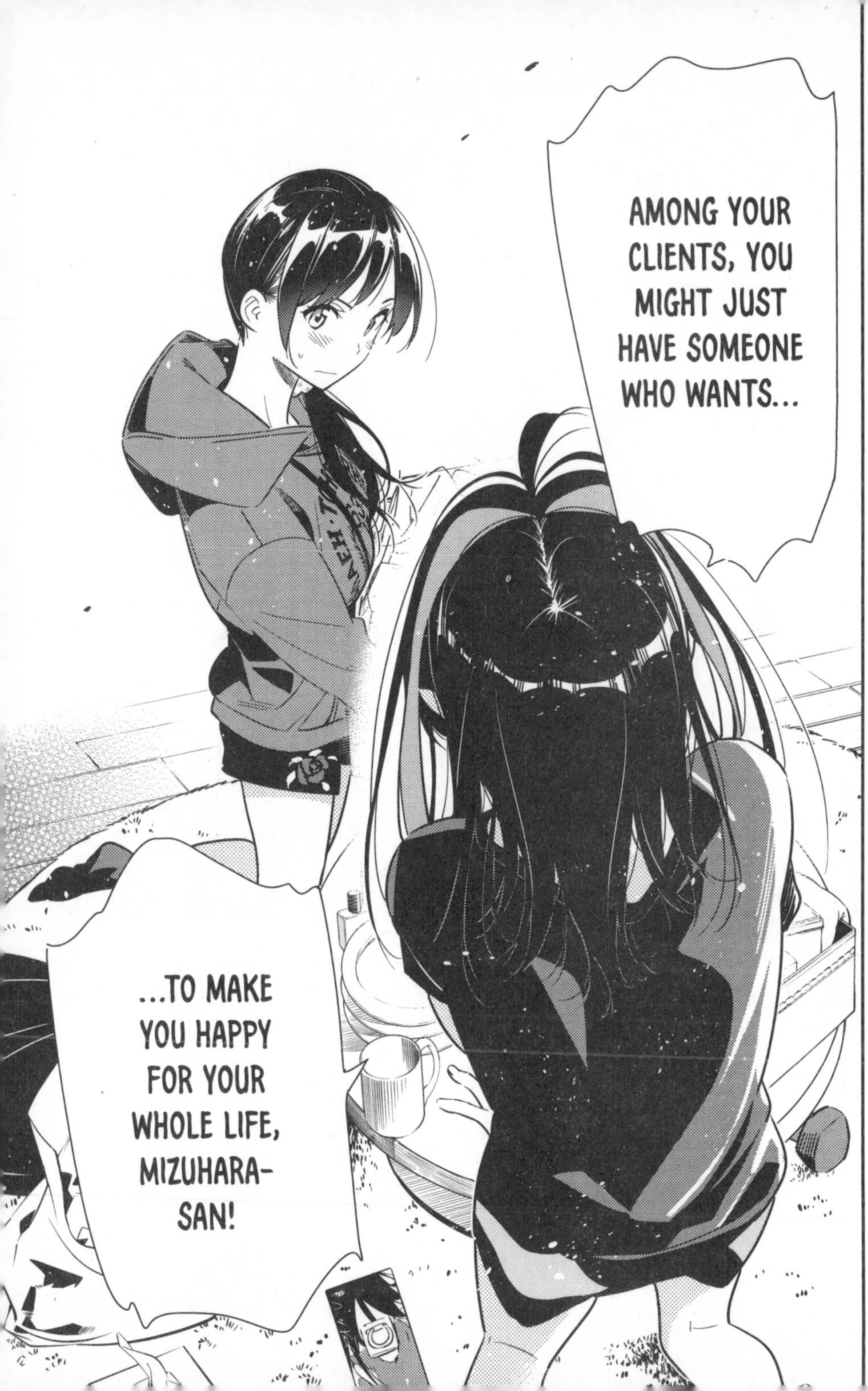
AMONG YOUR CLIENTS, YOU MIGHT JUST HAVE SOMEONE WHO WANTS...
...TO MAKE YOU HAPPY FOR YOUR WHOLE LIFE, MIZUHARA-SAN!

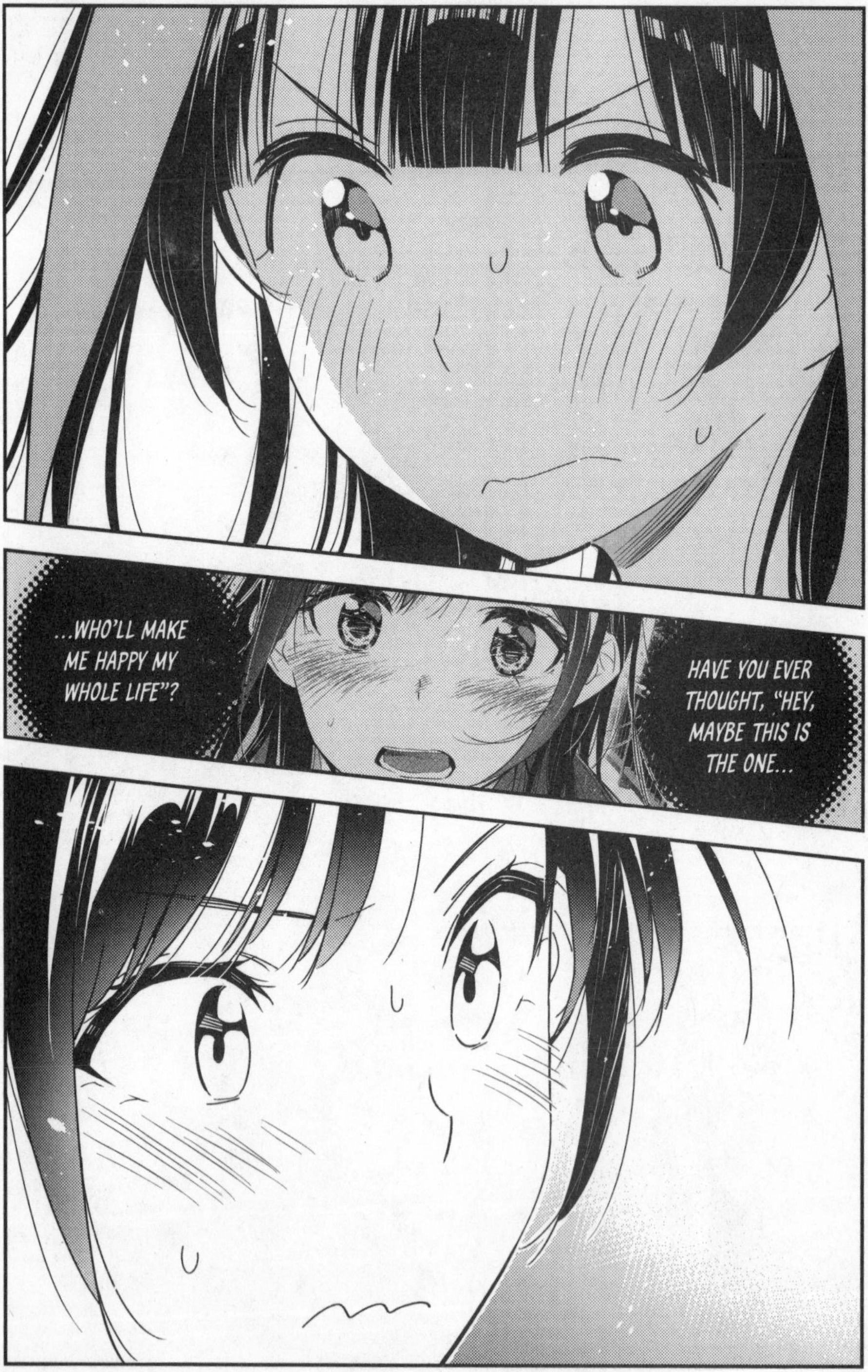
HAVE YOU EVER THOUGHT, "HEY, MAYBE THIS IS THE ONE...
...WHO'LL MAKE ME HAPPY MY WHOLE LIFE"?

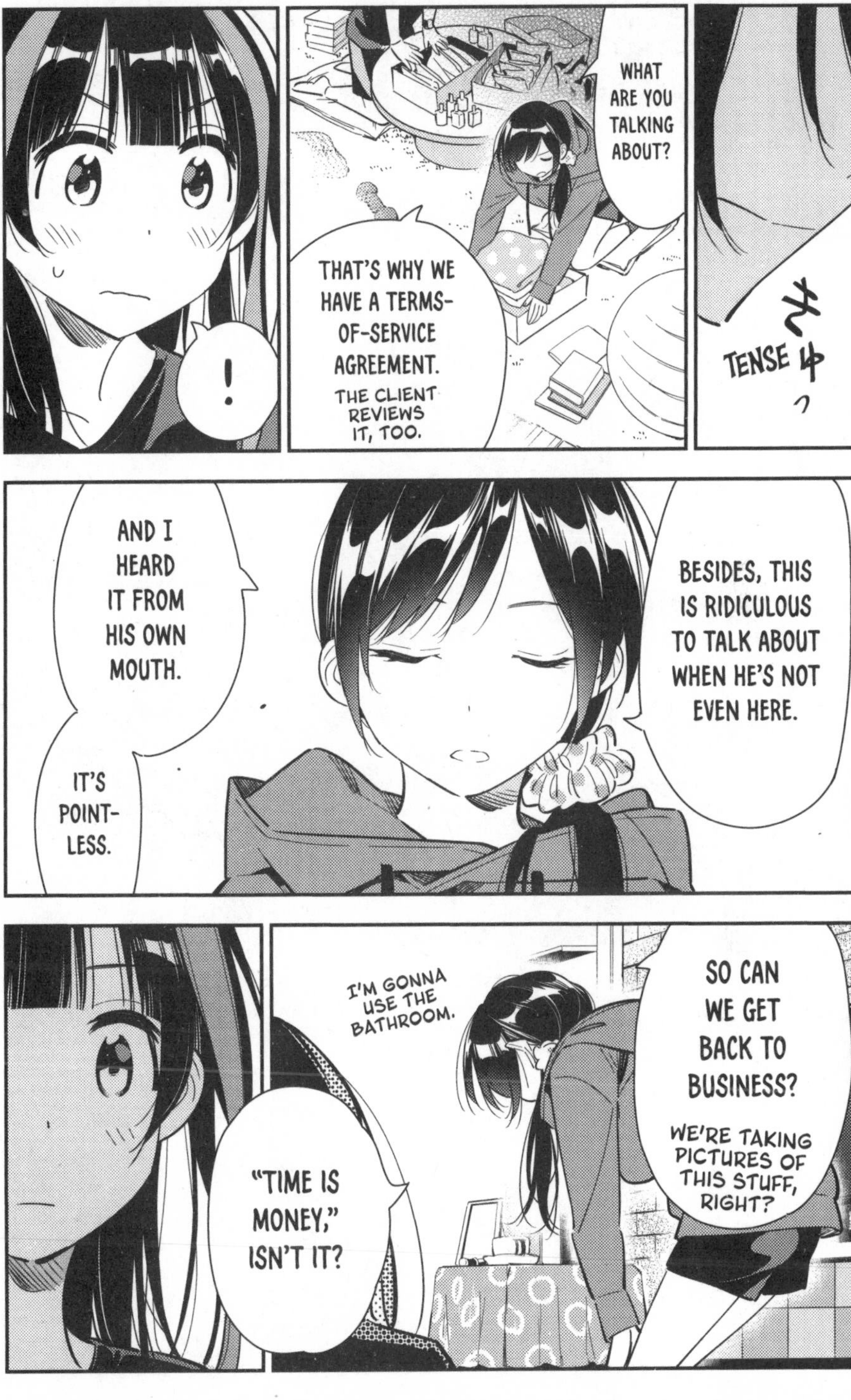
TENSE
きゅっ
WHAT ARE YOU TALKING ABOUT?
THAT'S WHY WE HAVE A TERMS-OF-SERVICE AGREEMENT.
THE CLIENT REVIEWS IT, TOO.
!
BESIDES, THIS IS RIDICULOUS TO TALK ABOUT WHEN HE'S NOT EVEN HERE.
AND I HEARD IT FROM HIS OWN MOUTH.
IT'S POINTLESS.
SO CAN WE GET BACK TO BUSINESS?
WE'RE TAKING PICTURES OF THIS STUFF, RIGHT?
I'M GONNA USE THE BATHROOM.
"TIME IS MONEY," ISN'T IT?

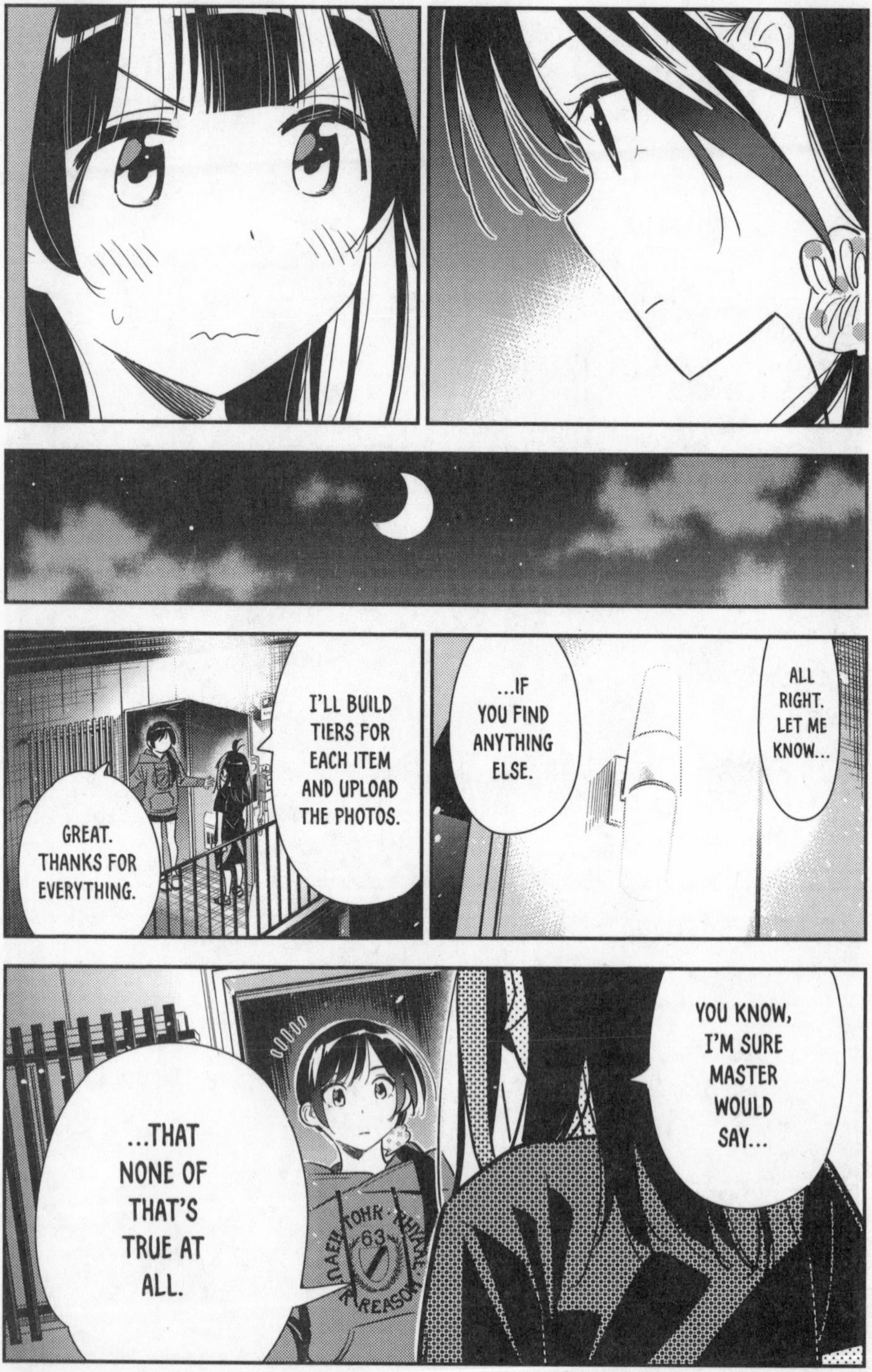
ALL RIGHT. LET ME KNOW...
...IF YOU FIND ANYTHING ELSE.
I'LL BUILD TIERS FOR EACH ITEM AND UPLOAD THE PHOTOS.
GREAT. THANKS FOR EVERYTHING.
YOU KNOW, I'M SURE MASTER WOULD SAY...
...THAT NONE OF THAT'S TRUE AT ALL.

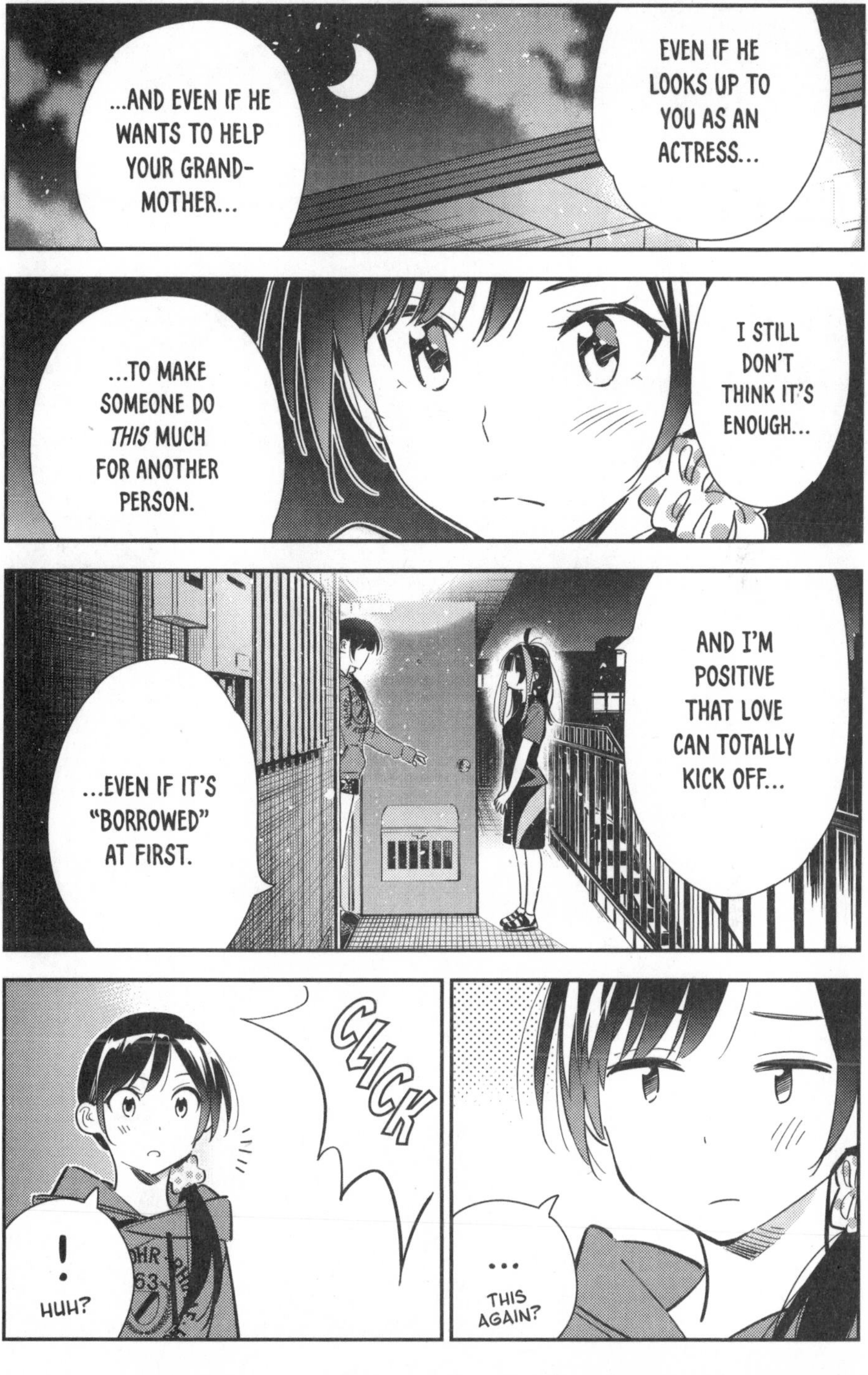
EVEN IF HE LOOKS UP TO YOU AS AN ACTRESS...
...AND EVEN IF HE WANTS TO HELP YOUR GRAND-MOTHER...
I STILL DON'T THINK IT'S ENOUGH...
...TO MAKE SOMEONE DO *THIS* MUCH FOR ANOTHER PERSON.
AND I'M POSITIVE THAT LOVE CAN TOTALLY KICK OFF...
...EVEN IF IT'S "BORROWED" AT FIRST.
... THIS AGAIN?
CLICK
! HUH?

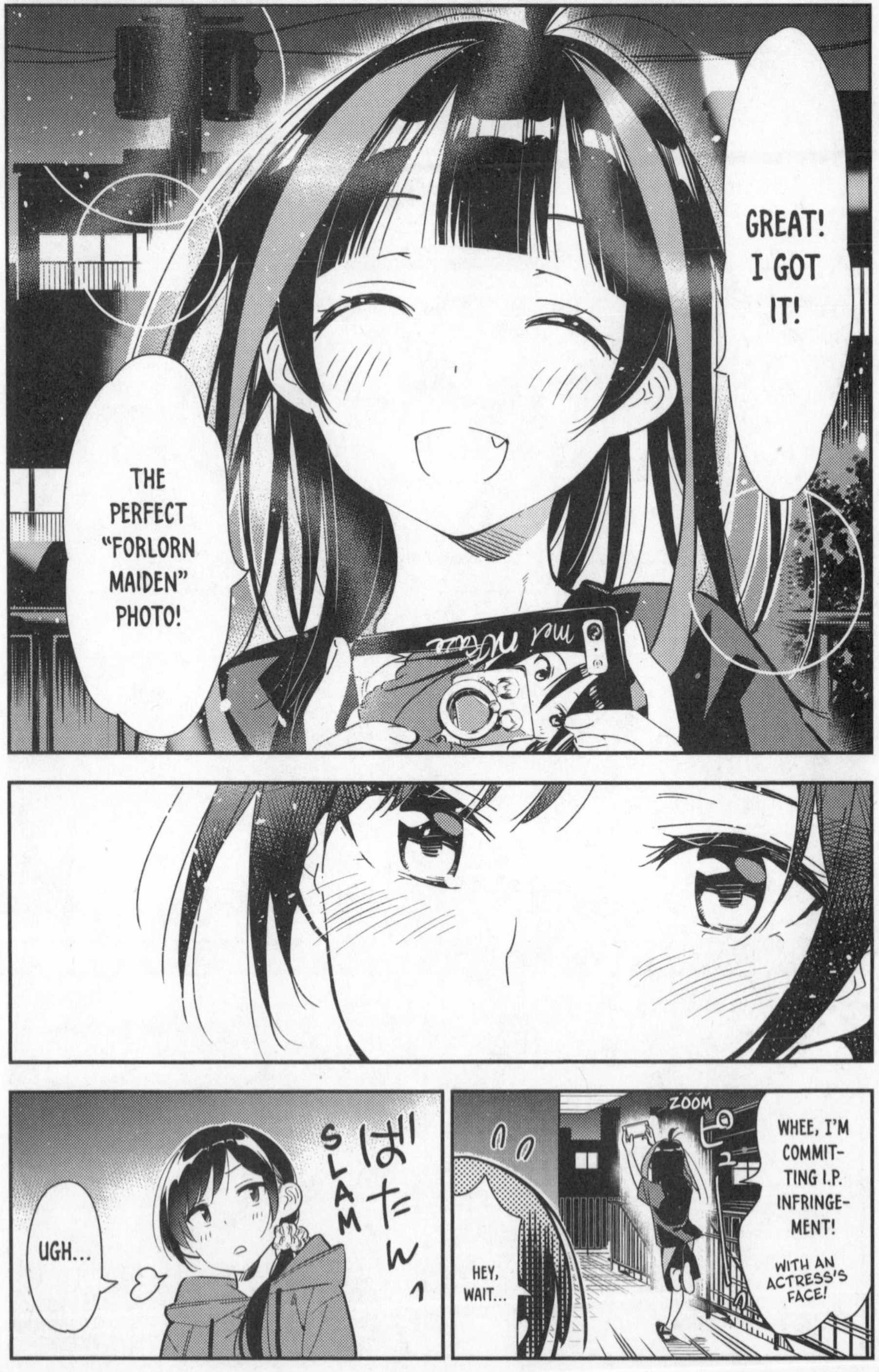
GREAT! I GOT IT!
THE PERFECT "FORLORN MAIDEN" PHOTO!
ZOOM
WHEE, I'M COMMITTING I.P. INFRINGEMENT!
WITH AN ACTRESS'S FACE!
HEY, WAIT...
ばたん
SLAM
UGH...

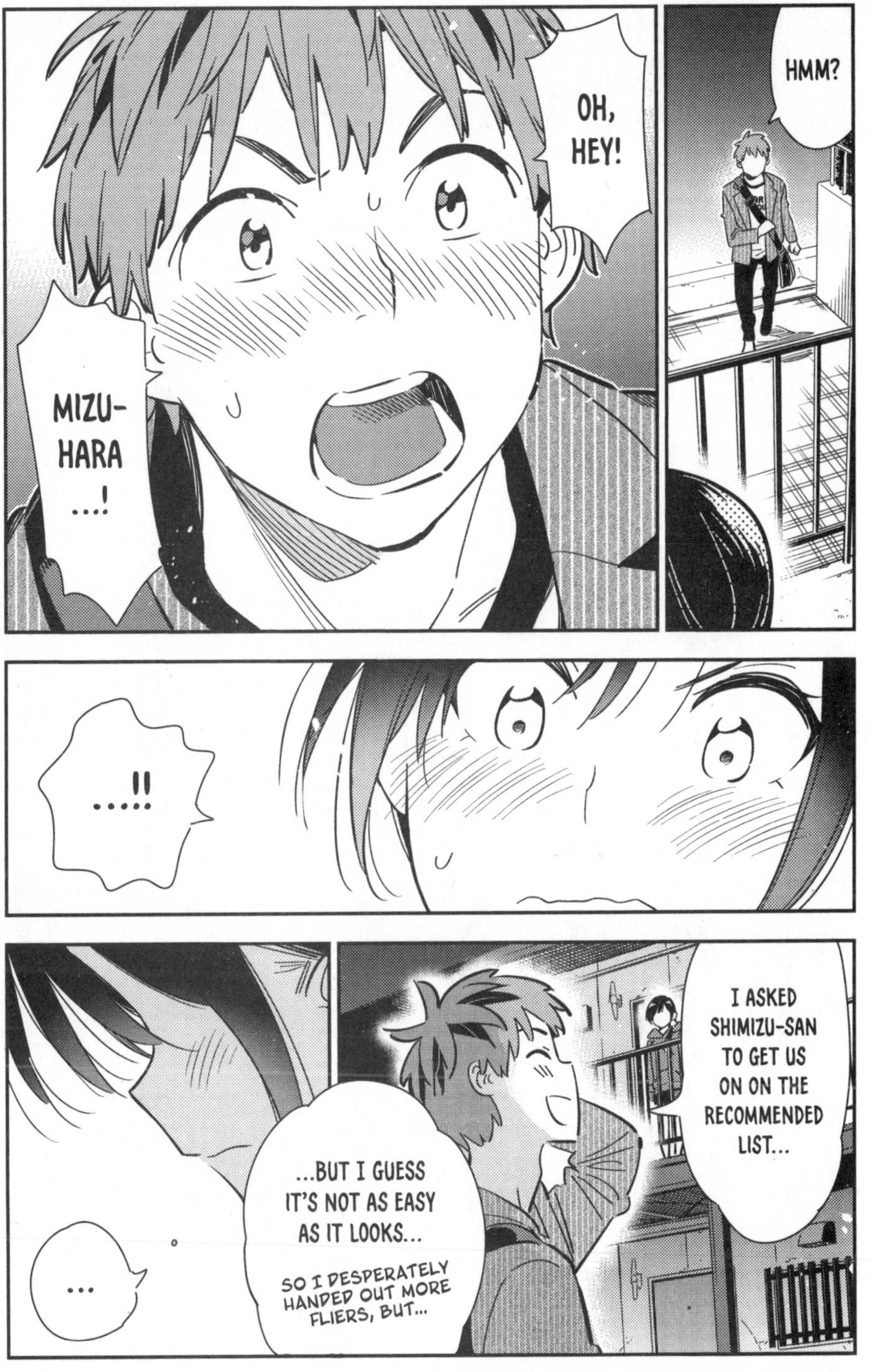
HMM?
OH, HEY!
MIZU-HARA ...!
....!!
I ASKED SHIMIZU-SAN TO GET US ON ON THE RECOMMENDED LIST...
...BUT I GUESS IT'S NOT AS EASY AS IT LOOKS...
SO I DESPERATELY HANDED OUT MORE FLIERS, BUT...
...

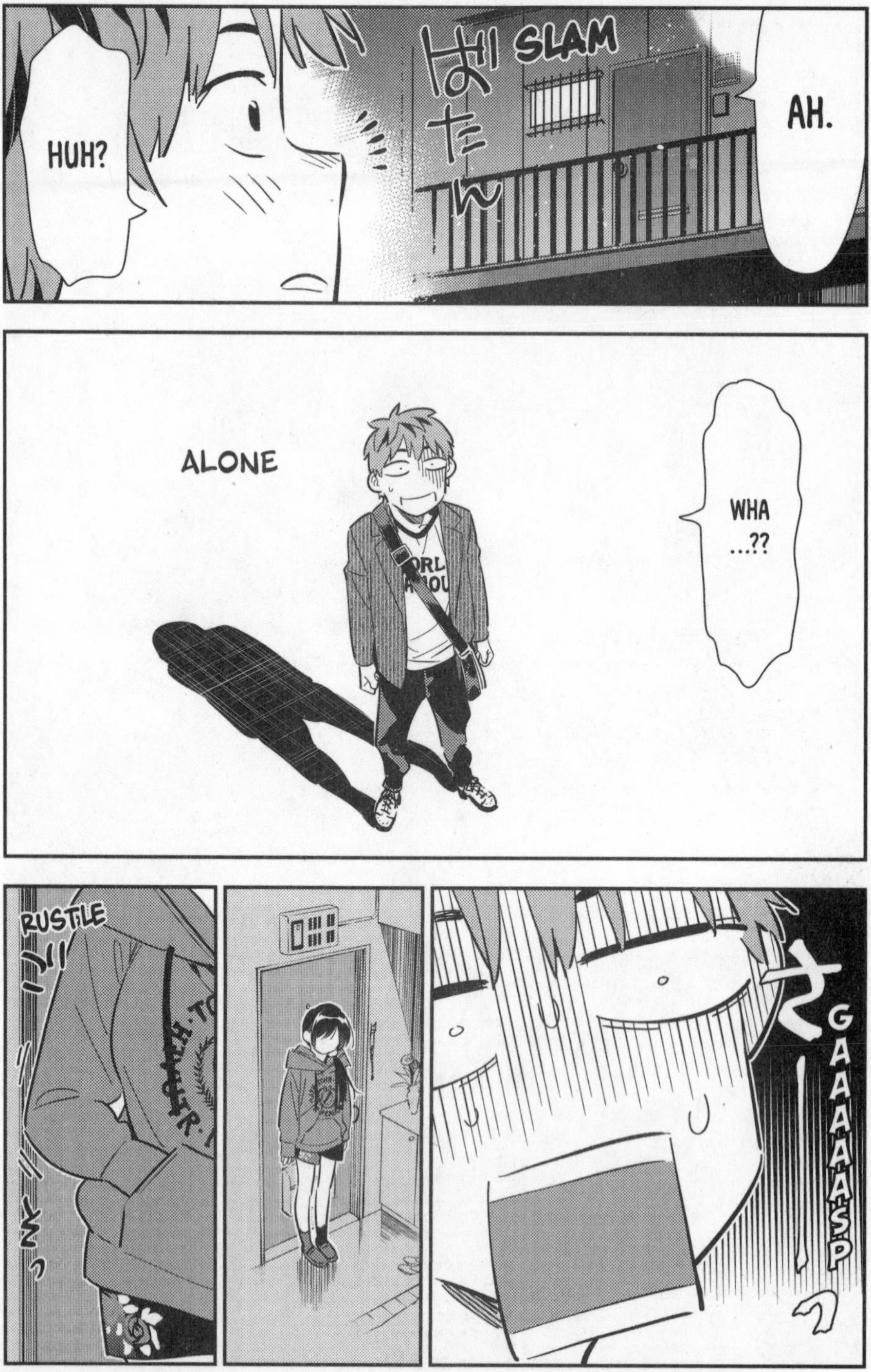
AH.
SLAM
ぱたん
HUH?
WHA ...??
ALONE
GAAAAAASP
RUSTLE

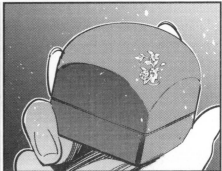

...EVEN IF IT'S "BORROWED" AT FIRST.

I'M POSITIVE THAT LOVE CAN TOTALLY KICK OFF...

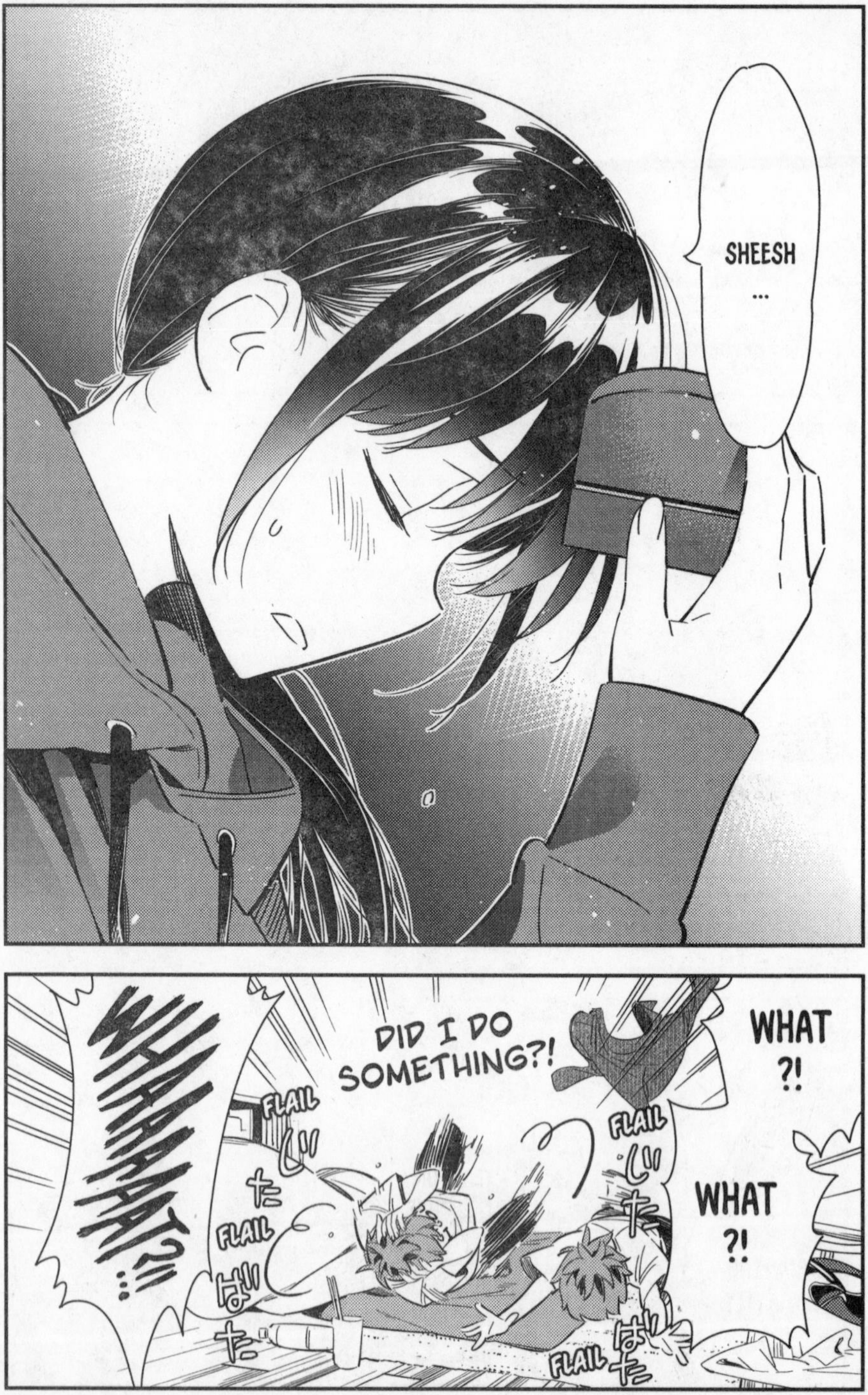
SHEESH ...
WHAT ?!
WHAT ?!
FLAIL
FLAIL
DID I DO SOMETHING?!
FLAIL
FLAIL
WHAAAAAT?!!

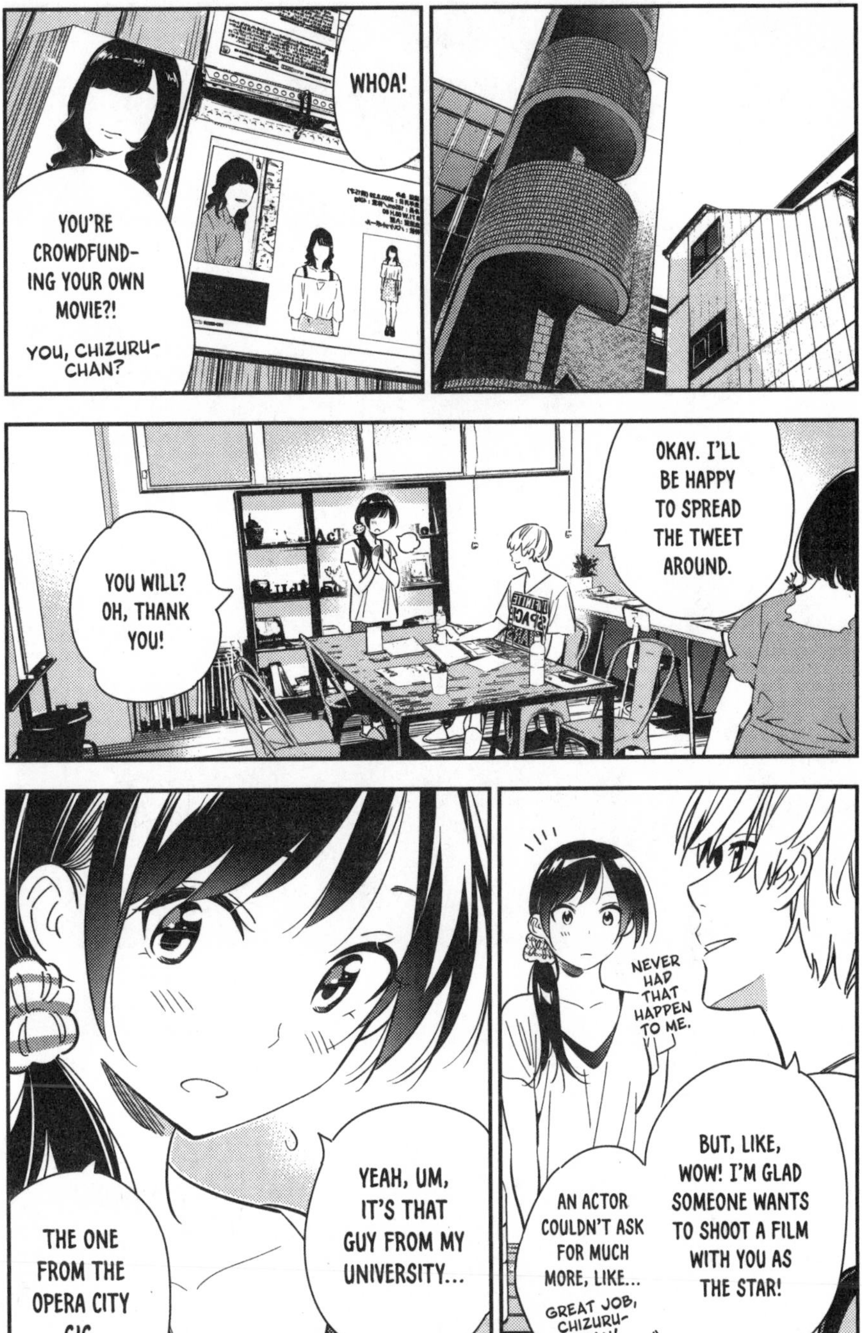
WHOA!
YOU'RE CROWDFUNDING YOUR OWN MOVIE?!
YOU, CHIZURU-CHAN?
OKAY. I'LL BE HAPPY TO SPREAD THE TWEET AROUND.
YOU WILL? OH, THANK YOU!
NEVER HAD THAT HAPPEN TO ME.
BUT, LIKE, WOW! I'M GLAD SOMEONE WANTS TO SHOOT A FILM WITH YOU AS THE STAR!
AN ACTOR COULDN'T ASK FOR MUCH MORE, LIKE...
GREAT JOB, CHIZURU-CHAN!
YEAH, UM, IT'S THAT GUY FROM MY UNIVERSITY...
THE ONE FROM THE OPERA CITY GIG.

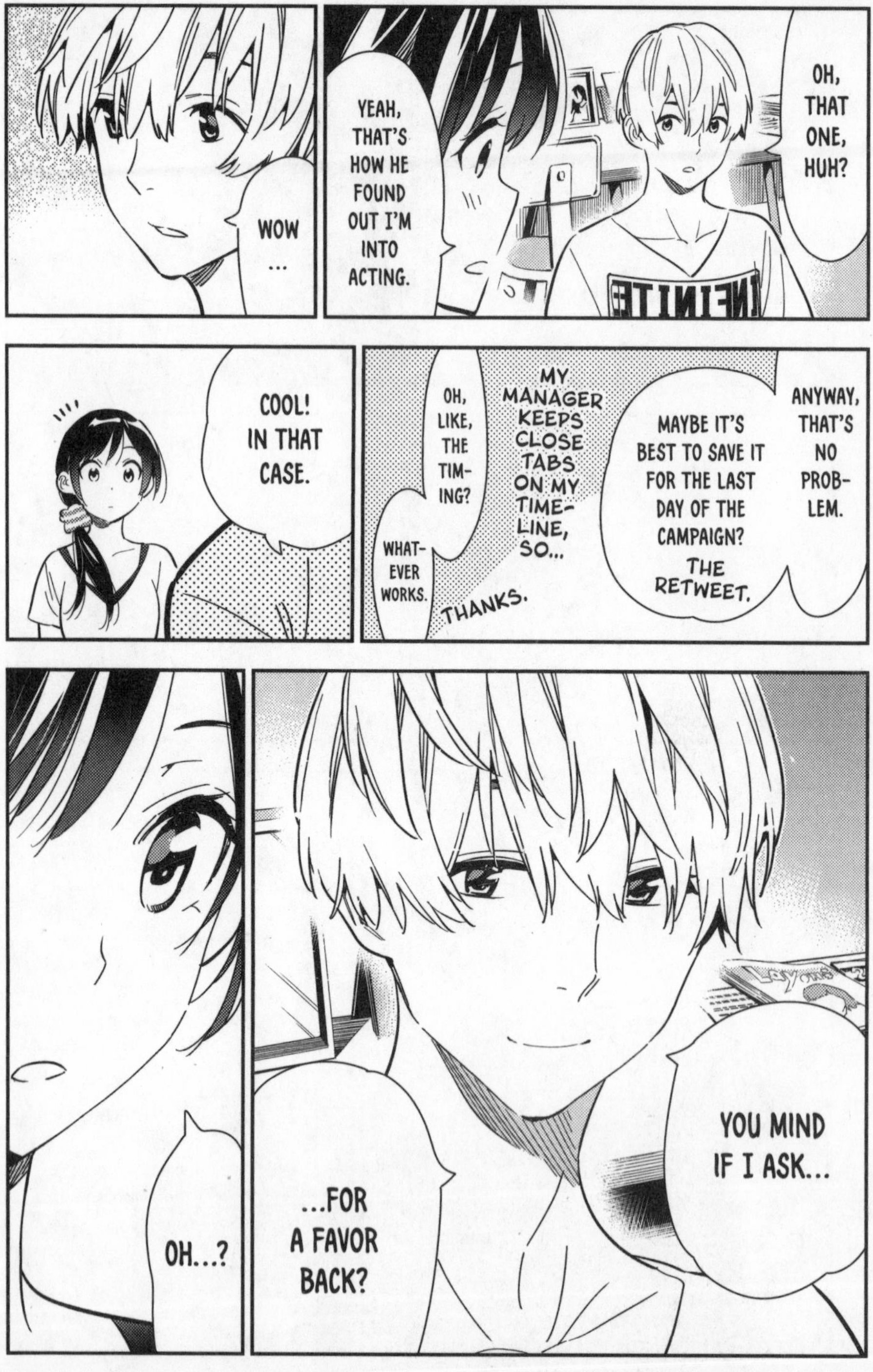
OH, THAT ONE, HUH?
YEAH, THAT'S HOW HE FOUND OUT I'M INTO ACTING.
WOW ...
ANYWAY, THAT'S NO PROBLEM.
MAYBE IT'S BEST TO SAVE IT FOR THE LAST DAY OF THE CAMPAIGN?
THE RETWEET.
MY MANAGER KEEPS CLOSE TABS ON MY TIMELINE, SO...
OH, LIKE, THE TIMING?
WHATEVER WORKS.
THANKS.
COOL! IN THAT CASE.
YOU MIND IF I ASK...
...FOR A FAVOR BACK?
OH...?

RATING 123
THE FINAL DAY AND MY GIRLFRIEND 1

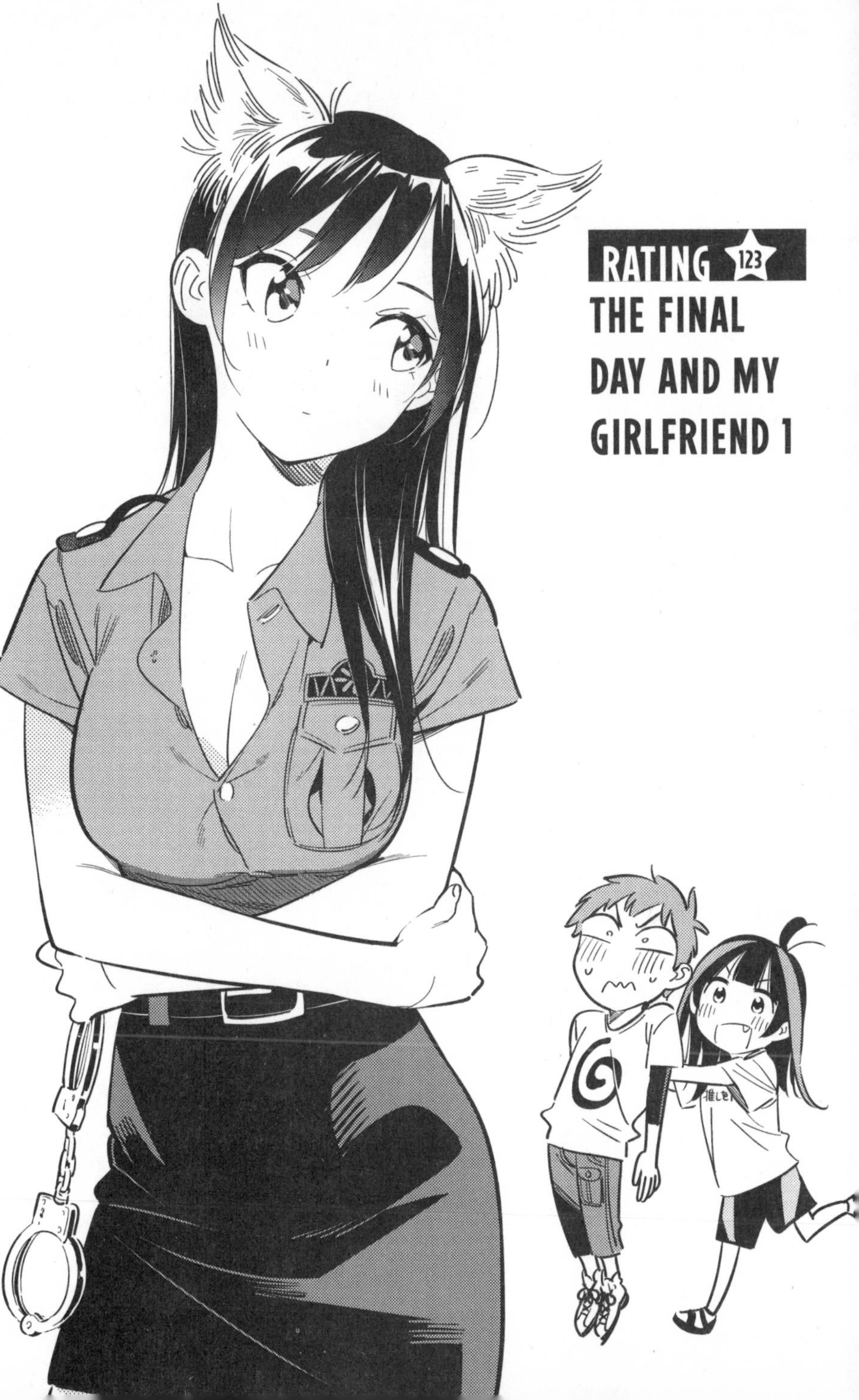

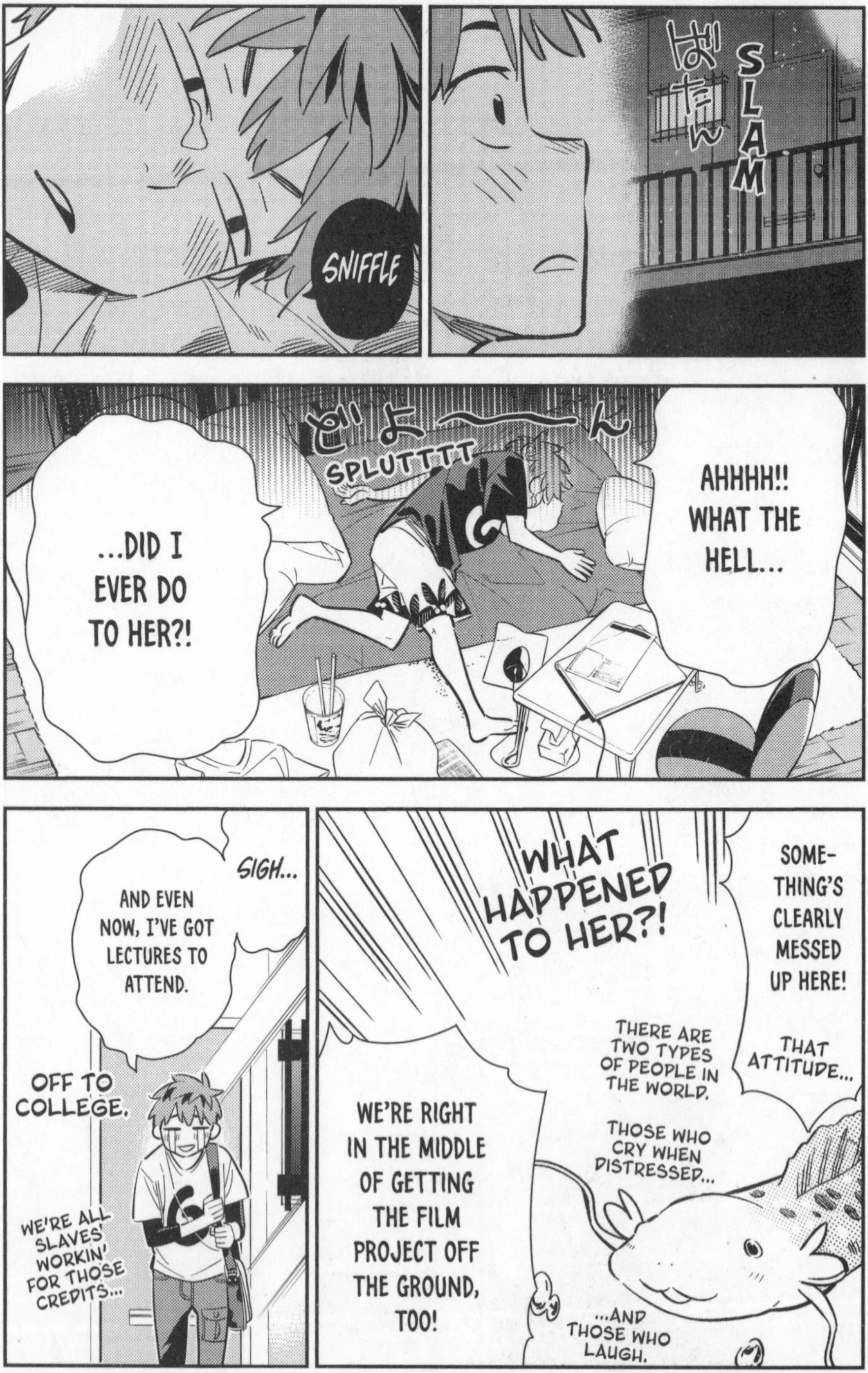
ばたん
SLAM
SNIFFLE
どよ〜〜ん
SPLUTTTT
AHHHH!! WHAT THE HELL...
...DID I EVER DO TO HER?!
SOME-THING'S CLEARLY MESSED UP HERE!
WHAT HAPPENED TO HER?!
THAT ATTITUDE...
THERE ARE TWO TYPES OF PEOPLE IN THE WORLD.
THOSE WHO CRY WHEN DISTRESSED...
...AND THOSE WHO LAUGH.
WE'RE RIGHT IN THE MIDDLE OF GETTING THE FILM PROJECT OFF THE GROUND, TOO!
SIGH...
AND EVEN NOW, I'VE GOT LECTURES TO ATTEND.
OFF TO COLLEGE.
WE'RE ALL SLAVES WORKIN' FOR THOSE CREDITS...

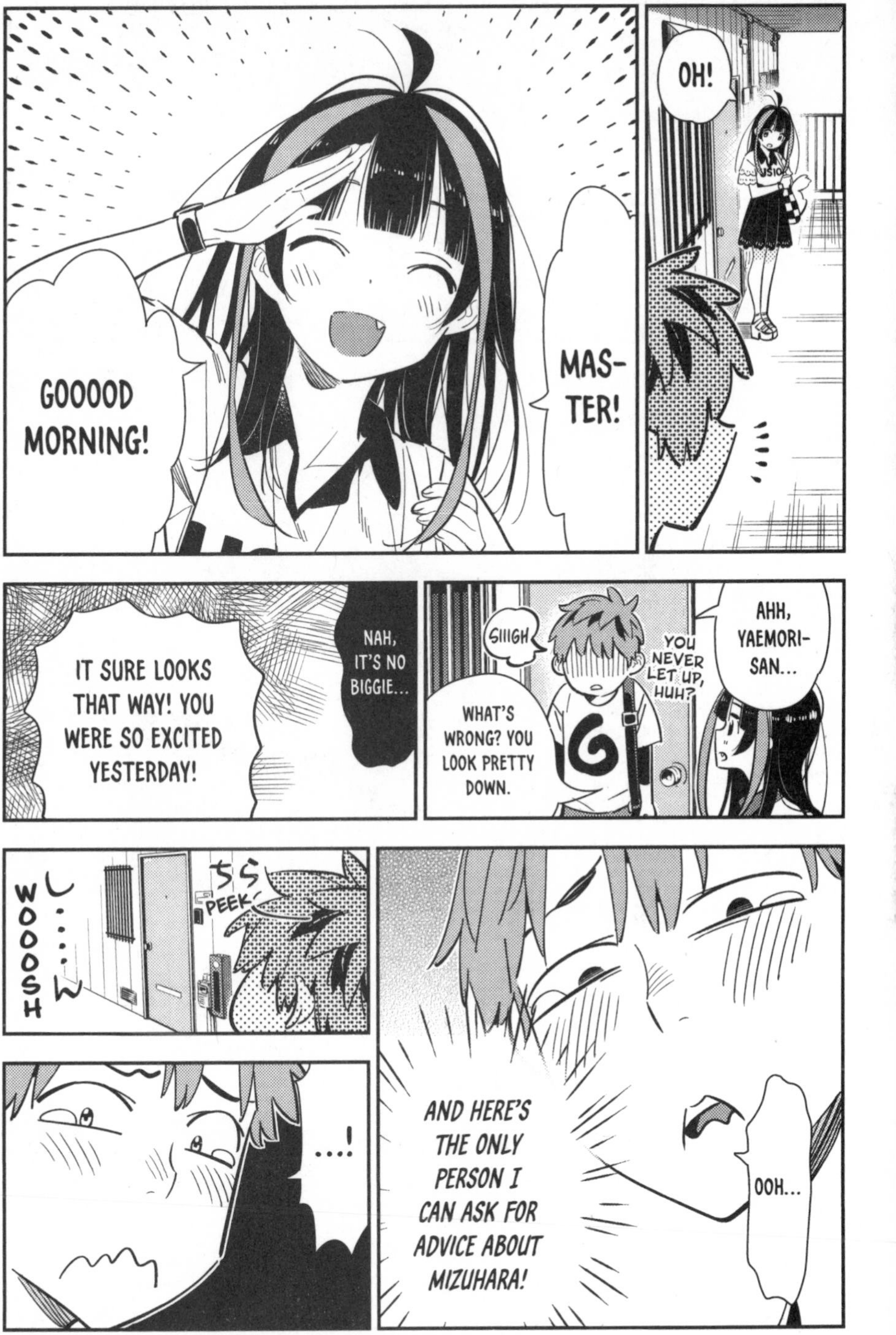
OH!
MAS-
TER!
GOOOOD MORNING!
AHH, YAEMORI-SAN...
YOU NEVER LET UP, HUH?
SIIIGH
WHAT'S WRONG? YOU LOOK PRETTY DOWN.
NAH, IT'S NO BIGGIE...
IT SURE LOOKS THAT WAY! YOU WERE SO EXCITED YESTERDAY!
OOH...
AND HERE'S THE ONLY PERSON I CAN ASK FOR ADVICE ABOUT MIZUHARA!
ちら
PEEK
し...ん
WOOOOSH
...!

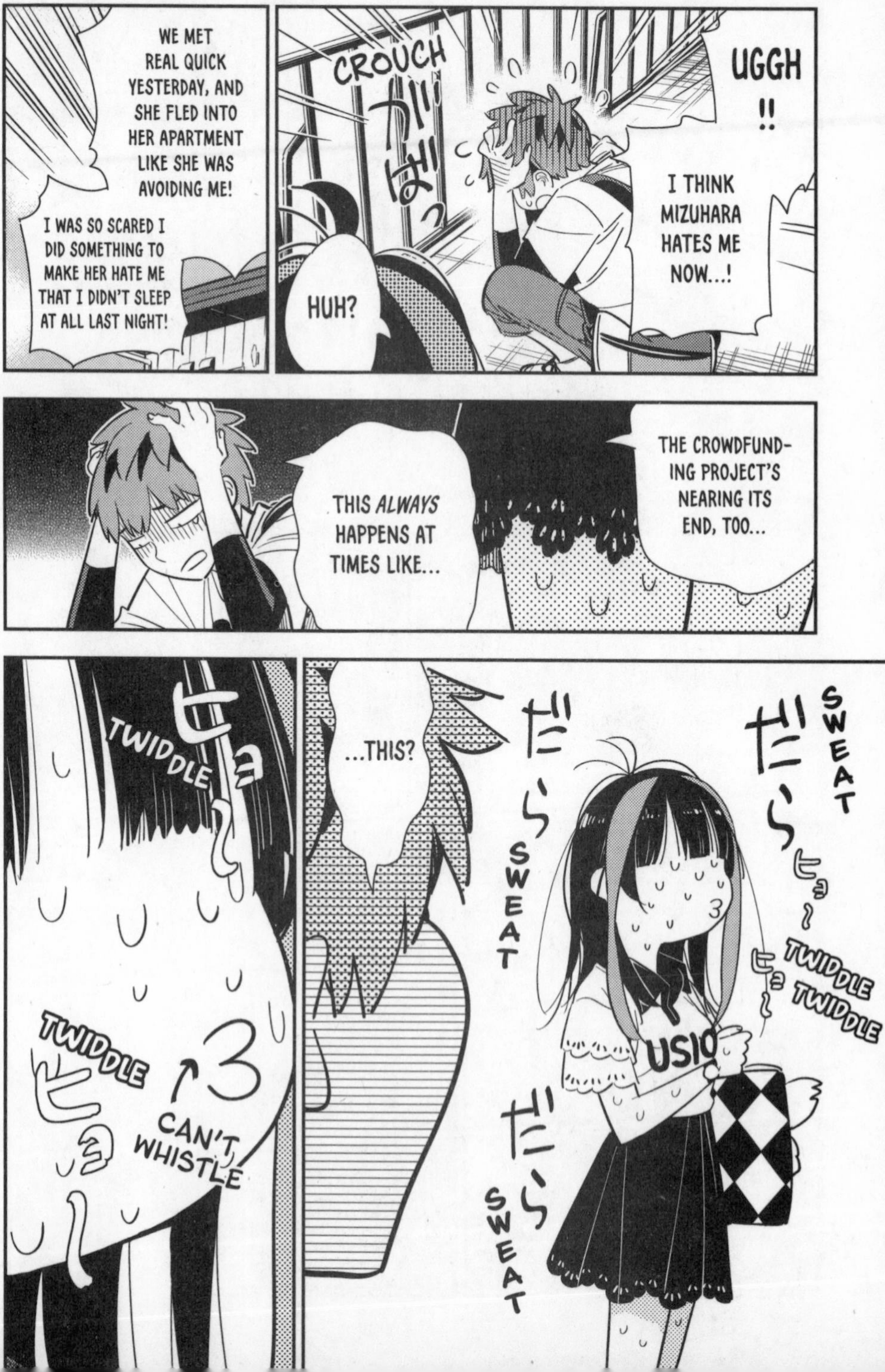
UGGH!!
CROUCH
I THINK MIZUHARA HATES ME NOW...!
HUH?
WE MET REAL QUICK YESTERDAY, AND SHE FLED INTO HER APARTMENT LIKE SHE WAS AVOIDING ME!
I WAS SO SCARED I DID SOMETHING TO MAKE HER HATE ME THAT I DIDN'T SLEEP AT ALL LAST NIGHT!
THE CROWDFUNDING-ING PROJECT'S NEARING ITS END, TOO...
THIS *ALWAYS* HAPPENS AT TIMES LIKE...
...THIS?
だら SWEAT
だら SWEAT
TWIDDLE TWIDDLE
USIO
だら SWEAT
TWIDDLE
TWIDDLE
CAN'T WHISTLE

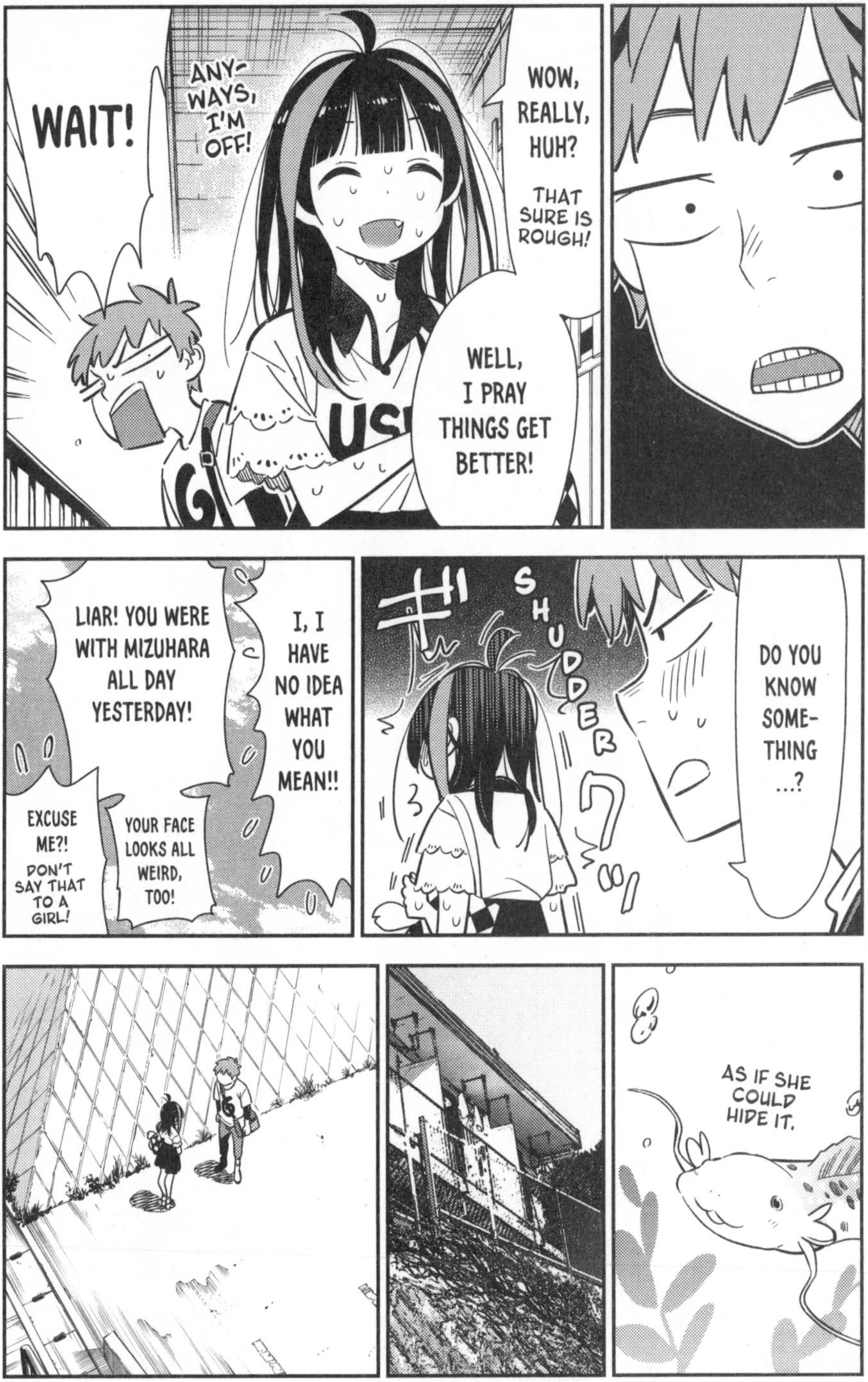
WOW, REALLY, HUH?
THAT SURE IS ROUGH!
WELL, I PRAY THINGS GET BETTER!
ANY-WAYS, I'M OFF!
WAIT!
DO YOU KNOW SOME-THING ...?
SHUDDER
I, I HAVE NO IDEA WHAT YOU MEAN!!
LIAR! YOU WERE WITH MIZUHARA ALL DAY YESTERDAY!
YOUR FACE LOOKS ALL WEIRD, TOO!
EXCUSE ME?!
DON'T SAY THAT TO A GIRL!
AS IF SHE COULD HIDE IT.

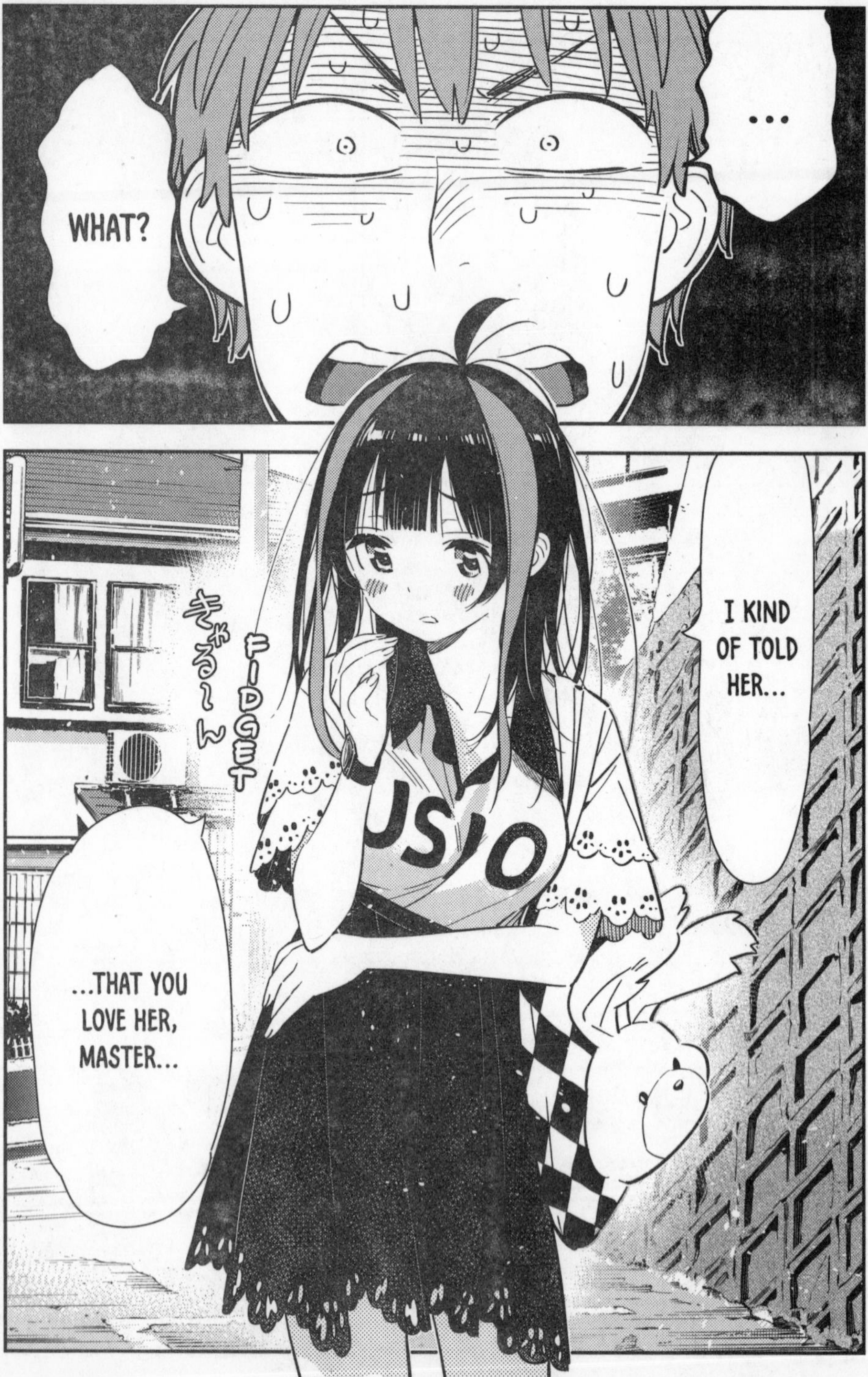
...
WHAT?
I KIND OF TOLD HER...
FIDGET
きゃる～ん
...THAT YOU LOVE HER, MASTER...

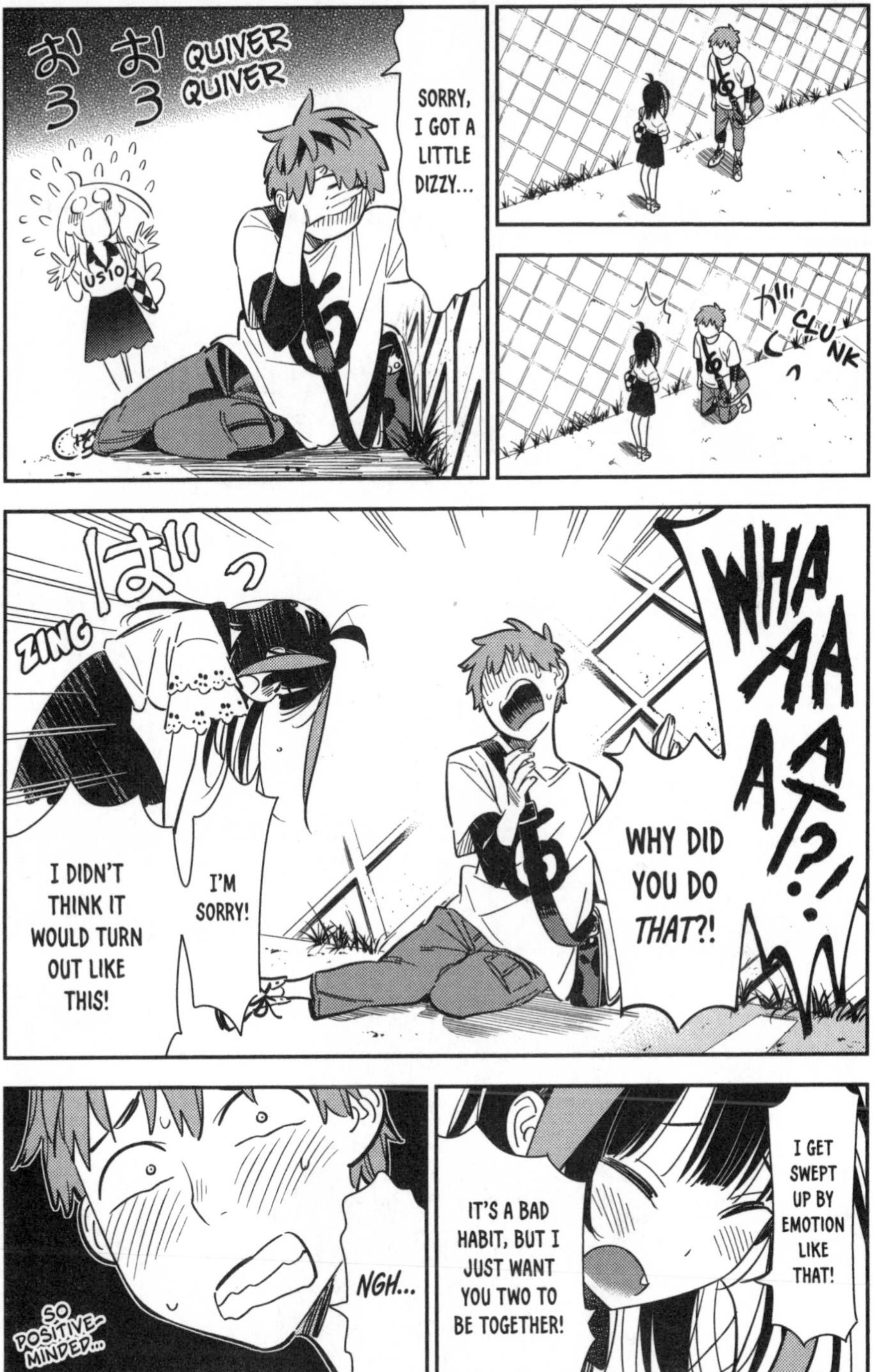
CLUNK
SORRY, I GOT A LITTLE DIZZY...
おろ おろ
QUIVER QUIVER
WHAAAAAT?!
はっ
ZING
WHY DID YOU DO THAT?!
I'M SORRY!
I DIDN'T THINK IT WOULD TURN OUT LIKE THIS!
I GET SWEPT UP BY EMOTION LIKE THAT!
IT'S A BAD HABIT, BUT I JUST WANT YOU TWO TO BE TOGETHER!
NGH...
SO POSITIVE-MINDED...

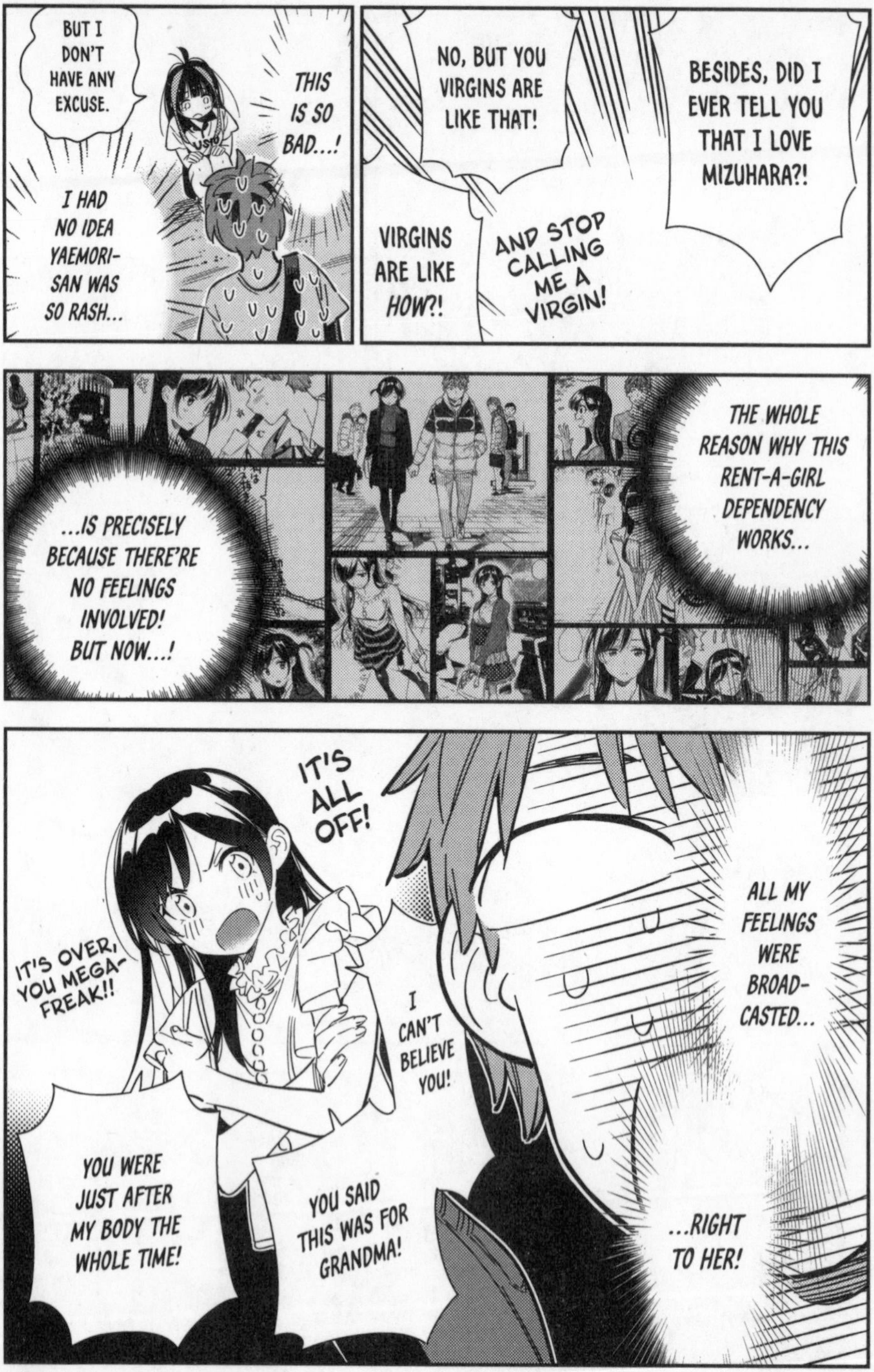
BESIDES, DID I EVER TELL YOU THAT I LOVE MIZUHARA?!
NO, BUT YOU VIRGINS ARE LIKE THAT!
AND STOP CALLING ME A VIRGIN!
VIRGINS ARE LIKE HOW?!
THIS IS SO BAD...!
BUT I DON'T HAVE ANY EXCUSE.
I HAD NO IDEA YAEMORI-SAN WAS SO RASH...
THE WHOLE REASON WHY THIS RENT-A-GIRL DEPENDENCY WORKS...
...IS PRECISELY BECAUSE THERE'RE NO FEELINGS INVOLVED! BUT NOW...!
ALL MY FEELINGS WERE BROAD-CASTED...
...RIGHT TO HER!
IT'S ALL OFF!
I CAN'T BELIEVE YOU!
IT'S OVER, YOU MEGA-FREAK!!
YOU SAID THIS WAS FOR GRANDMA!
YOU WERE JUST AFTER MY BODY THE WHOLE TIME!

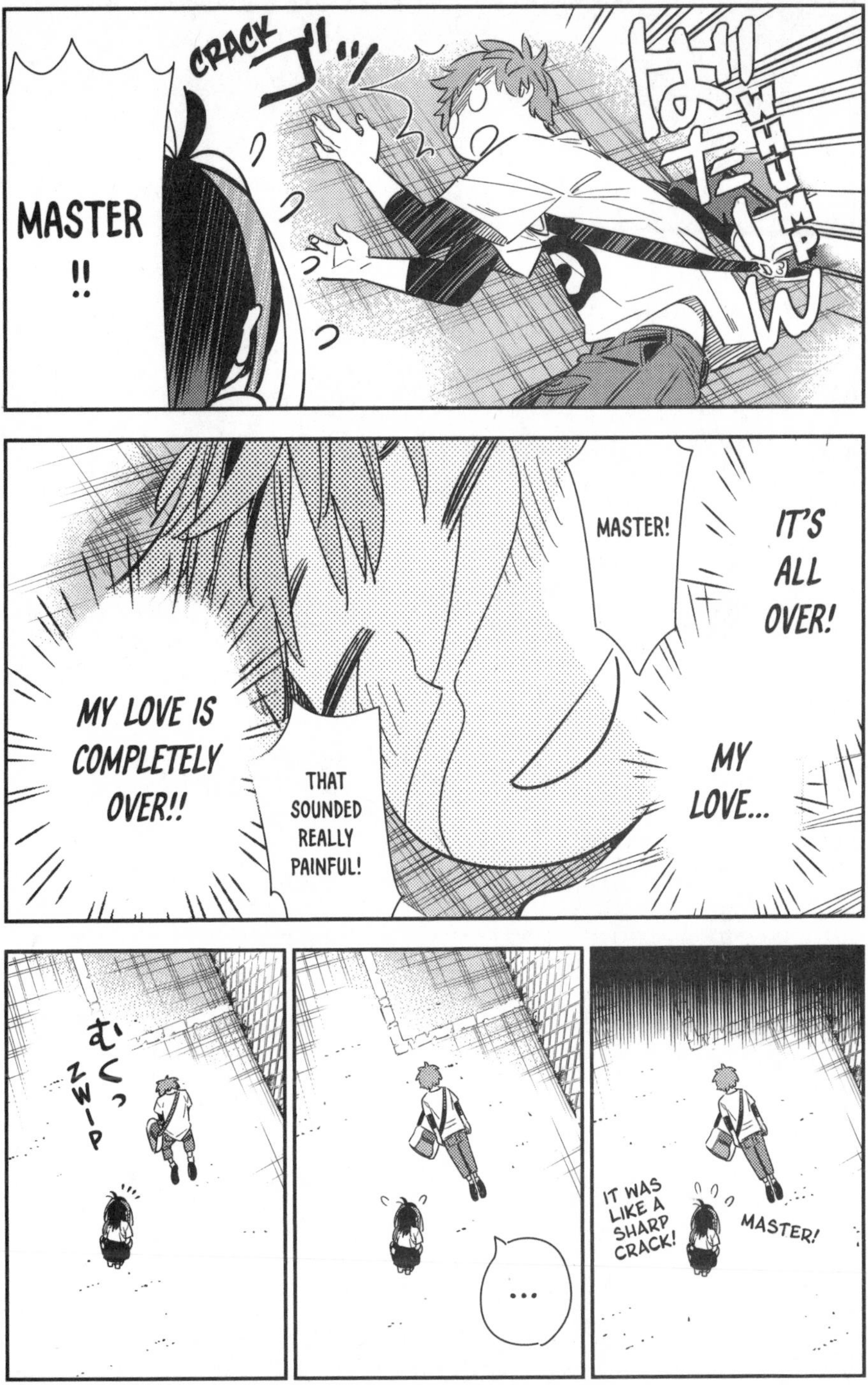
ばたーん
WHUMP
ゴッ
CRACK
MASTER !!
IT'S ALL OVER!
MASTER!
MY LOVE...
THAT SOUNDED REALLY PAINFUL!
MY LOVE IS COMPLETELY OVER!!
MASTER!
IT WAS LIKE A SHARP CRACK!
...
むくっ
ZWIP

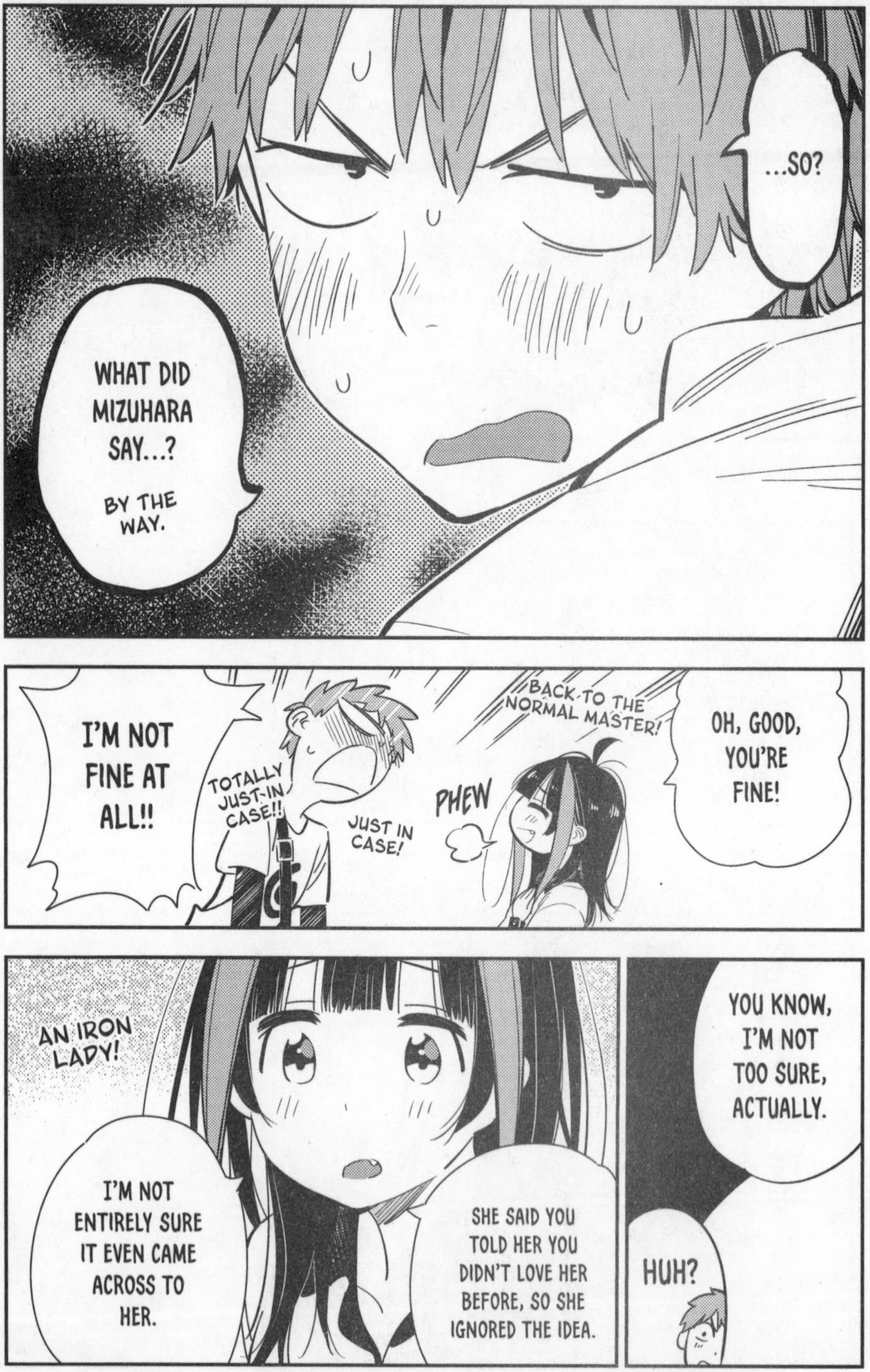
...SO?
WHAT DID MIZUHARA SAY...?
BY THE WAY.
OH, GOOD, YOU'RE FINE!
BACK TO THE NORMAL MASTER!
PHEW
JUST IN CASE!
TOTALLY JUST-IN CASE!!
I'M NOT FINE AT ALL!!
YOU KNOW, I'M NOT TOO SURE, ACTUALLY.
HUH?
SHE SAID YOU TOLD HER YOU DIDN'T LOVE HER BEFORE, SO SHE IGNORED THE IDEA.
I'M NOT ENTIRELY SURE IT EVEN CAME ACROSS TO HER.
AN IRON LADY!

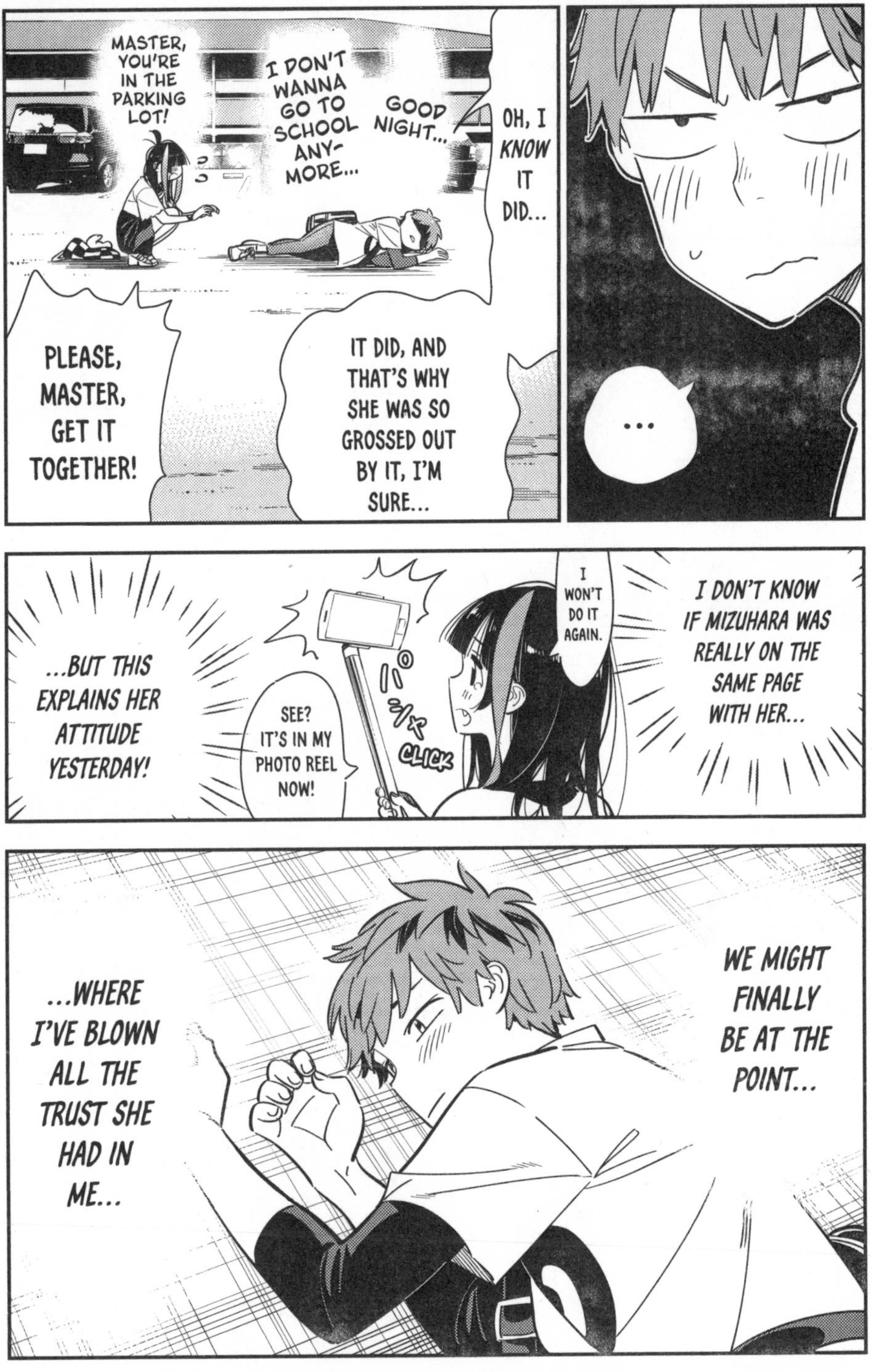
...
OH, I KNOW IT DID...
GOOD NIGHT...
I DON'T WANNA GO TO SCHOOL ANYMORE...
MASTER, YOU'RE IN THE PARKING LOT!
IT DID, AND THAT'S WHY SHE WAS SO GROSSED OUT BY IT, I'M SURE...
PLEASE, MASTER, GET IT TOGETHER!
I DON'T KNOW IF MIZUHARA WAS REALLY ON THE SAME PAGE WITH HER...
I WON'T DO IT AGAIN.
CLICK
SEE? IT'S IN MY PHOTO REEL NOW!
...BUT THIS EXPLAINS HER ATTITUDE YESTERDAY!
WE MIGHT FINALLY BE AT THE POINT...
...WHERE I'VE BLOWN ALL THE TRUST SHE HAD IN ME...

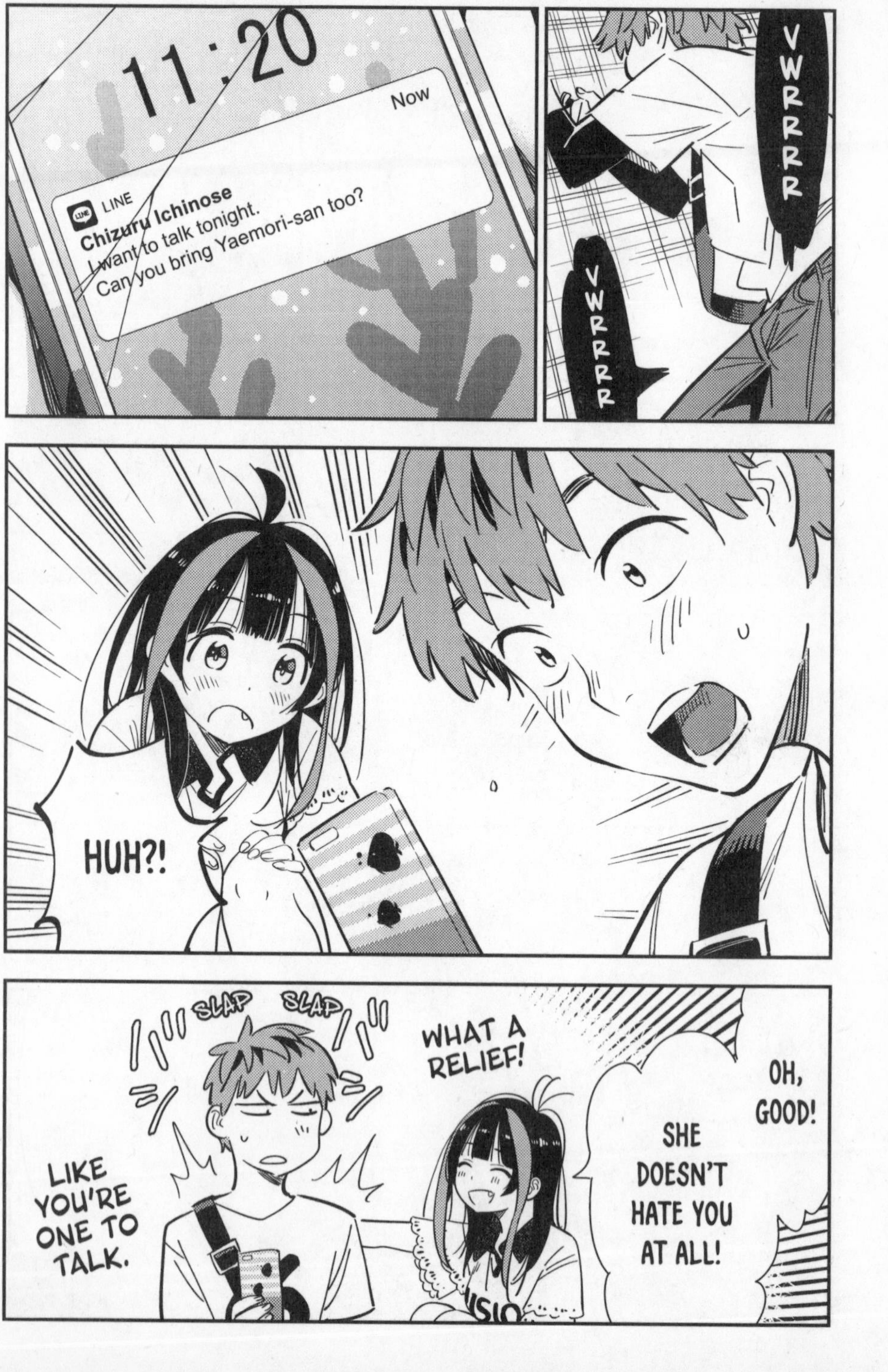

VWRRRR
VWRRRR
11:20
Now
LINE
Chizuru Ichinose
I want to talk tonight.
Can you bring Yaemori-san too?
HUH?!
OH, GOOD!
SHE DOESN'T HATE YOU AT ALL!
WHAT A RELIEF!
SLAP SLAP
LIKE YOU'RE ONE TO TALK.

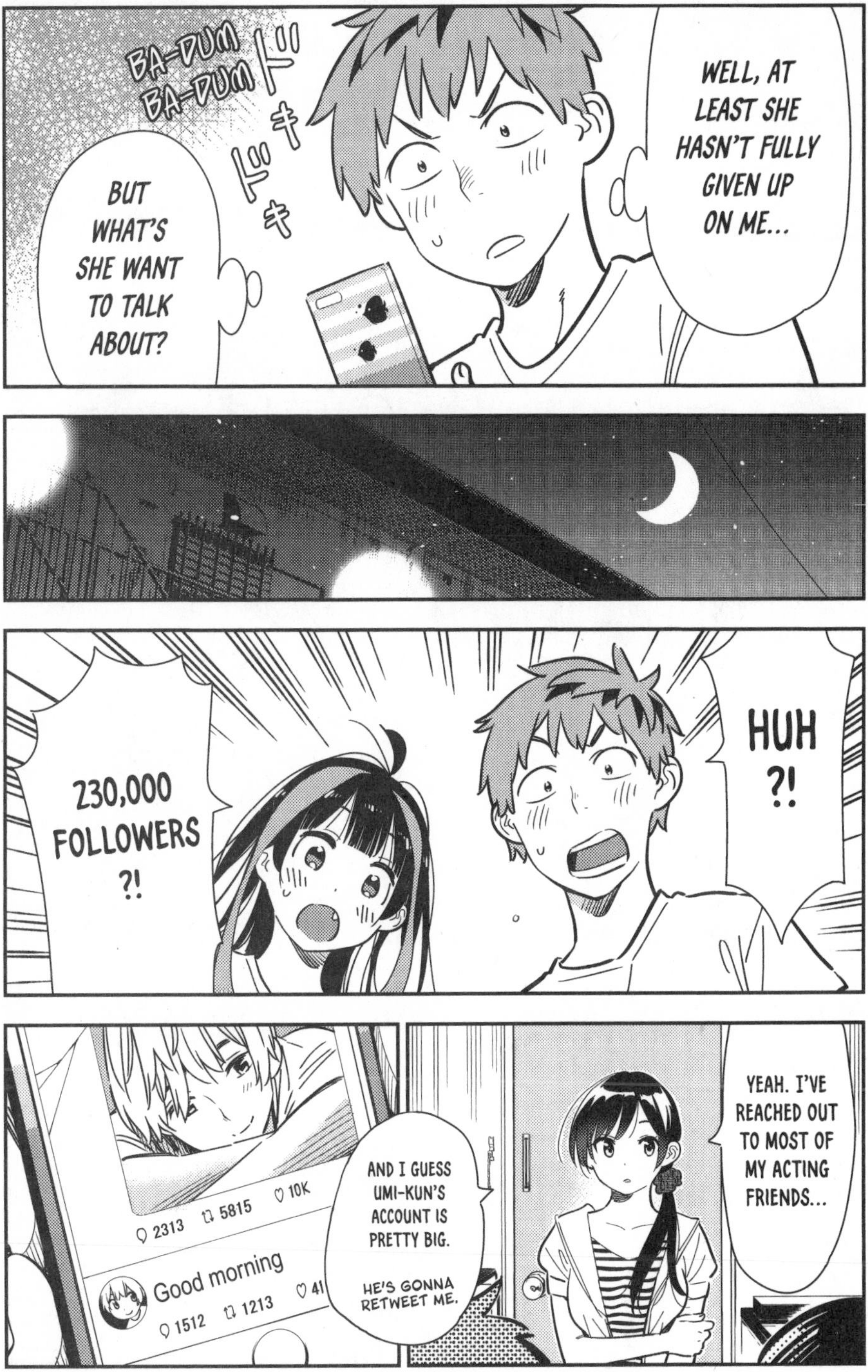
WELL, AT LEAST SHE HASN'T FULLY GIVEN UP ON ME...
BA-DUM BA-DUM
ドキドキ
BUT WHAT'S SHE WANT TO TALK ABOUT?
HUH ?!
230,000 FOLLOWERS ?!
YEAH. I'VE REACHED OUT TO MOST OF MY ACTING FRIENDS...
AND I GUESS UMI-KUN'S ACCOUNT IS PRETTY BIG.
HE'S GONNA RETWEET ME.
10K
5815
2313
Good morning
41
1213
1512

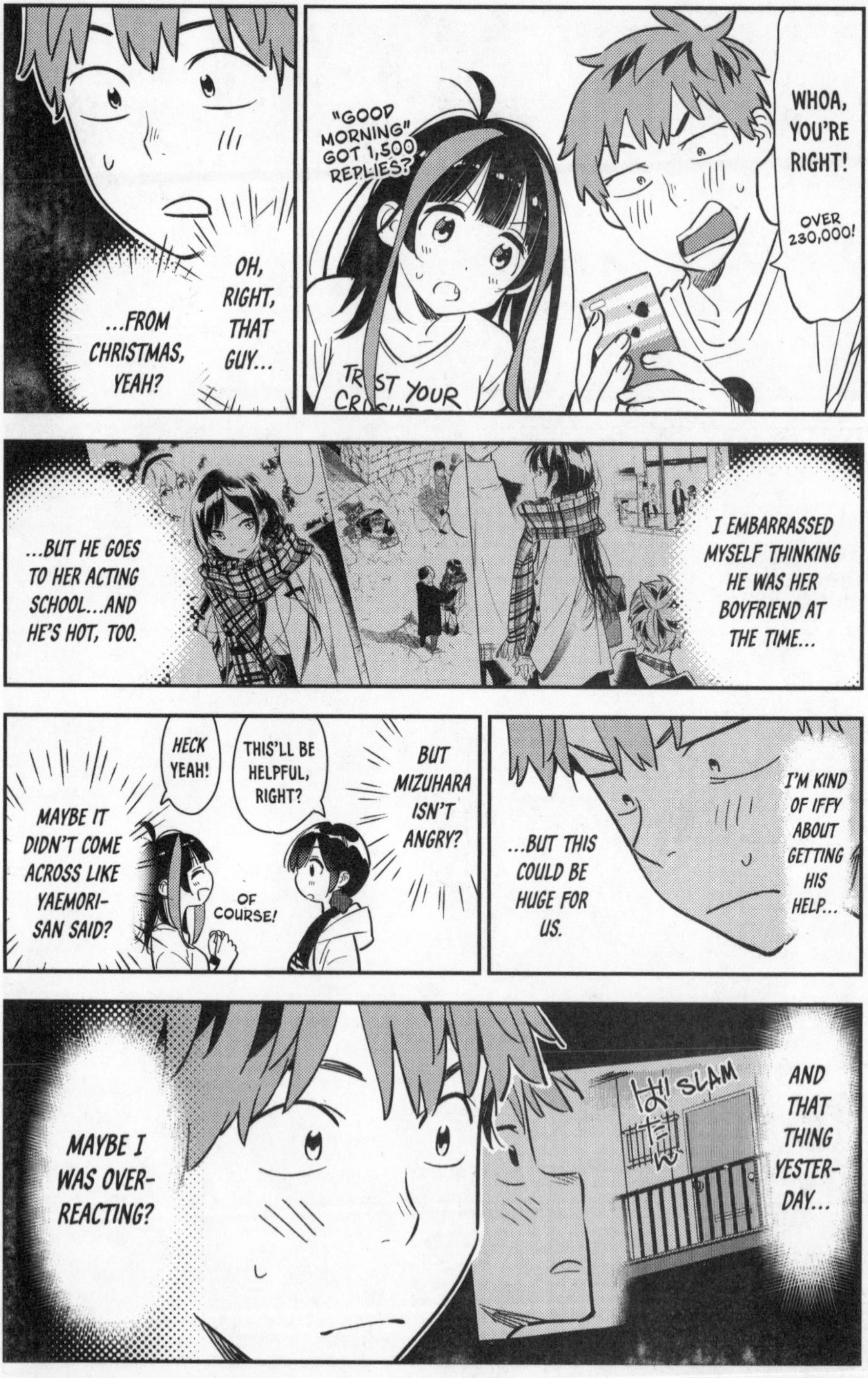
WHOA, YOU'RE RIGHT!
OVER 230,000!
"GOOD MORNING" GOT 1,500 REPLIES?
OH, RIGHT, THAT GUY...
...FROM CHRISTMAS, YEAH?
I EMBARRASSED MYSELF THINKING HE WAS HER BOYFRIEND AT THE TIME...
...BUT HE GOES TO HER ACTING SCHOOL...AND HE'S HOT, TOO.
I'M KIND OF IFFY ABOUT GETTING HIS HELP...
...BUT THIS COULD BE HUGE FOR US.
BUT MIZUHARA ISN'T ANGRY?
THIS'LL BE HELPFUL, RIGHT?
HECK YEAH!
OF COURSE!
MAYBE IT DIDN'T COME ACROSS LIKE YAEMORI-SAN SAID?
AND THAT THING YESTERDAY...
SLAM
MAYBE I WAS OVER-REACTING?

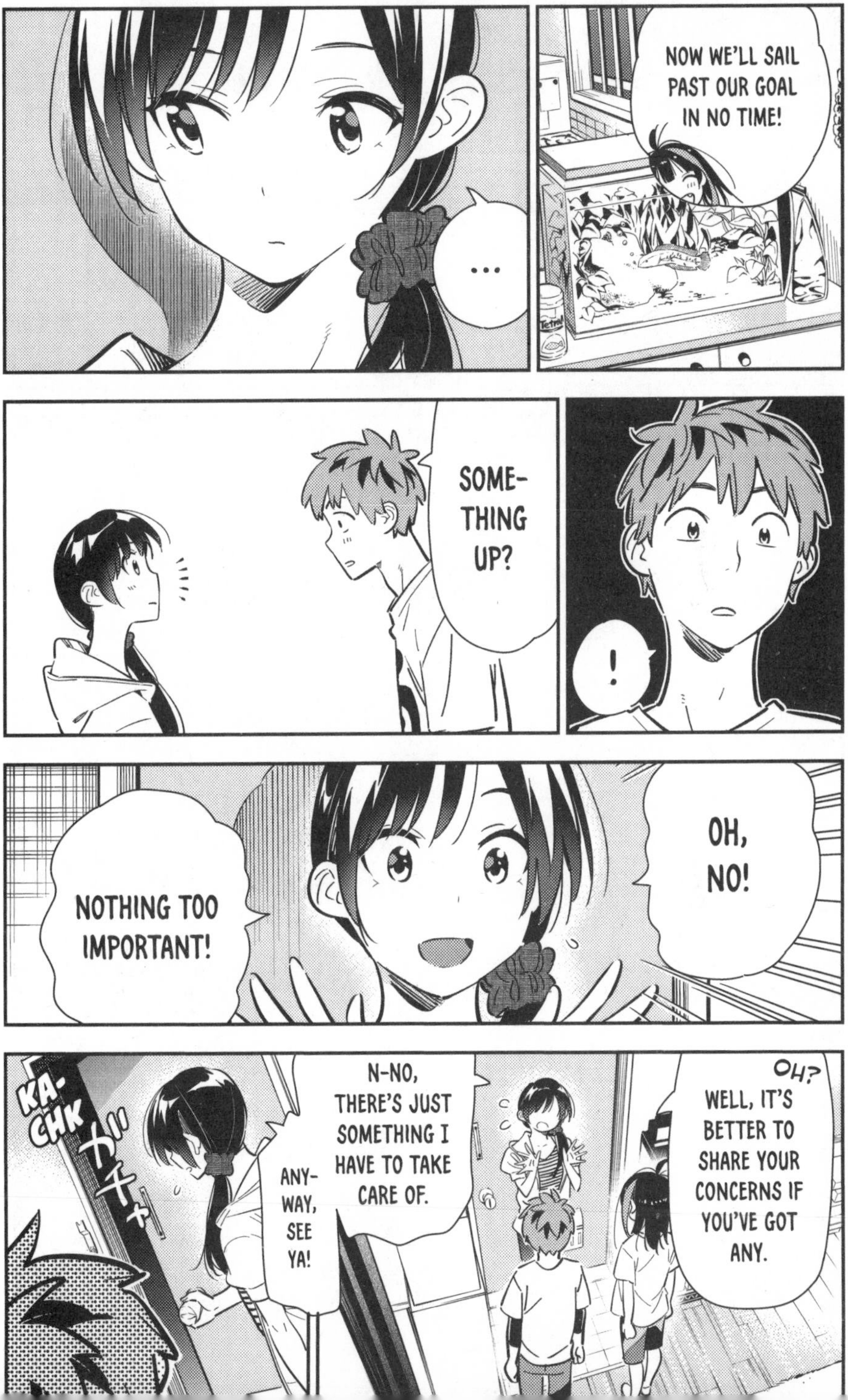
NOW WE'LL SAIL PAST OUR GOAL IN NO TIME!
...
!
SOME-THING UP?
OH, NO!
NOTHING TOO IMPORTANT!
OH?
WELL, IT'S BETTER TO SHARE YOUR CONCERNS IF YOU'VE GOT ANY.
N-NO, THERE'S JUST SOMETHING I HAVE TO TAKE CARE OF.
ANY-WAY, SEE YA!
KA-CHK

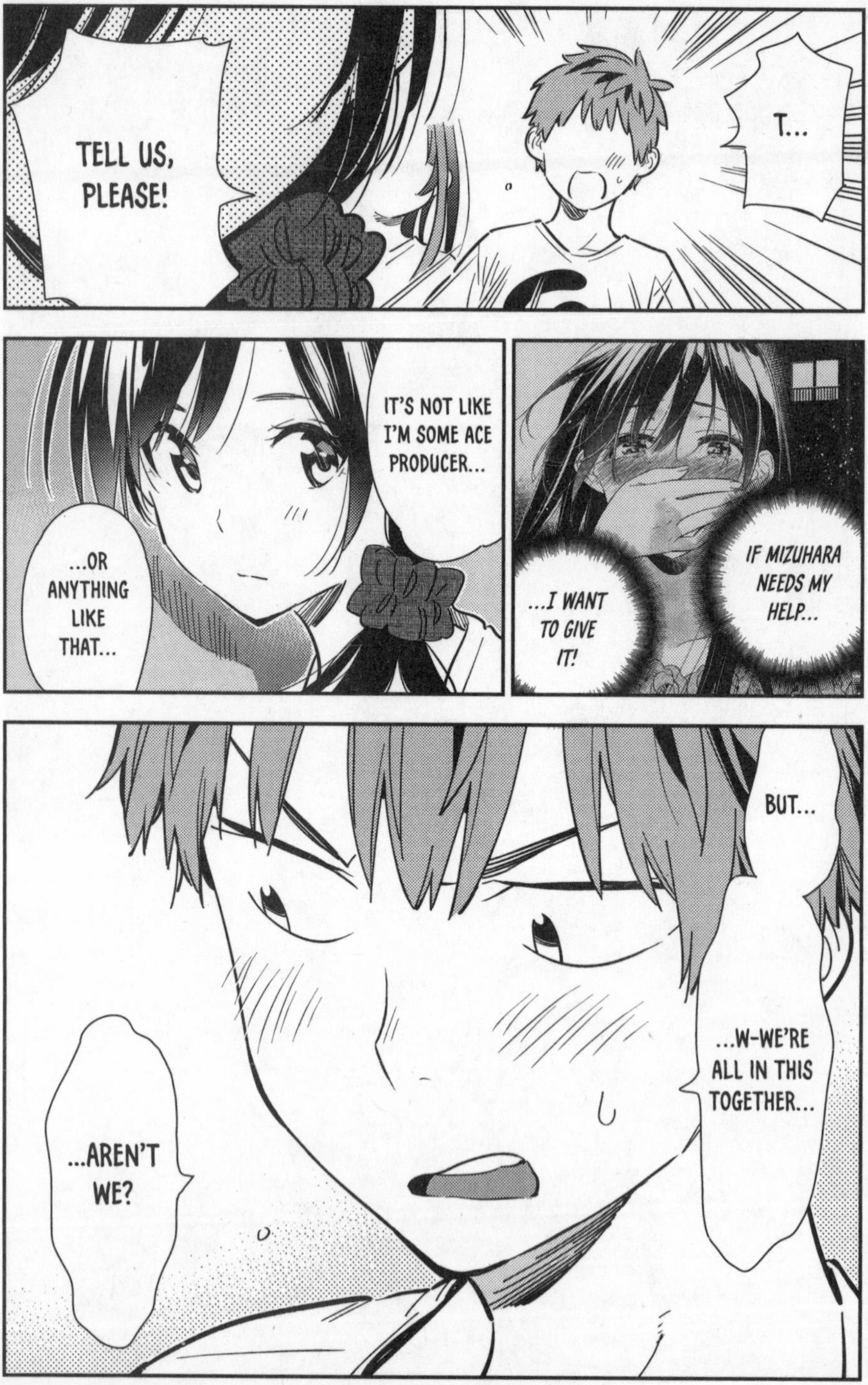

T...
TELL US, PLEASE!
IF MIZUHARA NEEDS MY HELP...
...I WANT TO GIVE IT!
IT'S NOT LIKE I'M SOME ACE PRODUCER...
...OR ANYTHING LIKE THAT...
BUT...
...W-WE'RE ALL IN THIS TOGETHER...
...AREN'T WE?

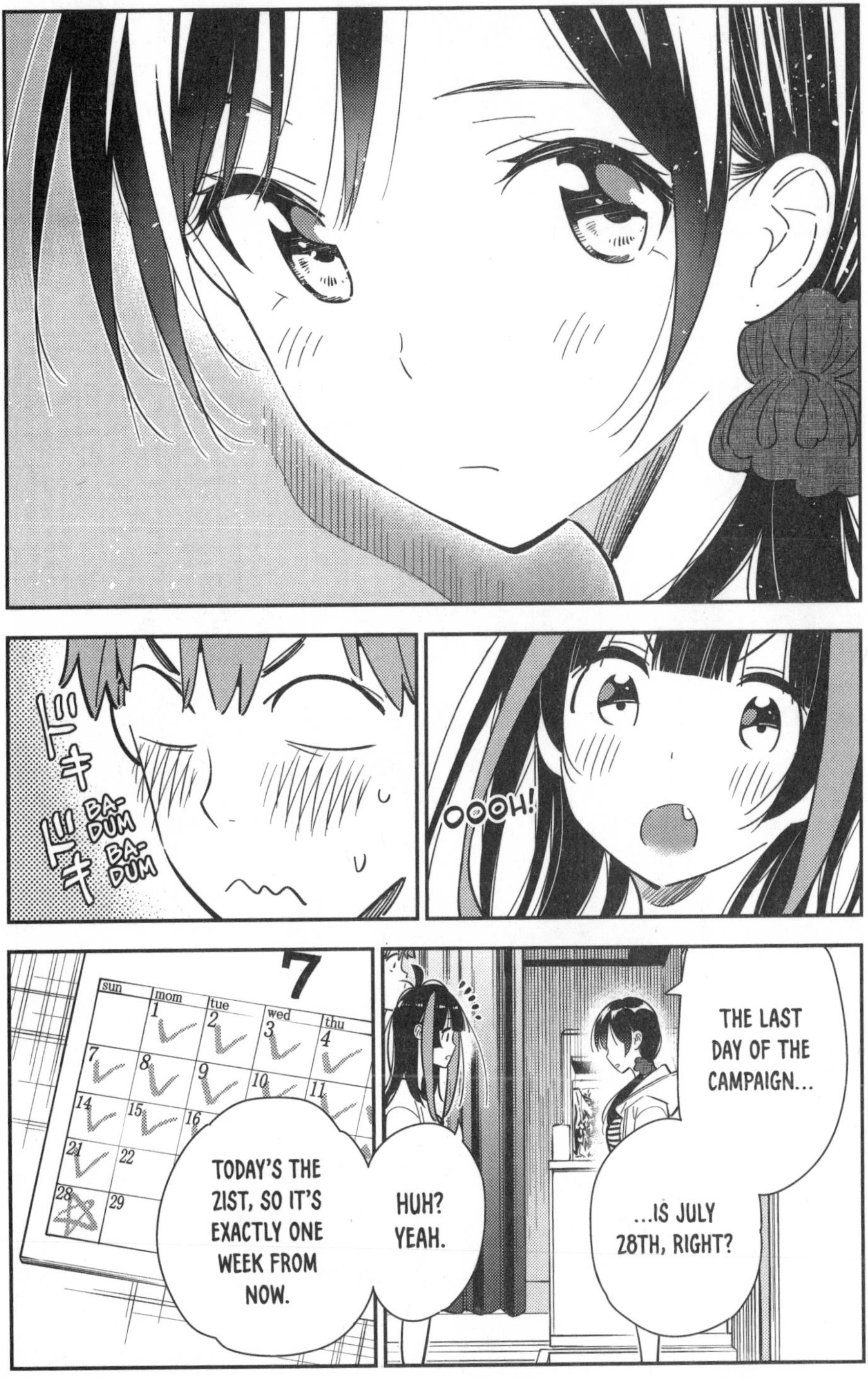

OOOH!
ドキ
ドキ
BA-DUM
BA-DUM
THE LAST DAY OF THE CAMPAIGN...
...IS JULY 28TH, RIGHT?
HUH? YEAH.
7
sun
mon
tue
wed
thu
TODAY'S THE 21ST, SO IT'S EXACTLY ONE WEEK FROM NOW.

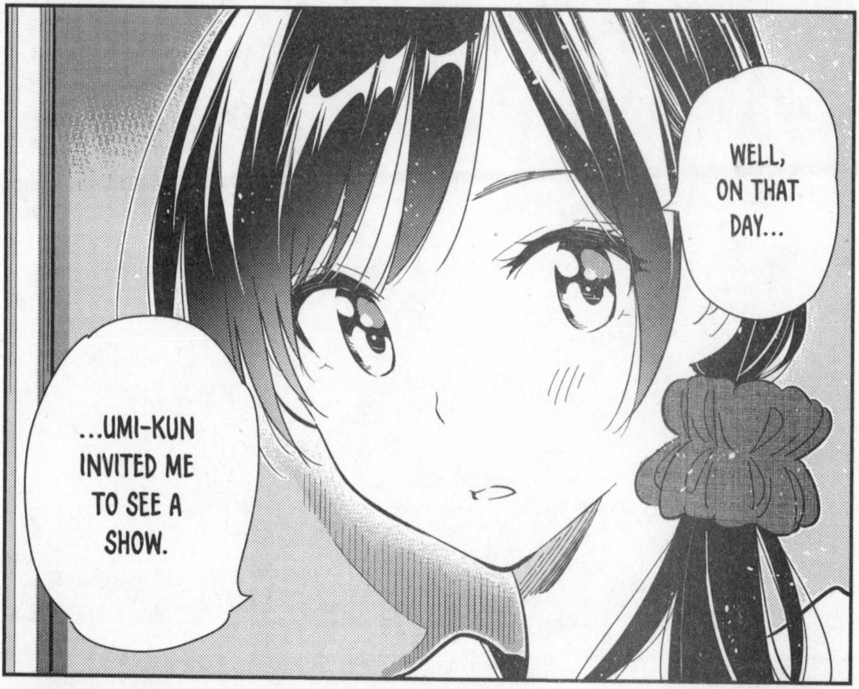
WELL, ON THAT DAY...
...UMI-KUN INVITED ME TO SEE A SHOW.
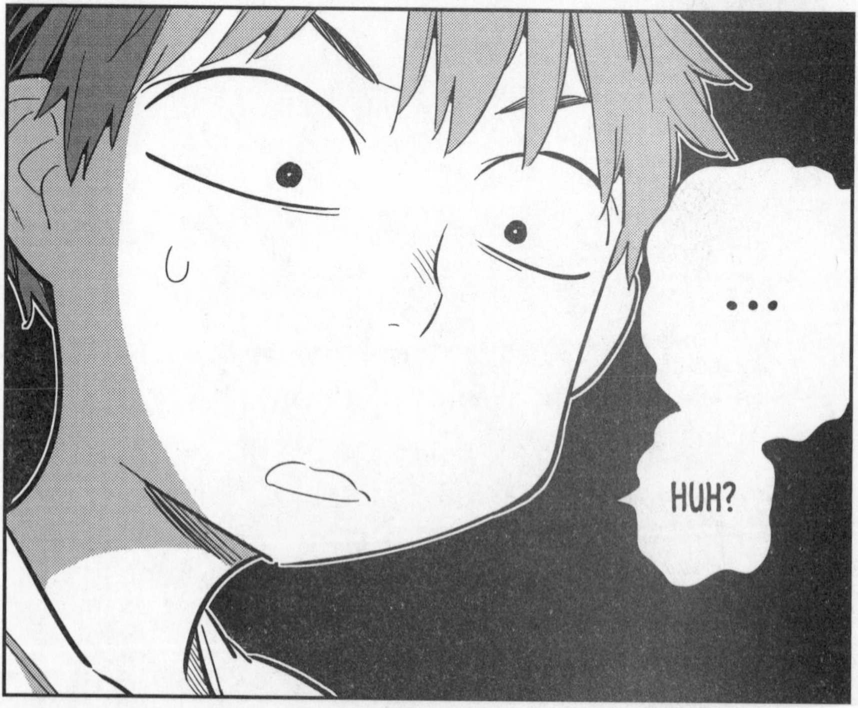
...
HUH?

RATING 124 THE FINAL DAY AND MY GIRLFRIEND 2

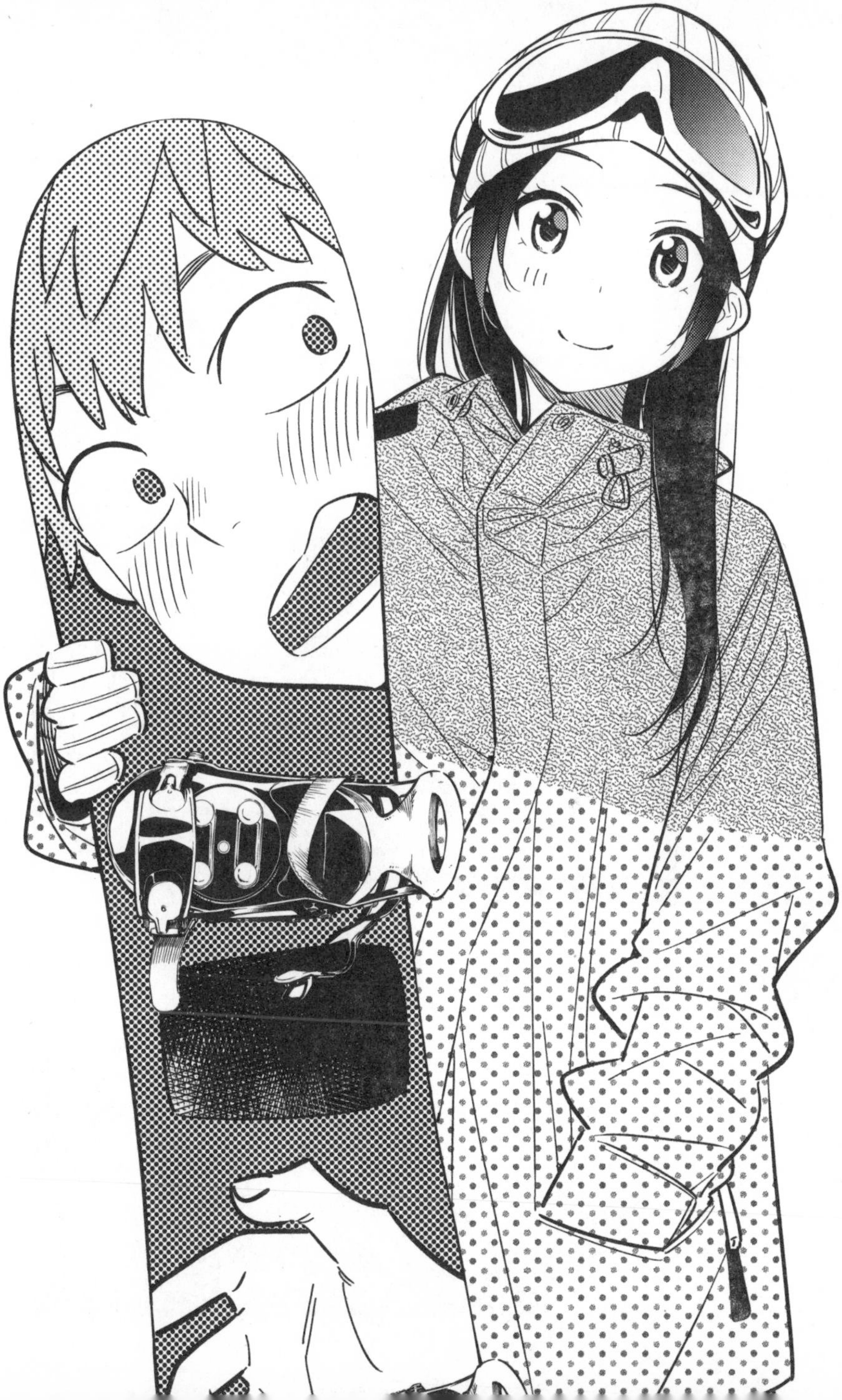

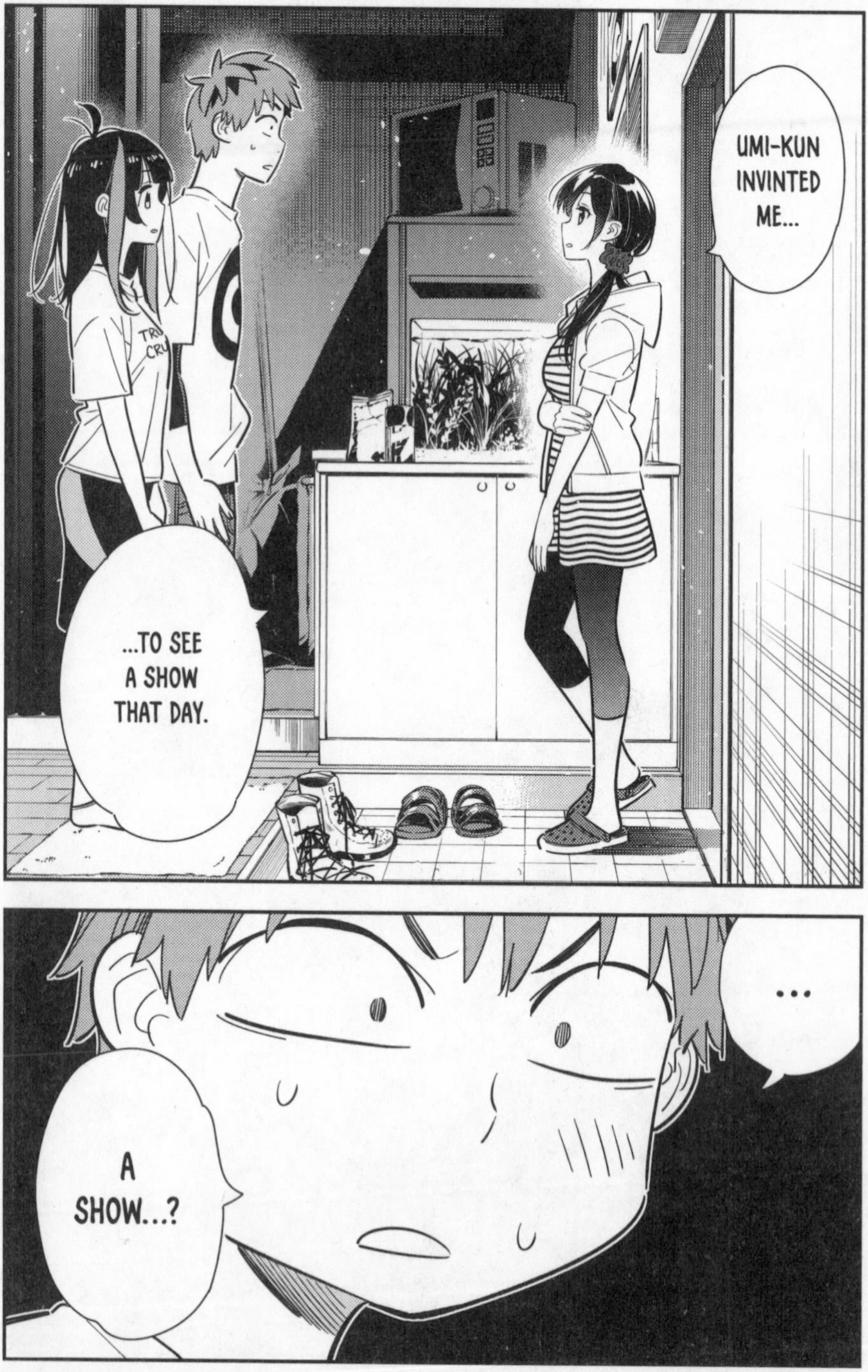
UMI-KUN INVINTED ME...
...TO SEE A SHOW THAT DAY.
...
A SHOW...?

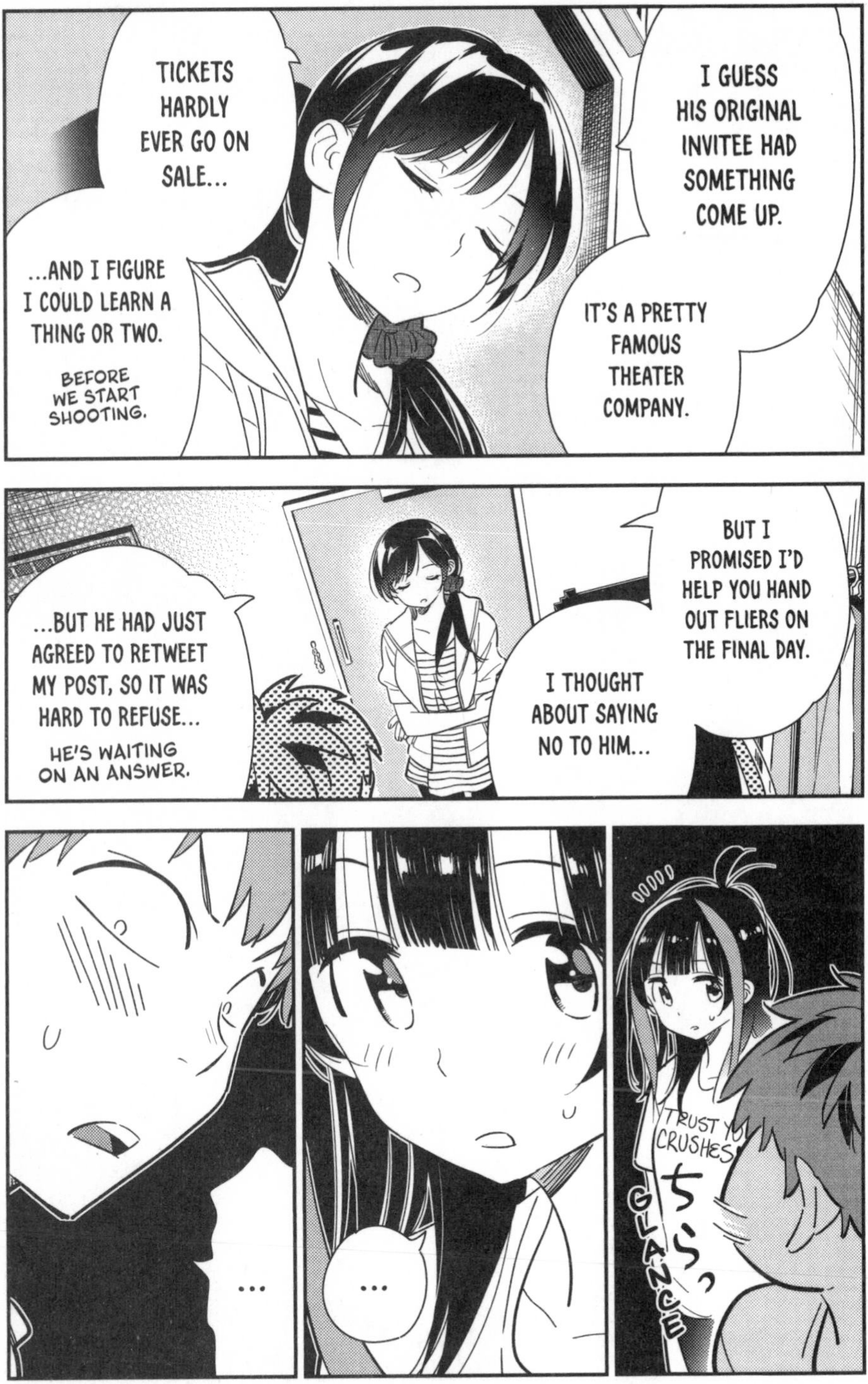
I GUESS HIS ORIGINAL INVITEE HAD SOMETHING COME UP.
IT'S A PRETTY FAMOUS THEATER COMPANY.
TICKETS HARDLY EVER GO ON SALE...
...AND I FIGURE I COULD LEARN A THING OR TWO.
BEFORE WE START SHOOTING.
BUT I PROMISED I'D HELP YOU HAND OUT FLIERS ON THE FINAL DAY.
I THOUGHT ABOUT SAYING NO TO HIM...
...BUT HE HAD JUST AGREED TO RETWEET MY POST, SO IT WAS HARD TO REFUSE...
HE'S WAITING ON AN ANSWER.
ちらっ
GLANCE
...
...

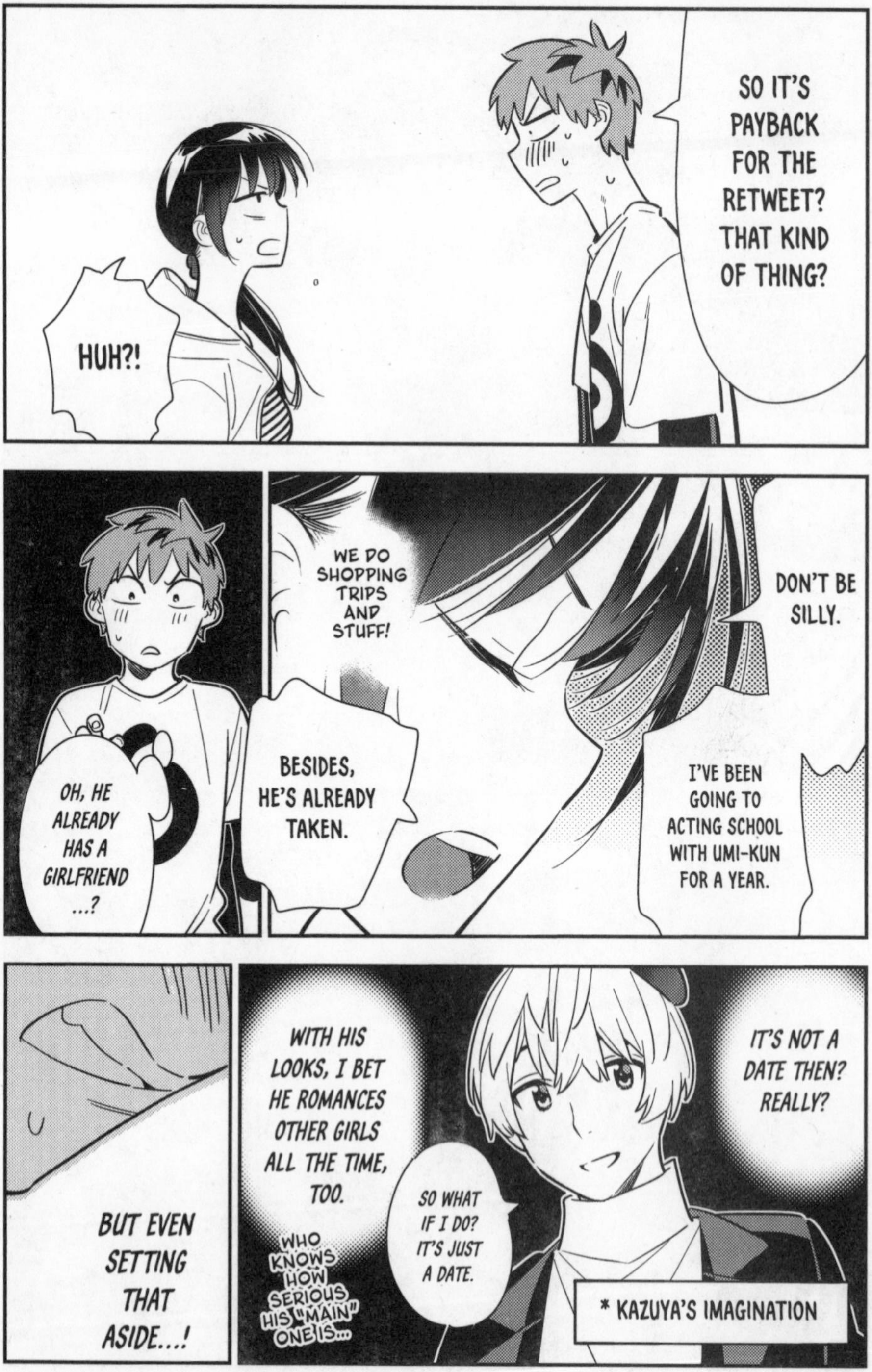
SO IT'S PAYBACK FOR THE RETWEET? THAT KIND OF THING?
HUH?!
DON'T BE SILLY.
I'VE BEEN GOING TO ACTING SCHOOL WITH UMI-KUN FOR A YEAR.
WE DO SHOPPING TRIPS AND STUFF!
BESIDES, HE'S ALREADY TAKEN.
OH, HE ALREADY HAS A GIRLFRIEND ...?
IT'S NOT A DATE THEN? REALLY?
SO WHAT IF I DO? IT'S JUST A DATE.
WITH HIS LOOKS, I BET HE ROMANCES OTHER GIRLS ALL THE TIME, TOO.
WHO KNOWS HOW SERIOUS HIS "MAIN" ONE IS...
* KAZUYA'S IMAGINATION
BUT EVEN SETTING THAT ASIDE...!

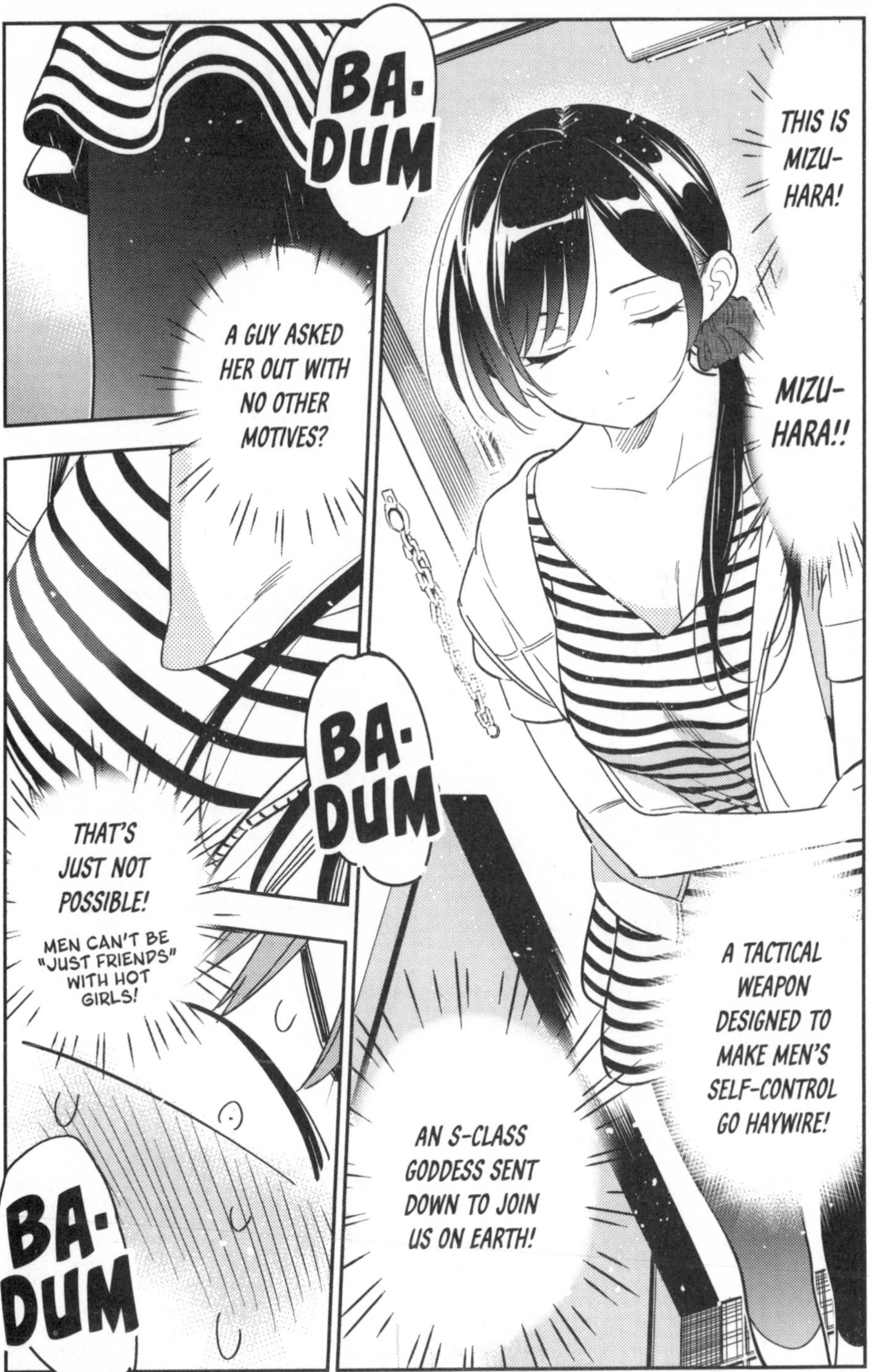
THIS IS MIZUHARA!
MIZUHARA!!
A TACTICAL WEAPON DESIGNED TO MAKE MEN'S SELF-CONTROL GO HAYWIRE!
AN S-CLASS GODDESS SENT DOWN TO JOIN US ON EARTH!
BA-DUM
A GUY ASKED HER OUT WITH NO OTHER MOTIVES?
BA-DUM
THAT'S JUST NOT POSSIBLE!
MEN CAN'T BE "JUST FRIENDS" WITH HOT GIRLS!
BA-DUM

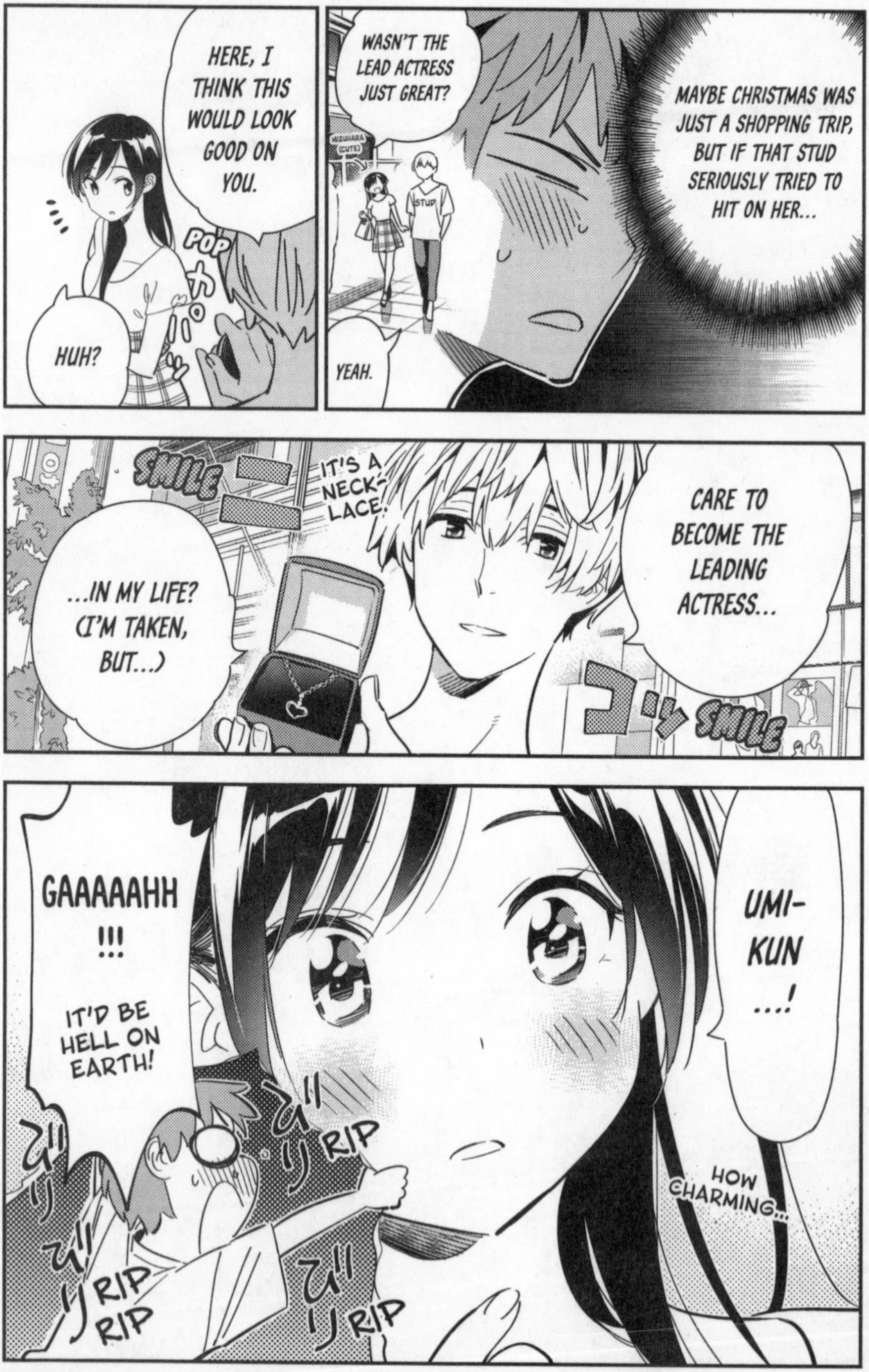

MAYBE CHRISTMAS WAS JUST A SHOPPING TRIP, BUT IF THAT STUD SERIOUSLY TRIED TO HIT ON HER...
WASN'T THE LEAD ACTRESS JUST GREAT?
MIZUHARA (CUTE)
STUD
YEAH.
HERE, I THINK THIS WOULD LOOK GOOD ON YOU.
POP
HUH?
CARE TO BECOME THE LEADING ACTRESS...
SMILE
IT'S A NECKLACE.
...IN MY LIFE? (I'M TAKEN, BUT...)
SMILE
UMI-KUN ...!
HOW CHARMING...
GAAAAAHH !!!
IT'D BE HELL ON EARTH!
RIP
RIP RIP
RIP

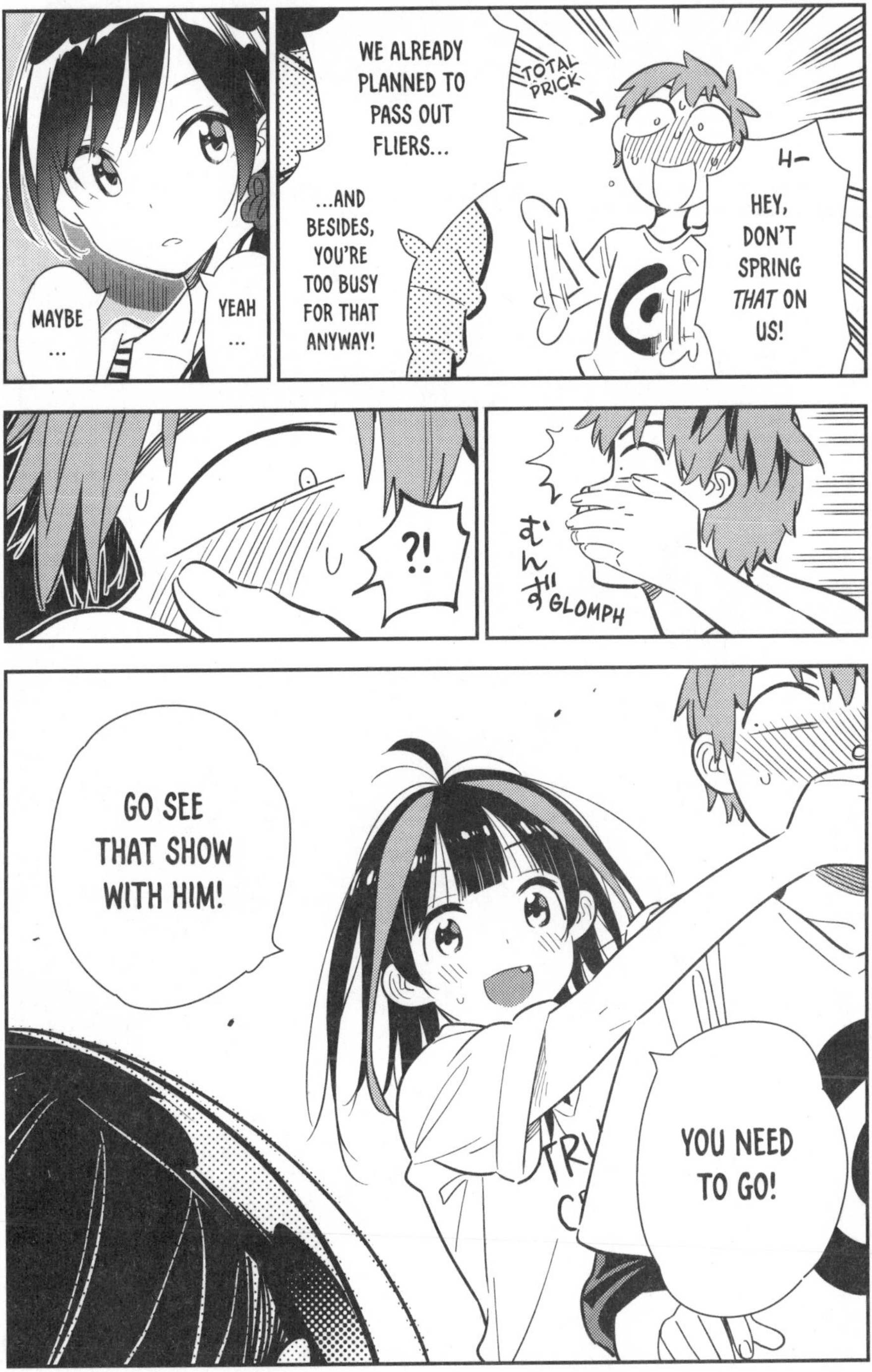
H– HEY, DON'T SPRING THAT ON US!
TOTAL PRICK
WE ALREADY PLANNED TO PASS OUT FLIERS...
...AND BESIDES, YOU'RE TOO BUSY FOR THAT ANYWAY!
YEAH ...
MAYBE ...
むんず GLOMPH
?!
GO SEE THAT SHOW WITH HIM!
YOU NEED TO GO!

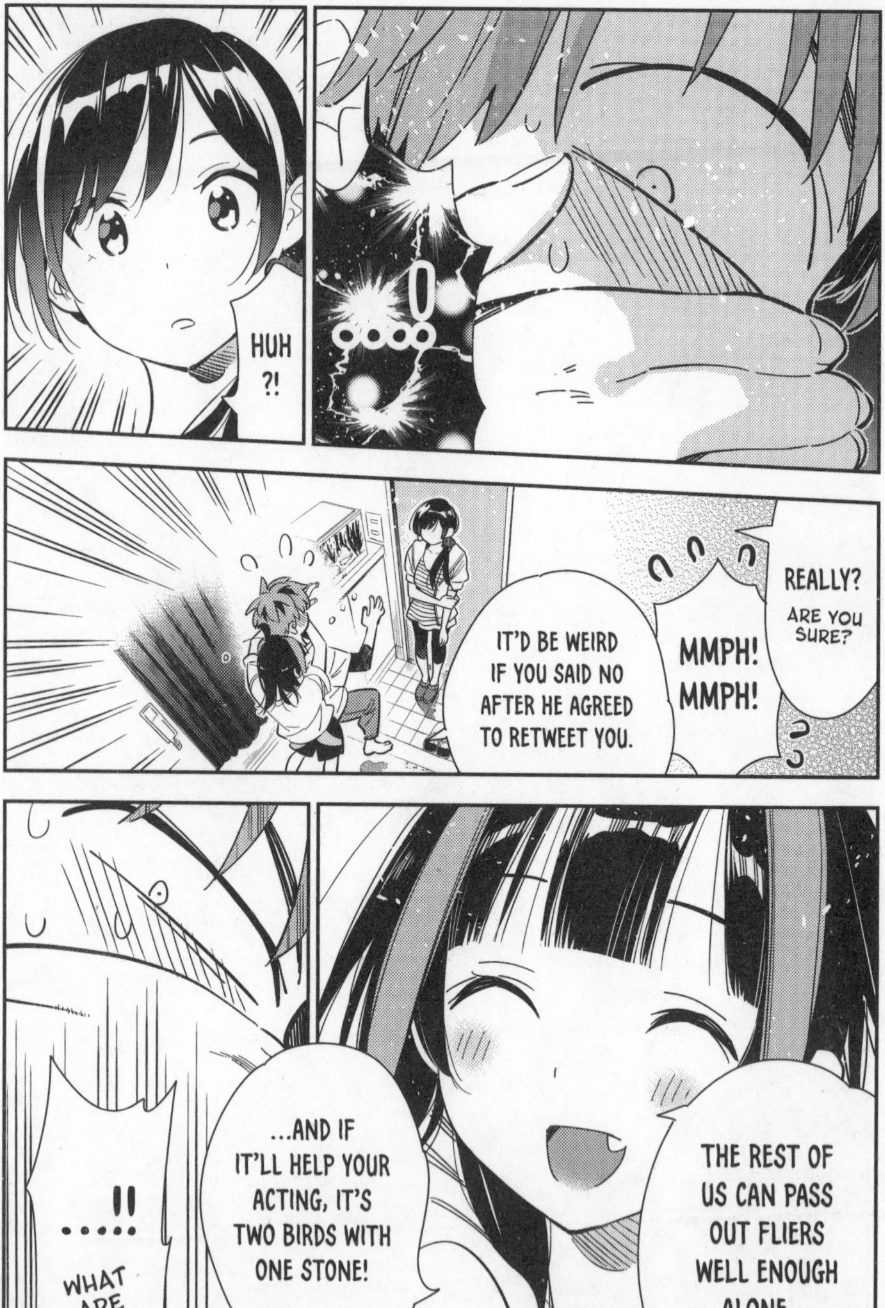
HUH ?!
REALLY? ARE YOU SURE?
MMPH! MMPH!
IT'D BE WEIRD IF YOU SAID NO AFTER HE AGREED TO RETWEET YOU.
THE REST OF US CAN PASS OUT FLIERS WELL ENOUGH ALONE...
...AND IF IT'LL HELP YOUR ACTING, IT'S TWO BIRDS WITH ONE STONE!
....!!
WHAT ARE YOU...

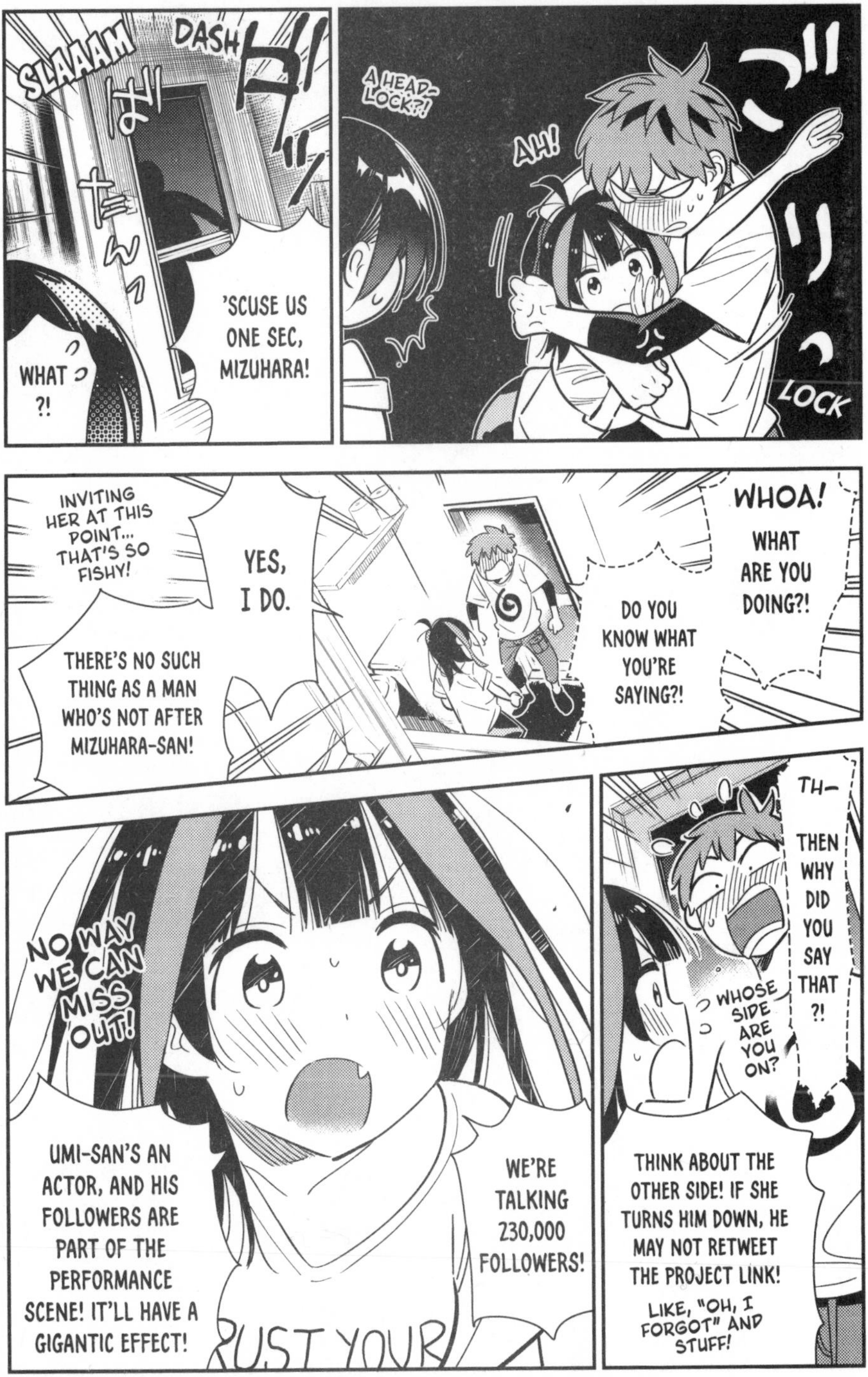
A HEAD-LOCK?!
AH!
LOCK
SLAAAAM
DASH
'SCUSE US ONE SEC, MIZUHARA!
WHAT ?!
WHOA!
WHAT ARE YOU DOING?!
DO YOU KNOW WHAT YOU'RE SAYING?!
YES, I DO.
INVITING HER AT THIS POINT... THAT'S SO FISHY!
THERE'S NO SUCH THING AS A MAN WHO'S NOT AFTER MIZUHARA-SAN!
TH—
THEN WHY DID YOU SAY THAT ?!
WHOSE SIDE ARE YOU ON?
THINK ABOUT THE OTHER SIDE! IF SHE TURNS HIM DOWN, HE MAY NOT RETWEET THE PROJECT LINK!
LIKE, "OH, I FORGOT" AND STUFF!
NO WAY WE CAN MISS OUT!
WE'RE TALKING 230,000 FOLLOWERS!
UMI-SAN'S AN ACTOR, AND HIS FOLLOWERS ARE PART OF THE PERFORMANCE SCENE! IT'LL HAVE A GIGANTIC EFFECT!
RUST YOUR

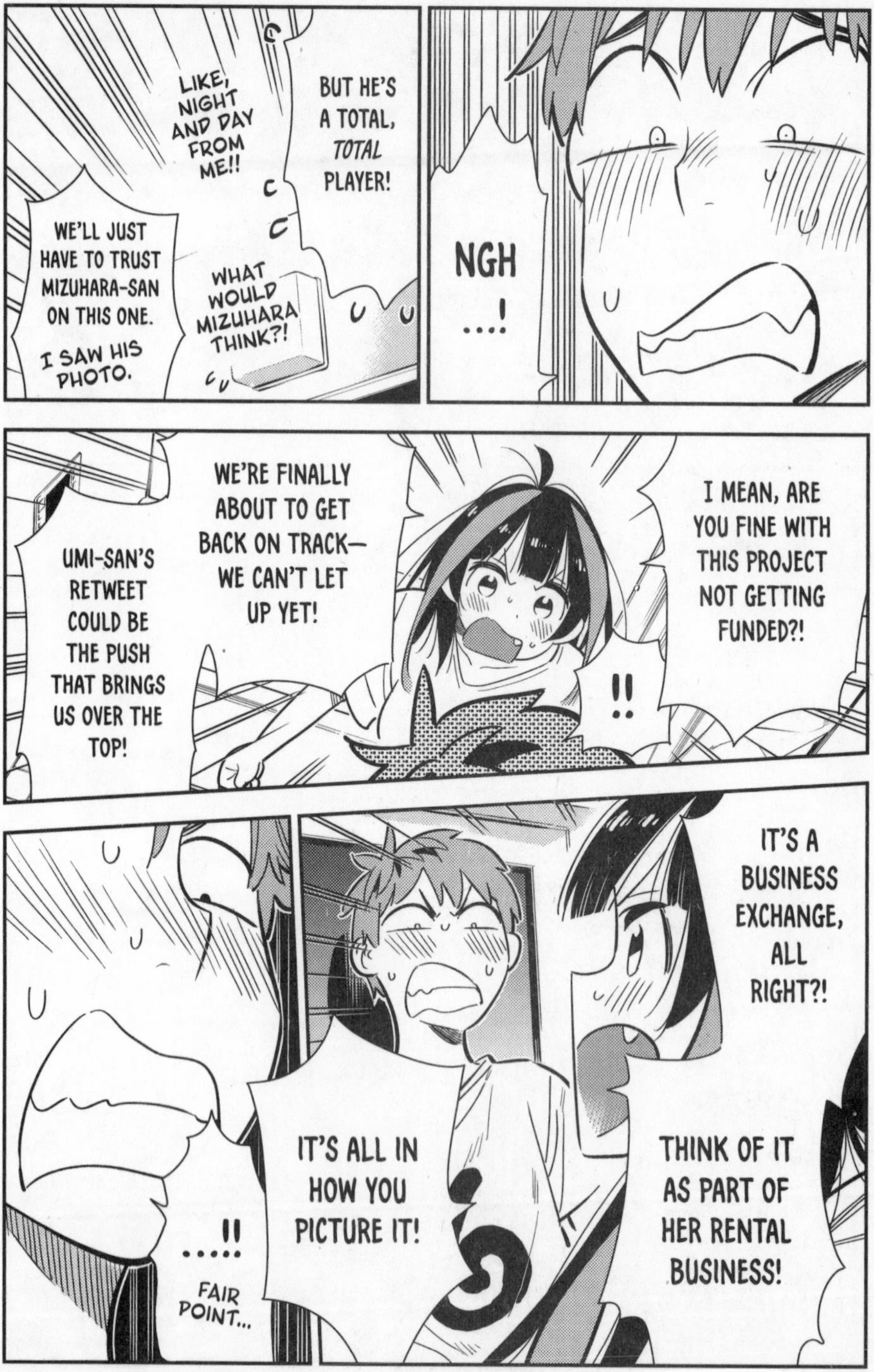
NGH ...!
BUT HE'S A TOTAL, *TOTAL* PLAYER!
LIKE, NIGHT AND DAY FROM ME!!
WHAT WOULD MIZUHARA THINK?!
WE'LL JUST HAVE TO TRUST MIZUHARA-SAN ON THIS ONE.
I SAW HIS PHOTO.
I MEAN, ARE YOU FINE WITH THIS PROJECT NOT GETTING FUNDED?!
!!
WE'RE FINALLY ABOUT TO GET BACK ON TRACK— WE CAN'T LET UP YET!
UMI-SAN'S RETWEET COULD BE THE PUSH THAT BRINGS US OVER THE TOP!
IT'S A BUSINESS EXCHANGE, ALL RIGHT?!
THINK OF IT AS PART OF HER RENTAL BUSINESS!
IT'S ALL IN HOW YOU PICTURE IT!
.....!!
FAIR POINT...

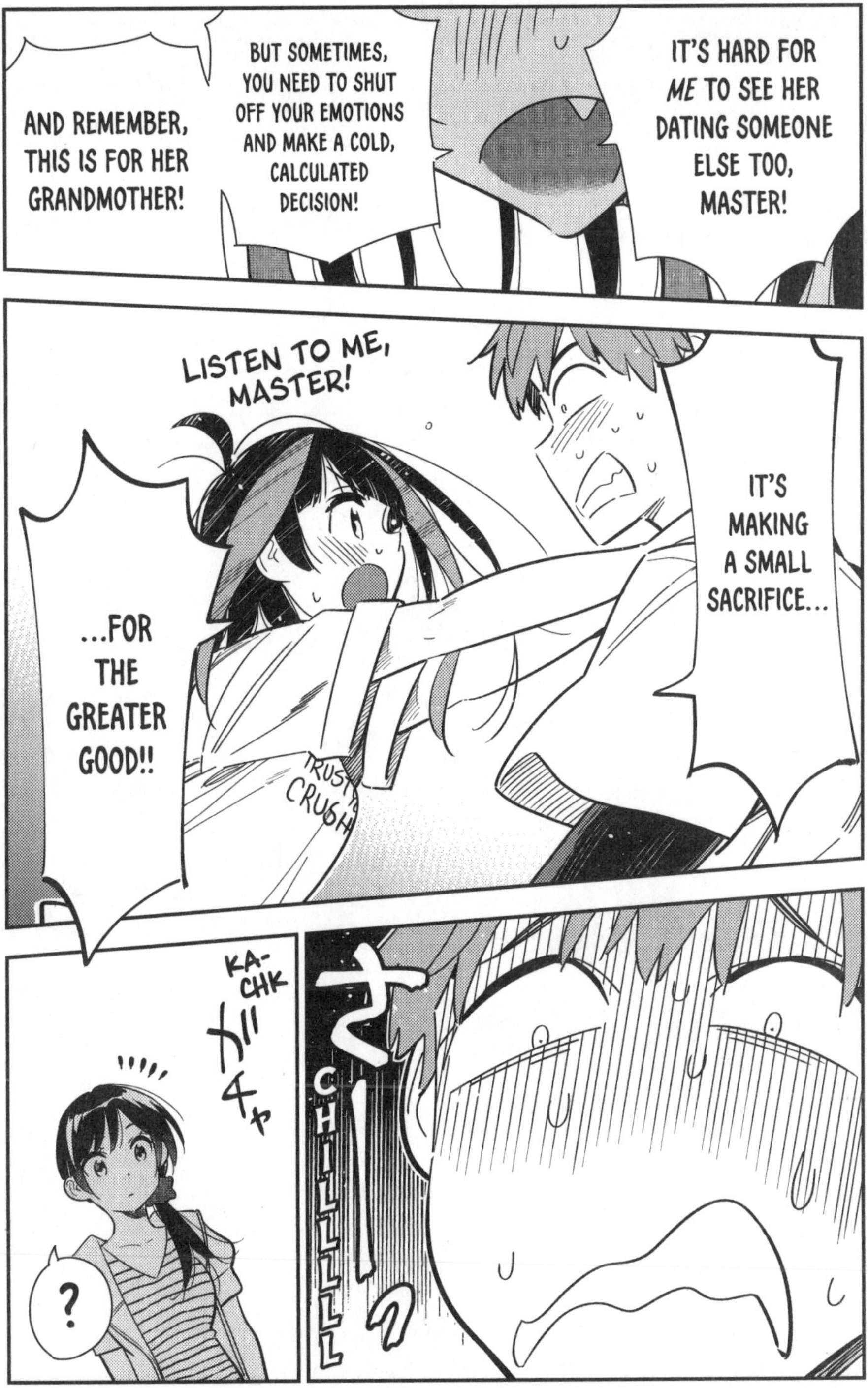
IT'S HARD FOR *ME* TO SEE HER DATING SOMEONE ELSE TOO, MASTER!
BUT SOMETIMES, YOU NEED TO SHUT OFF YOUR EMOTIONS AND MAKE A COLD, CALCULATED DECISION!
AND REMEMBER, THIS IS FOR HER GRANDMOTHER!
LISTEN TO ME, MASTER!
IT'S MAKING A SMALL SACRIFICE...
...FOR THE GREATER GOOD!!
CHILLLLLL
KA-CHK
?

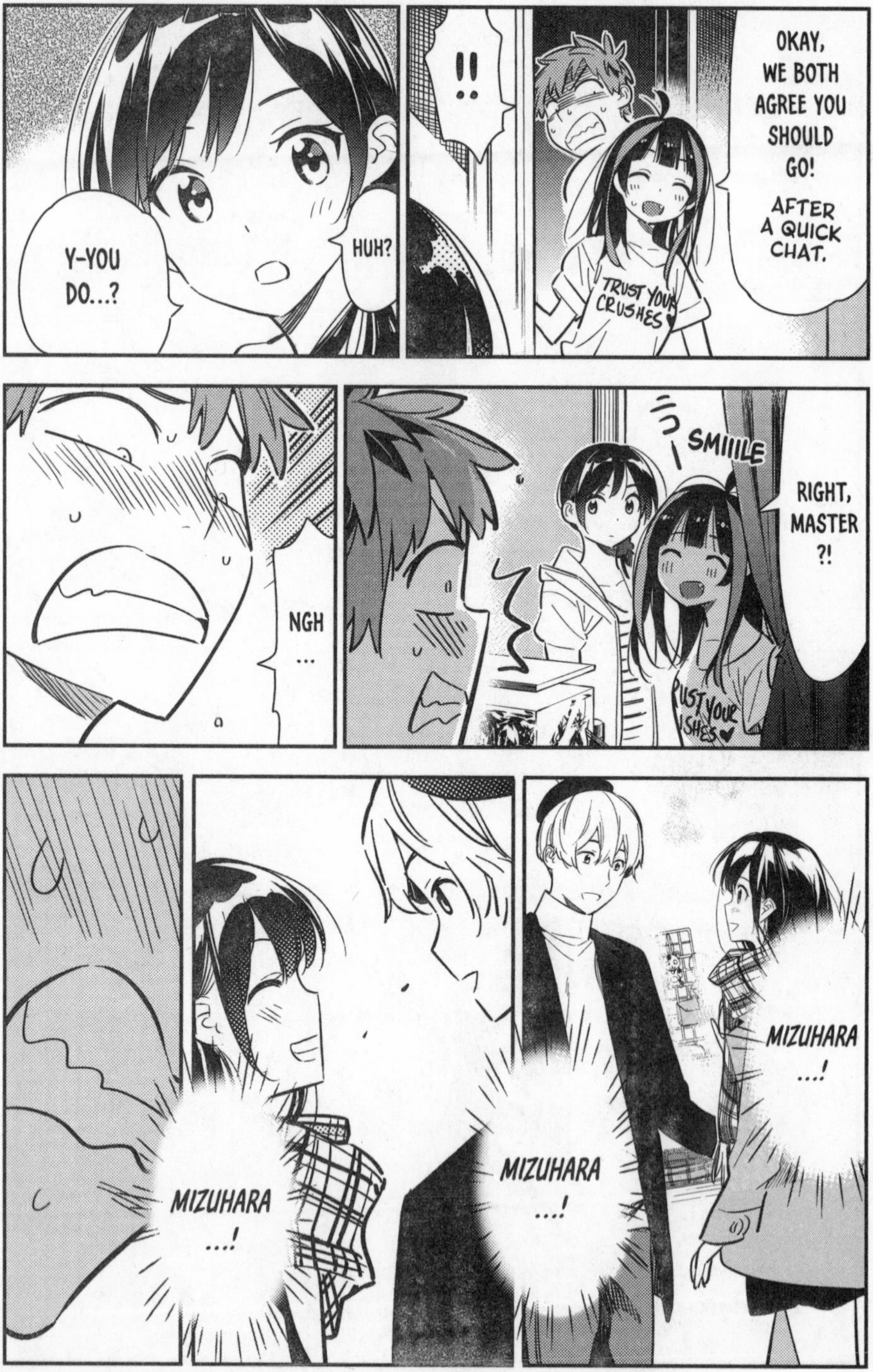
OKAY, WE BOTH AGREE YOU SHOULD GO! AFTER A QUICK CHAT.
TRUST YOUR CRUSHES
!!
HUH?
Y-YOU DO...?
RIGHT, MASTER?!
SMIIILE
NGH...
MIZUHARA...!
MIZUHARA...!
MIZUHARA...!

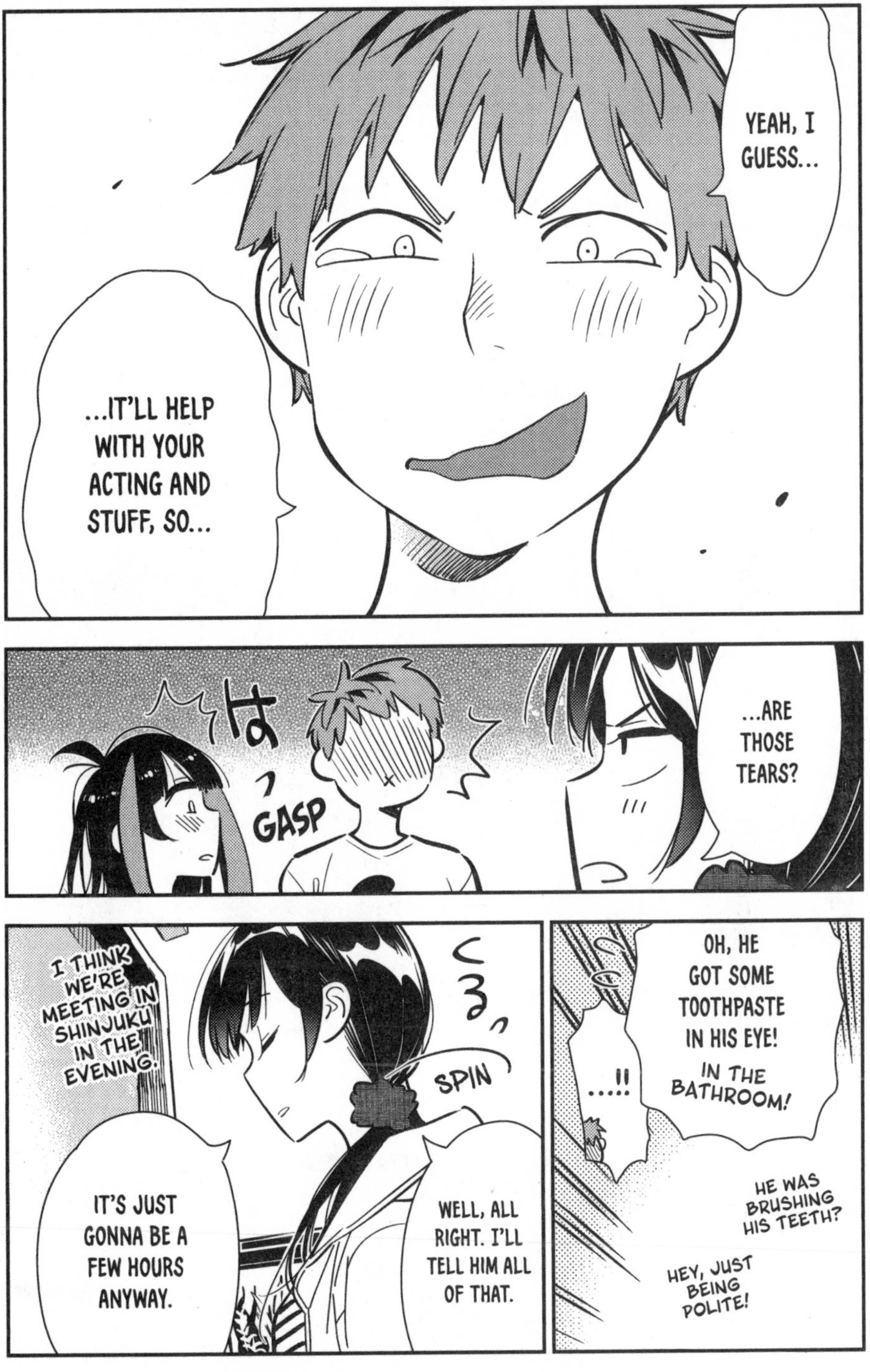
YEAH, I GUESS...
...IT'LL HELP WITH YOUR ACTING AND STUFF, SO...
...ARE THOSE TEARS?
は
GASP
OH, HE GOT SOME TOOTHPASTE IN HIS EYE!
IN THE BATHROOM!
....!!
HE WAS BRUSHING HIS TEETH?
HEY, JUST BEING POLITE!
くる
SPIN
WELL, ALL RIGHT. I'LL TELL HIM ALL OF THAT.
I THINK WE'RE MEETING IN SHINJUKU IN THE EVENING.
IT'S JUST GONNA BE A FEW HOURS ANYWAY.

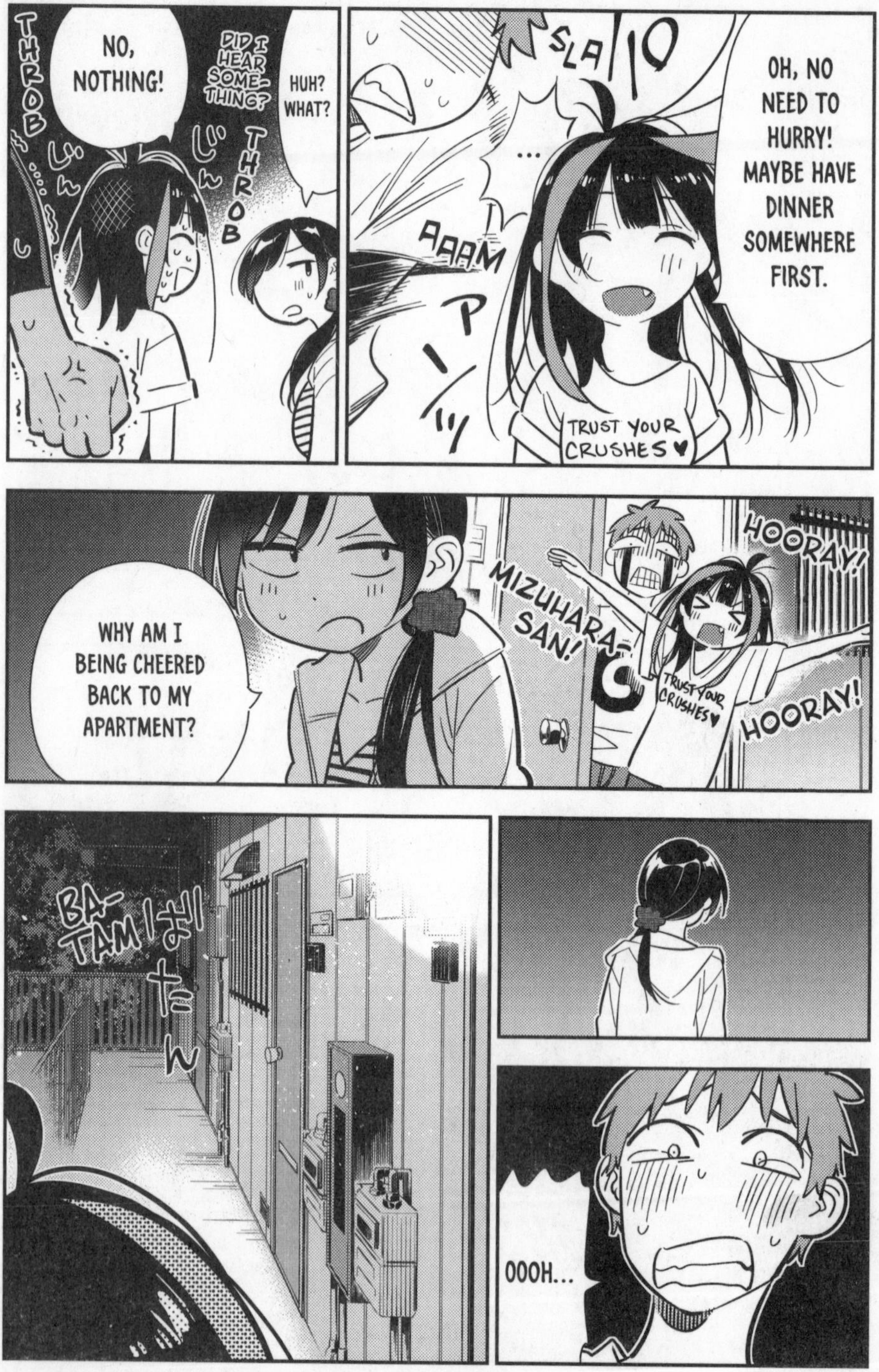
OH, NO NEED TO HURRY! MAYBE HAVE DINNER SOMEWHERE FIRST.
SLAM
...
AAAM
TRUST YOUR CRUSHES♥
HUH? WHAT?
DID I HEAR SOMETHING?
NO, NOTHING!
THROB
THROB
HOORAY!
MIZUHARA-SAN!
HOORAY!
TRUST YOUR CRUSHES♥
WHY AM I BEING CHEERED BACK TO MY APARTMENT?
OOOH...
BA-TAM ばたん

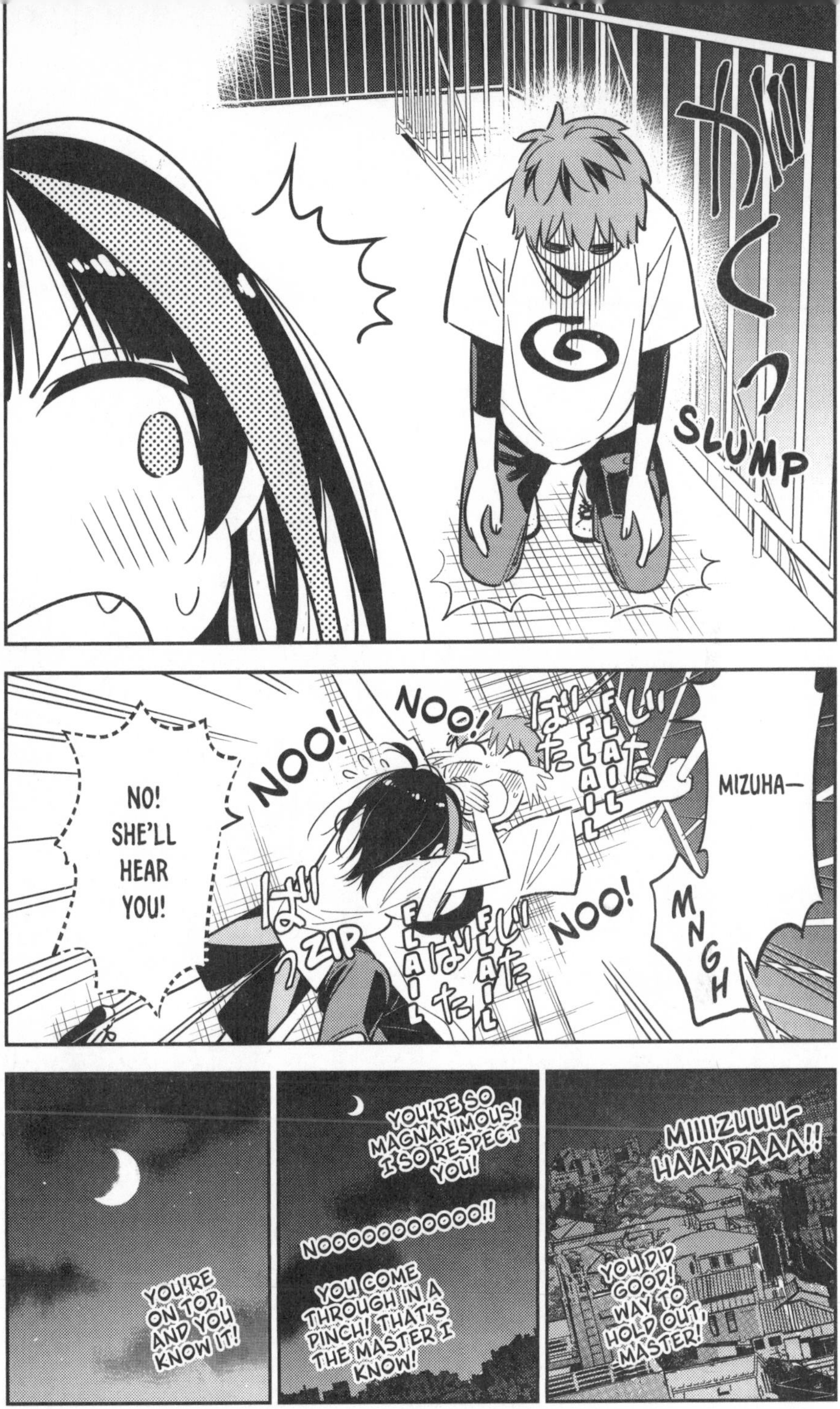
がくっ
SLUMP
MIZUHA—
じたばた
FLAIL FLAIL
NOO!
NOO!
NO! SHE'LL HEAR YOU!
MNGH
NOO!
じたばた
FLAIL FLAIL
ばっ
ZIP
MIIIIZUUU-HAAARAAA!!
YOU DID GOOD! WAY TO HOLD OUT, MASTER!
YOU'RE SO MAGNANIMOUS! I SO RESPECT YOU!
NOOOOOOOOOOO!!
YOU COME THROUGH IN A PINCH! THAT'S THE MASTER I KNOW!
YOU'RE ON TOP, AND YOU KNOW IT!

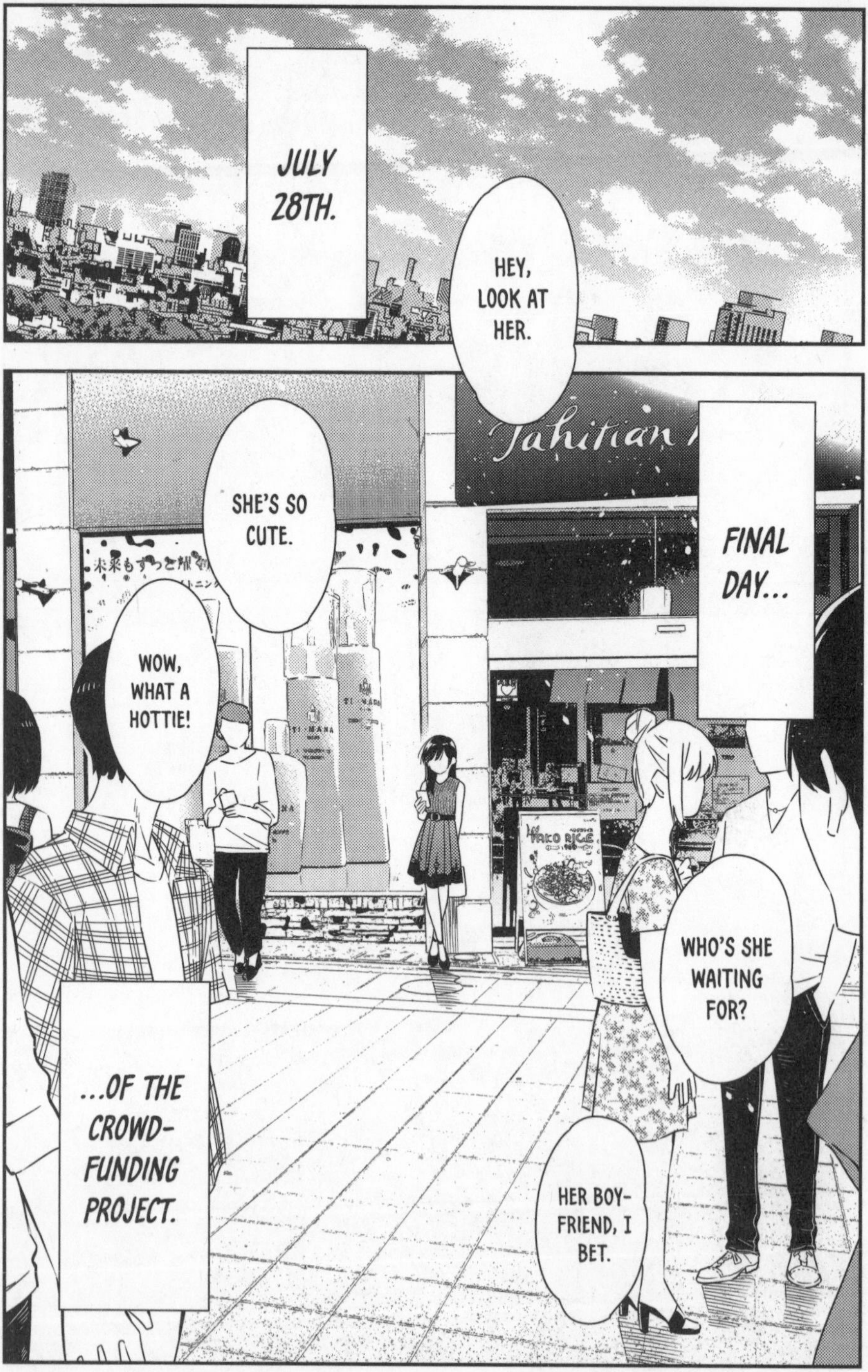
JULY 28TH.
HEY, LOOK AT HER.
FINAL DAY...
SHE'S SO CUTE.
WOW, WHAT A HOTTIE!
WHO'S SHE WAITING FOR?
HER BOY-FRIEND, I BET.
...OF THE CROWD-FUNDING PROJECT.

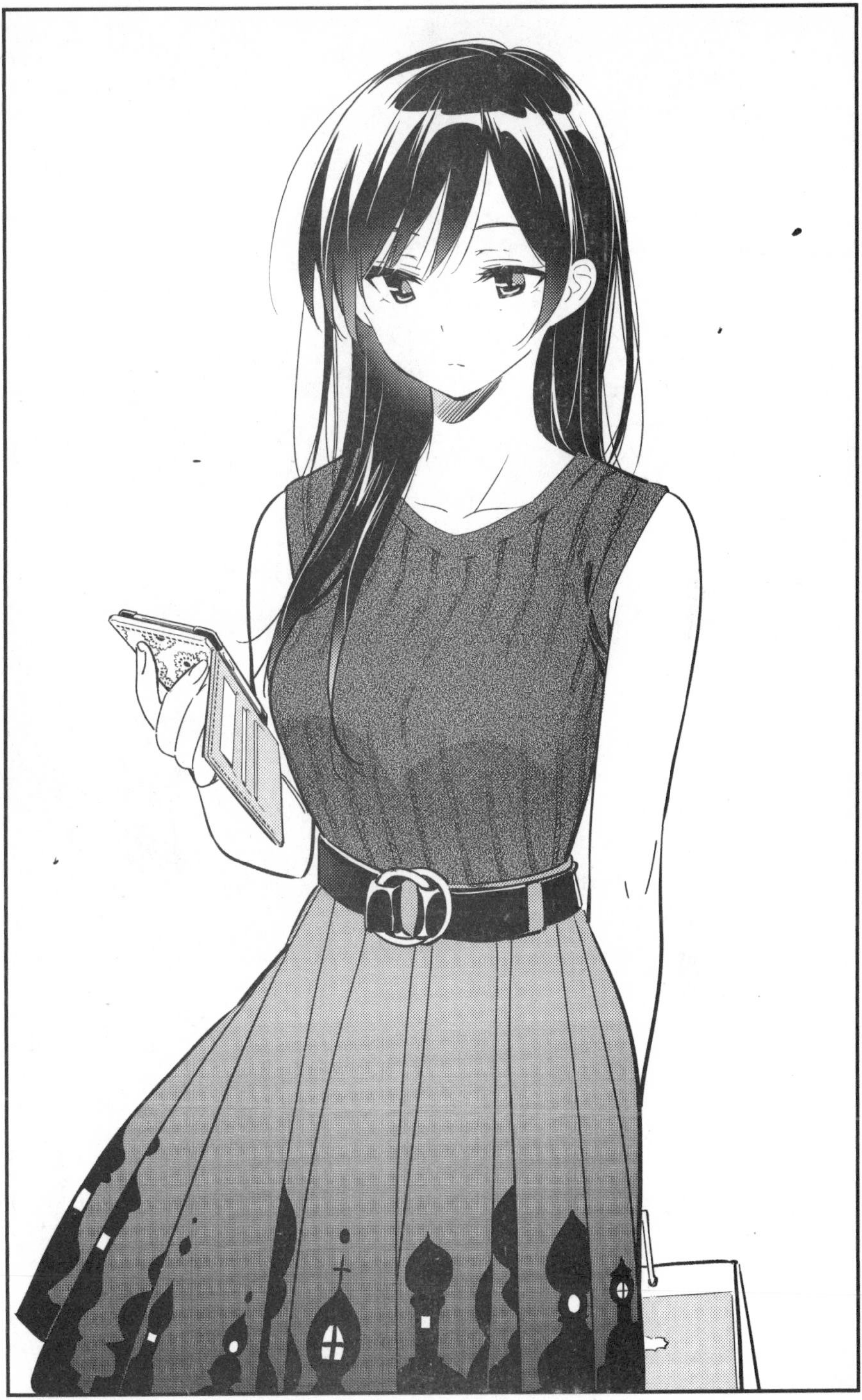

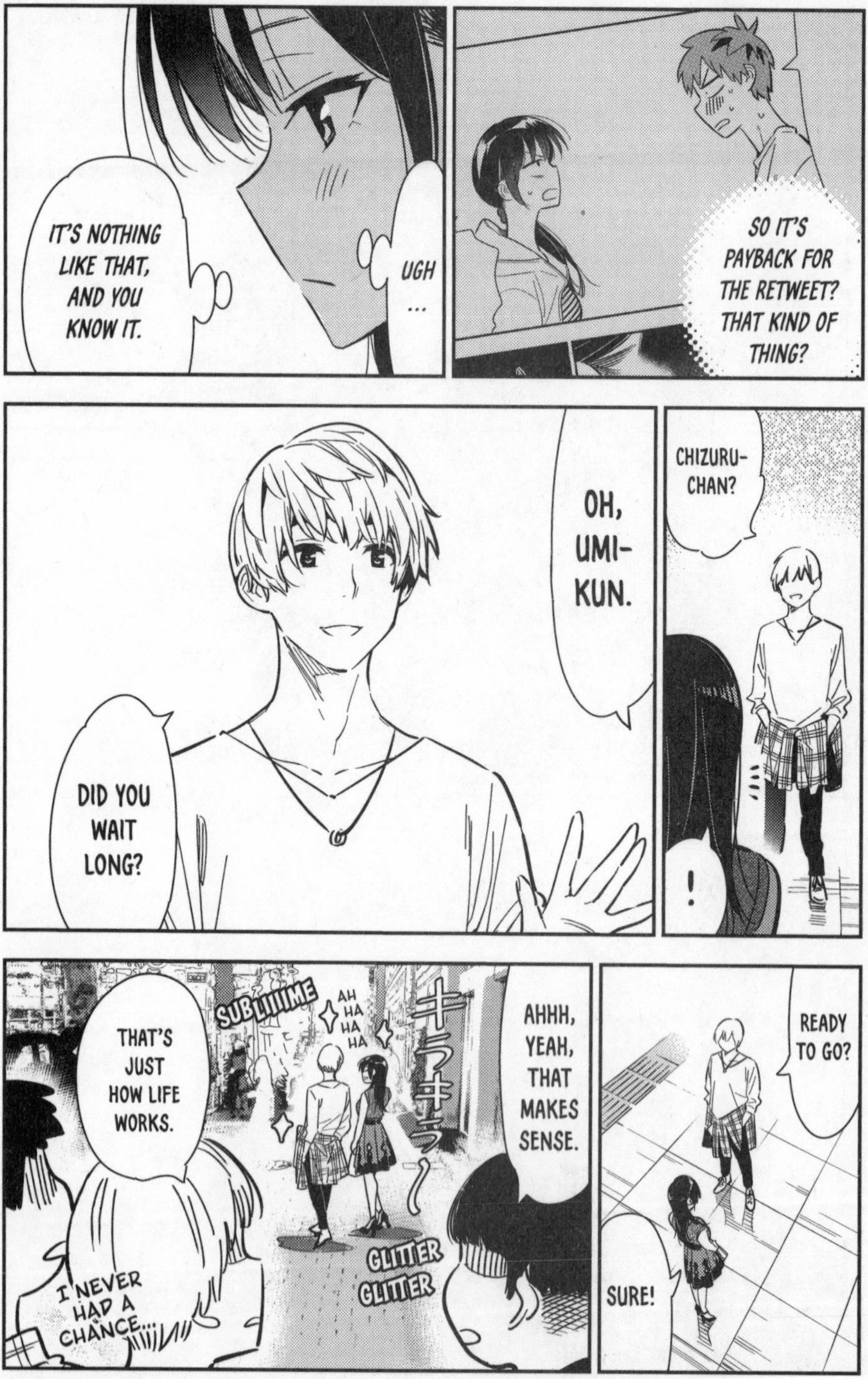
SO IT'S PAYBACK FOR THE RETWEET? THAT KIND OF THING?
UGH ...
IT'S NOTHING LIKE THAT, AND YOU KNOW IT.
CHIZURU-CHAN?
!
OH, UMI-KUN.
DID YOU WAIT LONG?
READY TO GO?
SURE!
AHHH, YEAH, THAT MAKES SENSE.
キラキラ
AH HA HA HA
SUBLIIIIME
GLITTER GLITTER
THAT'S JUST HOW LIFE WORKS.
I NEVER HAD A CHANCE...

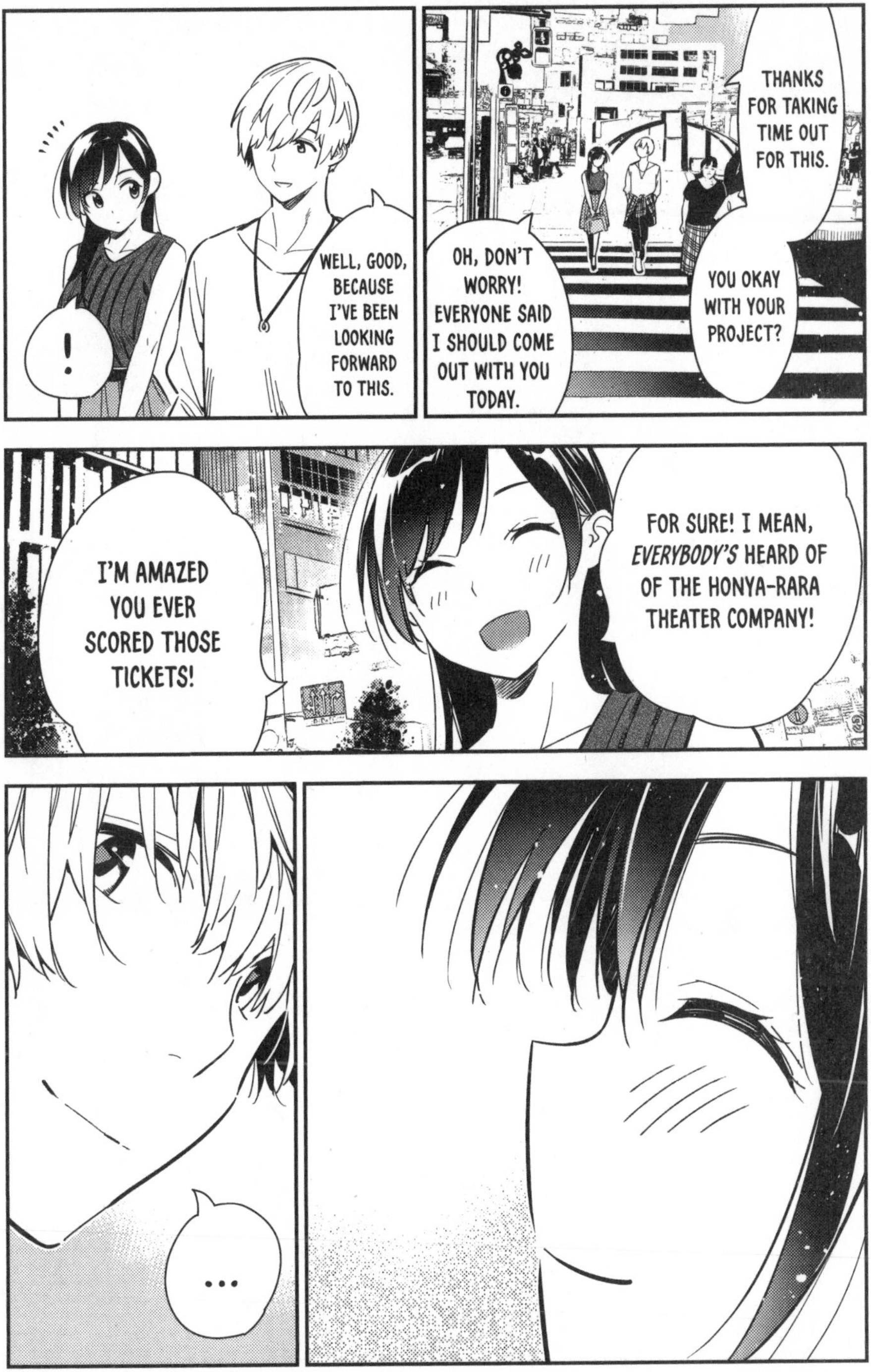
THANKS FOR TAKING TIME OUT FOR THIS.
YOU OKAY WITH YOUR PROJECT?
OH, DON'T WORRY! EVERYONE SAID I SHOULD COME OUT WITH YOU TODAY.
WELL, GOOD, BECAUSE I'VE BEEN LOOKING FORWARD TO THIS.
!
FOR SURE! I MEAN, *EVERYBODY'S* HEARD OF OF THE HONYA-RARA THEATER COMPANY!
I'M AMAZED YOU EVER SCORED THOSE TICKETS!
...

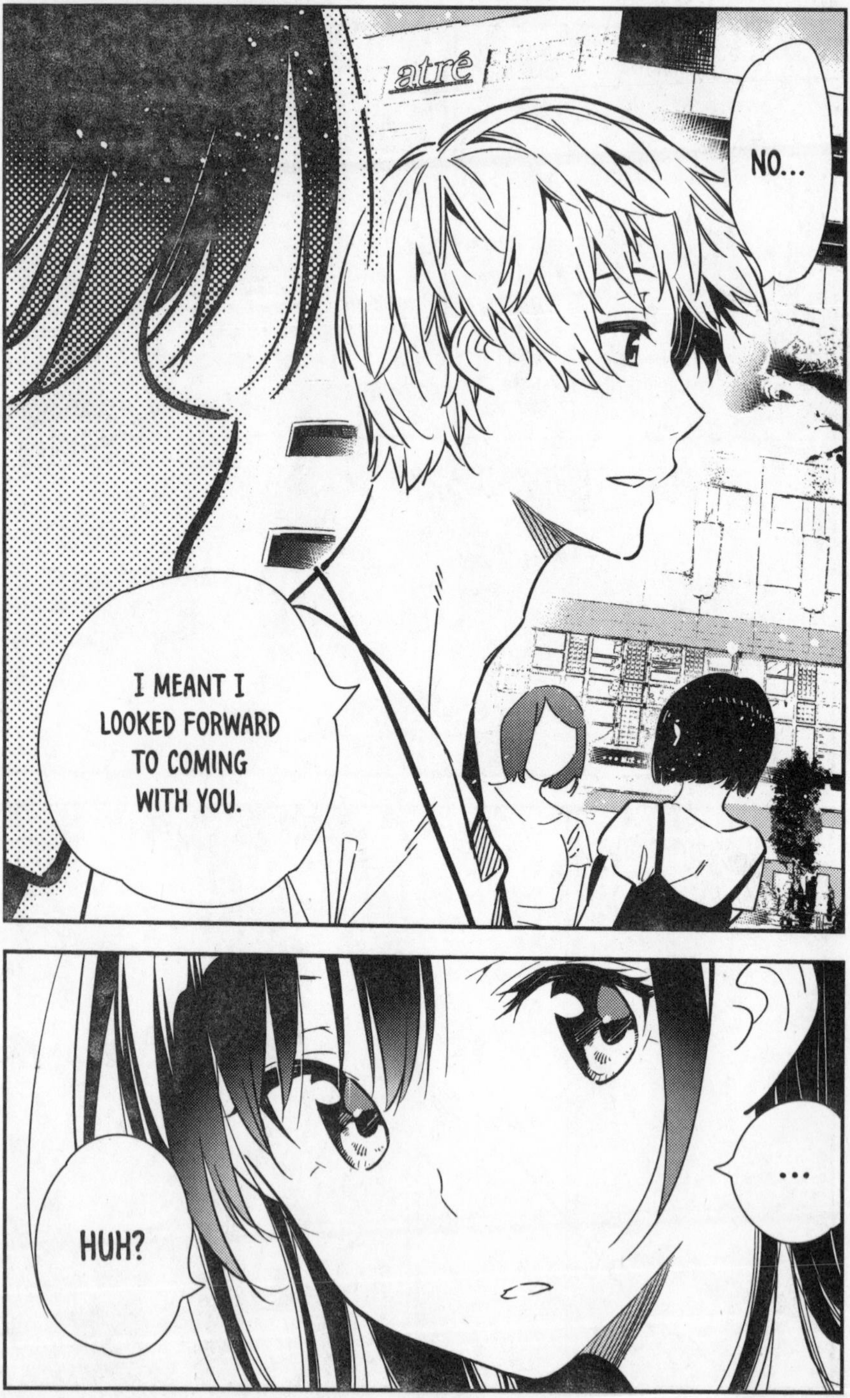
NO...
atré
I MEANT I LOOKED FORWARD TO COMING WITH YOU.
...
HUH?

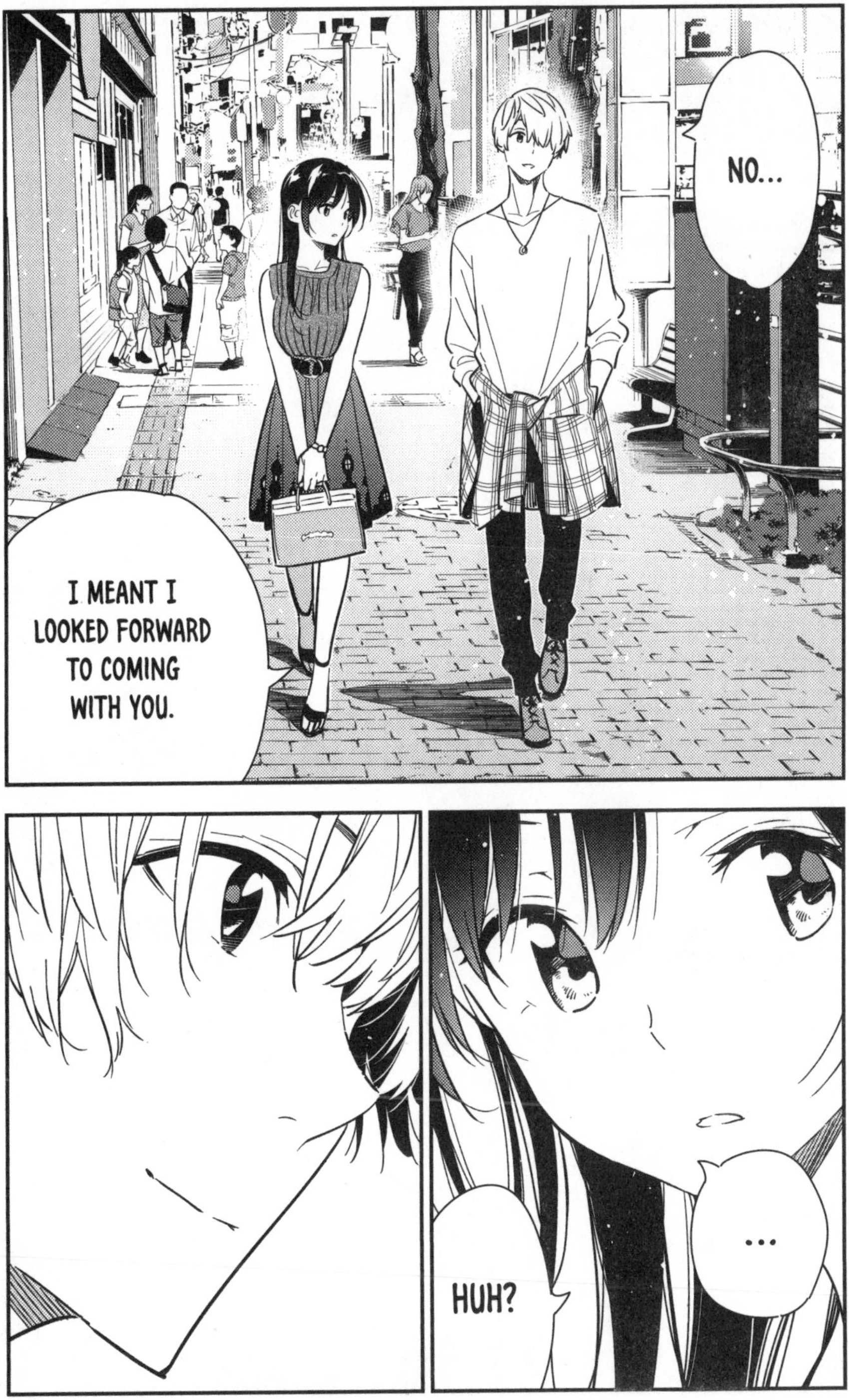
NO...
I MEANT I LOOKED FORWARD TO COMING WITH YOU.
...
HUH?

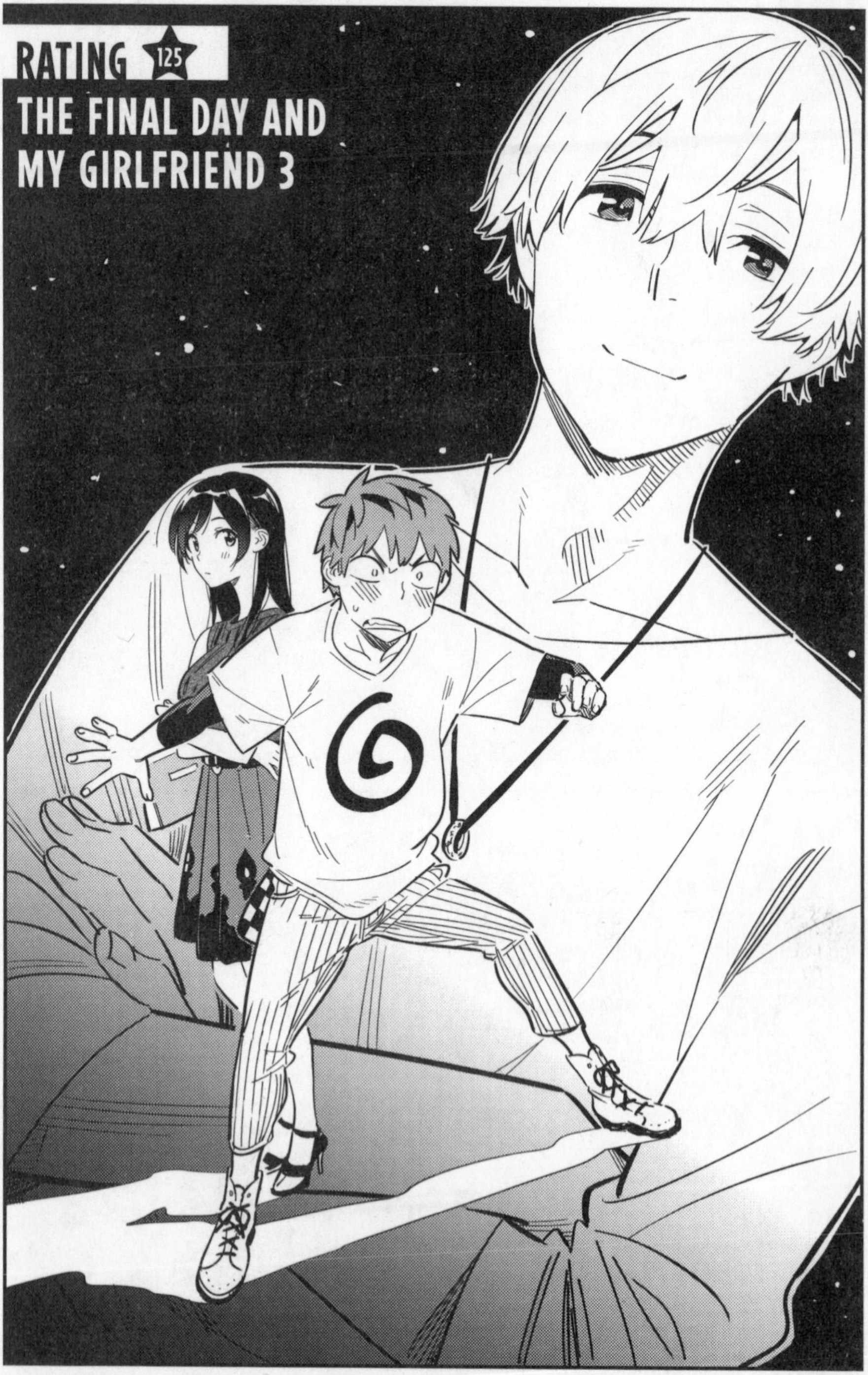
RATING 125
THE FINAL DAY AND MY GIRLFRIEND 3

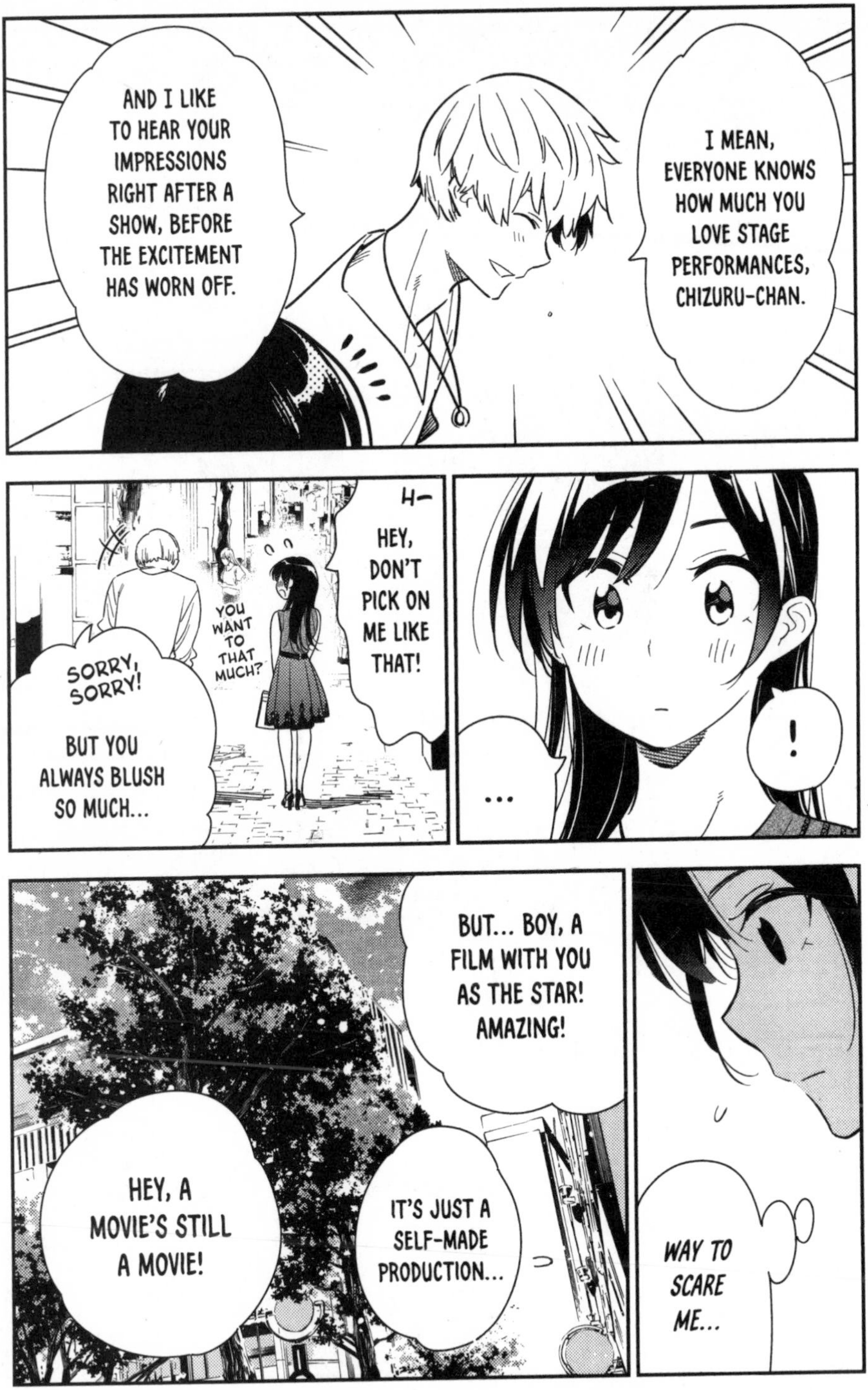
I MEAN, EVERYONE KNOWS HOW MUCH YOU LOVE STAGE PERFORMANCES, CHIZURU-CHAN.
AND I LIKE TO HEAR YOUR IMPRESSIONS RIGHT AFTER A SHOW, BEFORE THE EXCITEMENT HAS WORN OFF.
!
...
H— HEY, DON'T PICK ON ME LIKE THAT!
YOU WANT TO THAT MUCH?
SORRY, SORRY!
BUT YOU ALWAYS BLUSH SO MUCH...
WAY TO SCARE ME...
BUT... BOY, A FILM WITH YOU AS THE STAR! AMAZING!
IT'S JUST A SELF-MADE PRODUCTION...
HEY, A MOVIE'S STILL A MOVIE!

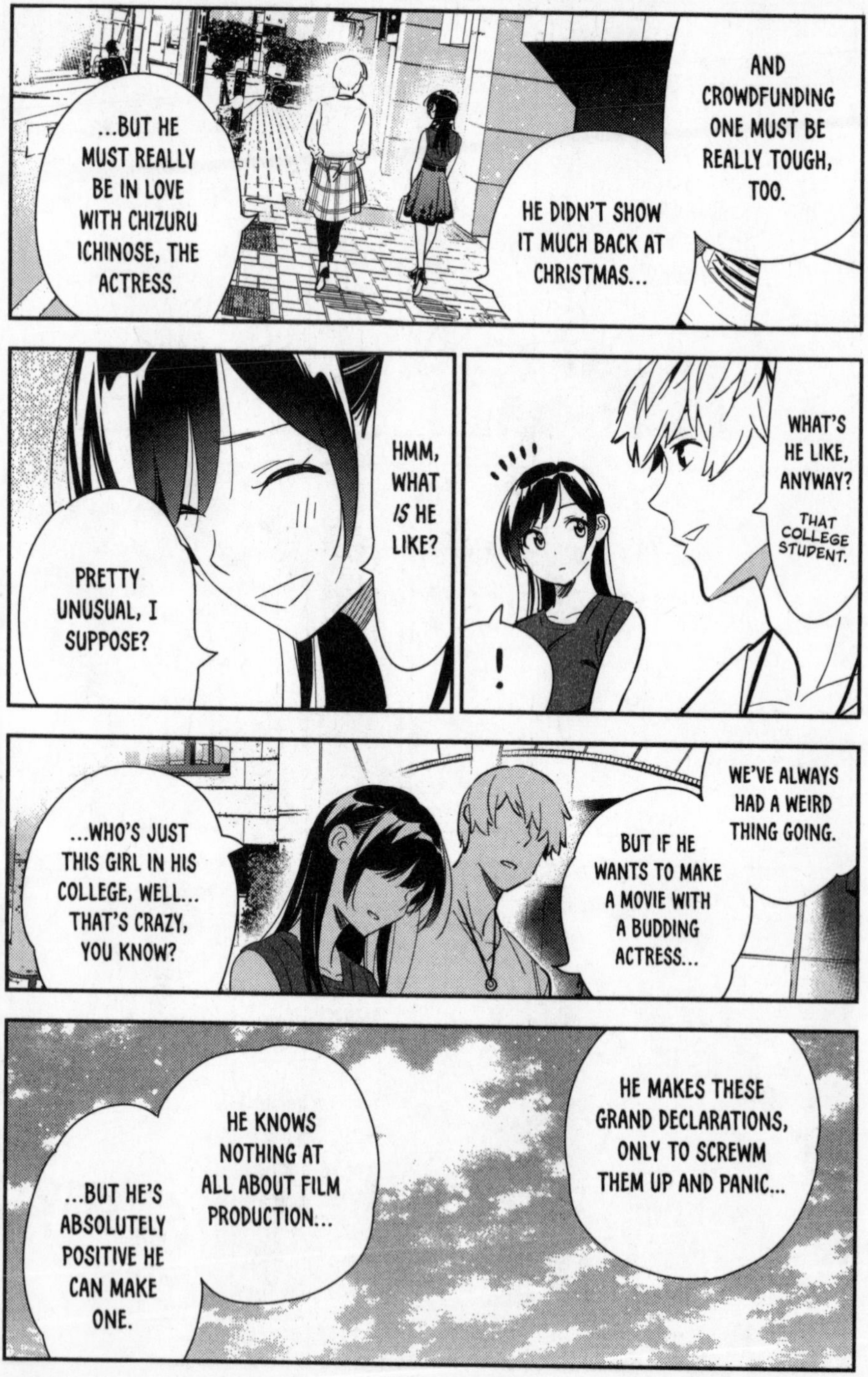
AND CROWDFUNDING ONE MUST BE REALLY TOUGH, TOO.
HE DIDN'T SHOW IT MUCH BACK AT CHRISTMAS...
...BUT HE MUST REALLY BE IN LOVE WITH CHIZURU ICHINOSE, THE ACTRESS.
WHAT'S HE LIKE, ANYWAY?
THAT COLLEGE STUDENT.
!
HMM, WHAT *IS* HE LIKE?
PRETTY UNUSUAL, I SUPPOSE?
WE'VE ALWAYS HAD A WEIRD THING GOING.
BUT IF HE WANTS TO MAKE A MOVIE WITH A BUDDING ACTRESS...
...WHO'S JUST THIS GIRL IN HIS COLLEGE, WELL... THAT'S CRAZY, YOU KNOW?
HE MAKES THESE GRAND DECLARATIONS, ONLY TO SCREWM THEM UP AND PANIC...
HE KNOWS NOTHING AT ALL ABOUT FILM PRODUCTION...
...BUT HE'S ABSOLUTELY POSITIVE HE CAN MAKE ONE.

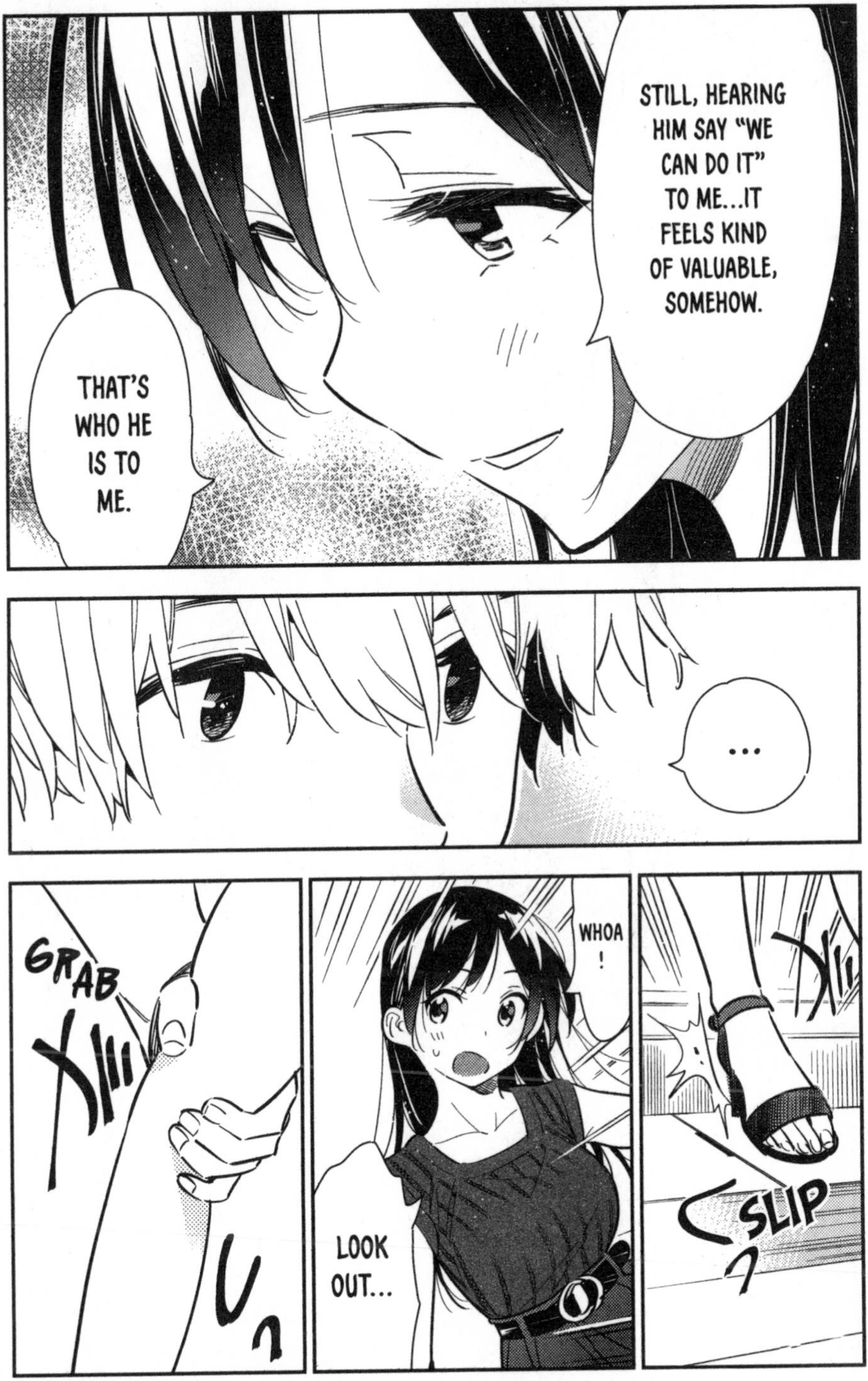
STILL, HEARING HIM SAY "WE CAN DO IT" TO ME...IT FEELS KIND OF VALUABLE, SOMEHOW.
THAT'S WHO HE IS TO ME.
...
SLIP
WHOA!
LOOK OUT...
GRAB

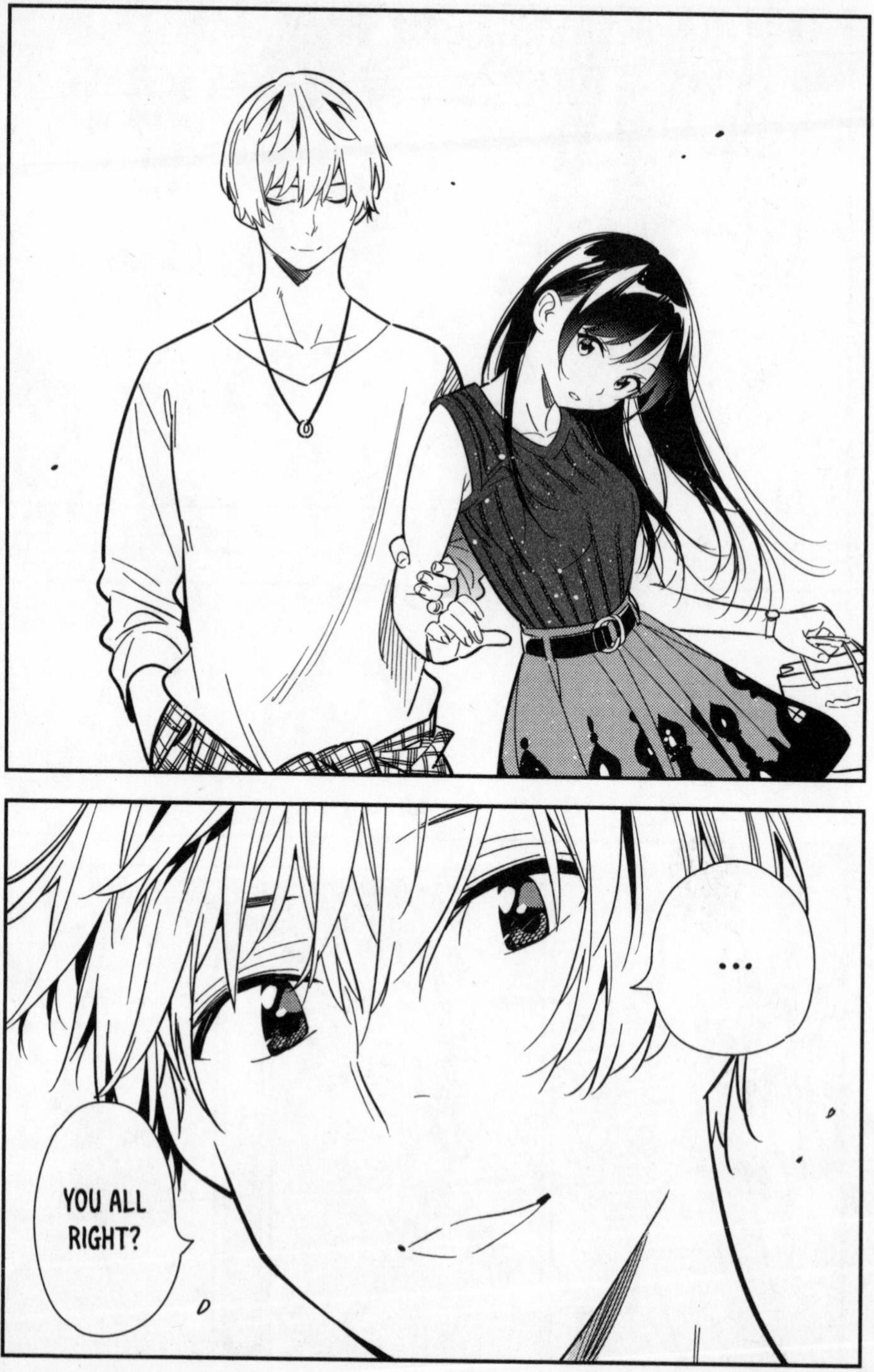
...
YOU ALL RIGHT?

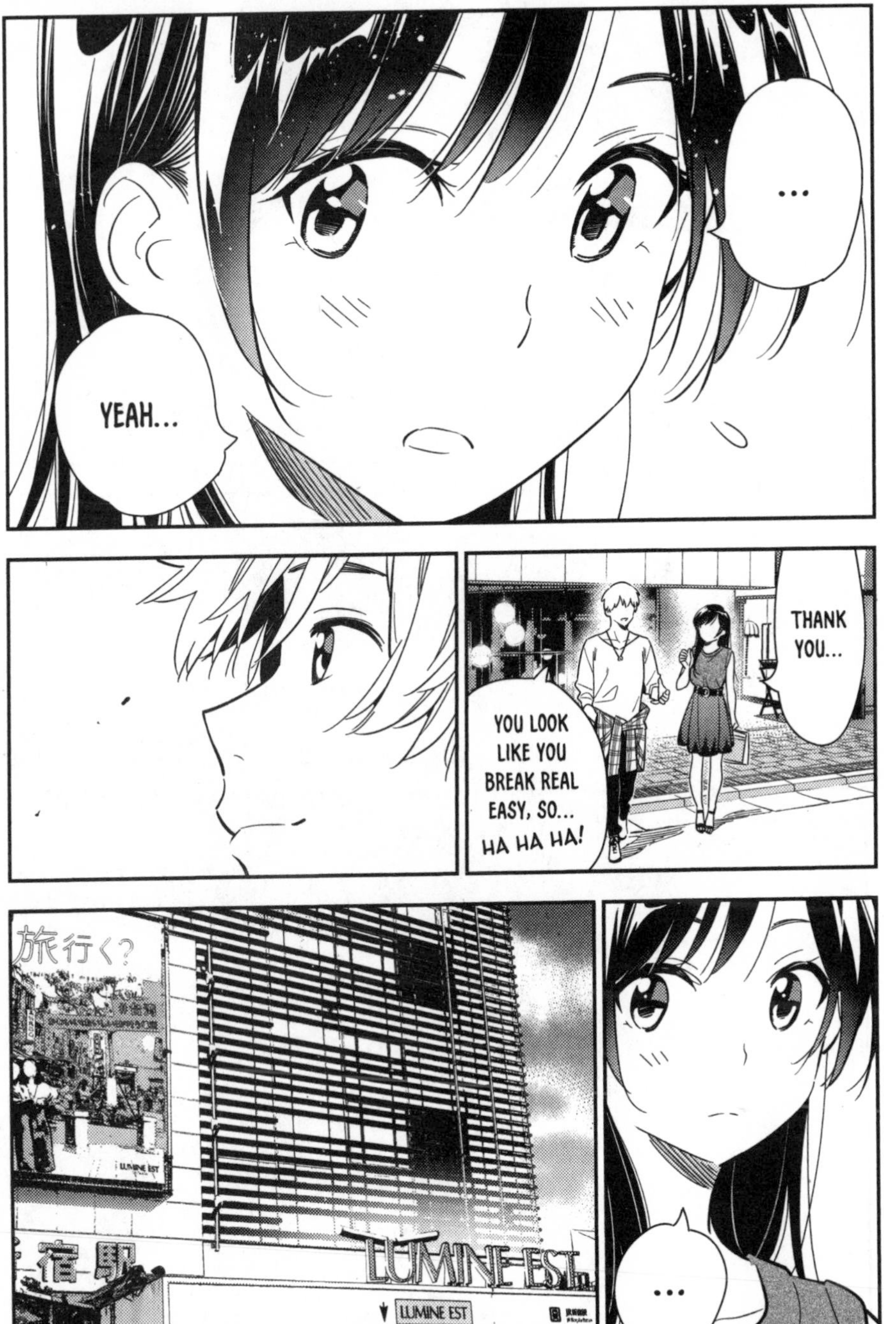
...
YEAH...
THANK YOU...
YOU LOOK LIKE YOU BREAK REAL EASY, SO... HA HA HA!
...
旅行く?
LUMINE EST
LUMINE EST

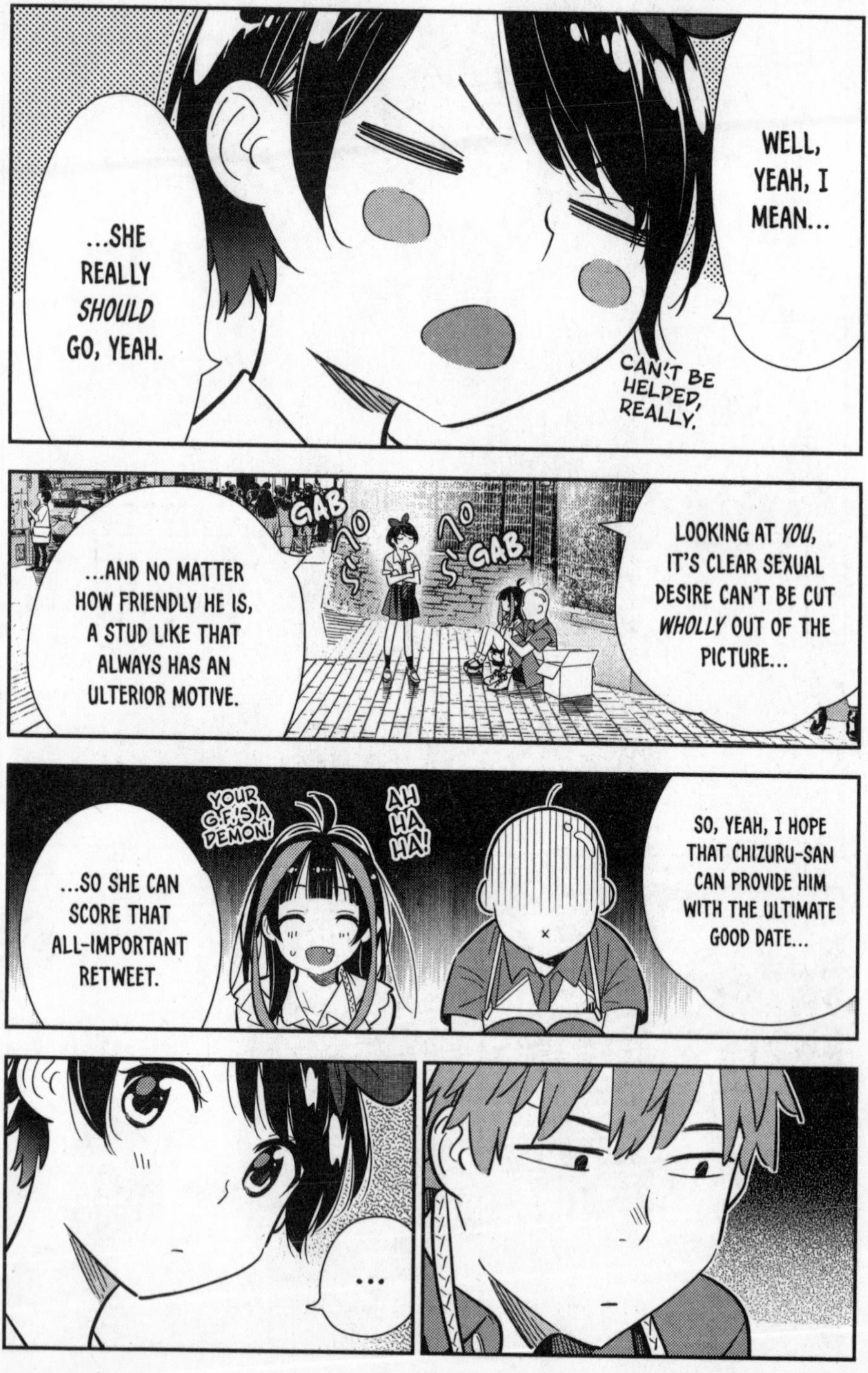
WELL, YEAH, I MEAN...
CAN'T BE HELPED, REALLY.
...SHE REALLY *SHOULD* GO, YEAH.
LOOKING AT *YOU*, IT'S CLEAR SEXUAL DESIRE CAN'T BE CUT *WHOLLY* OUT OF THE PICTURE...
GAB
GAB
...AND NO MATTER HOW FRIENDLY HE IS, A STUD LIKE THAT ALWAYS HAS AN ULTERIOR MOTIVE.
SO, YEAH, I HOPE THAT CHIZURU-SAN CAN PROVIDE HIM WITH THE ULTIMATE GOOD DATE...
AH HA HA!
YOUR G.F.'S A DEMON!
...SO SHE CAN SCORE THAT ALL-IMPORTANT RETWEET.
...

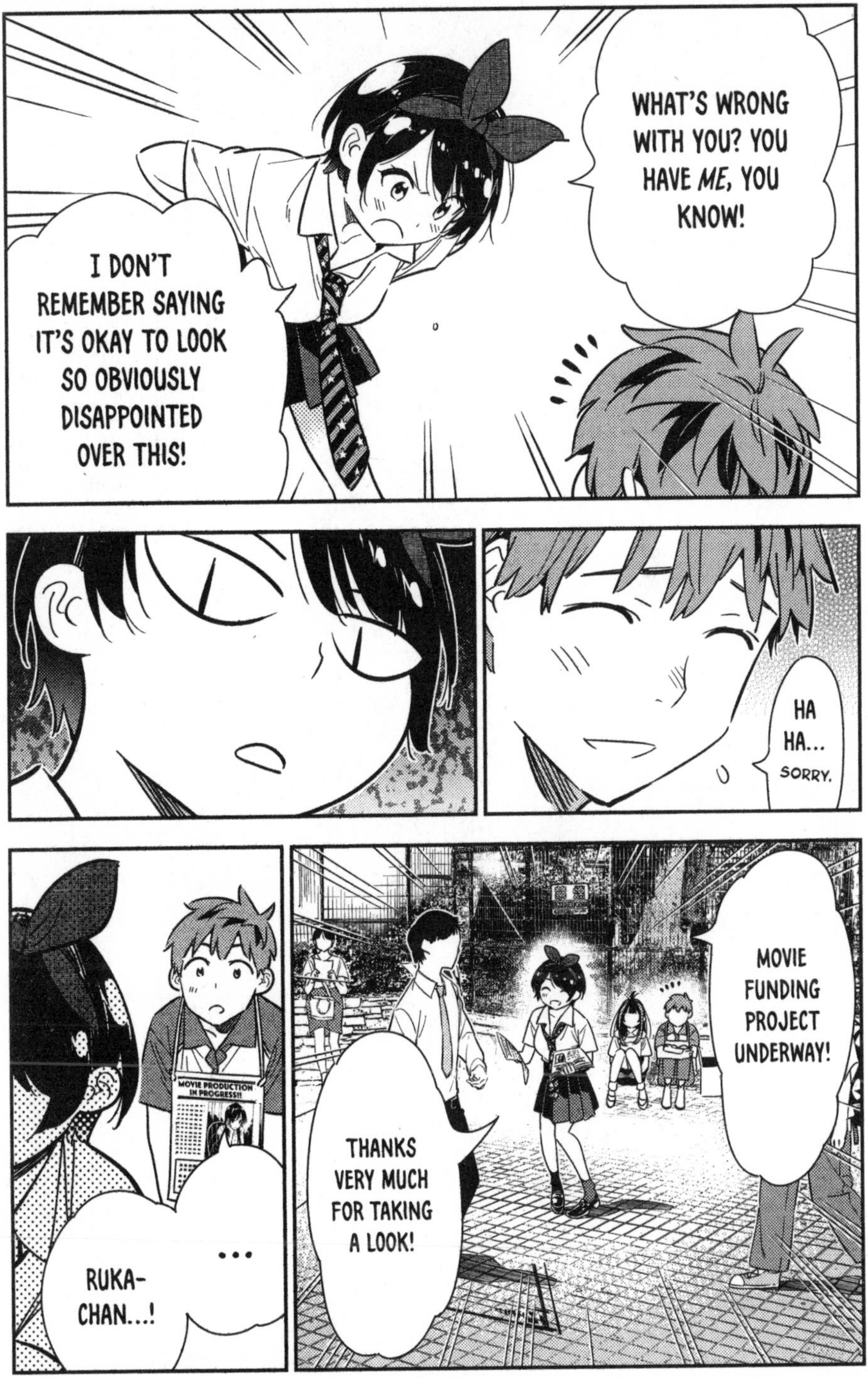
WHAT'S WRONG WITH YOU? YOU HAVE *ME*, YOU KNOW!
I DON'T REMEMBER SAYING IT'S OKAY TO LOOK SO OBVIOUSLY DISAPPOINTED OVER THIS!
HA HA... SORRY.
MOVIE FUNDING PROJECT UNDERWAY!
THANKS VERY MUCH FOR TAKING A LOOK!
MOVIE PRODUCTION IN PROGRESS!!
...
RUKA-CHAN...!

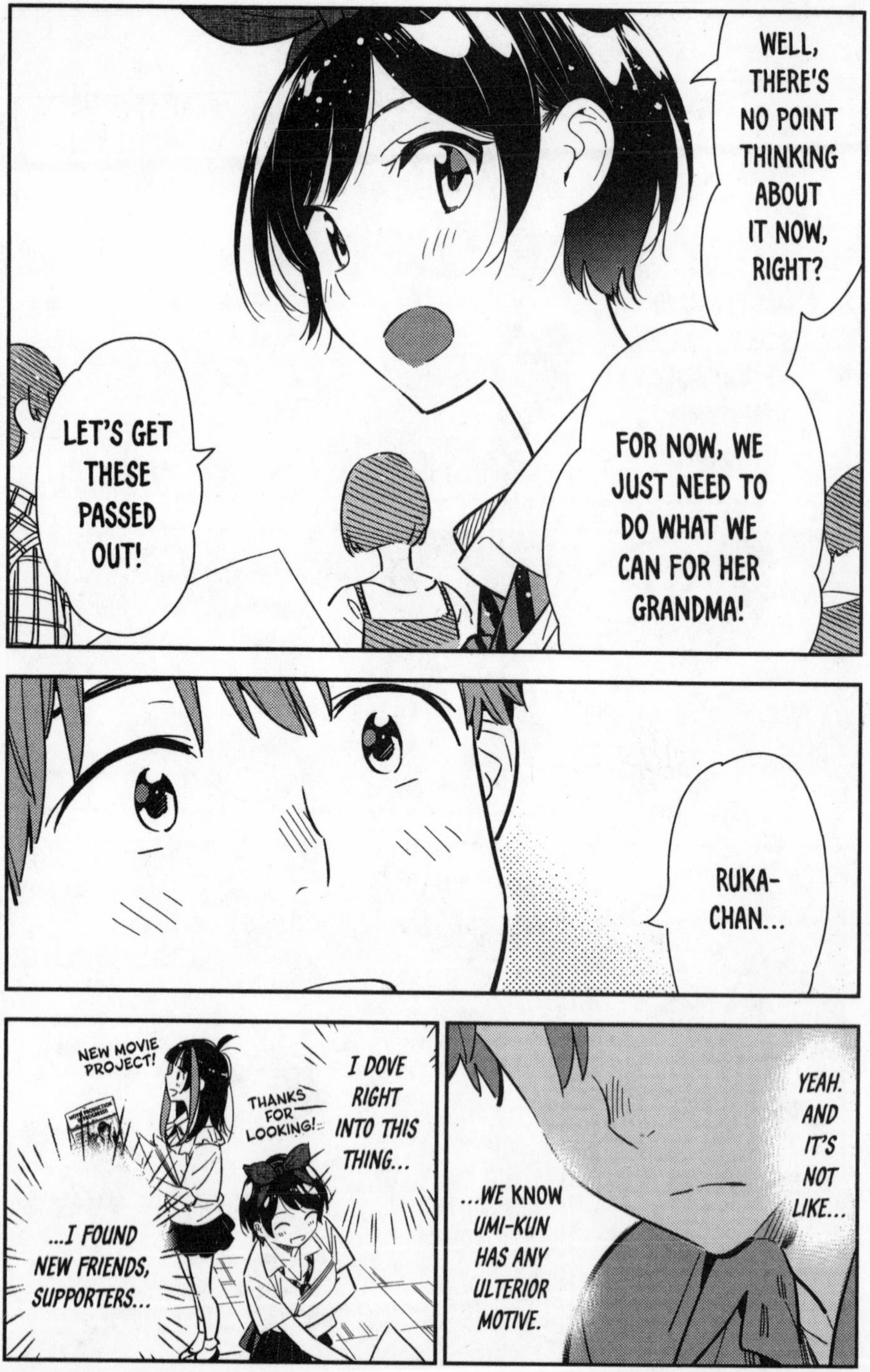
WELL, THERE'S NO POINT THINKING ABOUT IT NOW, RIGHT?
FOR NOW, WE JUST NEED TO DO WHAT WE CAN FOR HER GRANDMA!
LET'S GET THESE PASSED OUT!
RUKA-CHAN...
YEAH. AND IT'S NOT LIKE...
...WE KNOW UMI-KUN HAS ANY ULTERIOR MOTIVE.
I DOVE RIGHT INTO THIS THING...
THANKS FOR LOOKING!
NEW MOVIE PROJECT!
...I FOUND NEW FRIENDS, SUPPORTERS...

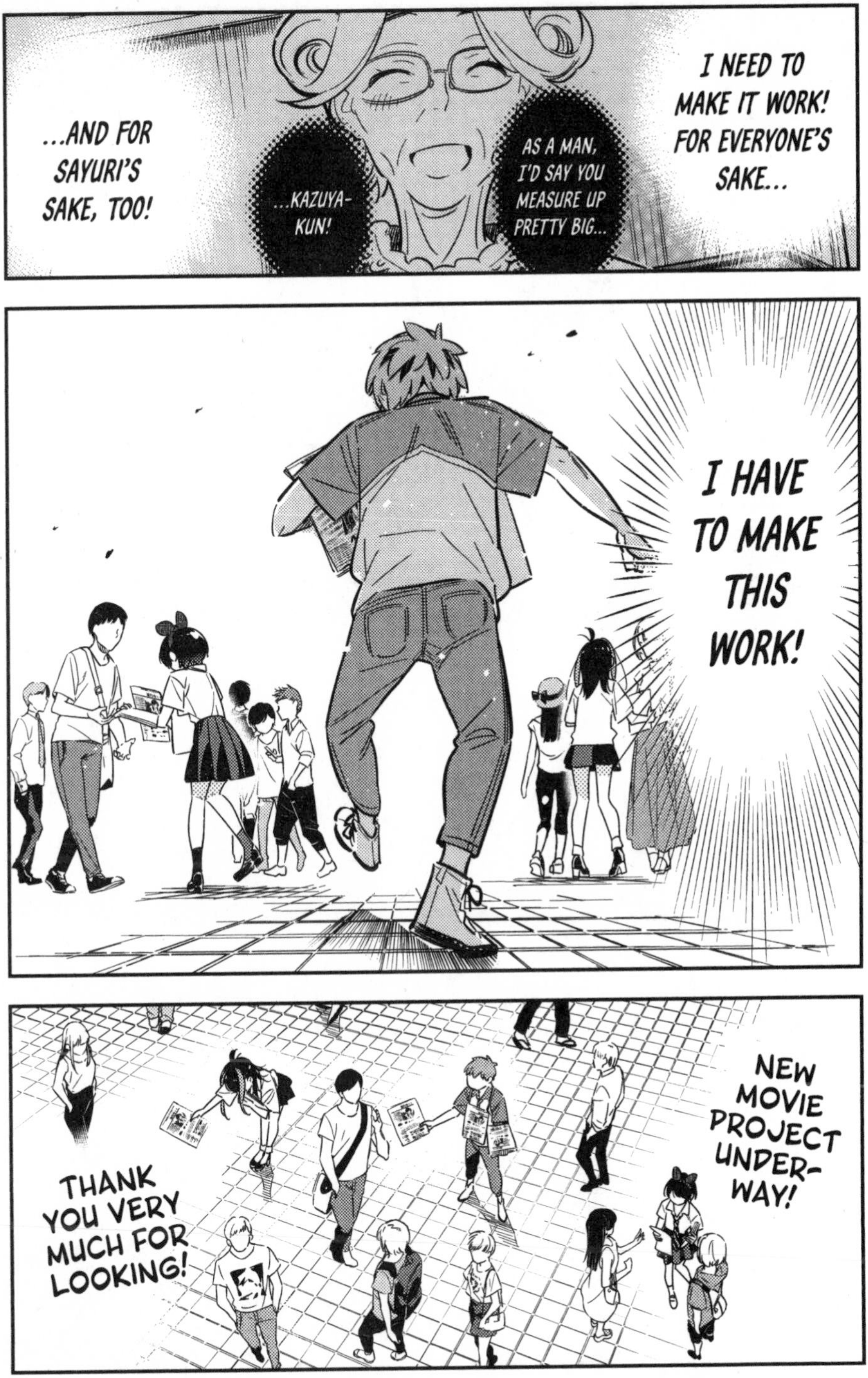
I NEED TO MAKE IT WORK! FOR EVERYONE'S SAKE...
AS A MAN, I'D SAY YOU MEASURE UP PRETTY BIG...
...KAZUYA-KUN!
...AND FOR SAYURI'S SAKE, TOO!
I HAVE TO MAKE THIS WORK!
NEW MOVIE PROJECT UNDER-WAY!
THANK YOU VERY MUCH FOR LOOKING!

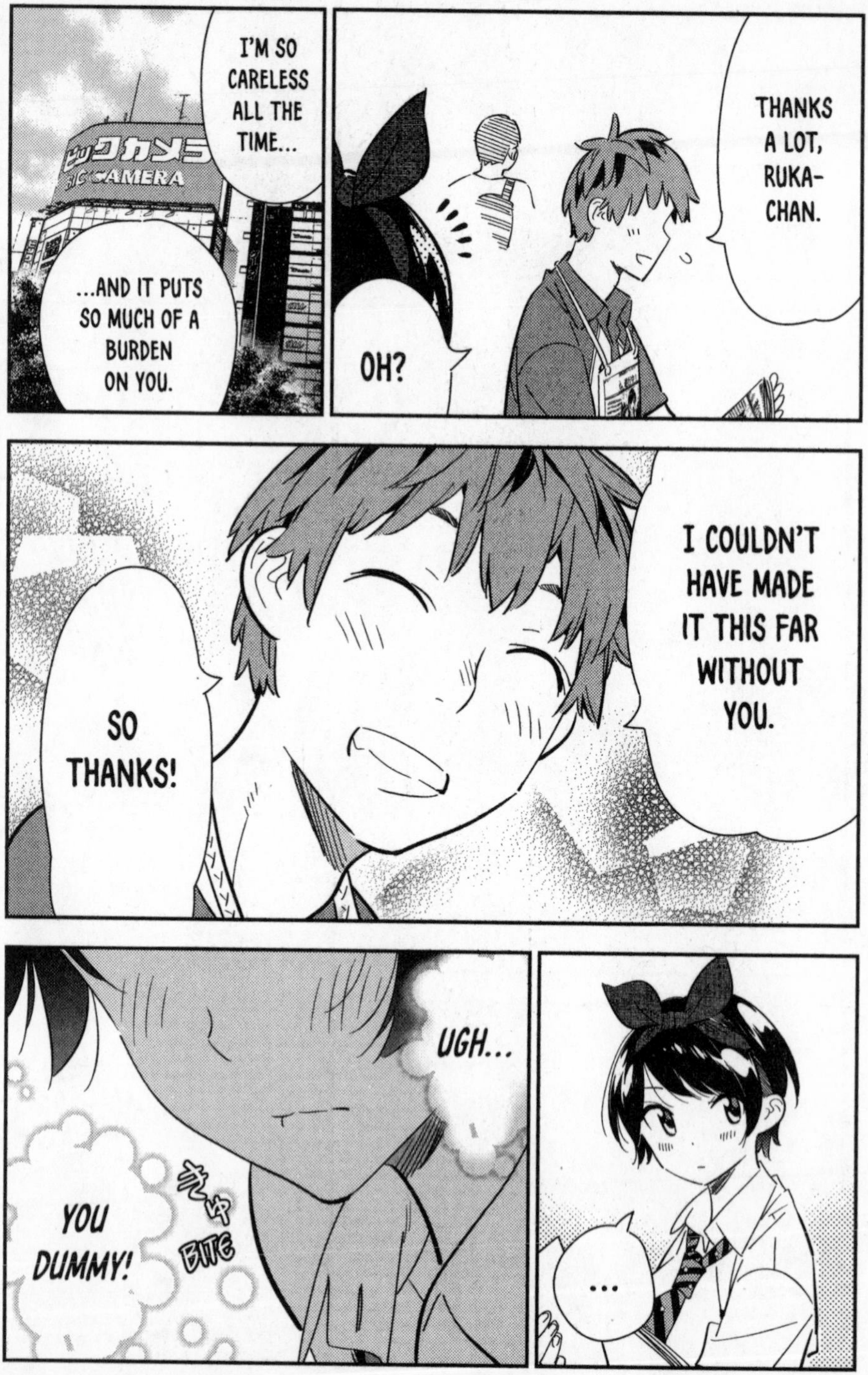
THANKS A LOT, RUKA-CHAN.
OH?
I'M SO CARELESS ALL THE TIME...
...AND IT PUTS SO MUCH OF A BURDEN ON YOU.
I COULDN'T HAVE MADE IT THIS FAR WITHOUT YOU.
SO THANKS!
...
UGH...
きゅ
BITE
YOU DUMMY!

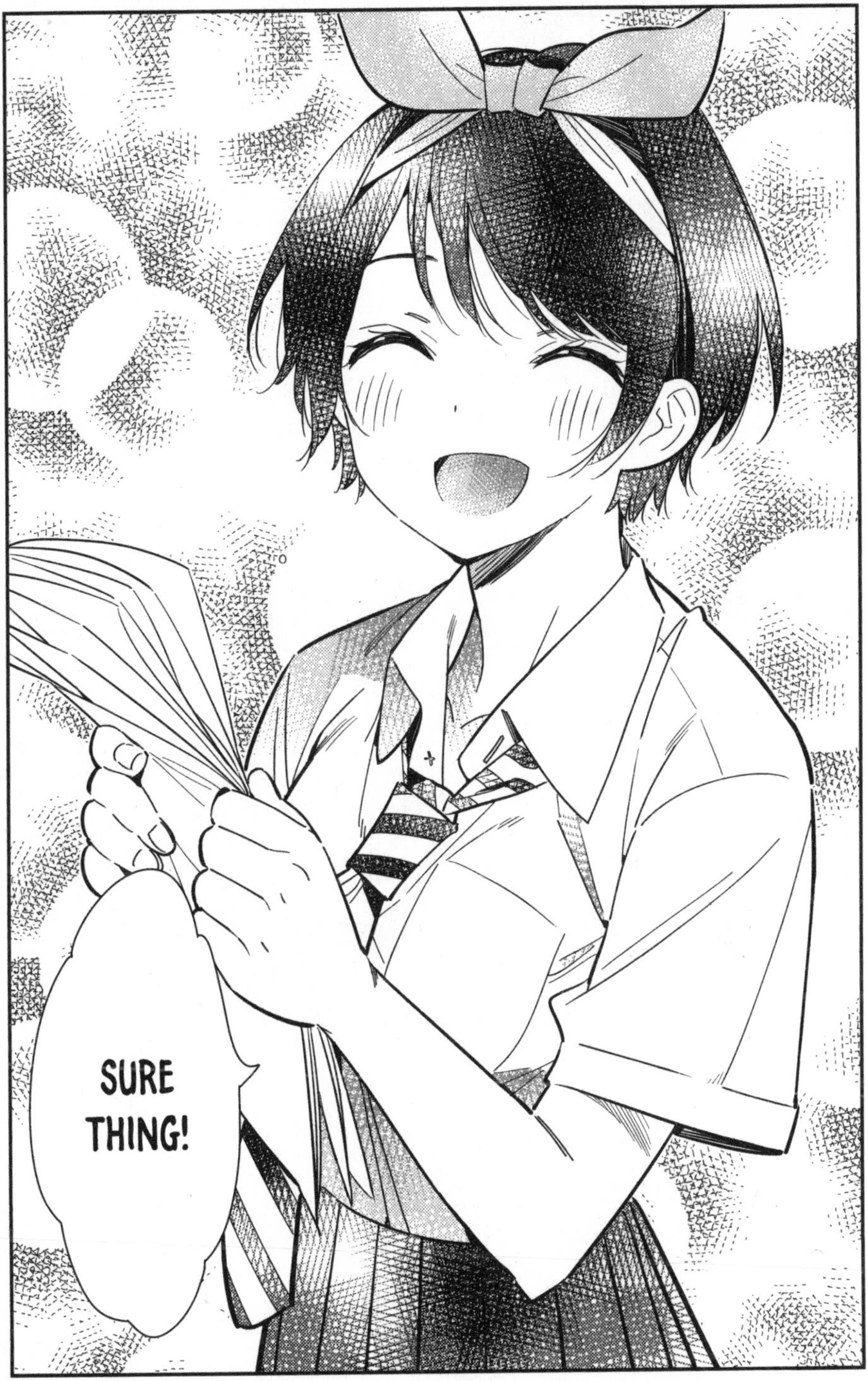
SURE THING!

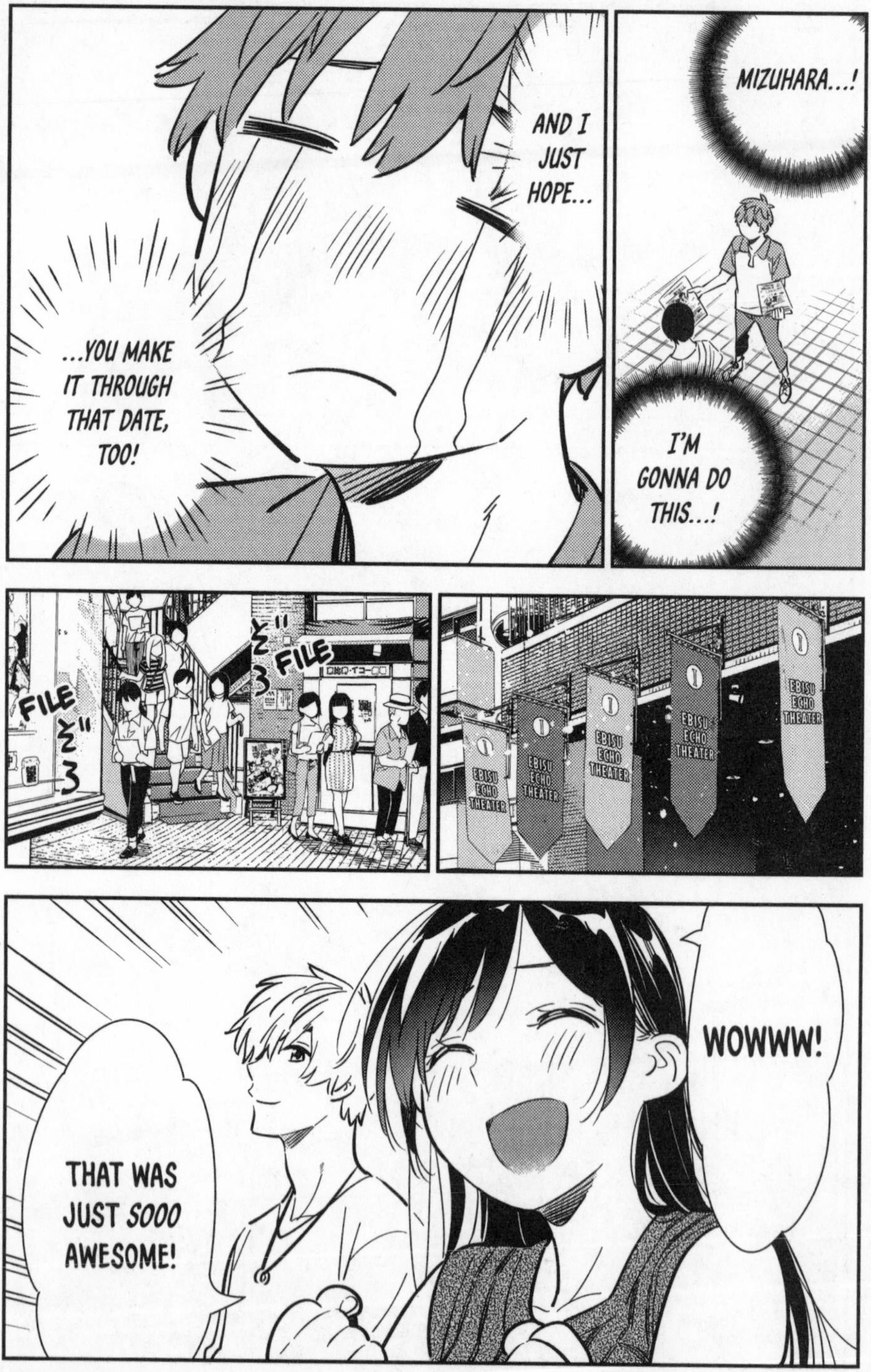
MIZUHARA...!
I'M GONNA DO THIS...!
AND I JUST HOPE...
...YOU MAKE IT THROUGH THAT DATE, TOO!
EBISU ECHO THEATER
FILE
FILE
WOWWW!
THAT WAS JUST SOOO AWESOME!

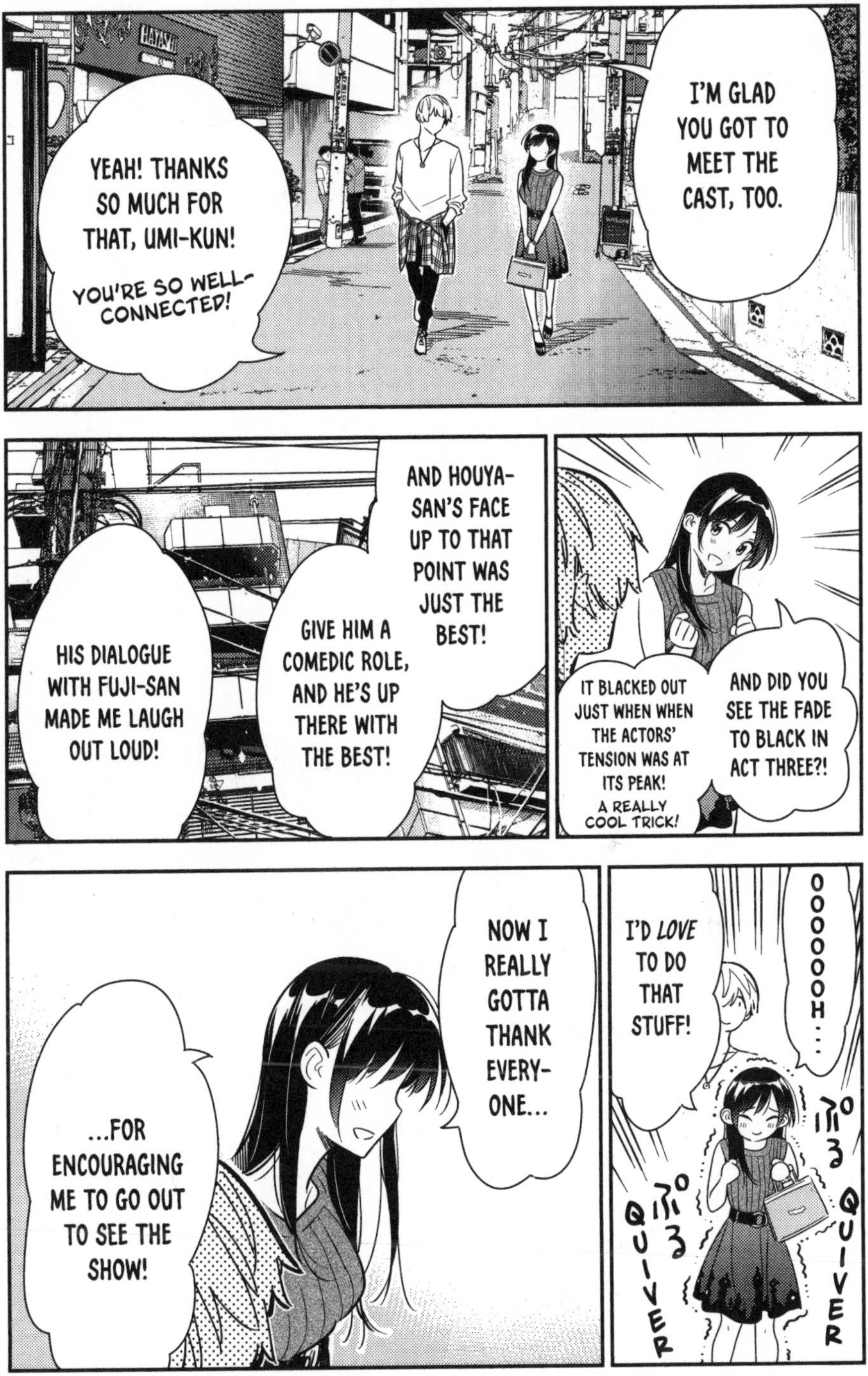
I'M GLAD YOU GOT TO MEET THE CAST, TOO.
YEAH! THANKS SO MUCH FOR THAT, UMI-KUN!
YOU'RE SO WELL-CONNECTED!
AND DID YOU SEE THE FADE TO BLACK IN ACT THREE?!
IT BLACKED OUT JUST WHEN WHEN THE ACTORS' TENSION WAS AT ITS PEAK!
A REALLY COOL TRICK!
AND HOUYA-SAN'S FACE UP TO THAT POINT WAS JUST THE BEST!
GIVE HIM A COMEDIC ROLE, AND HE'S UP THERE WITH THE BEST!
HIS DIALOGUE WITH FUJI-SAN MADE ME LAUGH OUT LOUD!
OOOOOOOH...
I'D *LOVE* TO DO THAT STUFF!
ぷる QUIVER
ぷる QUIVER
NOW I REALLY GOTTA THANK EVERY-ONE...
...FOR ENCOURAGING ME TO GO OUT TO SEE THE SHOW!

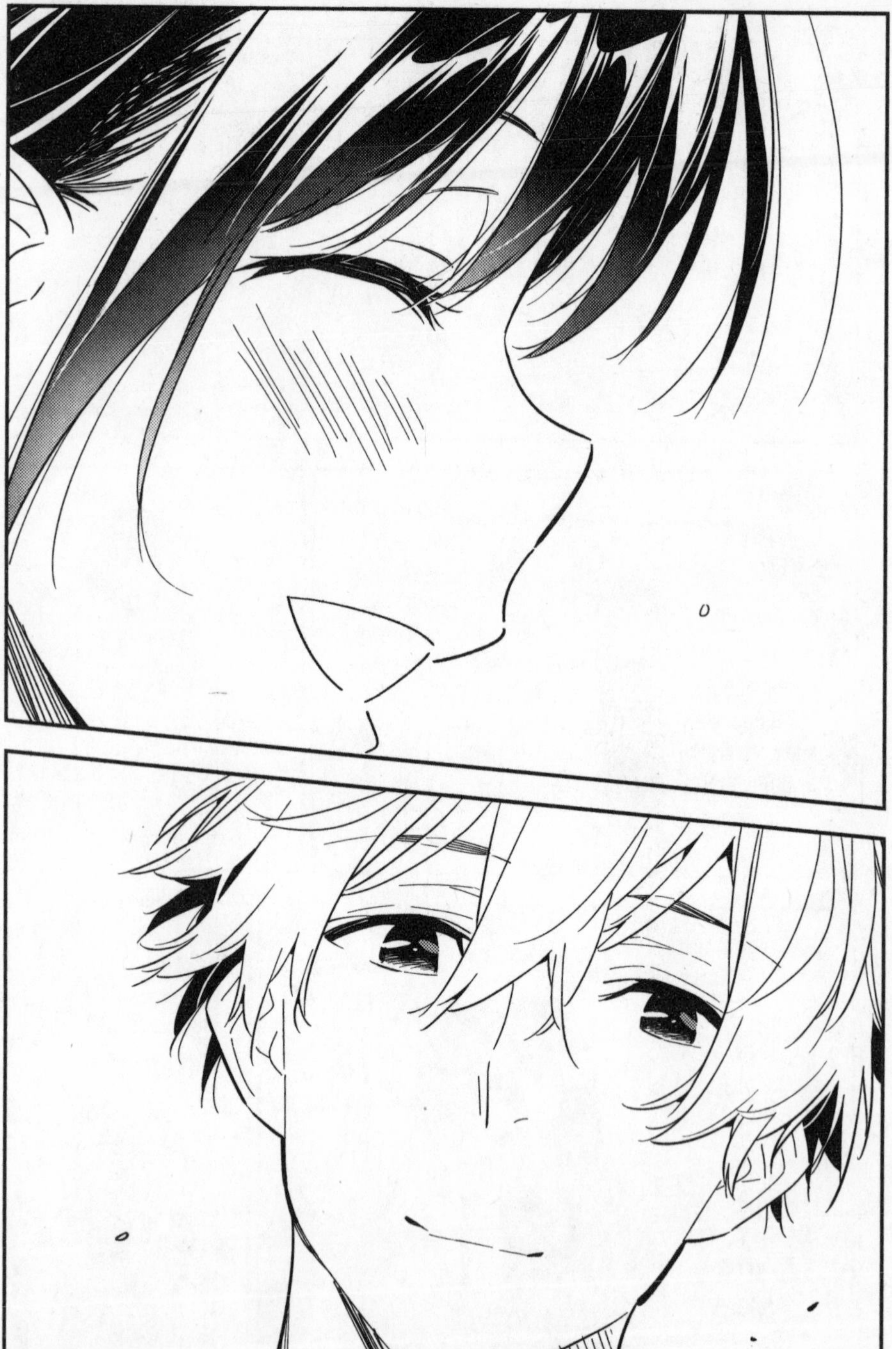

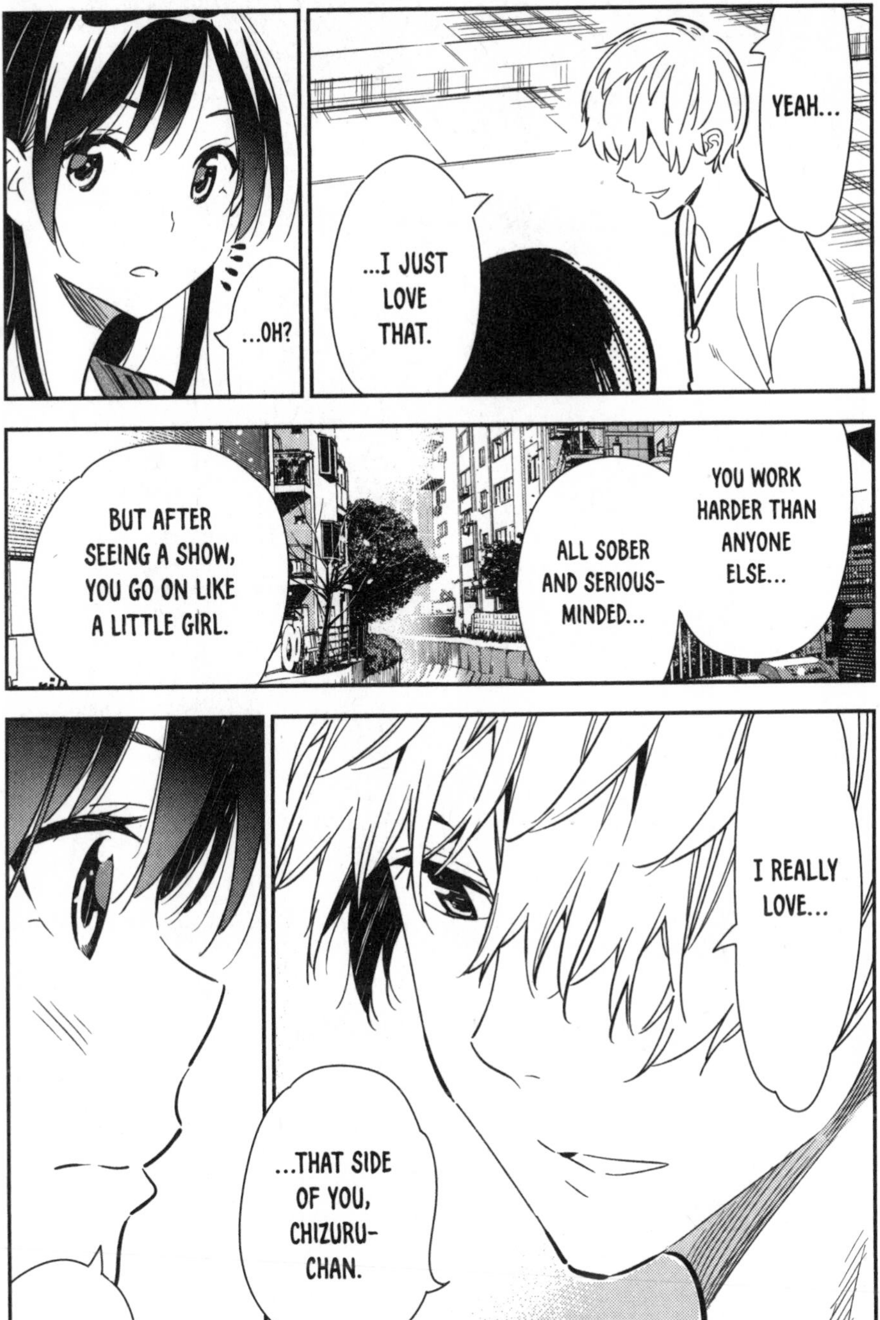
YEAH...
...I JUST LOVE THAT.
...OH?
YOU WORK HARDER THAN ANYONE ELSE...
ALL SOBER AND SERIOUS-MINDED...
BUT AFTER SEEING A SHOW, YOU GO ON LIKE A LITTLE GIRL.
I REALLY LOVE...
...THAT SIDE OF YOU, CHIZURU-CHAN.
...

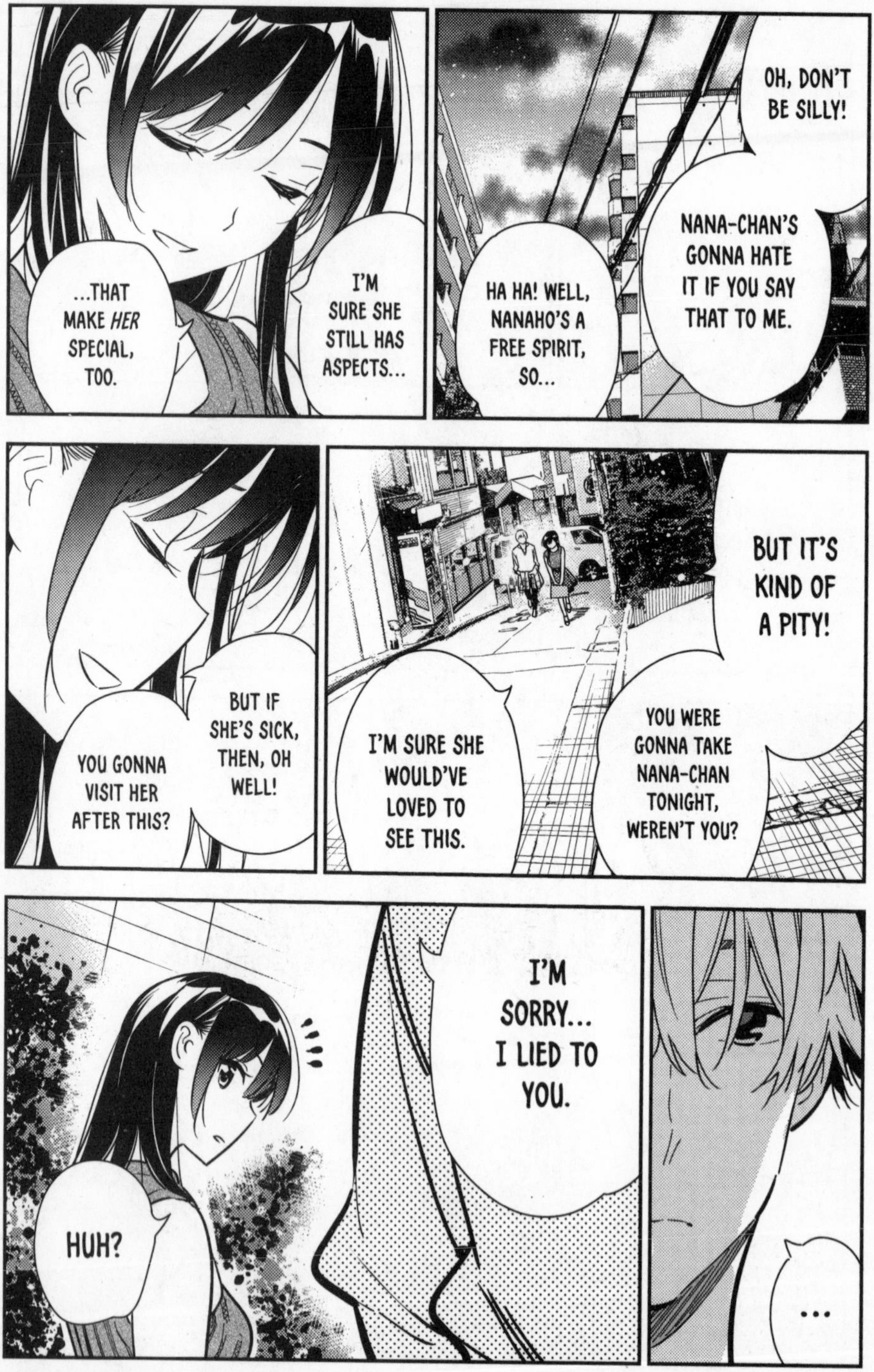
OH, DON'T BE SILLY!
NANA-CHAN'S GONNA HATE IT IF YOU SAY THAT TO ME.
HA HA! WELL, NANAHO'S A FREE SPIRIT, SO...
I'M SURE SHE STILL HAS ASPECTS...
...THAT MAKE *HER* SPECIAL, TOO.
BUT IT'S KIND OF A PITY!
YOU WERE GONNA TAKE NANA-CHAN TONIGHT, WEREN'T YOU?
I'M SURE SHE WOULD'VE LOVED TO SEE THIS.
BUT IF SHE'S SICK, THEN, OH WELL!
YOU GONNA VISIT HER AFTER THIS?
...
I'M SORRY... I LIED TO YOU.
HUH?

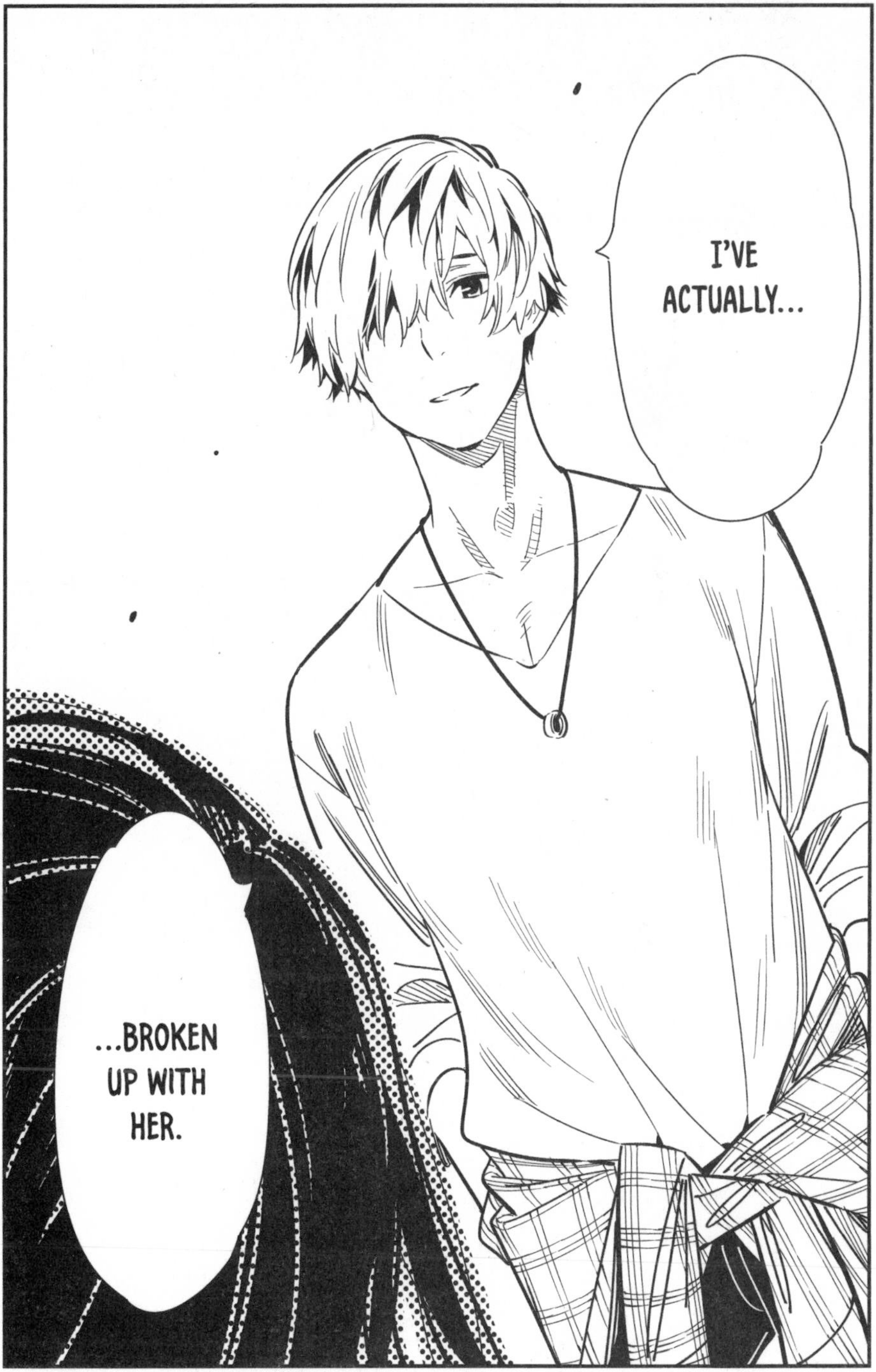
I'VE ACTUALLY...
...BROKEN UP WITH HER.

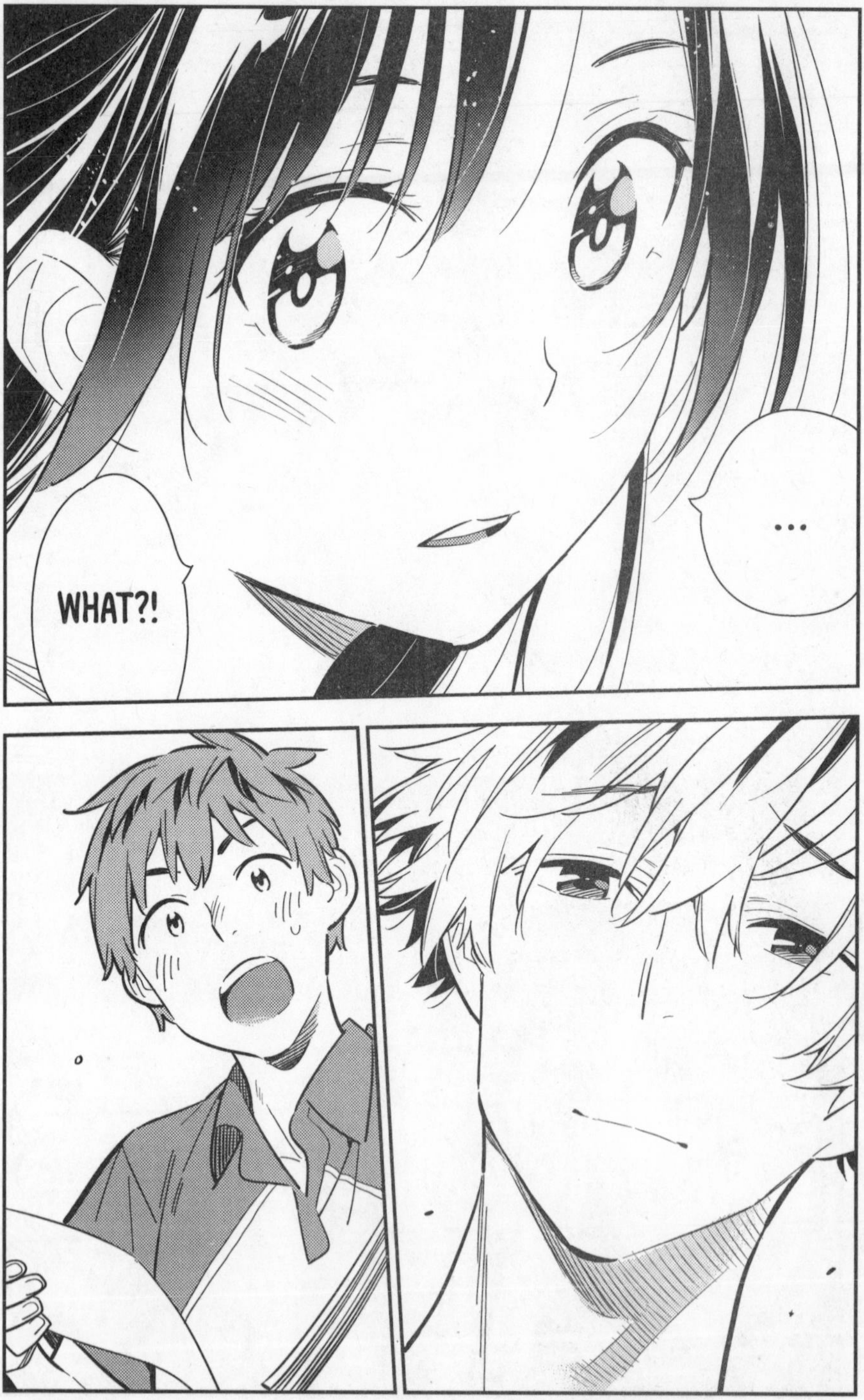
...
WHAT?!

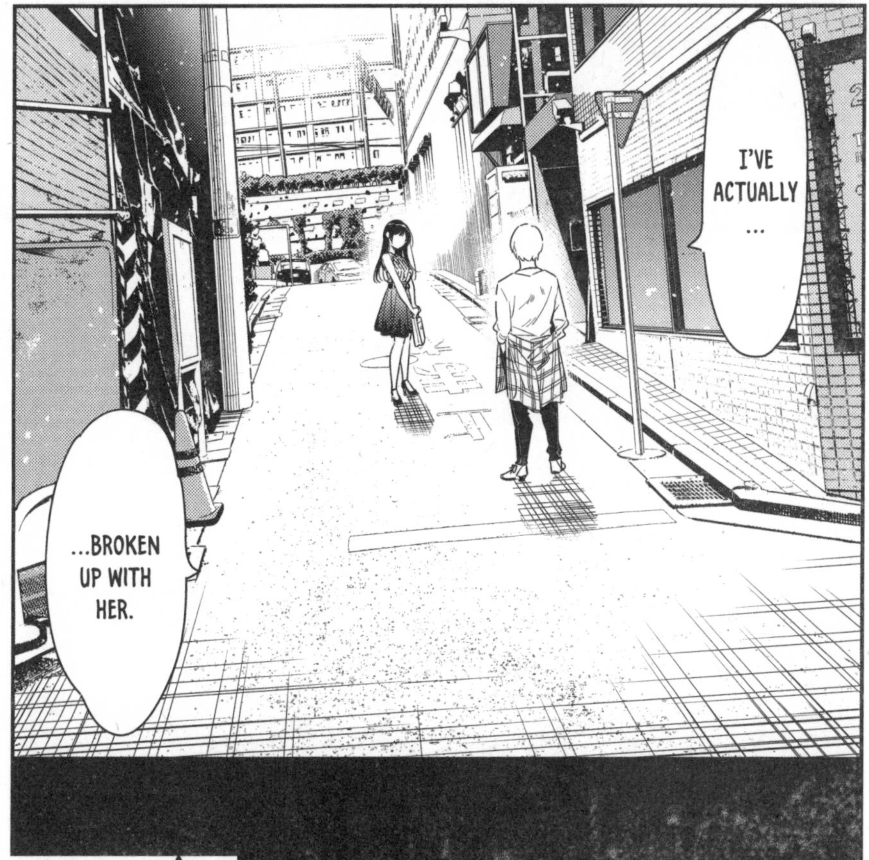
I'VE ACTUALLY ...
...BROKEN UP WITH HER.

RATING 126
THE FINAL DAY AND MY GIRLFRIEND 4

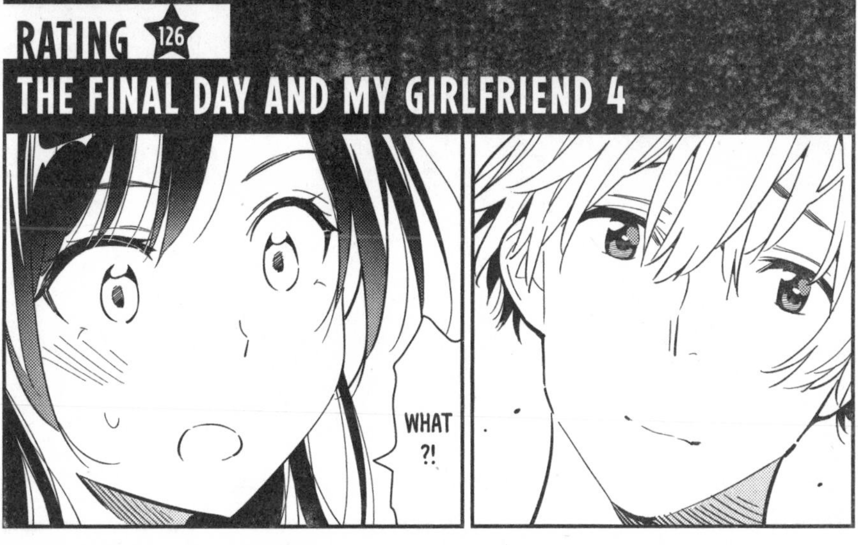
WHAT ?!

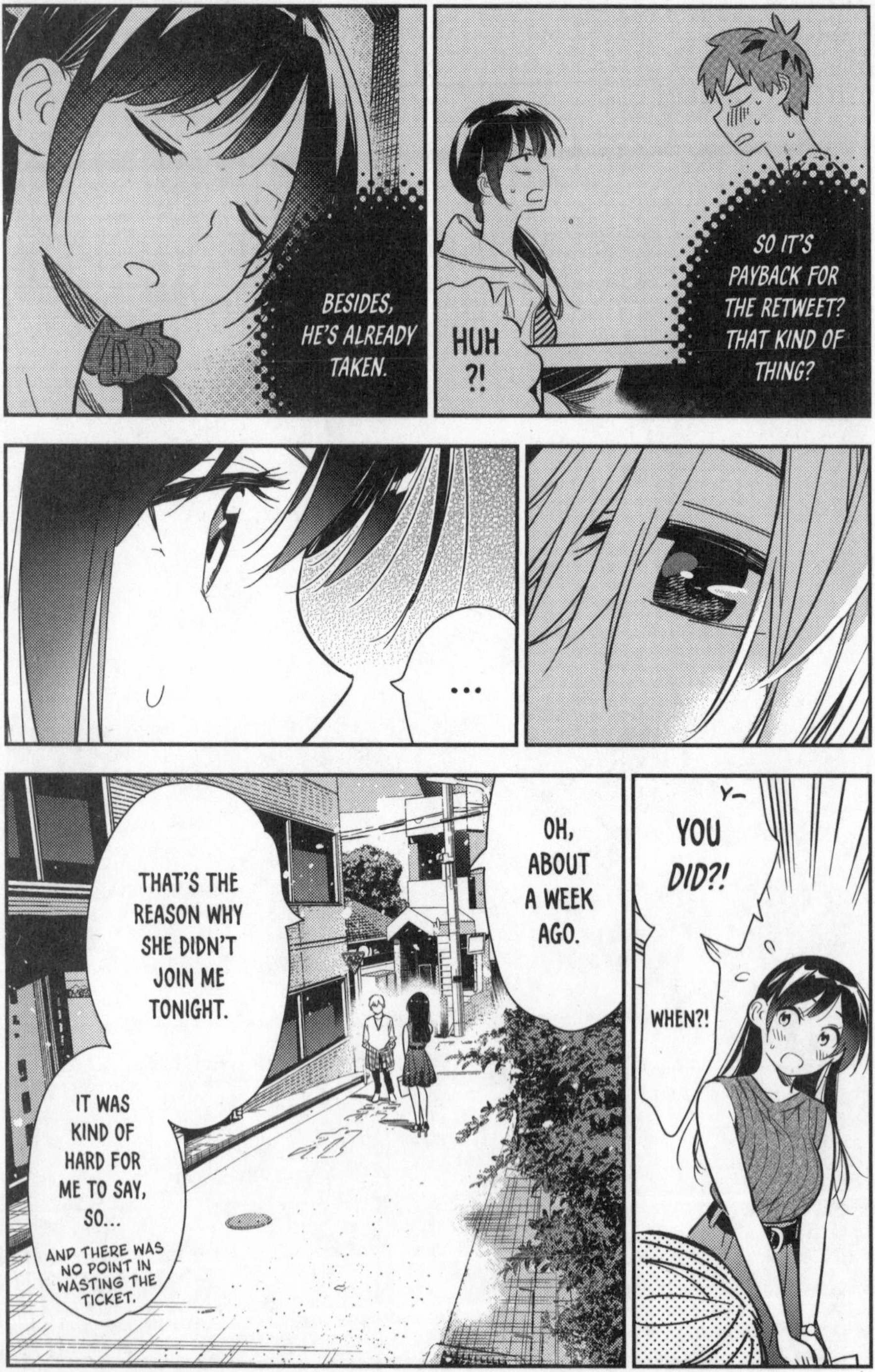
SO IT'S PAYBACK FOR THE RETWEET? THAT KIND OF THING?
HUH ?!
BESIDES, HE'S ALREADY TAKEN.
...
Y— YOU DID?!
WHEN?!
OH, ABOUT A WEEK AGO.
THAT'S THE REASON WHY SHE DIDN'T JOIN ME TONIGHT.
IT WAS KIND OF HARD FOR ME TO SAY, SO...
AND THERE WAS NO POINT IN WASTING THE TICKET.

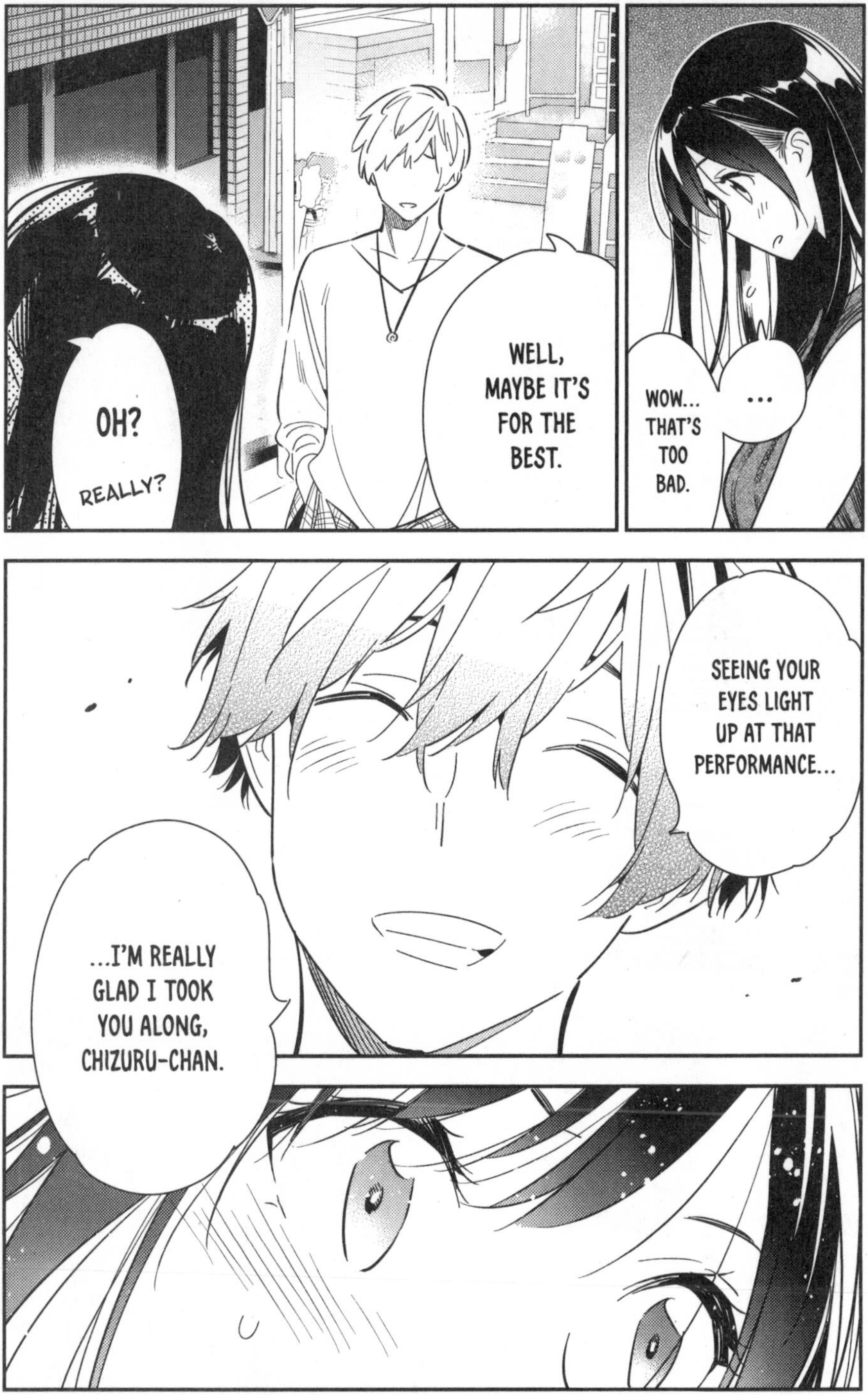
...
WOW... THAT'S TOO BAD.
WELL, MAYBE IT'S FOR THE BEST.
OH?
REALLY?
SEEING YOUR EYES LIGHT UP AT THAT PERFORMANCE...
...I'M REALLY GLAD I TOOK YOU ALONG, CHIZURU-CHAN.

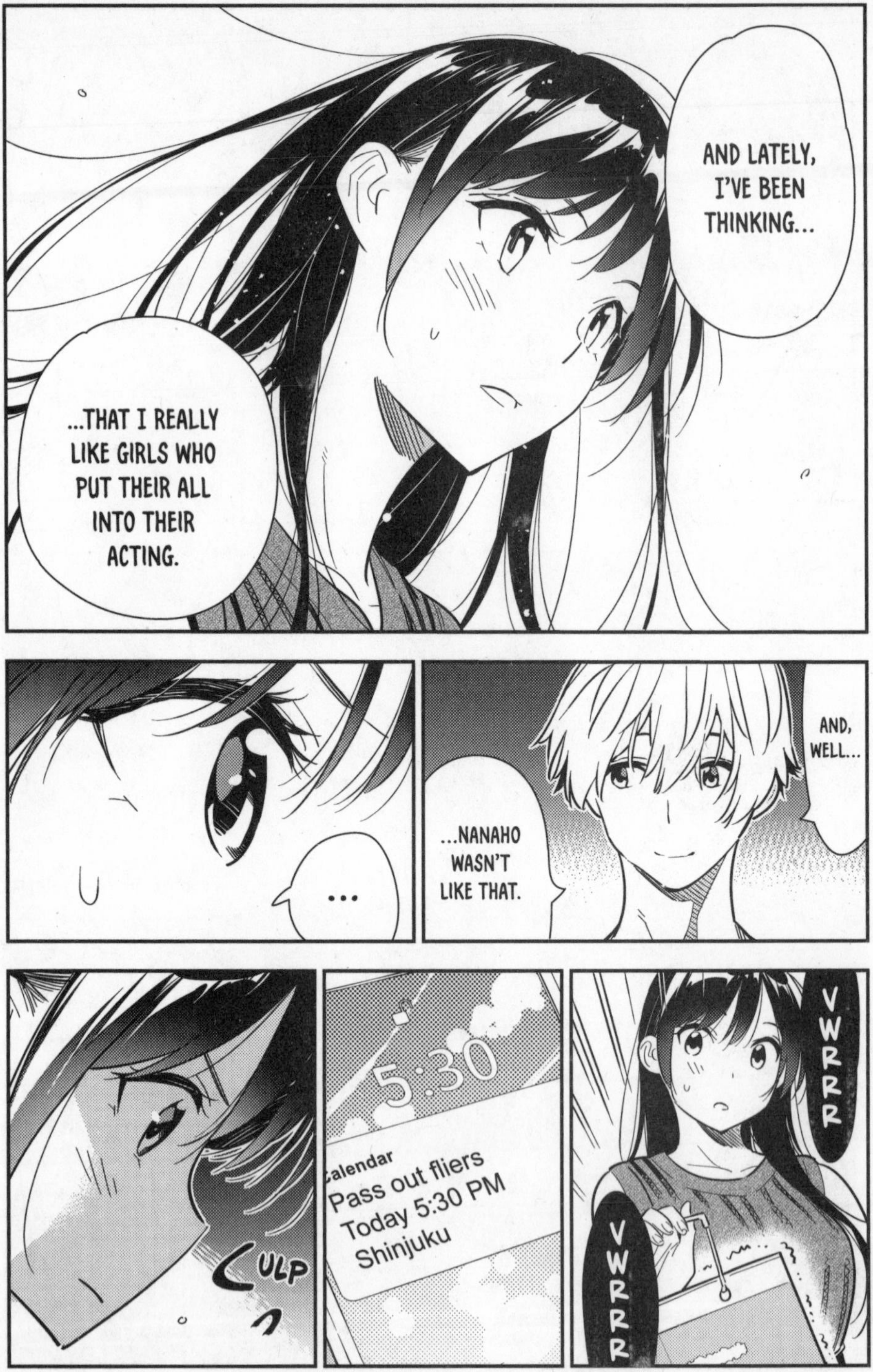
AND LATELY, I'VE BEEN THINKING...
...THAT I REALLY LIKE GIRLS WHO PUT THEIR ALL INTO THEIR ACTING.
AND, WELL...
...NANAHO WASN'T LIKE THAT.
...
VWRRR
VWRRR
5:30
Calendar
Pass out fliers
Today 5:30 PM
Shinjuku
GULP

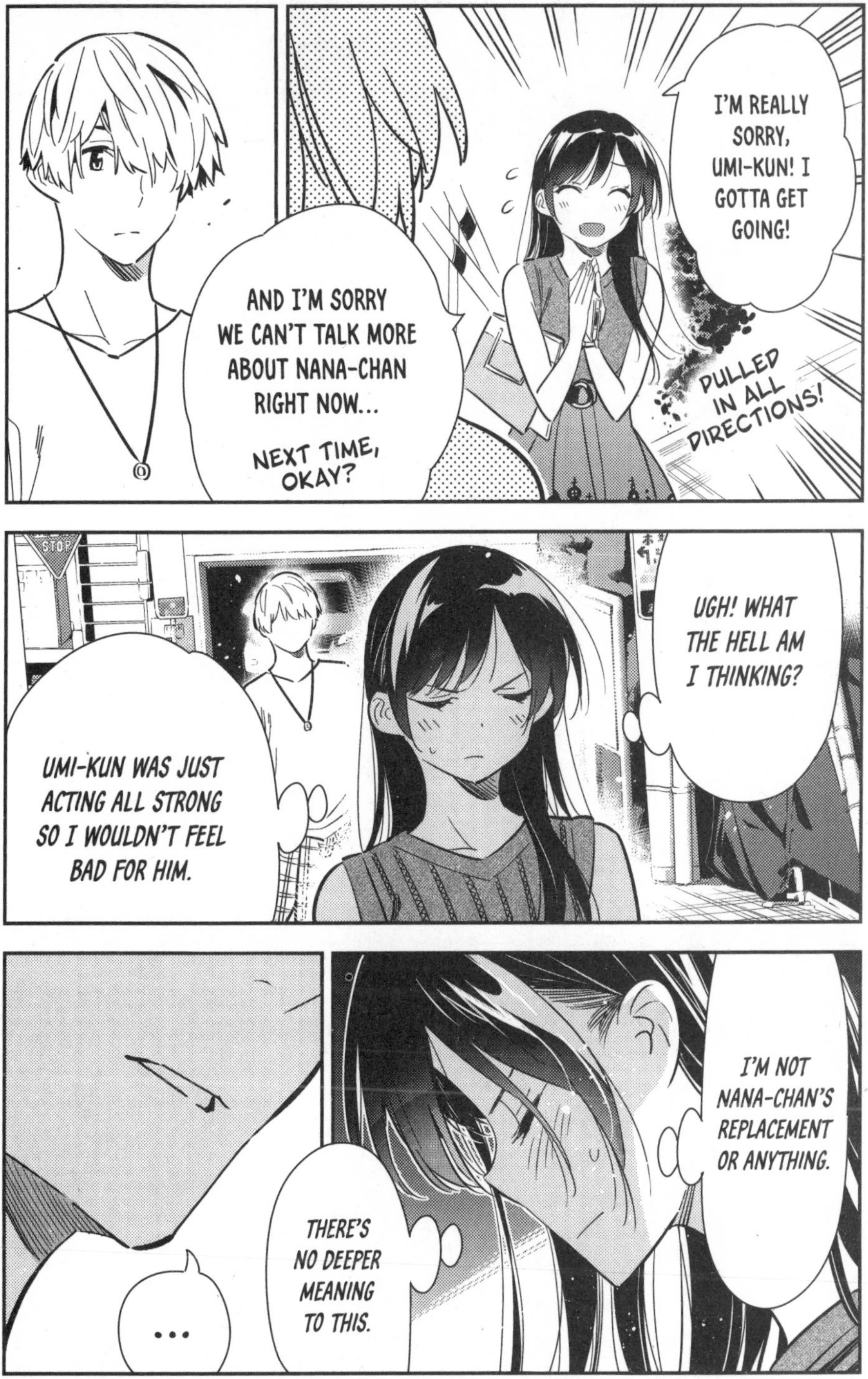
I'M REALLY SORRY, UMI-KUN! I GOTTA GET GOING!
PULLED IN ALL DIRECTIONS!
AND I'M SORRY WE CAN'T TALK MORE ABOUT NANA-CHAN RIGHT NOW...
NEXT TIME, OKAY?
UGH! WHAT THE HELL AM I THINKING?
UMI-KUN WAS JUST ACTING ALL STRONG SO I WOULDN'T FEEL BAD FOR HIM.
I'M NOT NANA-CHAN'S REPLACEMENT OR ANYTHING.
THERE'S NO DEEPER MEANING TO THIS.
...

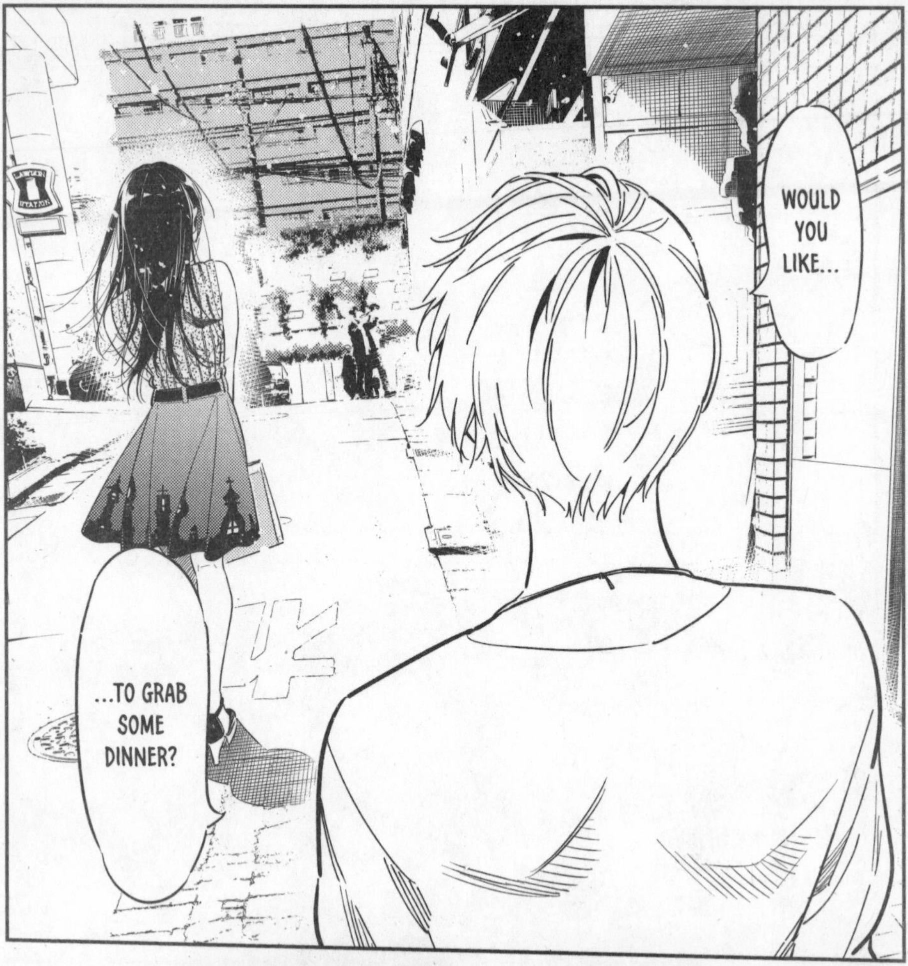
WOULD YOU LIKE...
...TO GRAB SOME DINNER?
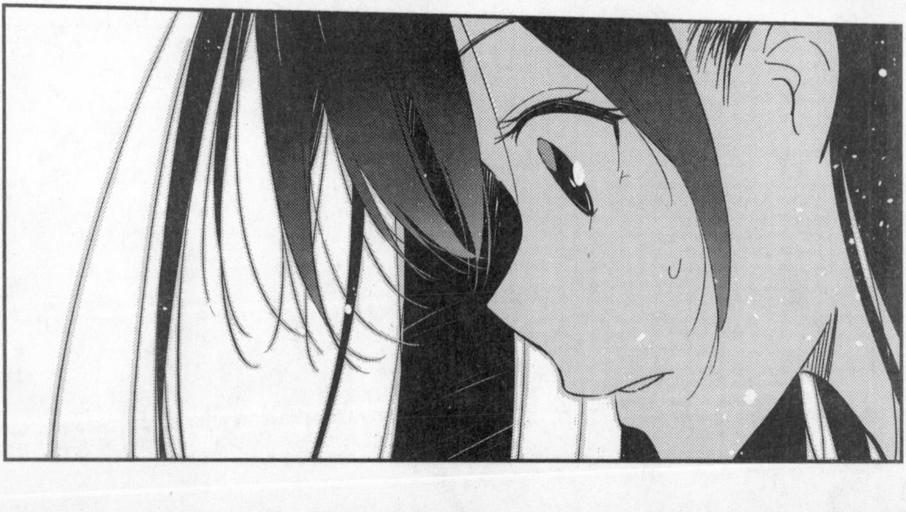

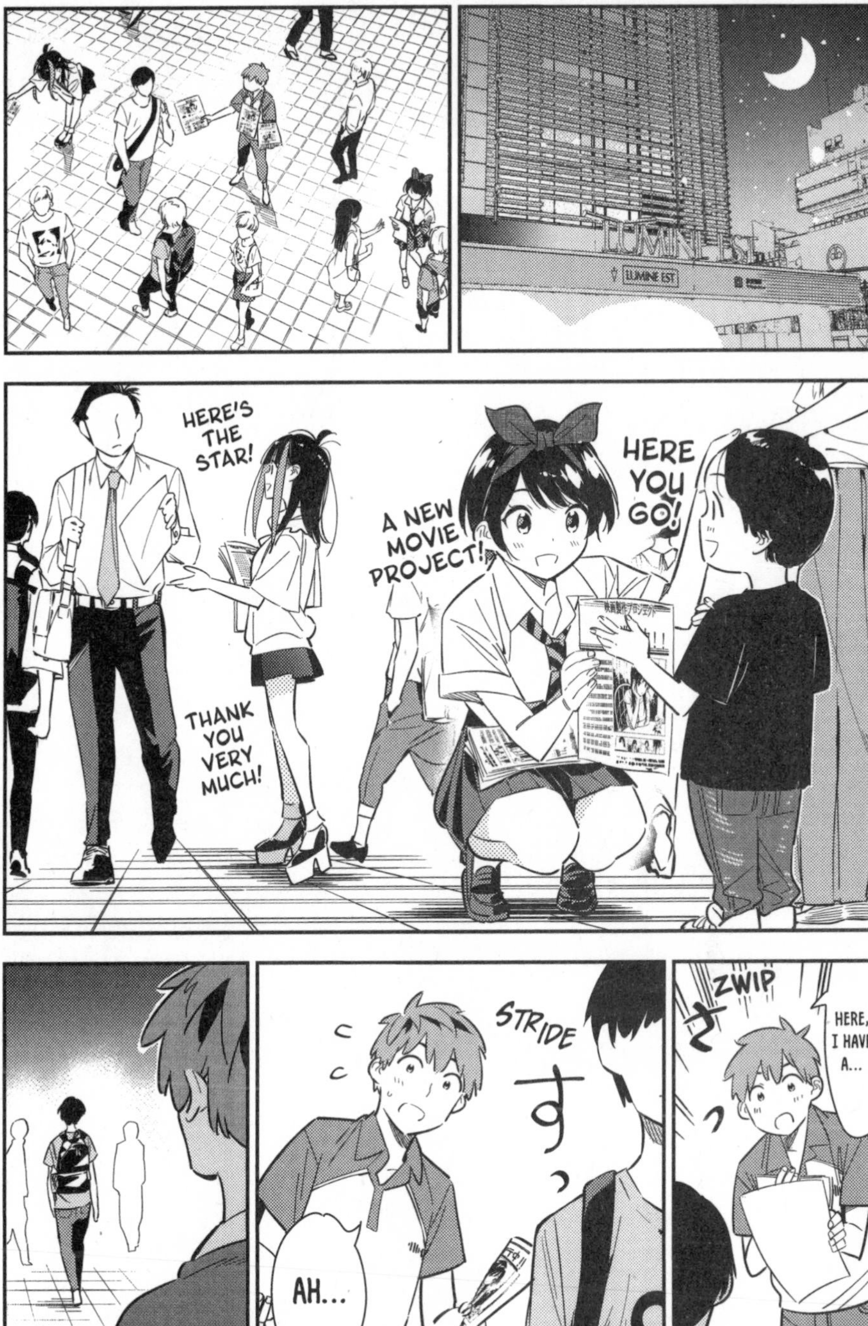
LUMINE EST
LUMINE EST
HERE YOU GO!
A NEW MOVIE PROJECT!
HERE'S THE STAR!
THANK YOU VERY MUCH!
ZWIP
さ
HERE, I HAVE A...
STRIDE
す
AH...

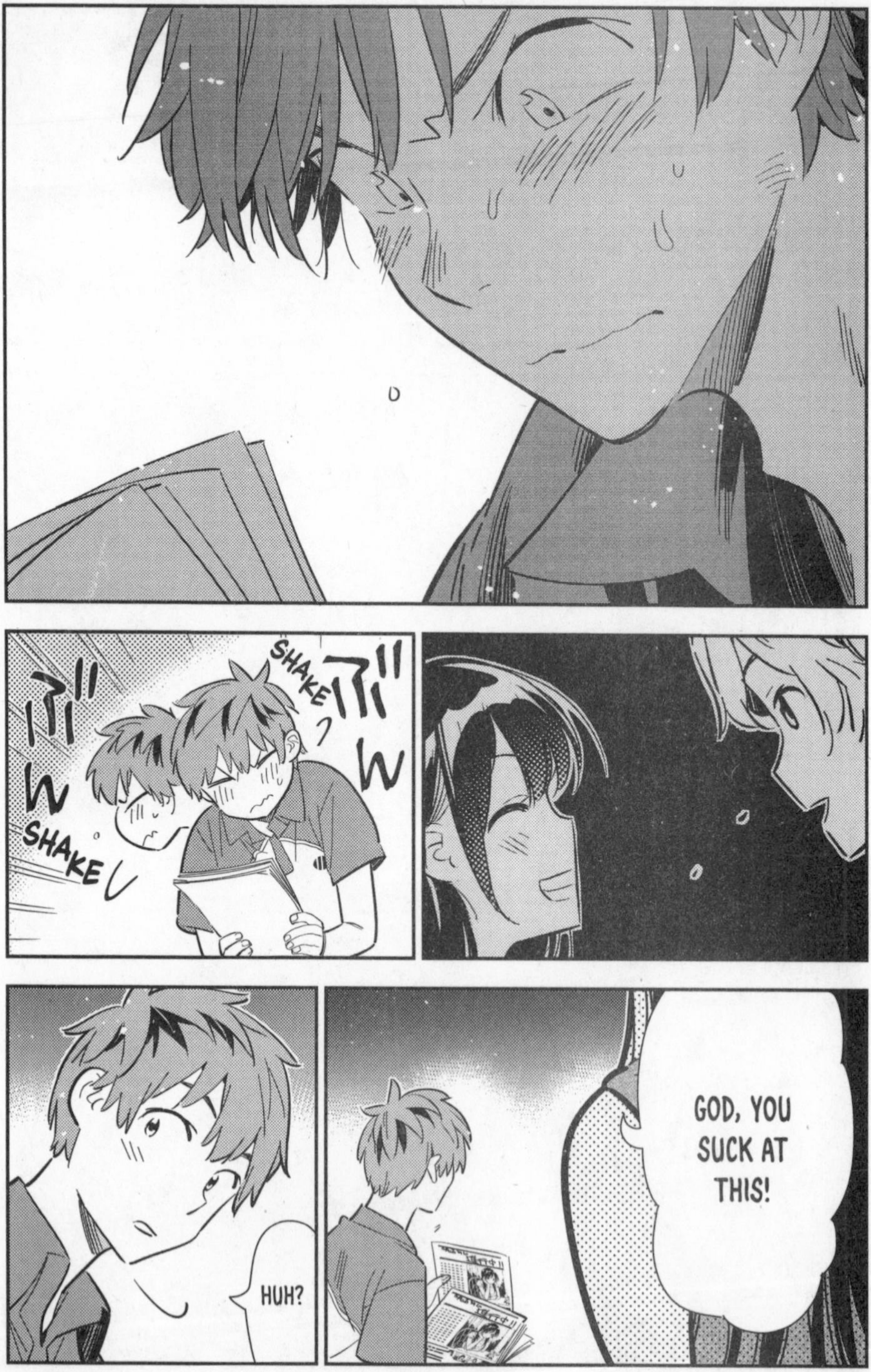
SHAKE
SHAKE
GOD, YOU SUCK AT THIS!
HUH?

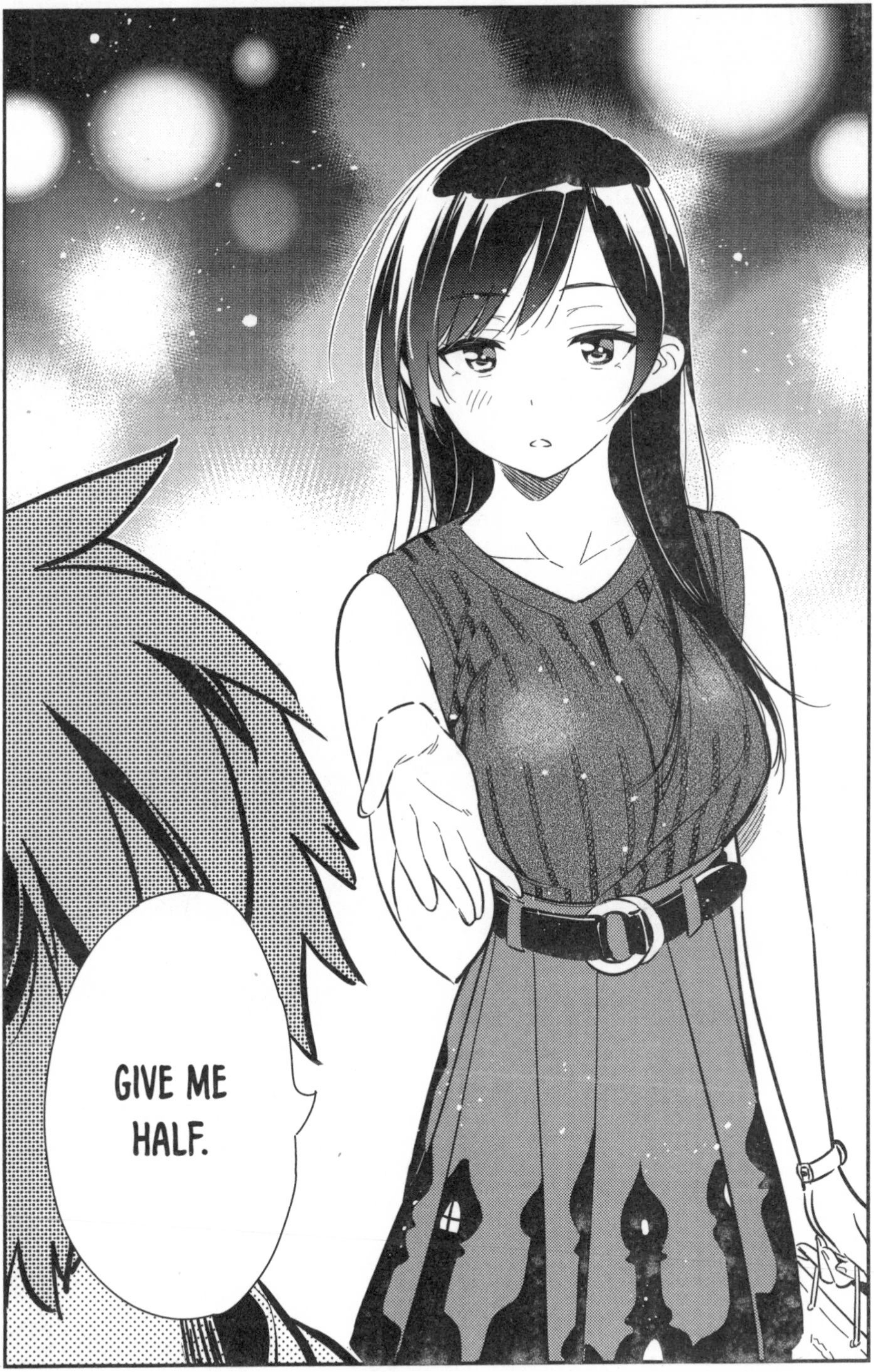
GIVE ME HALF.

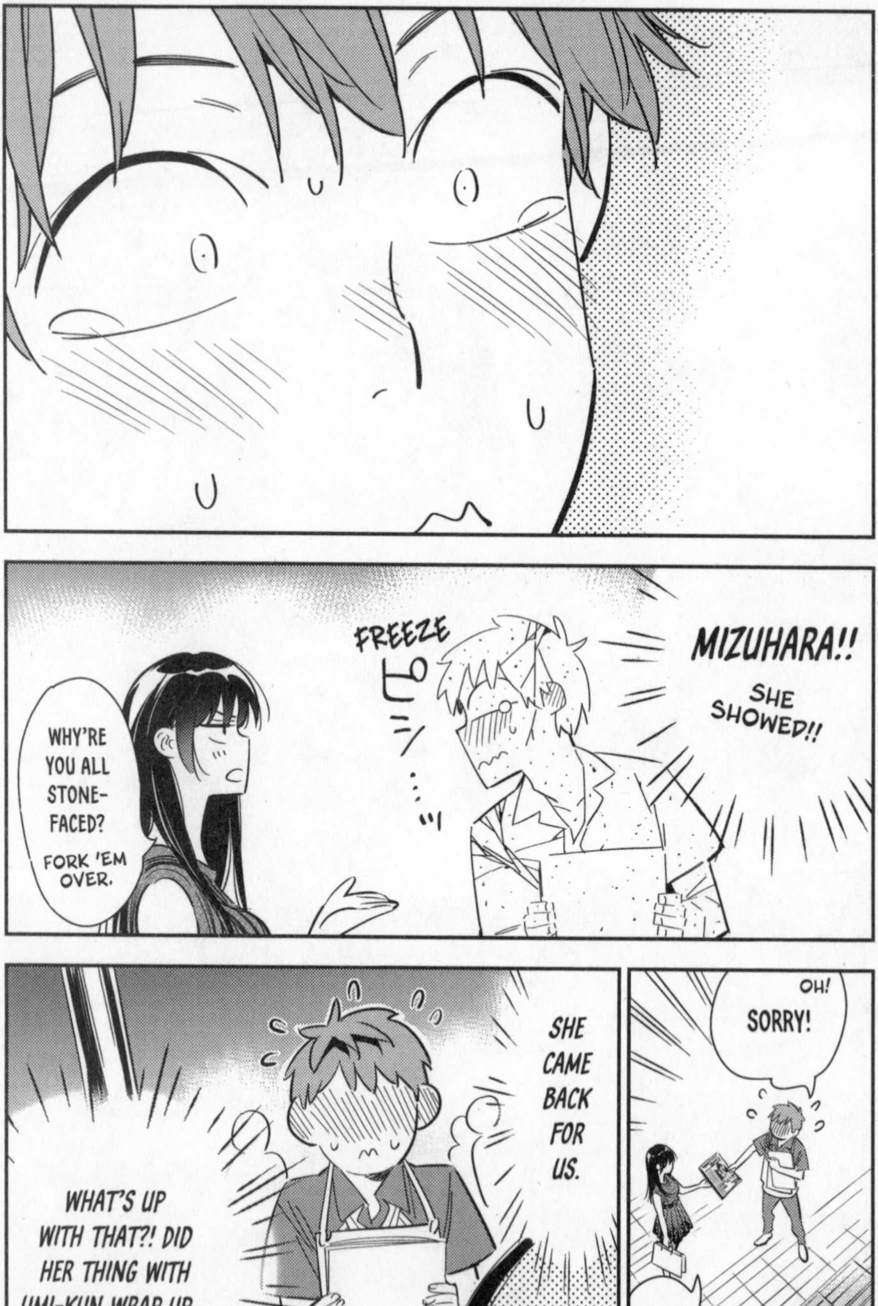
MIZUHARA!!
SHE SHOWED!!
FREEZE
ピ
...!
WHY'RE YOU ALL STONE-FACED?
FORK 'EM OVER.
OH!
SORRY!
HERE.
SHE CAME BACK FOR US.
WHAT'S UP WITH THAT?! DID HER THING WITH UMI-KUN WRAP UP... UNEVENTFULLY?!

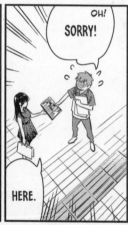

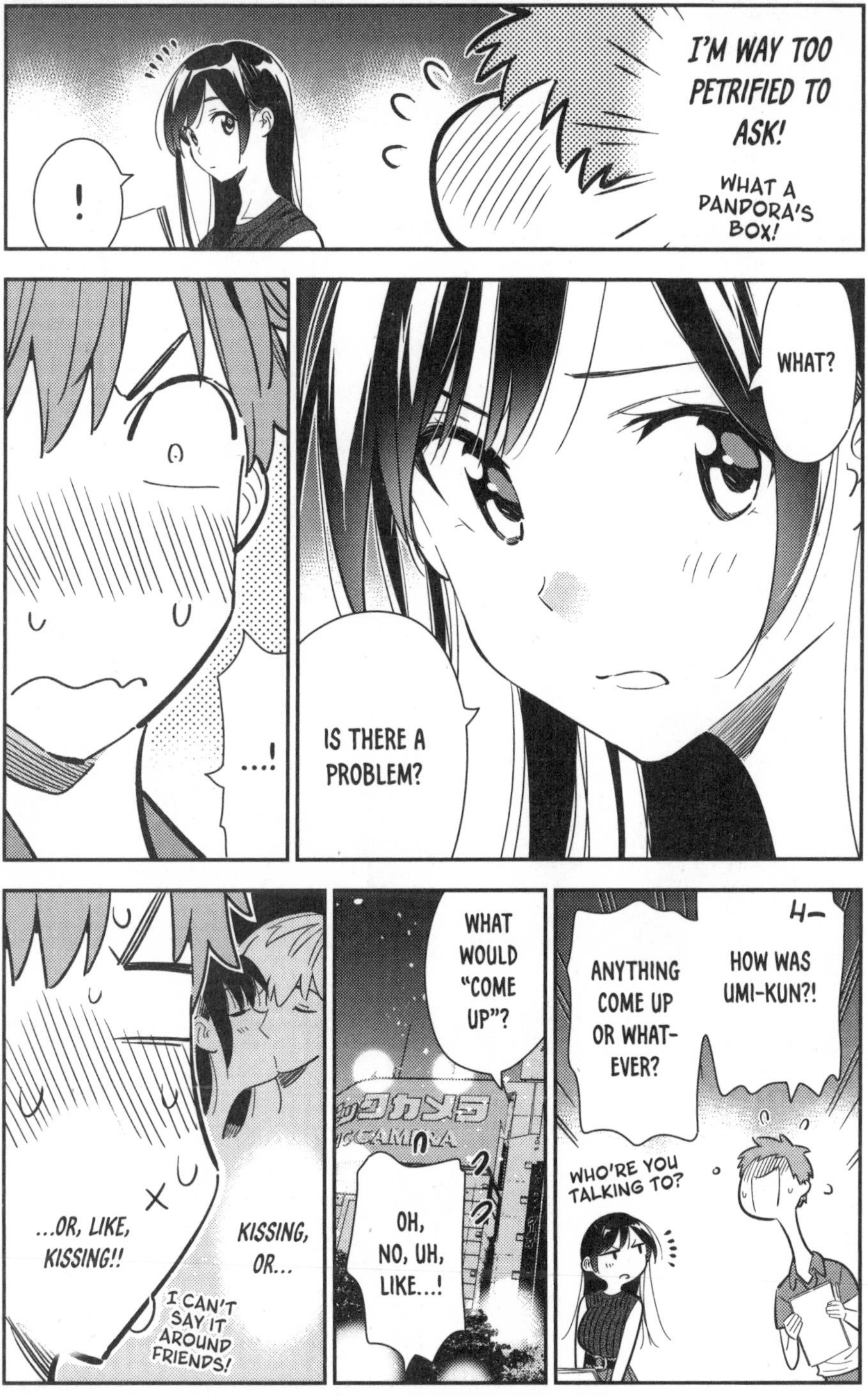
I'M WAY TOO PETRIFIED TO ASK!
WHAT A PANDORA'S BOX!
!
WHAT?
IS THERE A PROBLEM?
...!
H—
HOW WAS UMI-KUN?!
ANYTHING COME UP OR WHAT-EVER?
WHO'RE YOU TALKING TO?
WHAT WOULD "COME UP"?
OH, NO, UH, LIKE...!
KISSING, OR...
...OR, LIKE, KISSING!!
I CAN'T SAY IT AROUND FRIENDS!

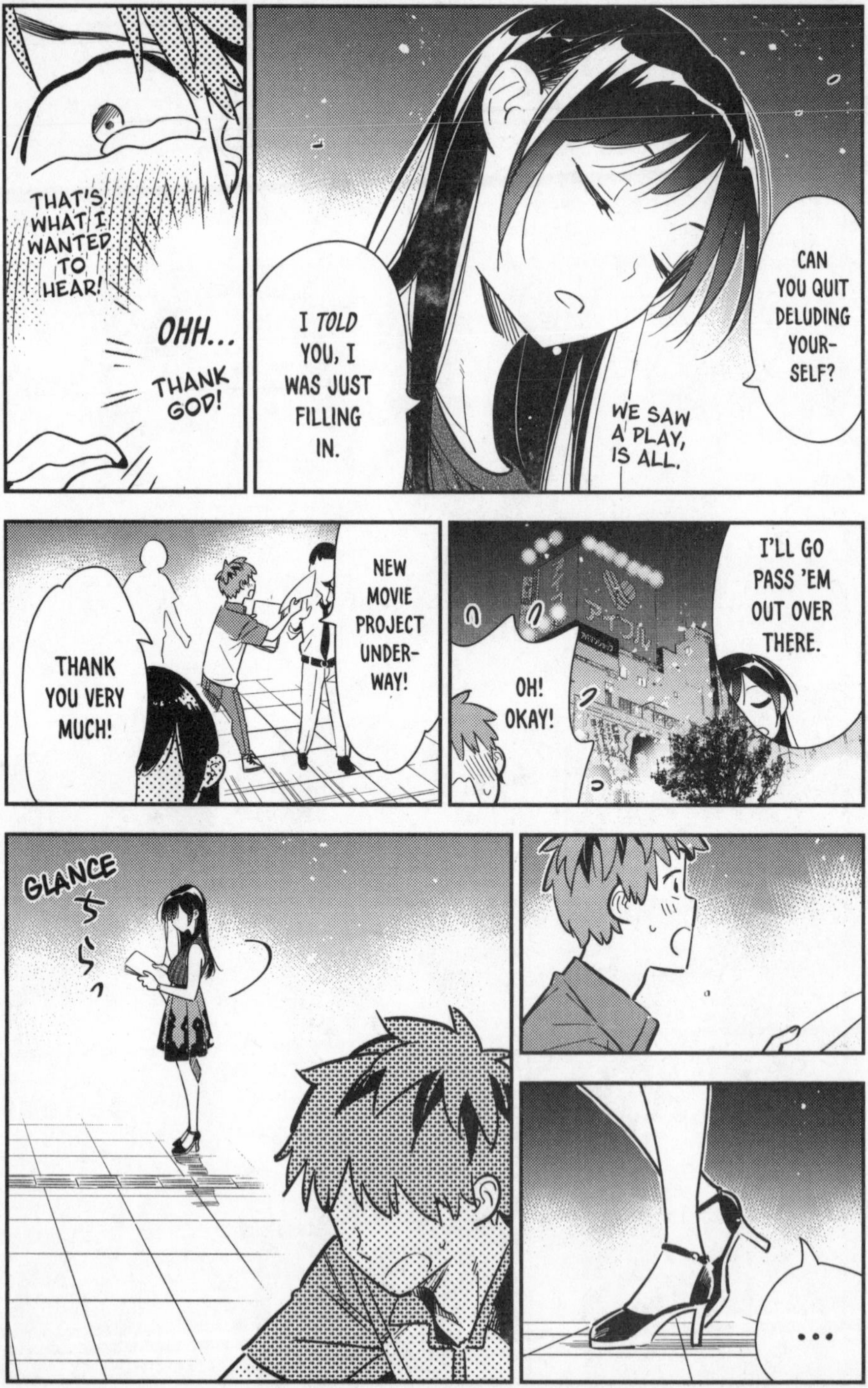
CAN YOU QUIT DELUDING YOUR-SELF?
WE SAW A PLAY, IS ALL.
I *TOLD* YOU, I WAS JUST FILLING IN.
THAT'S WHAT I WANTED TO HEAR!
OHH...
THANK GOD!
I'LL GO PASS 'EM OUT OVER THERE.
OH! OKAY!
NEW MOVIE PROJECT UNDER-WAY!
THANK YOU VERY MUCH!
...
GLANCE
ちらっ

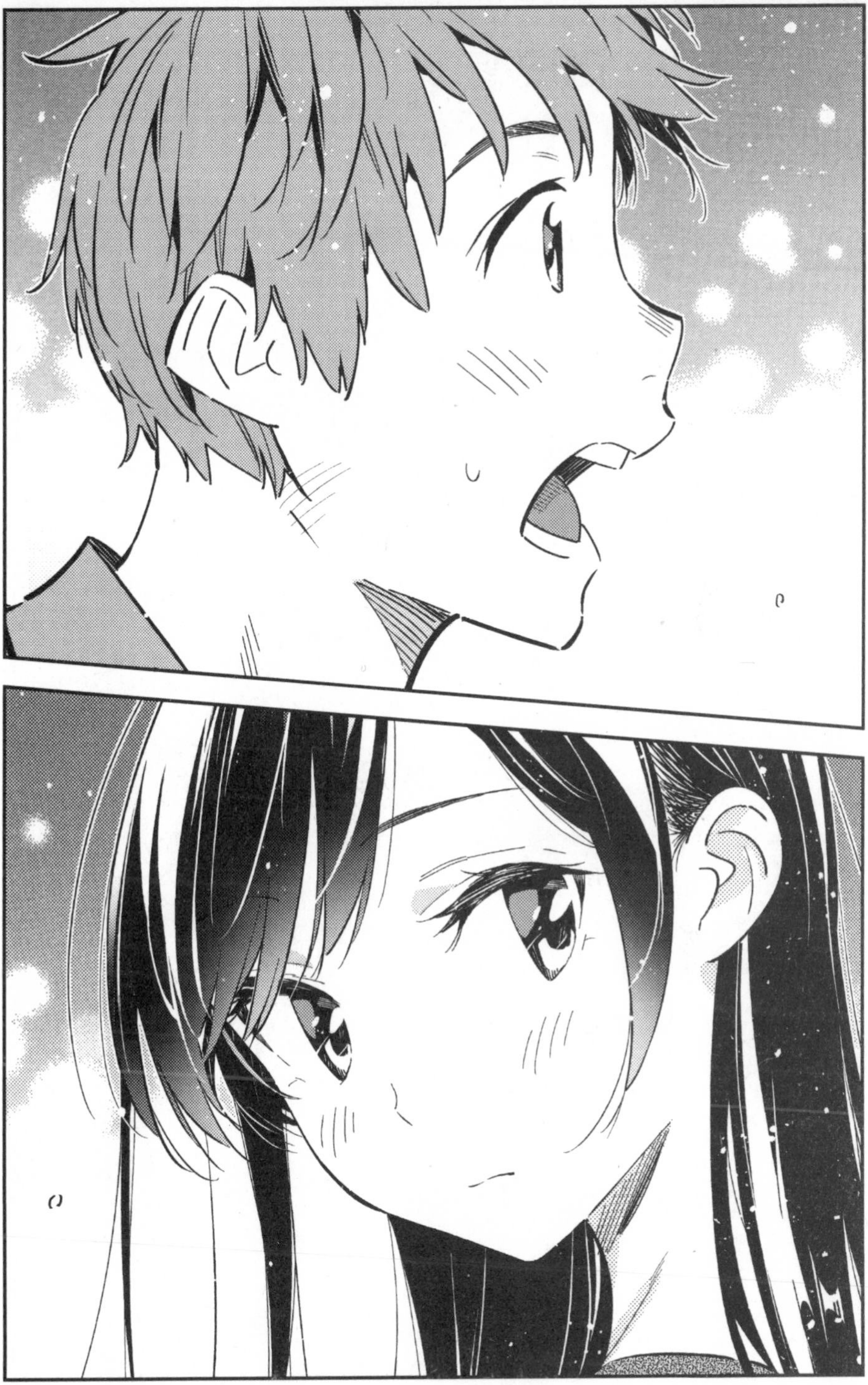

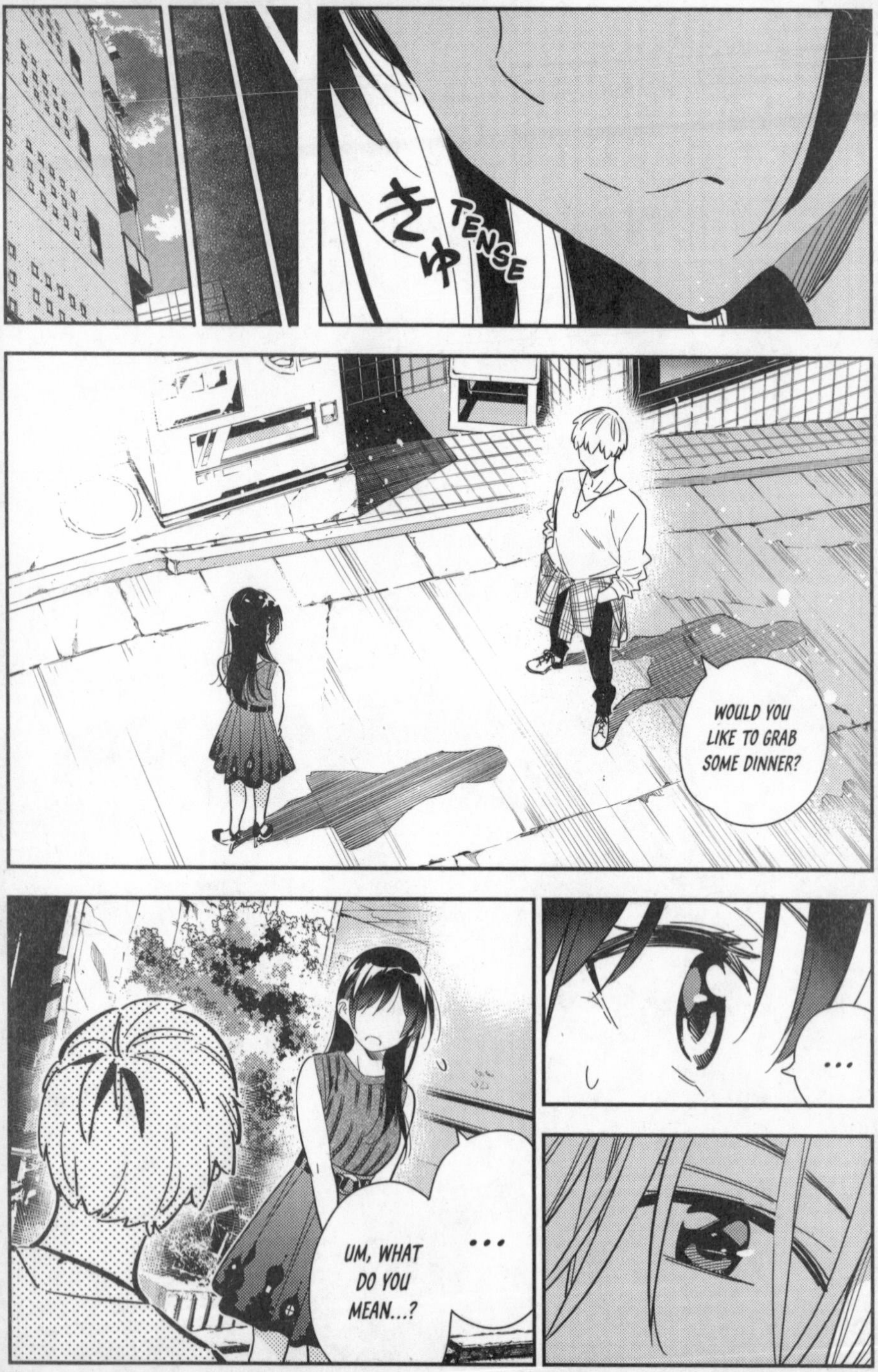
きゅ
TENSE
WOULD YOU LIKE TO GRAB SOME DINNER?
...
...
UM, WHAT DO YOU MEAN...?

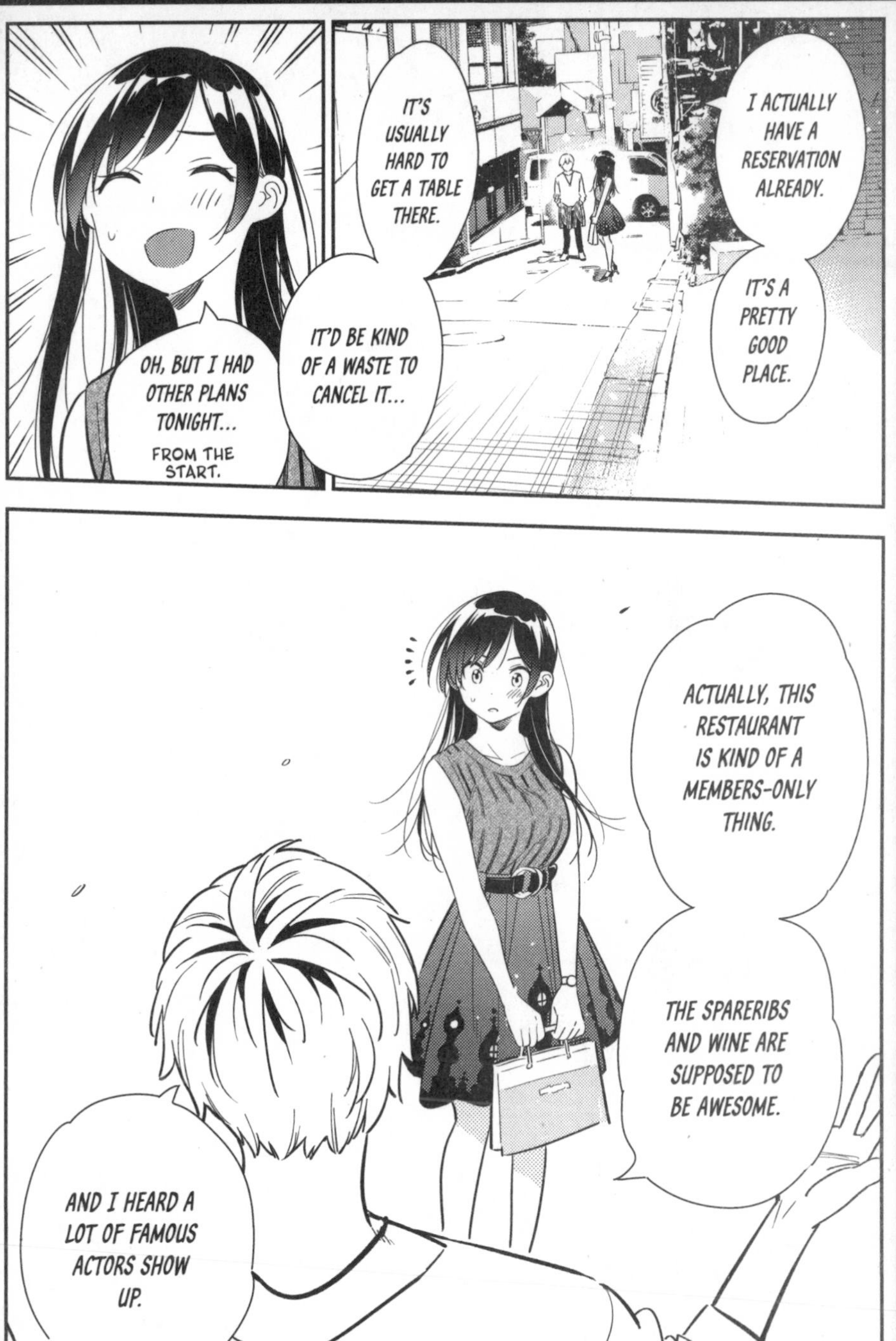
I ACTUALLY HAVE A RESERVATION ALREADY.
IT'S A PRETTY GOOD PLACE.
IT'S USUALLY HARD TO GET A TABLE THERE.
IT'D BE KIND OF A WASTE TO CANCEL IT...
OH, BUT I HAD OTHER PLANS TONIGHT...
FROM THE START.
ACTUALLY, THIS RESTAURANT IS KIND OF A MEMBERS-ONLY THING.
THE SPARERIBS AND WINE ARE SUPPOSED TO BE AWESOME.
AND I HEARD A LOT OF FAMOUS ACTORS SHOW UP.

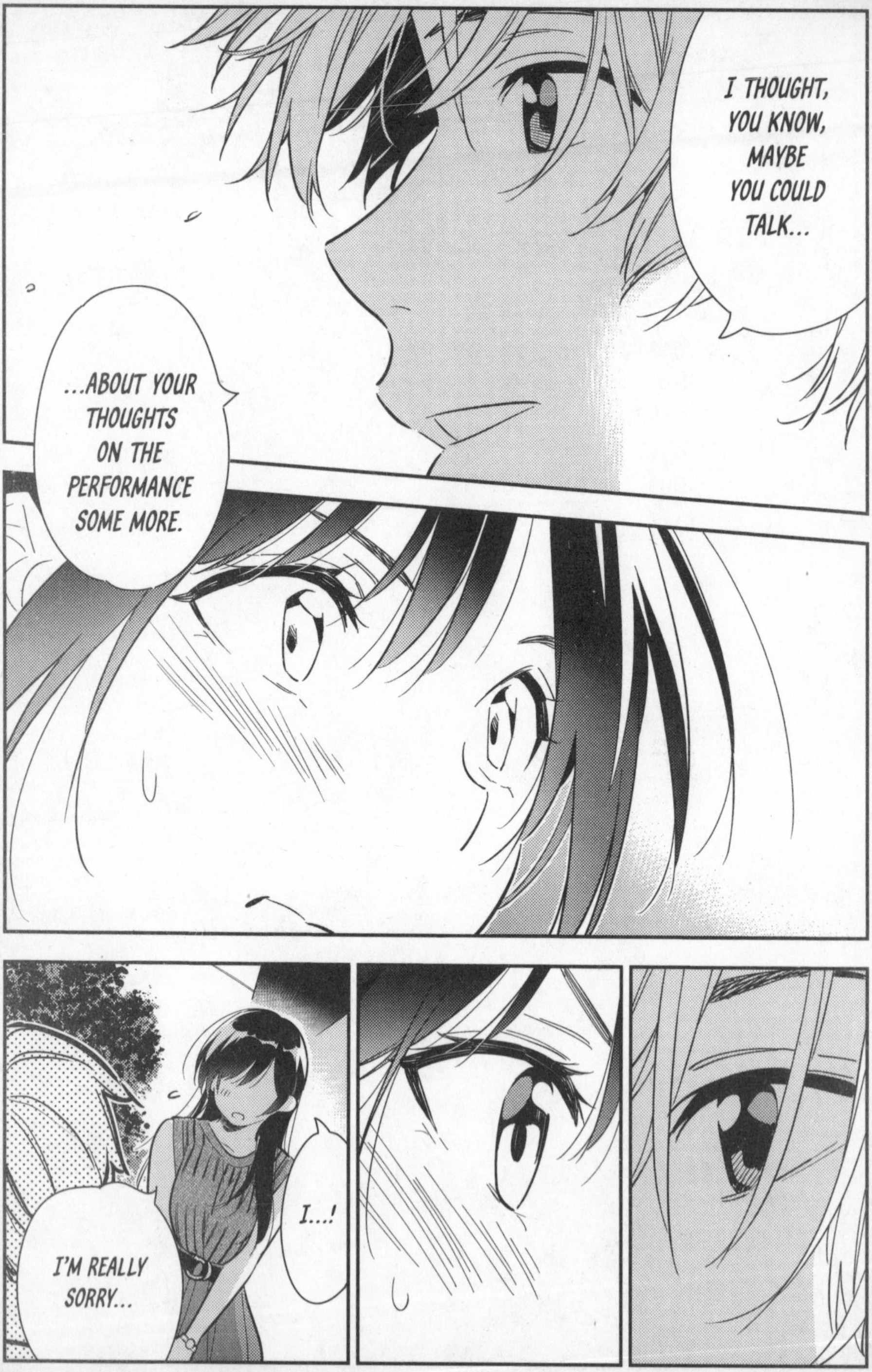
I THOUGHT, YOU KNOW, MAYBE YOU COULD TALK...
...ABOUT YOUR THOUGHTS ON THE PERFORMANCE SOME MORE.
I...!
I'M REALLY SORRY...

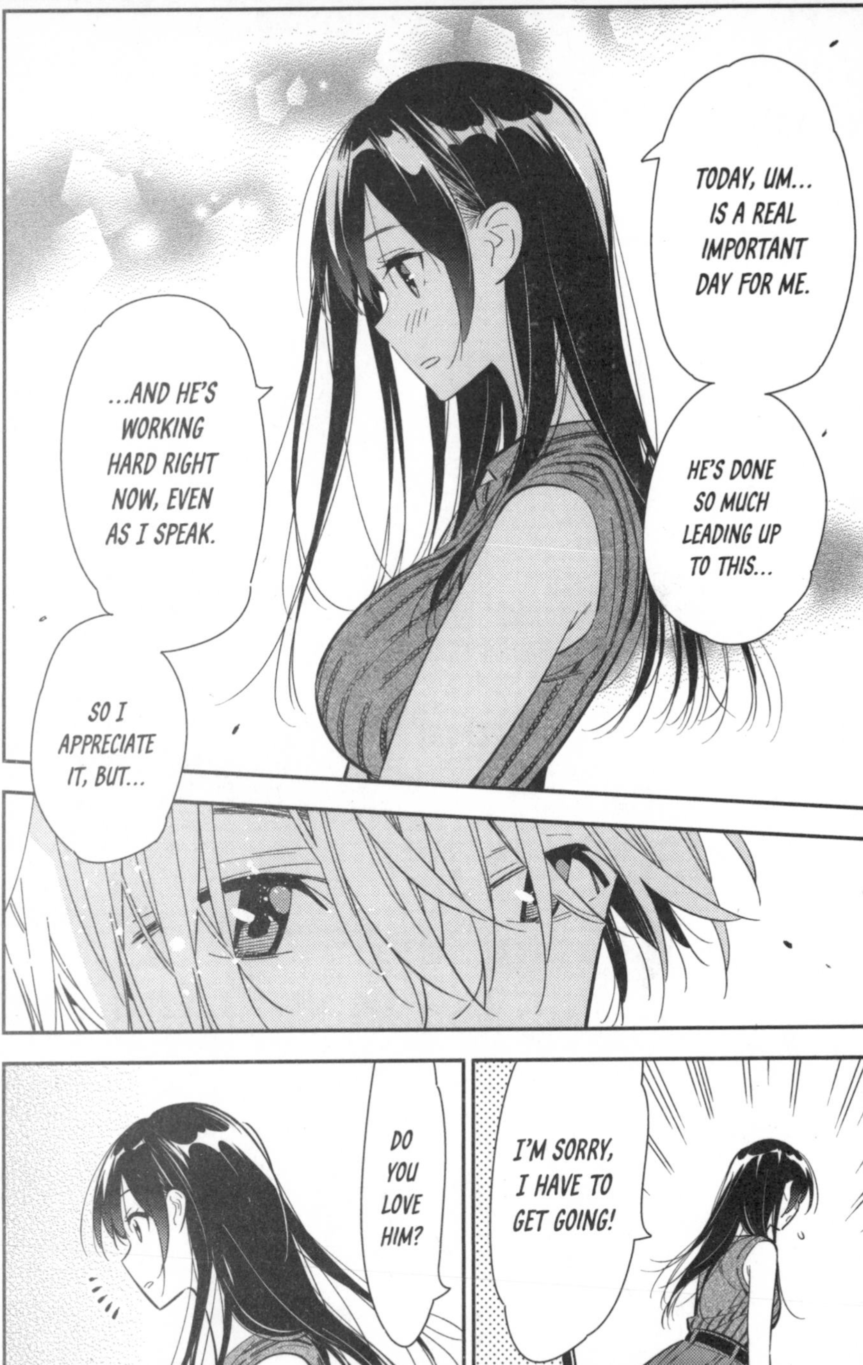
TODAY, UM... IS A REAL IMPORTANT DAY FOR ME.
HE'S DONE SO MUCH LEADING UP TO THIS...
...AND HE'S WORKING HARD RIGHT NOW, EVEN AS I SPEAK.
SO I APPRECIATE IT, BUT...
I'M SORRY, I HAVE TO GET GOING!
DO YOU LOVE HIM?

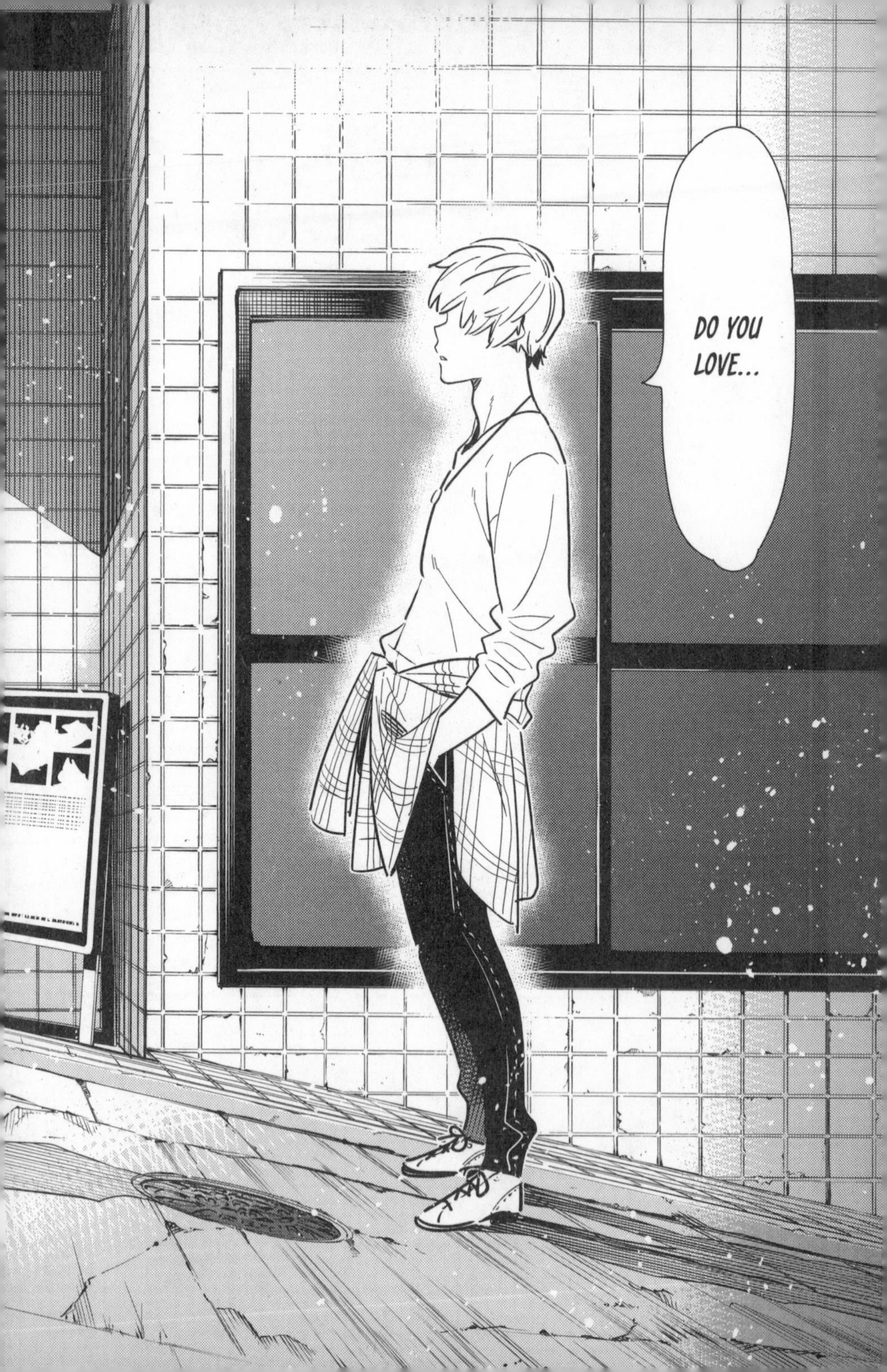
DO YOU LOVE...

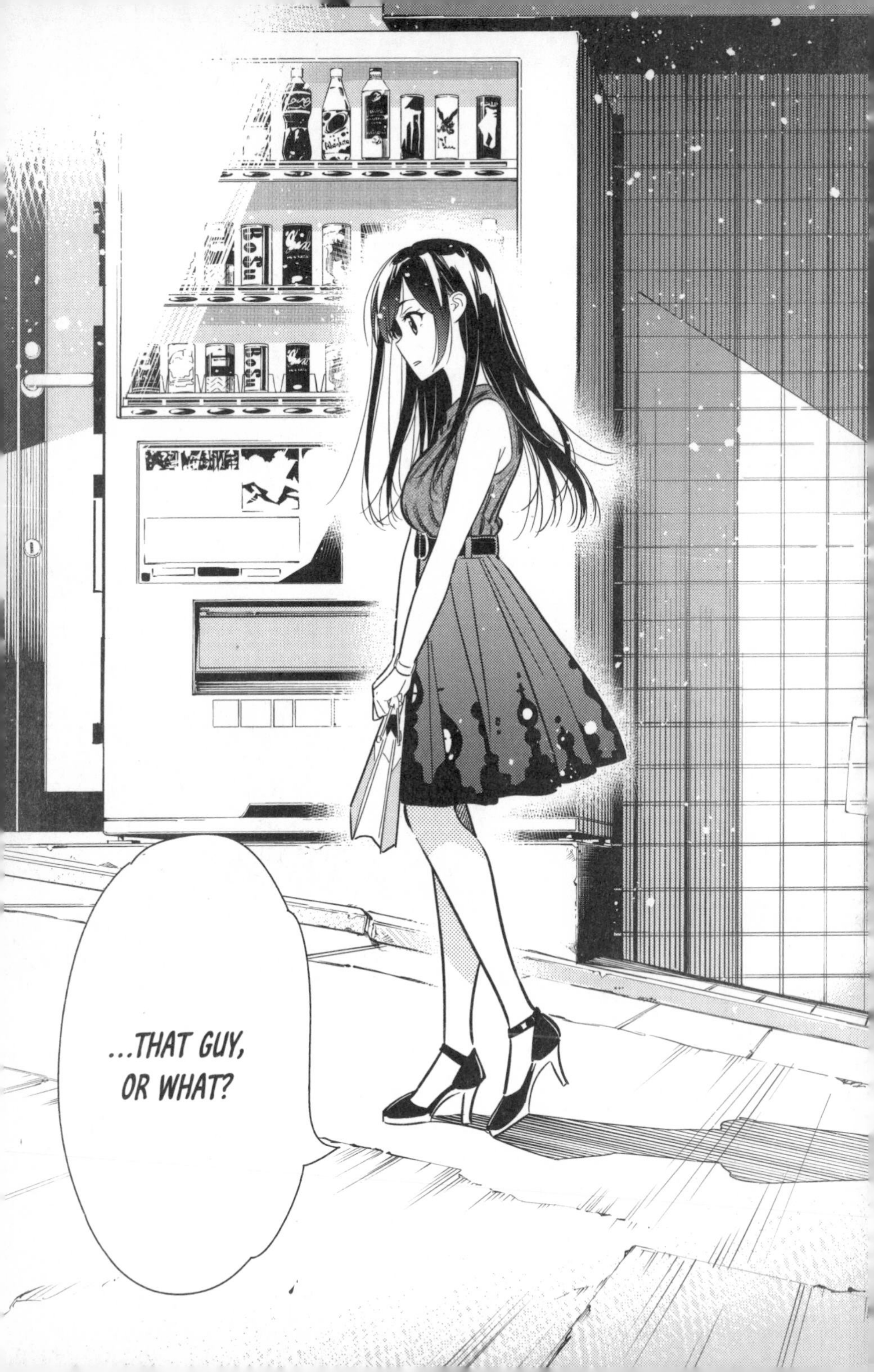
...THAT GUY, OR WHAT?

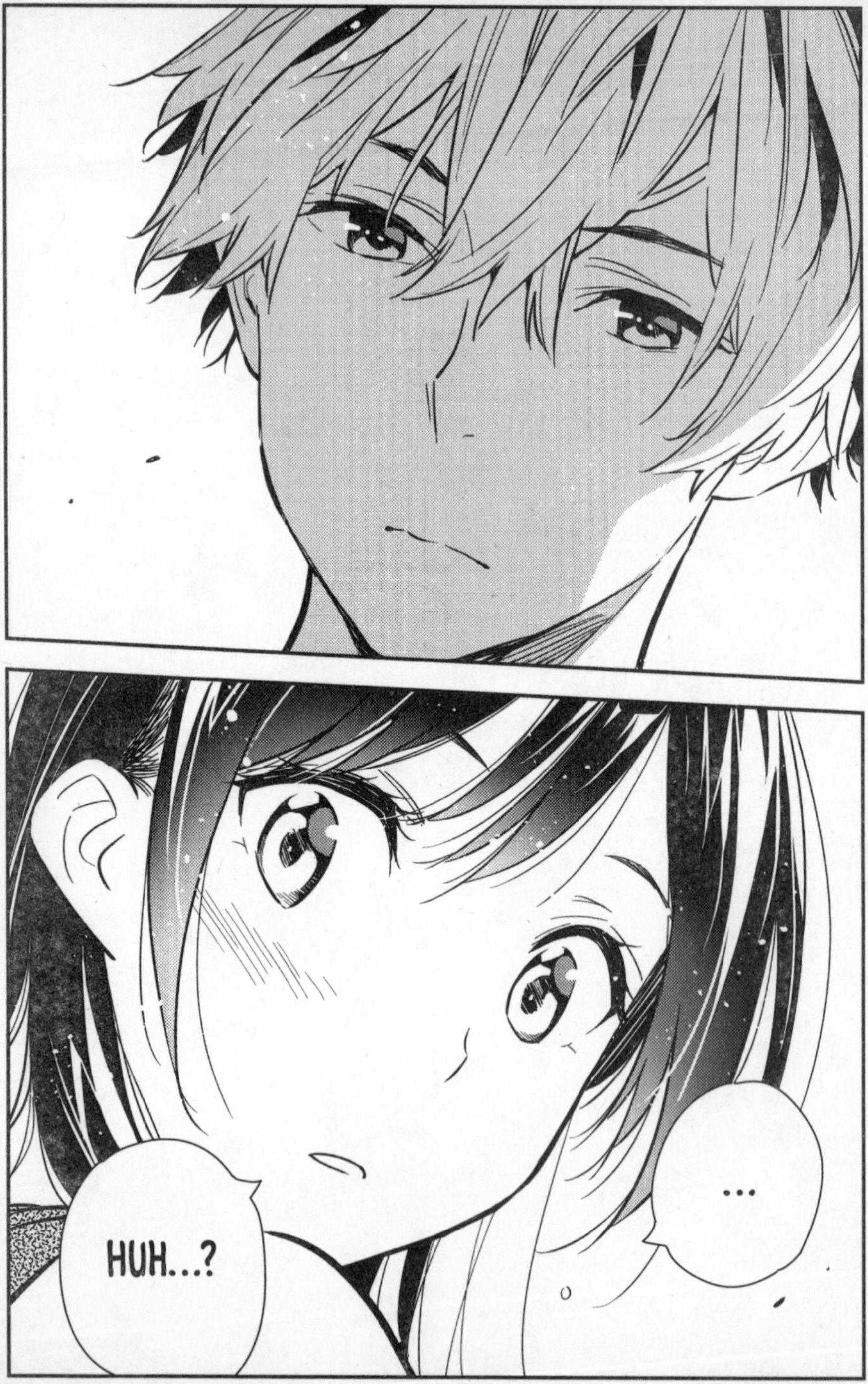
...
HUH...?

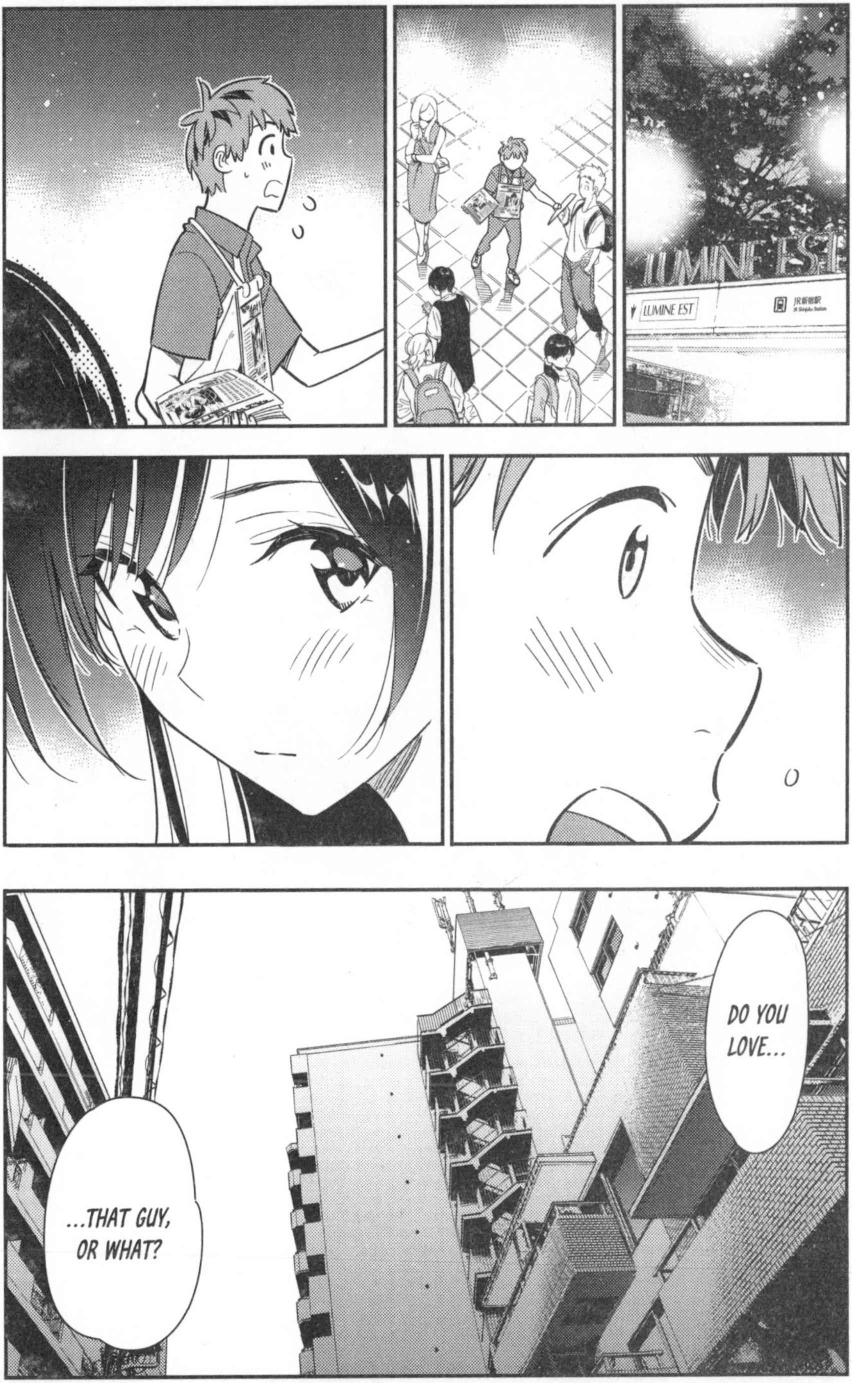
LUMINE EST
LUMINE EST
JR新宿駅
DO YOU LOVE...
...THAT GUY, OR WHAT?

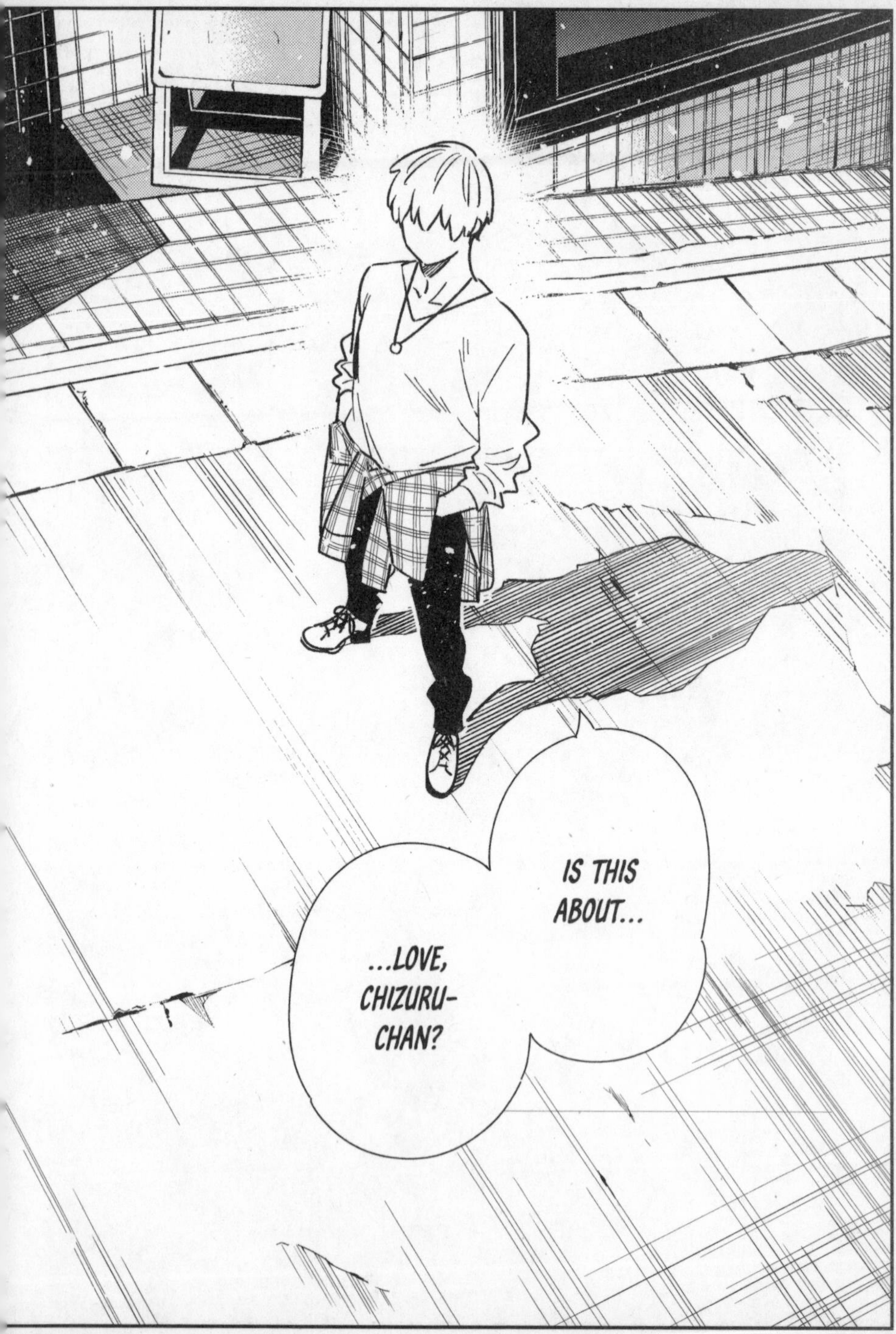
IS THIS ABOUT...
...LOVE, CHIZURU-CHAN?

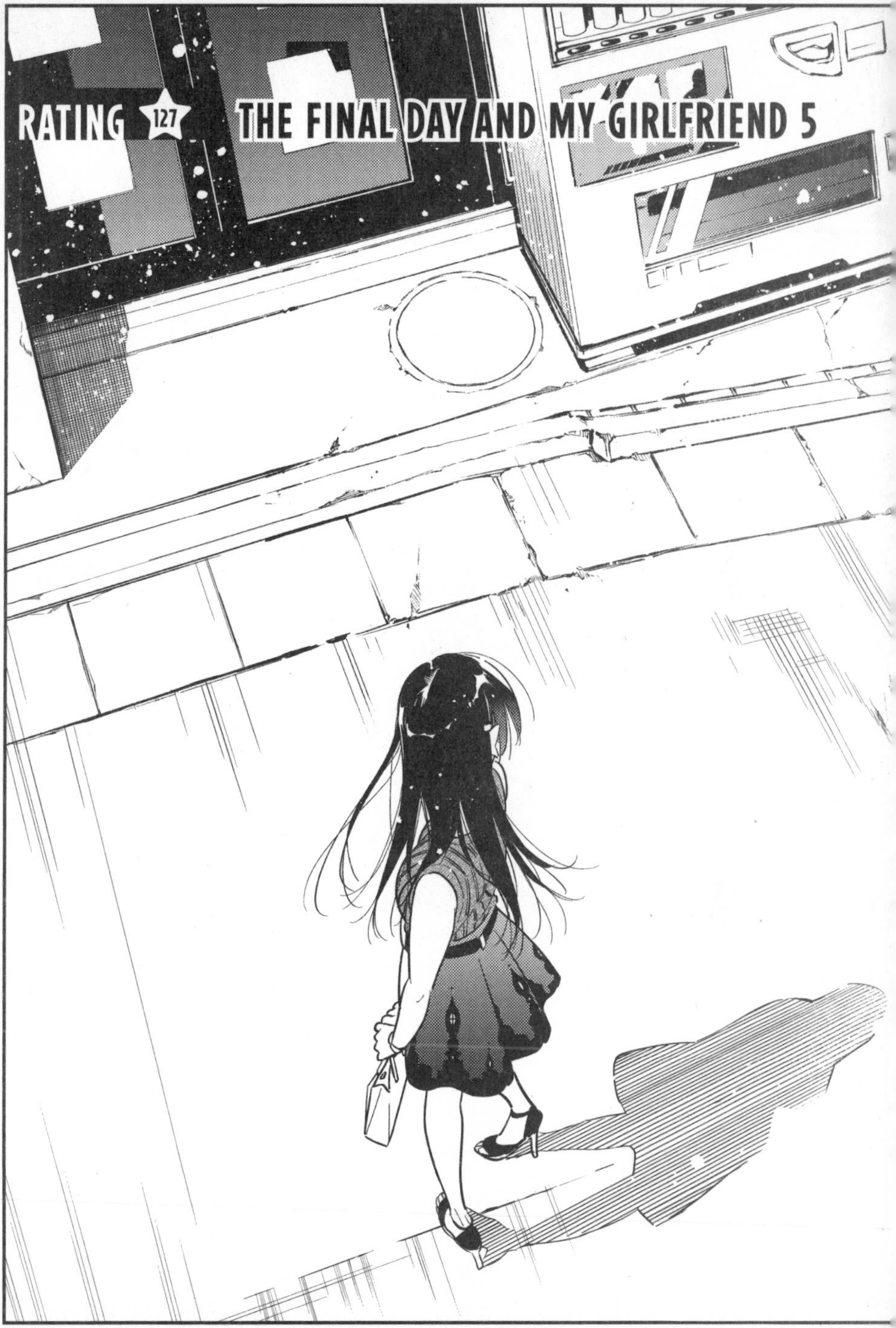
RATING 127 THE FINAL DAY AND MY GIRLFRIEND 5

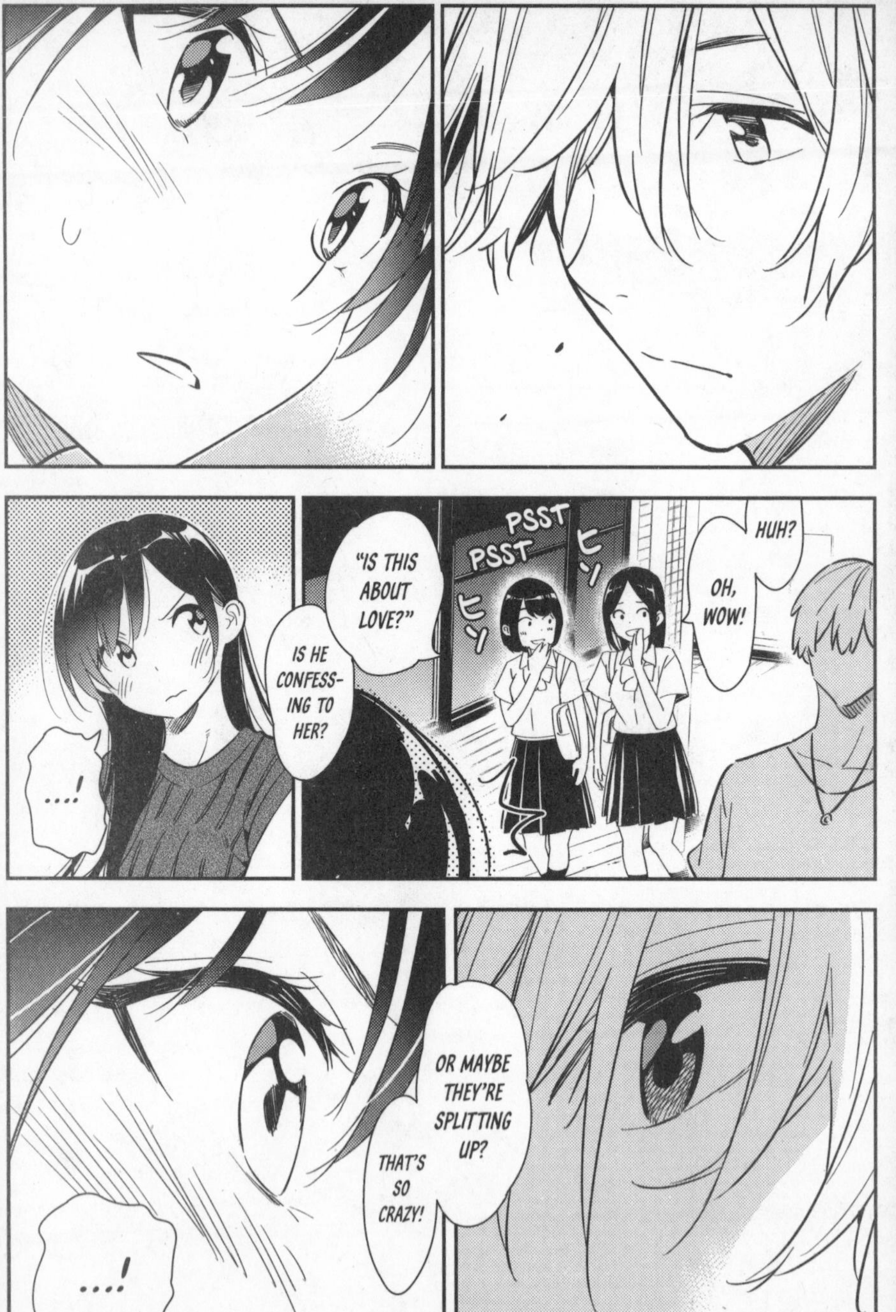
HUH?
OH, WOW!
PSST
ヒソ
PSST
ヒソ
"IS THIS ABOUT LOVE?"
IS HE CONFESSING TO HER?
...!
OR MAYBE THEY'RE SPLITTING UP?
THAT'S SO CRAZY!
...!

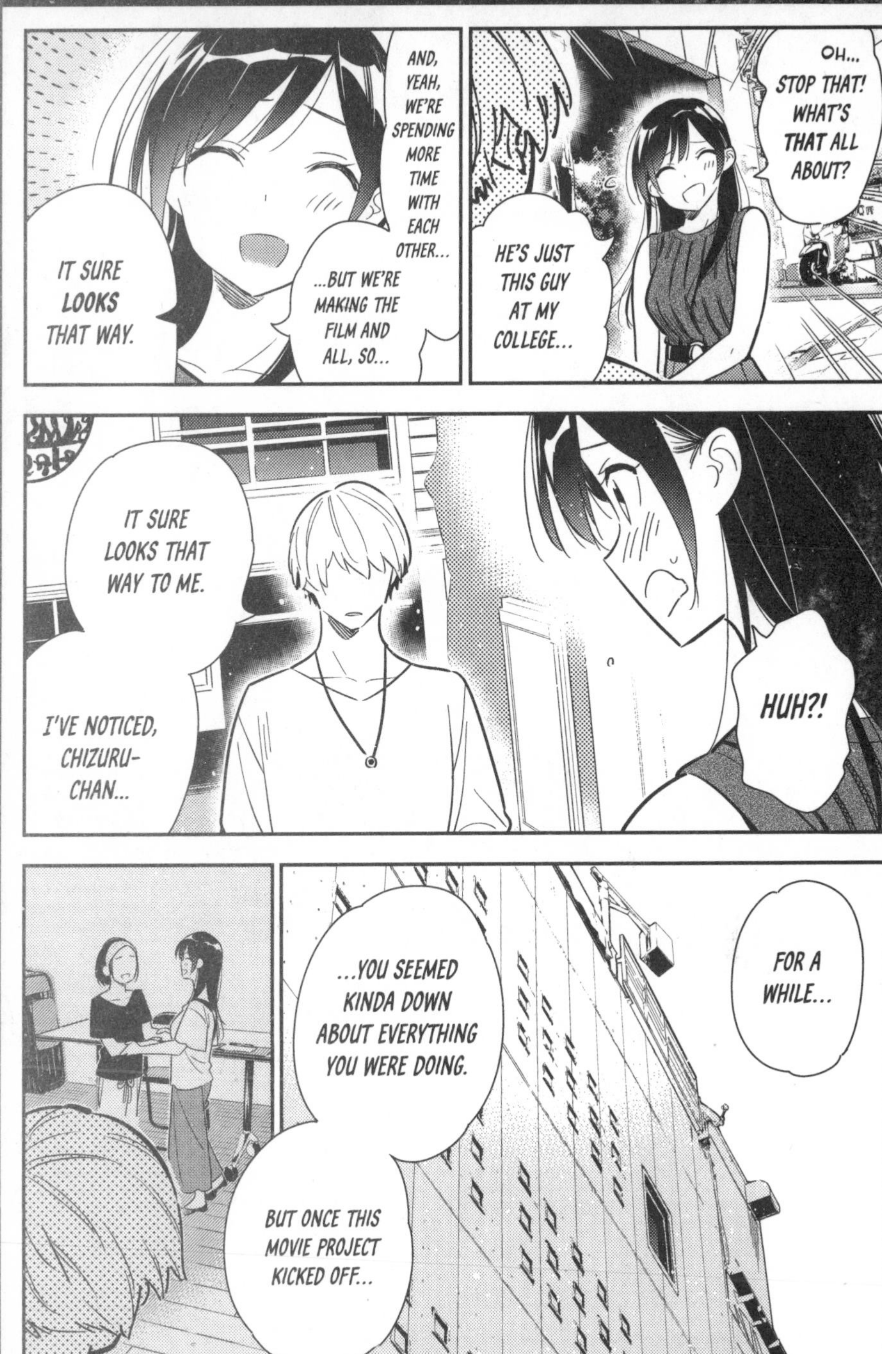
OH... STOP THAT! WHAT'S THAT ALL ABOUT?
HE'S JUST THIS GUY AT MY COLLEGE...
AND, YEAH, WE'RE SPENDING MORE TIME WITH EACH OTHER...
...BUT WE'RE MAKING THE FILM AND ALL, SO...
IT SURE LOOKS THAT WAY.
HUH?!
IT SURE LOOKS THAT WAY TO ME.
I'VE NOTICED, CHIZURU-CHAN...
FOR A WHILE...
...YOU SEEMED KINDA DOWN ABOUT EVERYTHING YOU WERE DOING.
BUT ONCE THIS MOVIE PROJECT KICKED OFF...

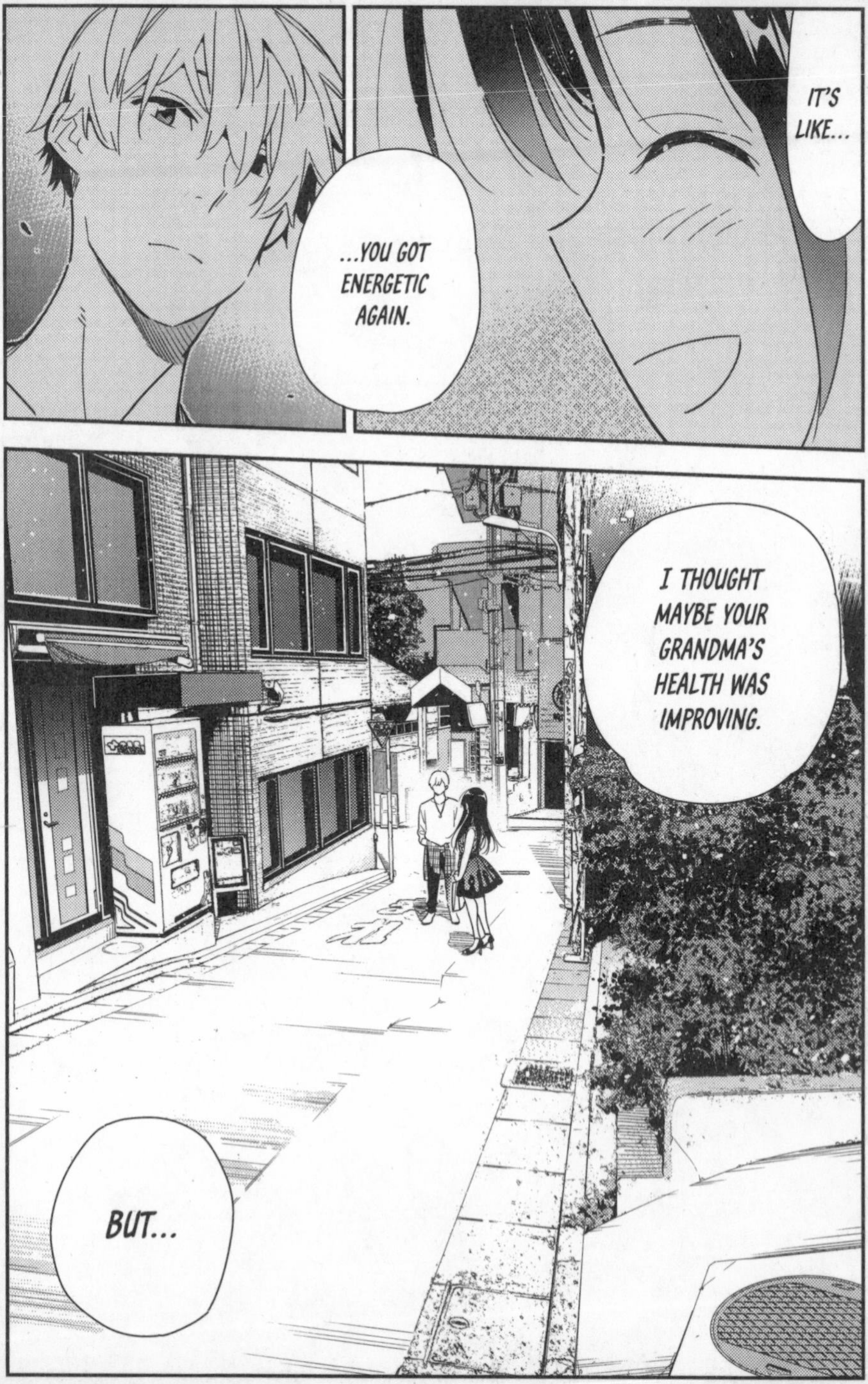
IT'S LIKE...
...YOU GOT ENERGETIC AGAIN.
I THOUGHT MAYBE YOUR GRANDMA'S HEALTH WAS IMPROVING.
BUT...

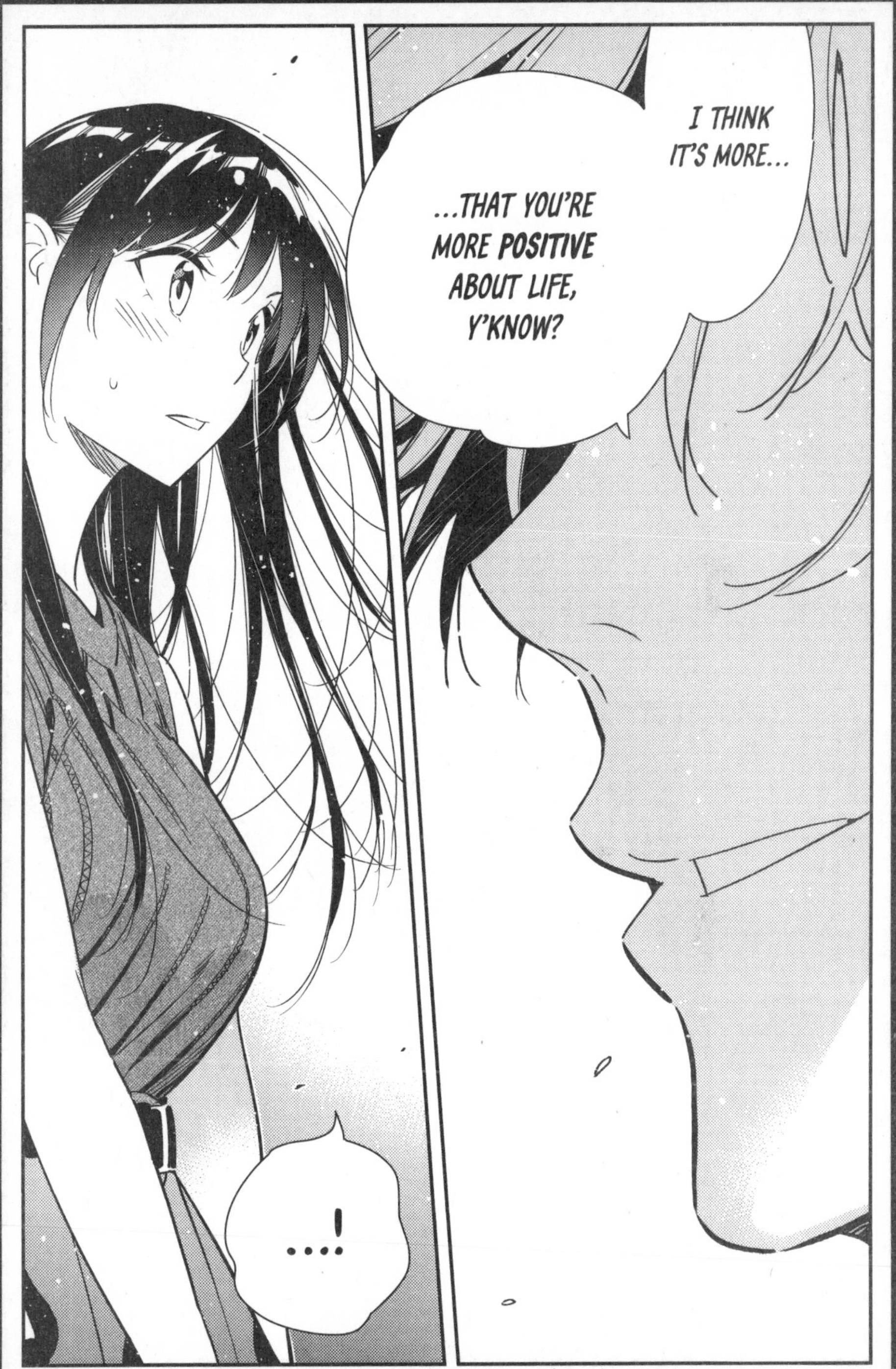
I THINK IT'S MORE...
...THAT YOU'RE MORE **POSITIVE** ABOUT LIFE, Y'KNOW?
...!

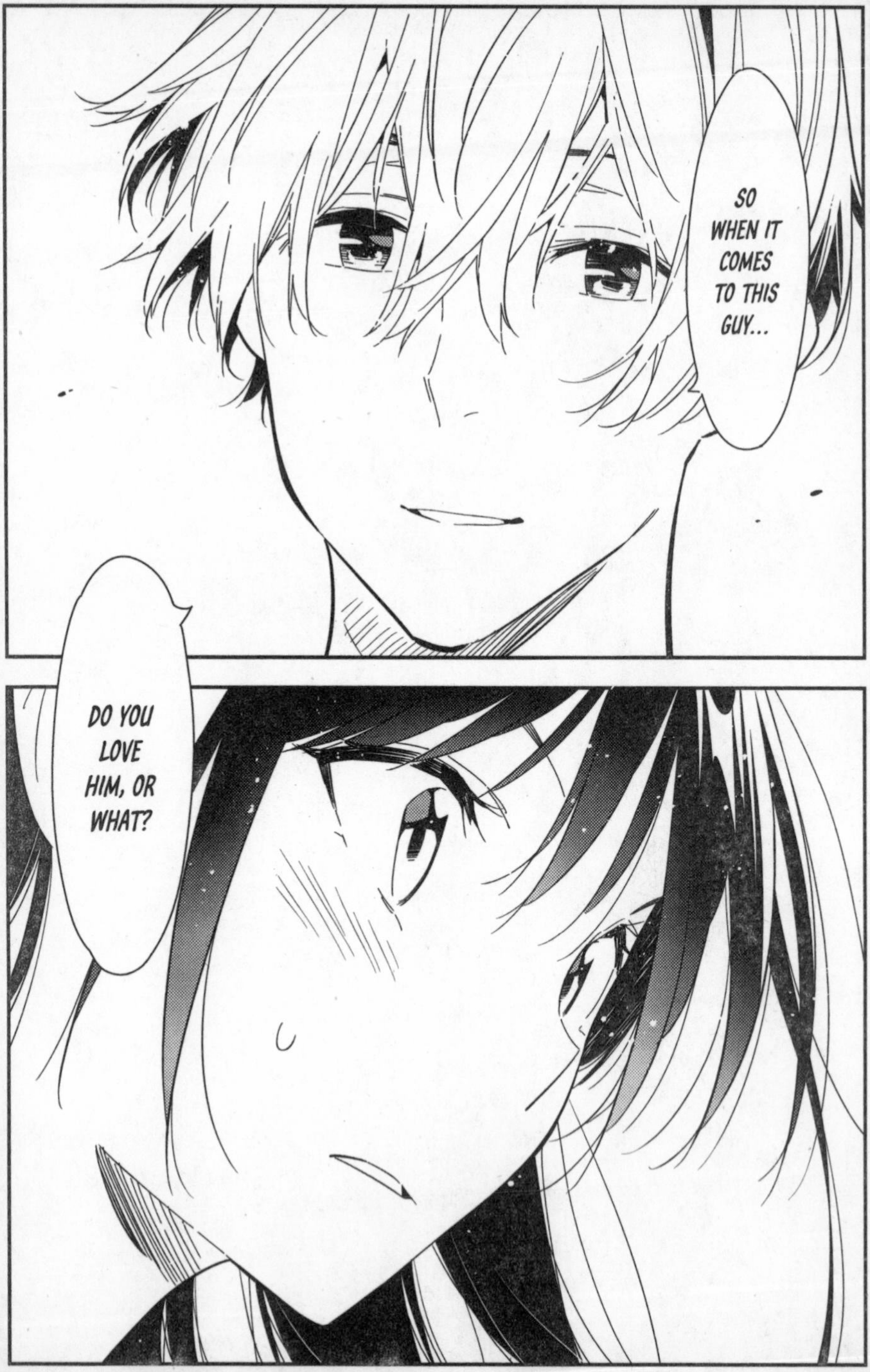
SO WHEN IT COMES TO THIS GUY...
DO YOU LOVE HIM, OR WHAT?

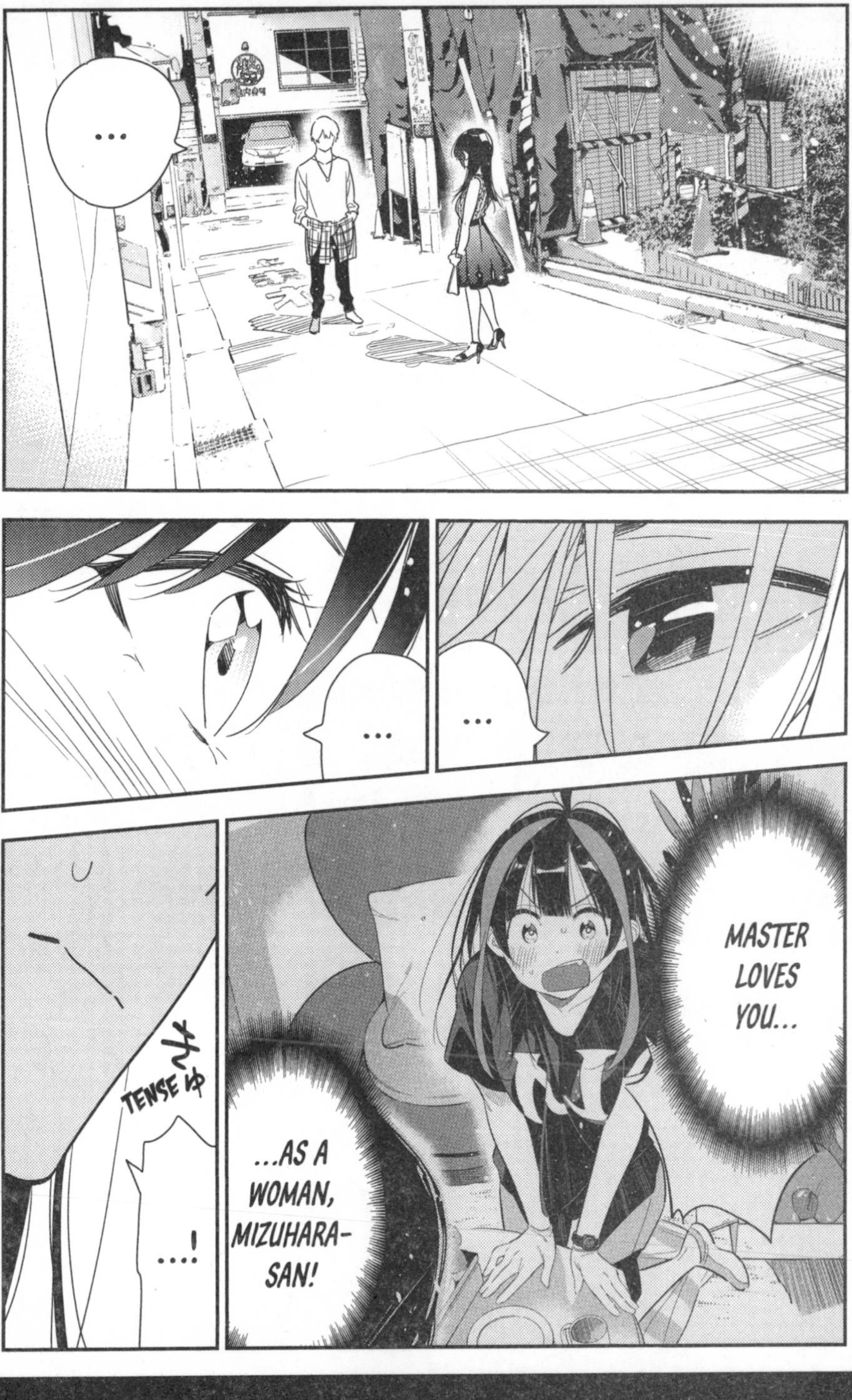
...
...
...
MASTER LOVES YOU...
...AS A WOMAN, MIZUHARA-SAN!
TENSE
...!

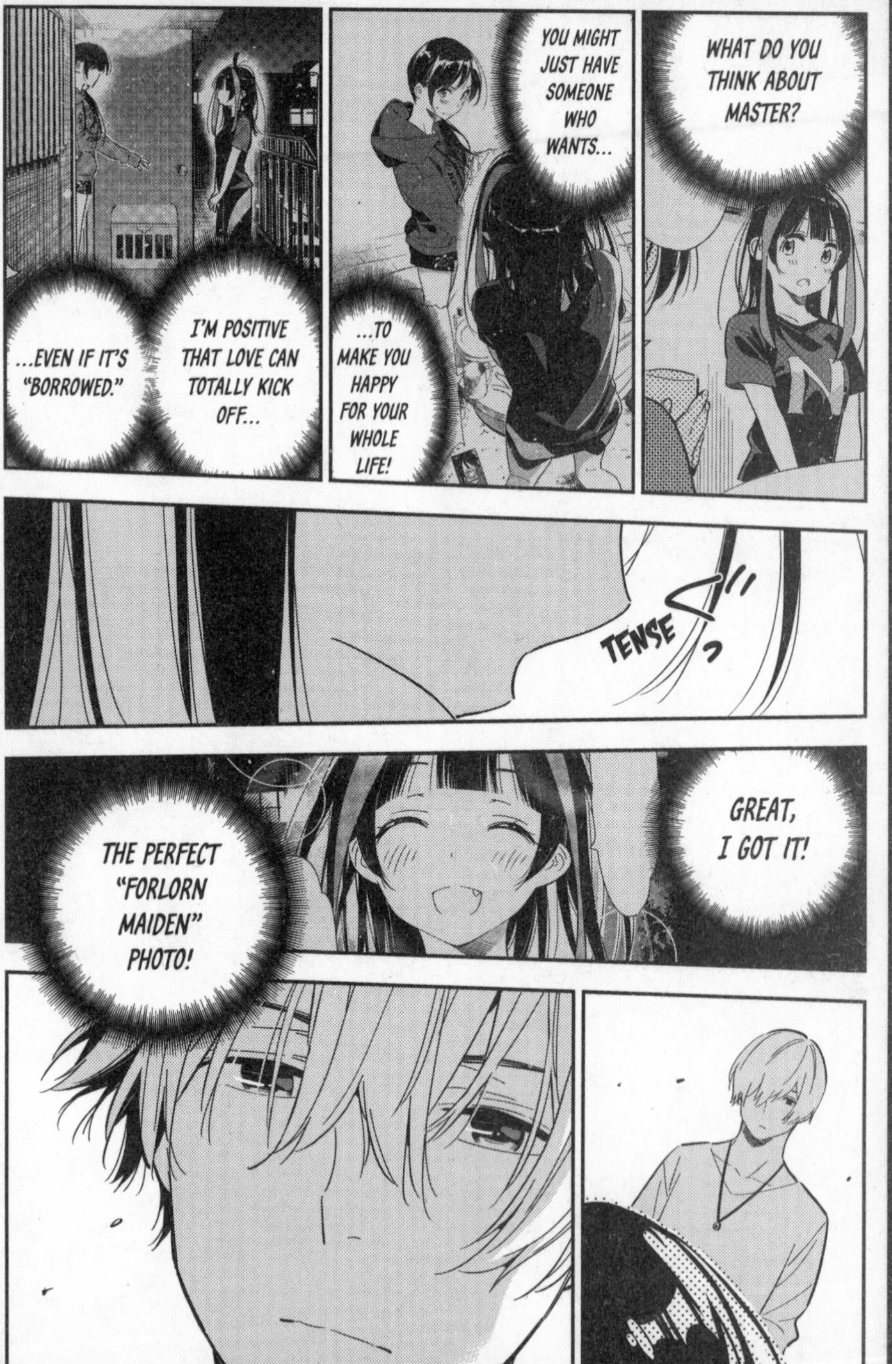
WHAT DO YOU THINK ABOUT MASTER?
YOU MIGHT JUST HAVE SOMEONE WHO WANTS...
...TO MAKE YOU HAPPY FOR YOUR WHOLE LIFE!
I'M POSITIVE THAT LOVE CAN TOTALLY KICK OFF...
...EVEN IF IT'S "BORROWED."
TENSE
GREAT, I GOT IT!
THE PERFECT "FORLORN MAIDEN" PHOTO!

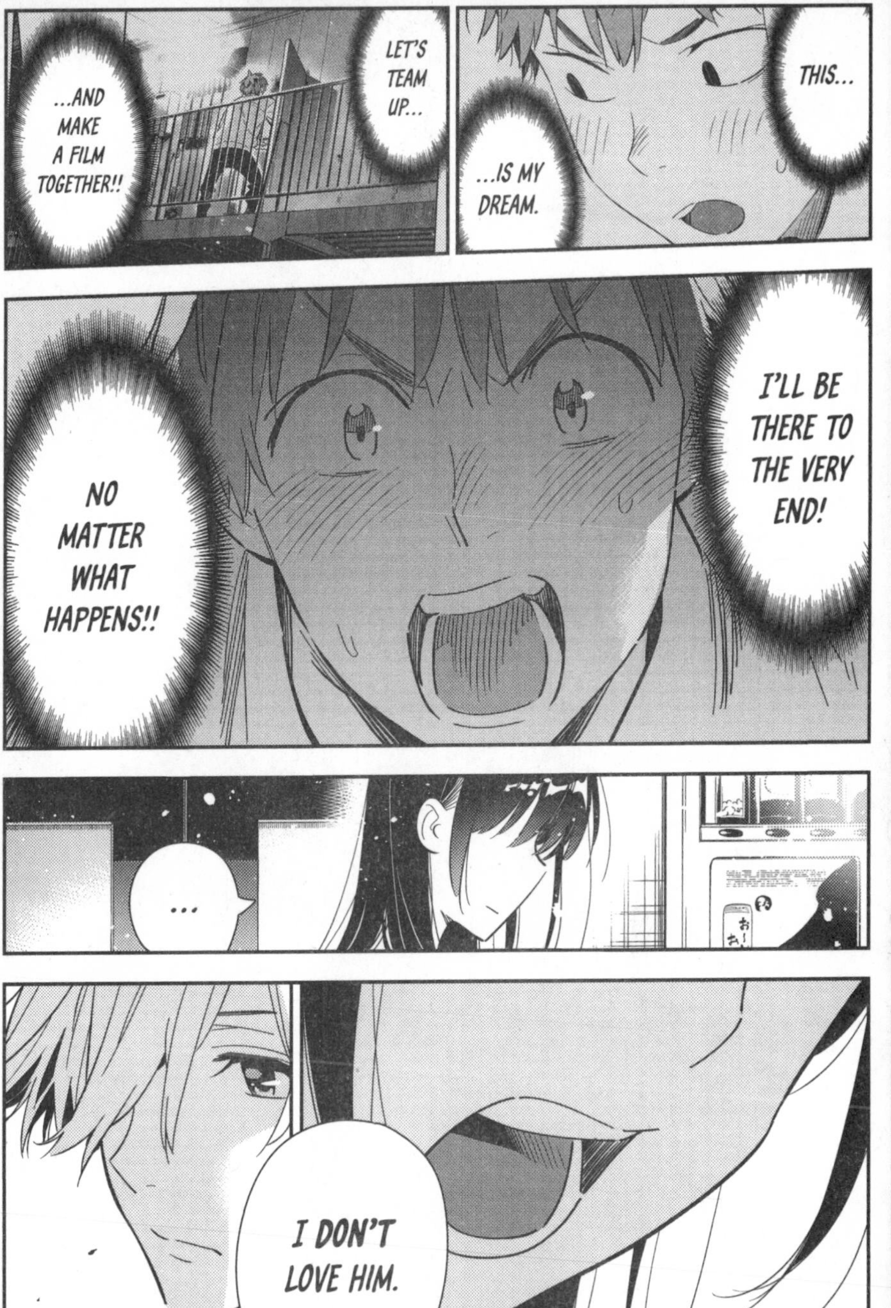
THIS...
...IS MY DREAM.
LET'S TEAM UP...
...AND MAKE A FILM TOGETHER!!
I'LL BE THERE TO THE VERY END!
NO MATTER WHAT HAPPENS!!
...
I DON'T LOVE HIM.

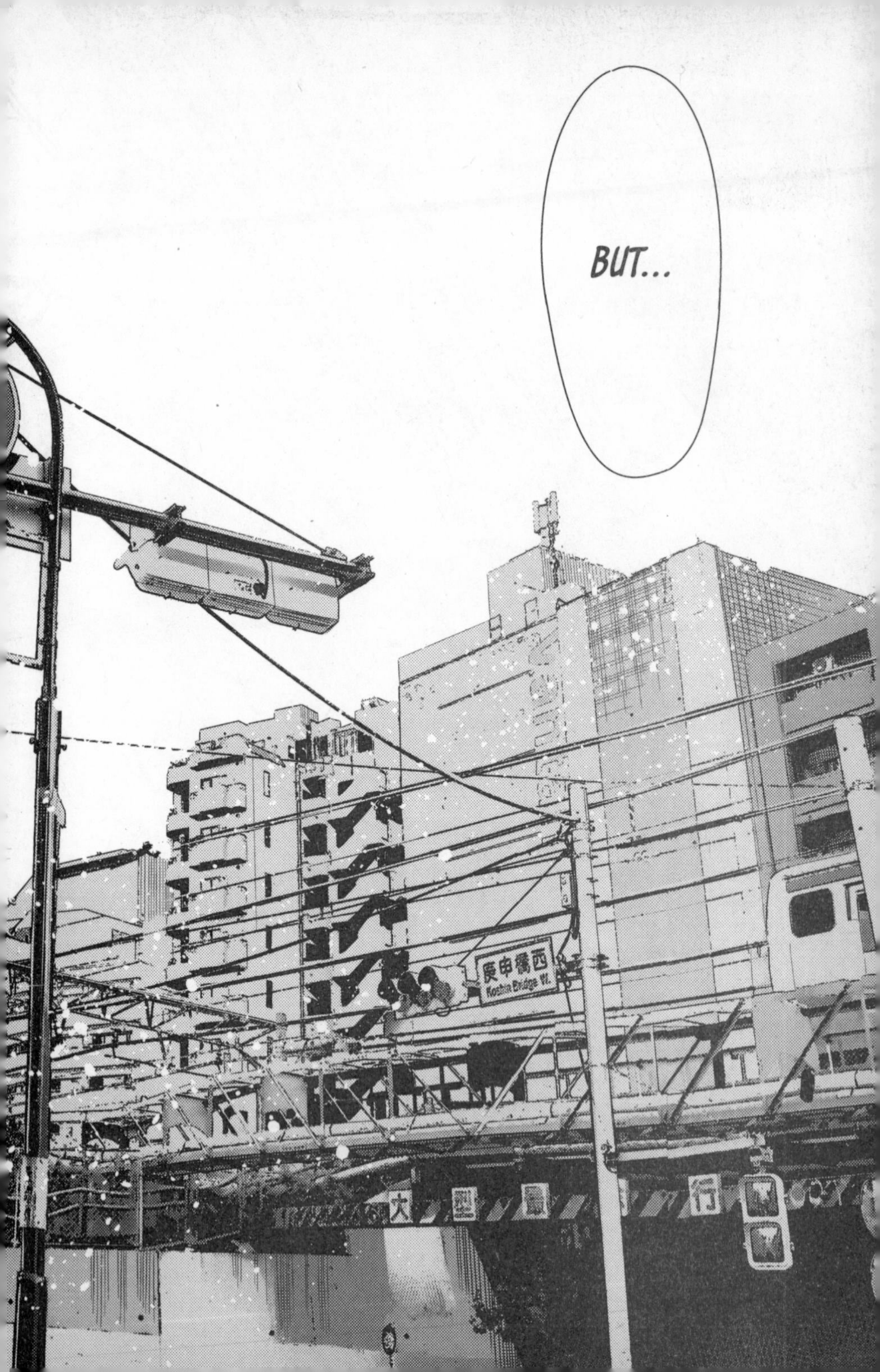
BUT...
庚申橋西
Koshin Bridge W.

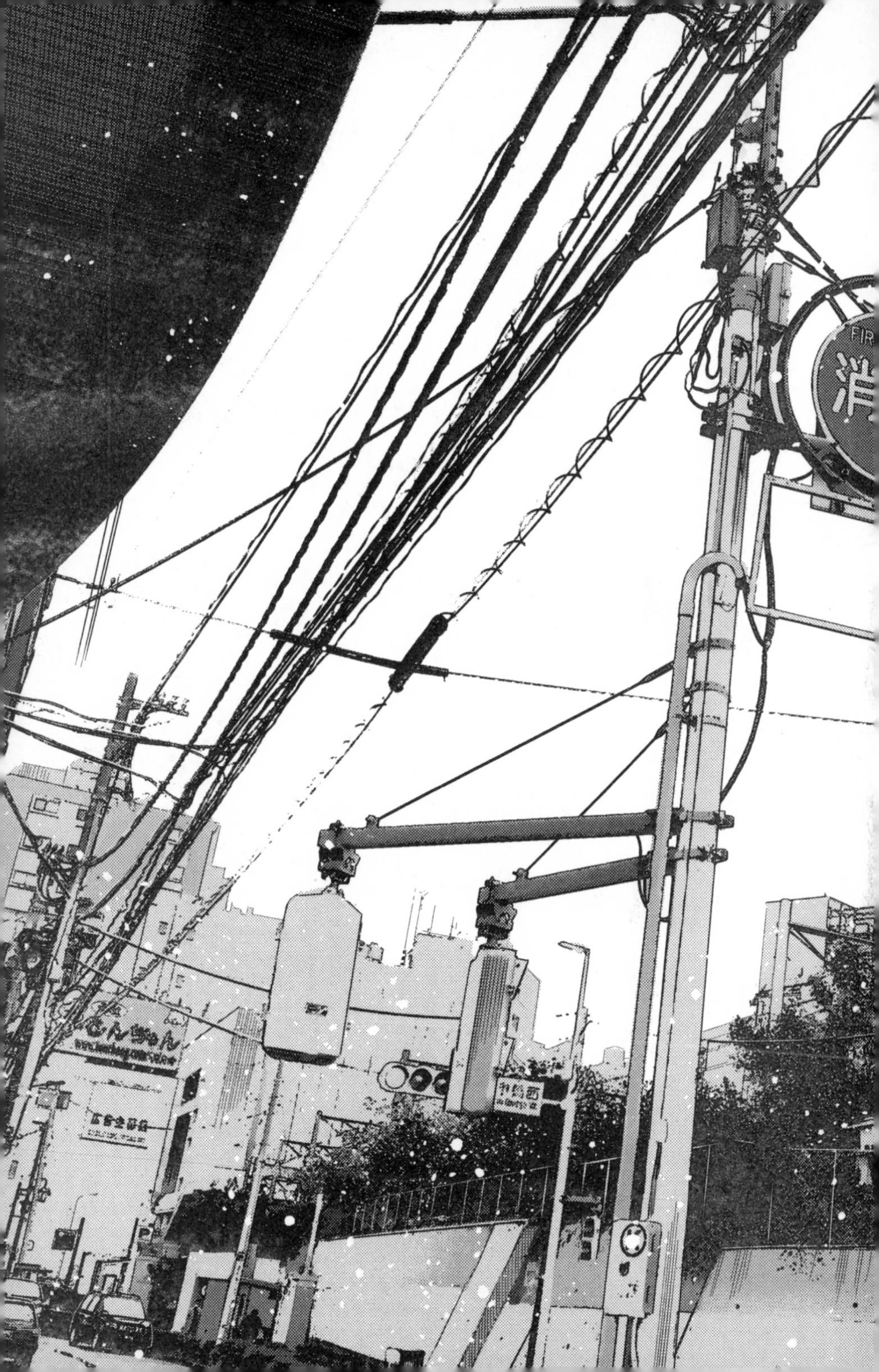

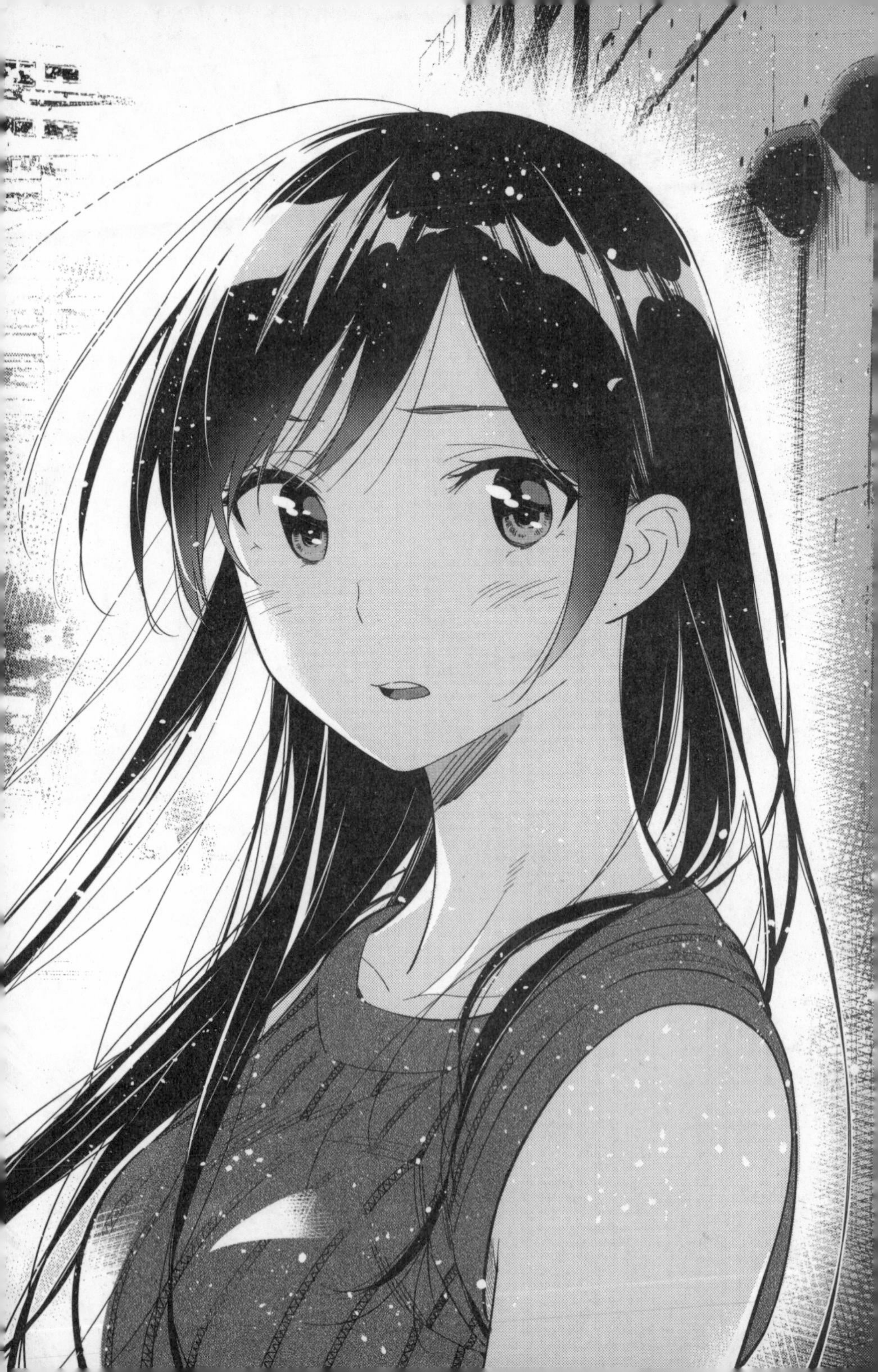

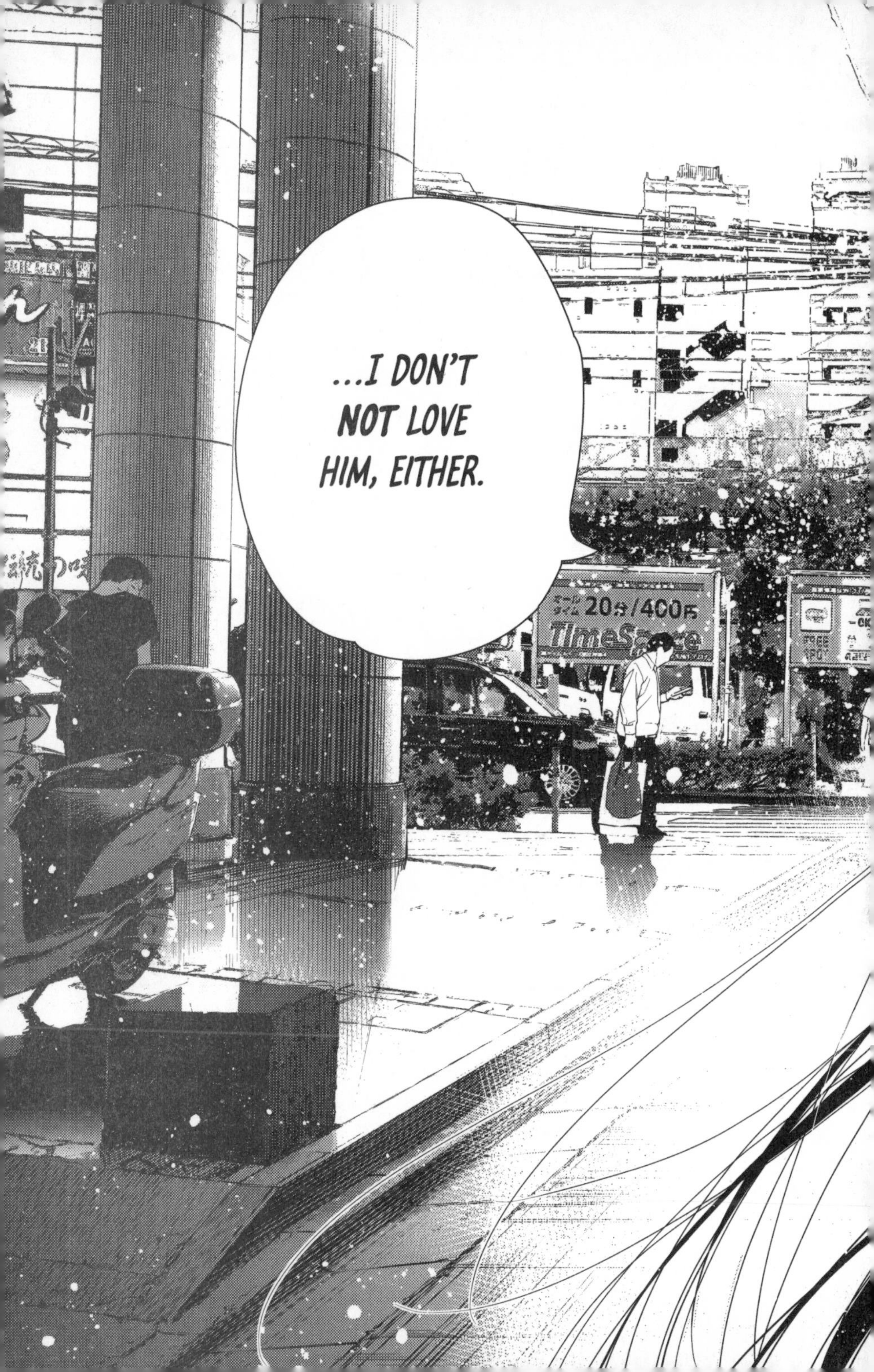
...I DON'T NOT LOVE HIM, EITHER.
20分/400円

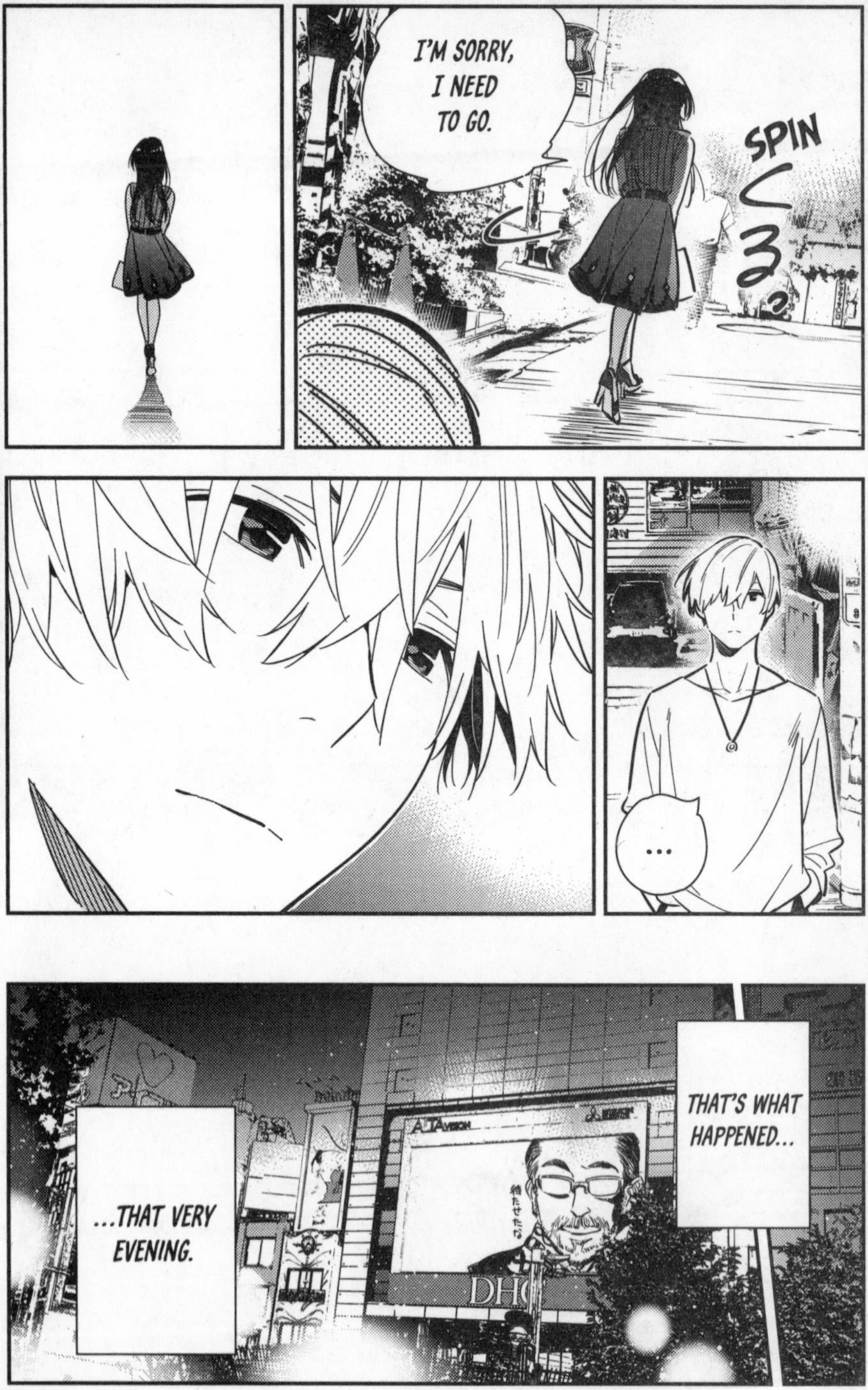
I'M SORRY, I NEED TO GO.
SPIN
くるっ
...
THAT'S WHAT HAPPENED...
...THAT VERY EVENING.

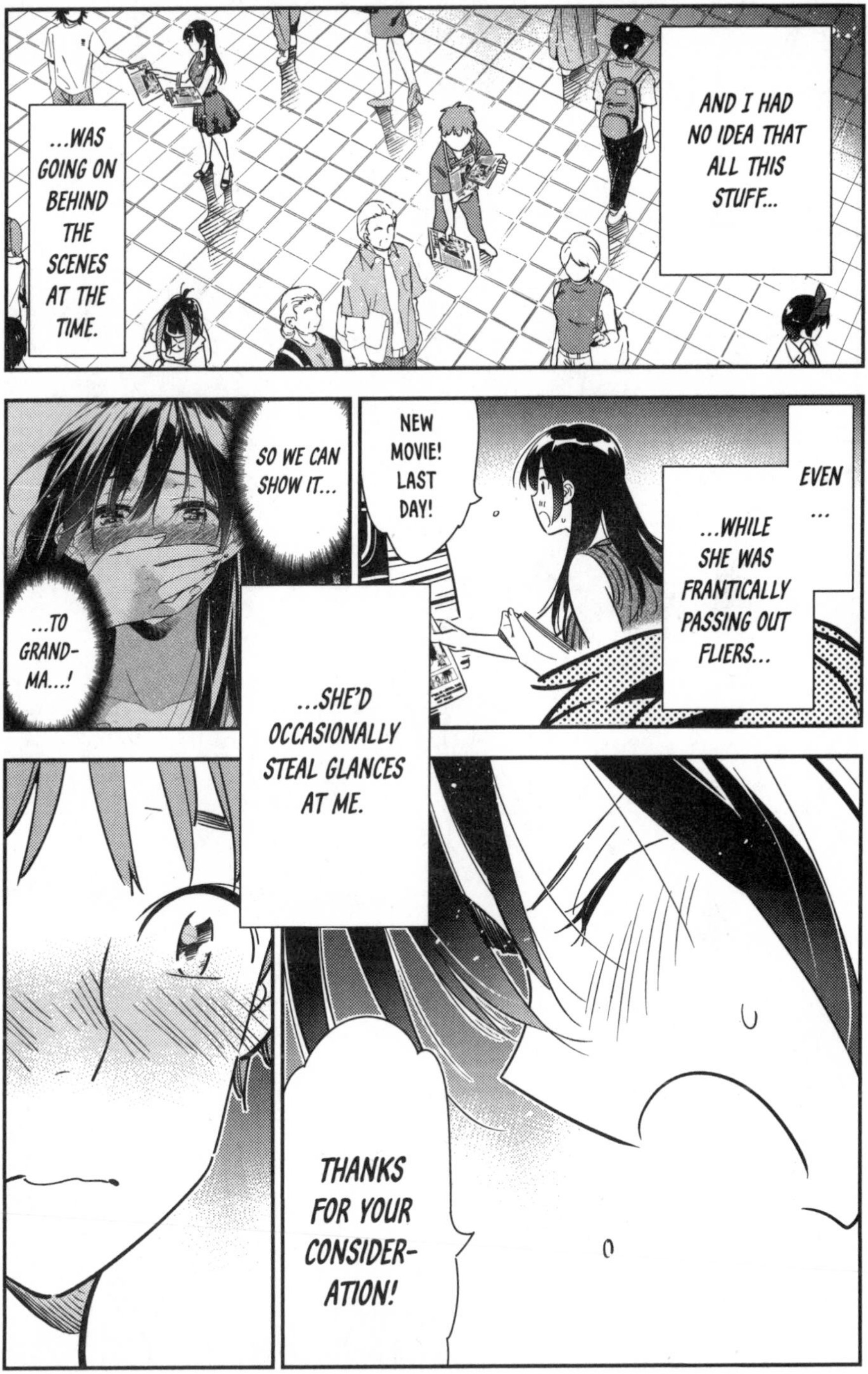
AND I HAD NO IDEA THAT ALL THIS STUFF...
...WAS GOING ON BEHIND THE SCENES AT THE TIME.
EVEN...
...WHILE SHE WAS FRANTICALLY PASSING OUT FLIERS...
NEW MOVIE! LAST DAY!
...SHE'D OCCASIONALLY STEAL GLANCES AT ME.
SO WE CAN SHOW IT...
...TO GRAND-MA...!
THANKS FOR YOUR CONSIDER-ATION!

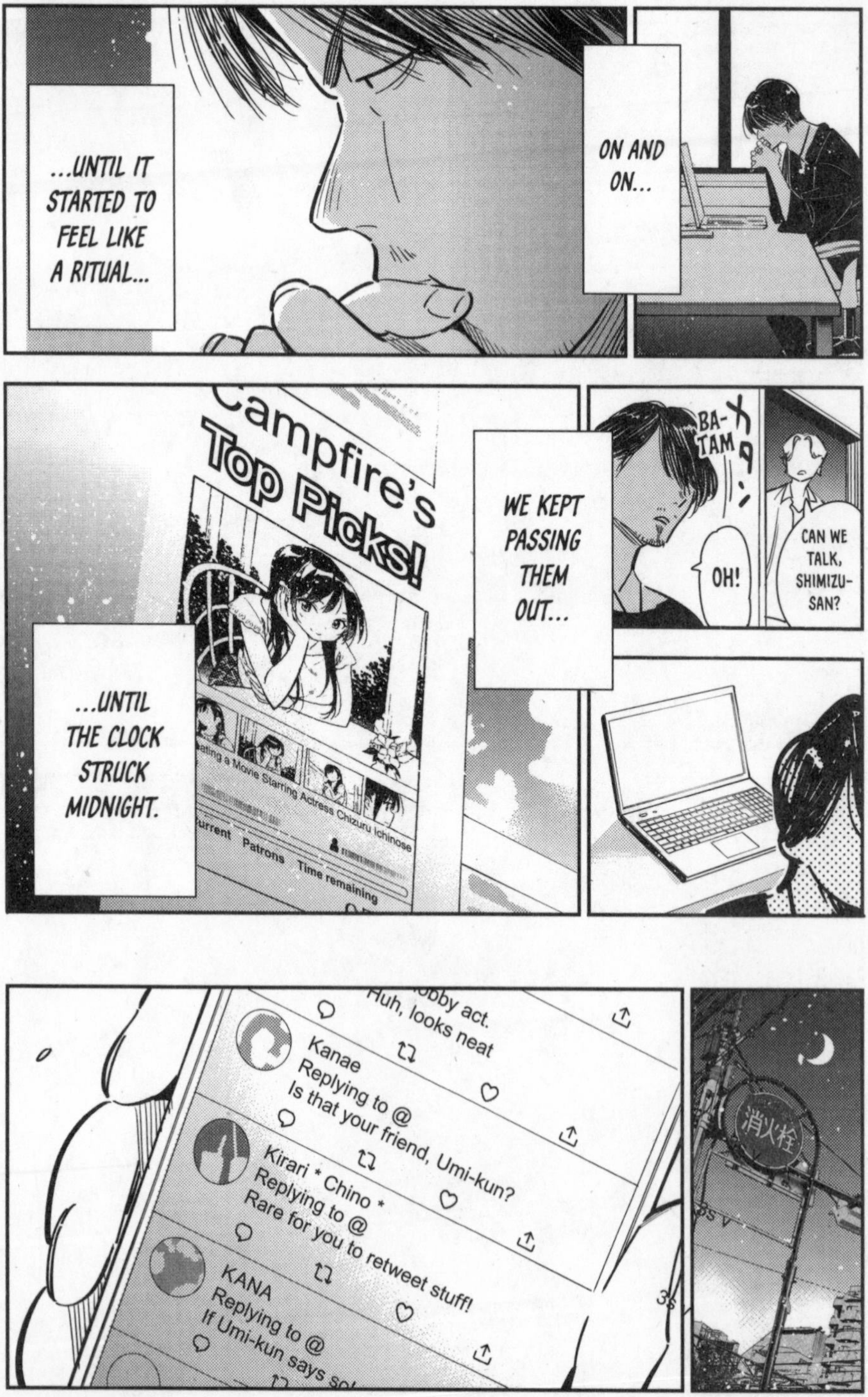
ON AND ON...
...UNTIL IT STARTED TO FEEL LIKE A RITUAL...
BA-TAM
CAN WE TALK, SHIMIZU-SAN?
OH!
WE KEPT PASSING THEM OUT...
Campfire's Top Picks!
Patrons
Time remaining
...UNTIL THE CLOCK STRUCK MIDNIGHT.
消火栓
Huh, looks neat
Kanae
Replying to @
Is that your friend, Umi-kun?
Kirari * Chino *
Replying to @
Rare for you to retweet stuff!
KANA
Replying to @

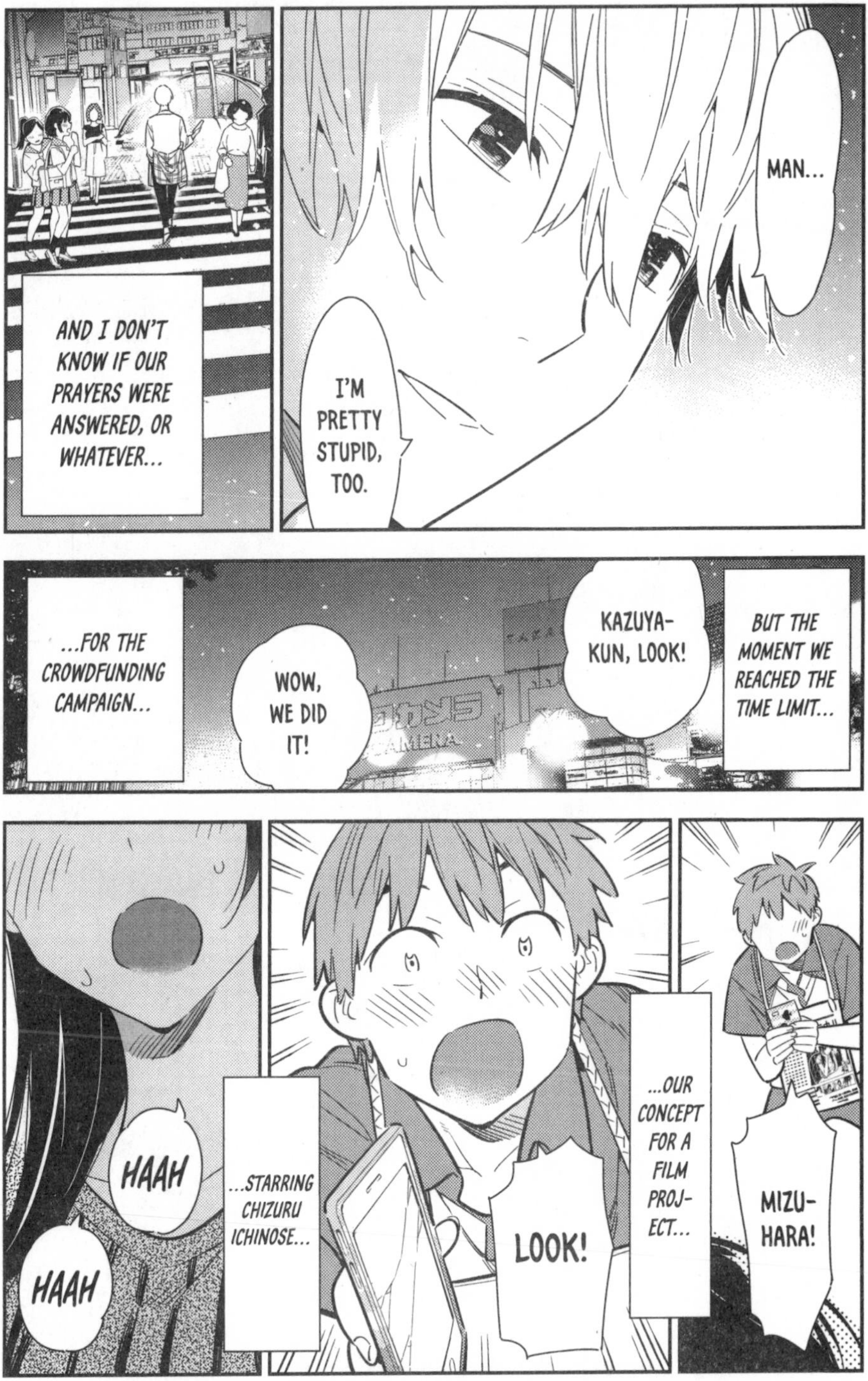
MAN...
I'M PRETTY STUPID, TOO.
AND I DON'T KNOW IF OUR PRAYERS WERE ANSWERED, OR WHATEVER...
BUT THE MOMENT WE REACHED THE TIME LIMIT...
KAZUYA-KUN, LOOK!
WOW, WE DID IT!
...FOR THE CROWDFUNDING CAMPAIGN...
MIZU-HARA!
...OUR CONCEPT FOR A FILM PROJ-ECT...
LOOK!
...STARRING CHIZURU ICHINOSE...
HAAH
HAAH

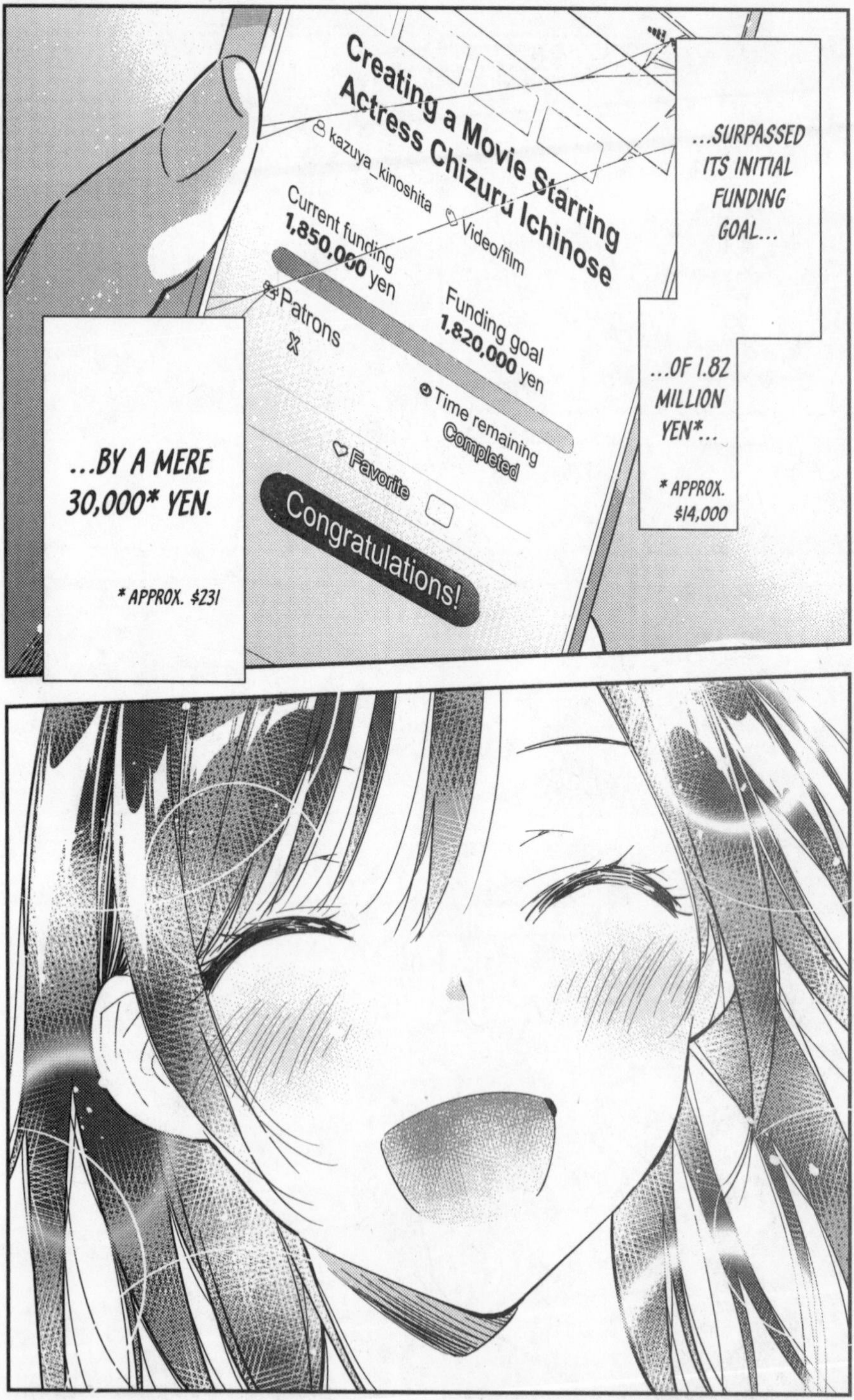
...SURPASSED ITS INITIAL FUNDING GOAL...
...OF 1.82 MILLION YEN*...
* APPROX. $14,000
Creating a Movie Starring Actress Chizuru Ichinose
kazuya_kinoshita
Video/film
Current funding
1,850,000 yen
Funding goal
1,820,000 yen
Patrons
Time remaining
Completed
Favorite
Congratulations!
...BY A MERE 30,000* YEN.
* APPROX. $231

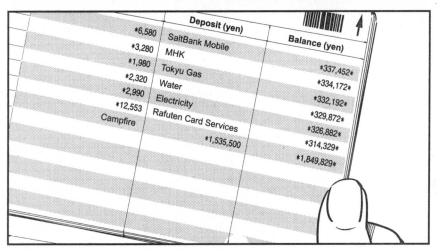

	Deposit (yen)		Balance (yen)
*6,580	SaltBank Mobile		
*3,280	MHK		*337,452*
*1,980	Tokyu Gas		*334,172*
*2,320	Water		*332,192*
*2,990	Electricity		*329,872*
*12,553	Rafuten Card Services		*326,882*
Campfire			*314,329*
		*1,535,500	*1,849,829*

*1,849,

RATING 128 INTRODUCTIONS AND MY GIRLFRIEND

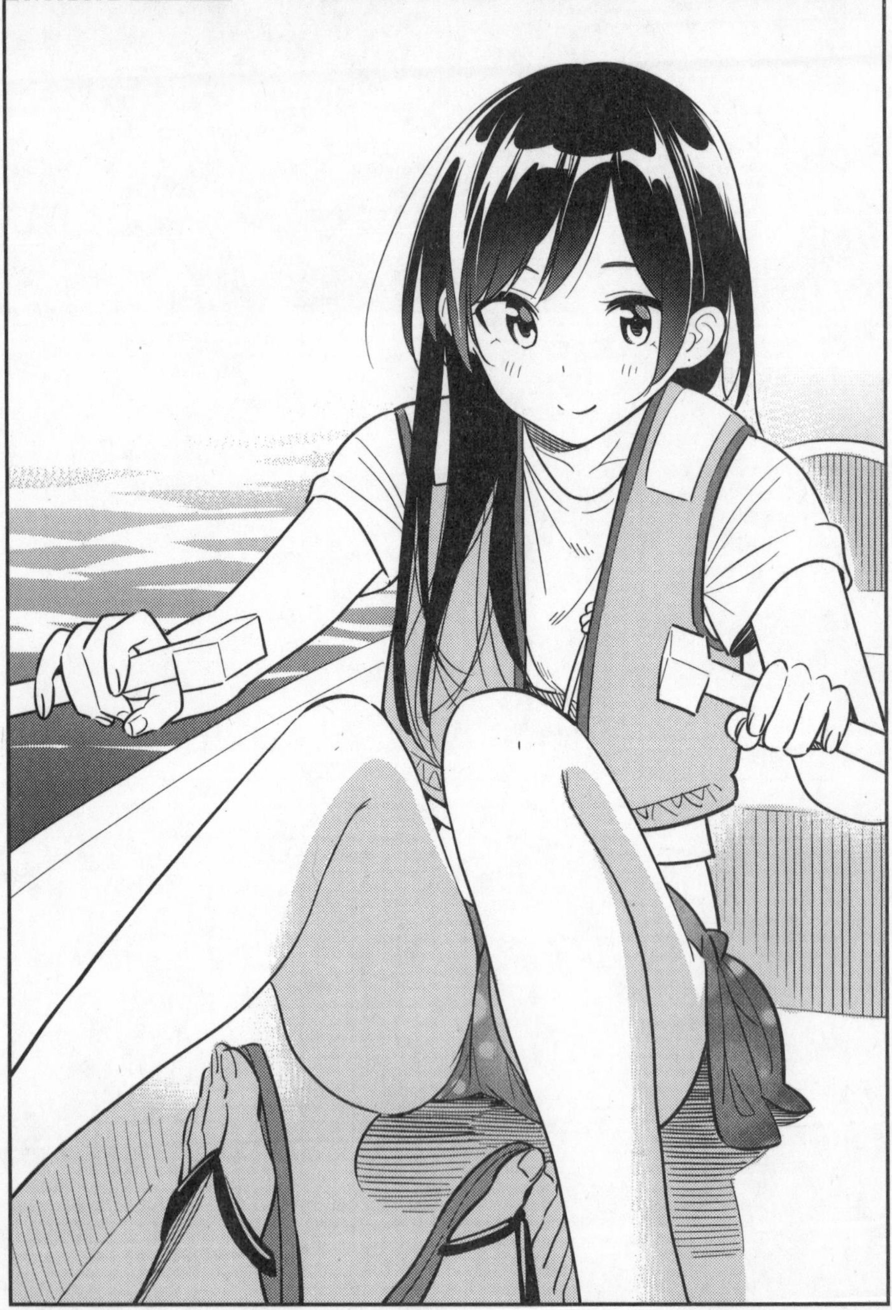

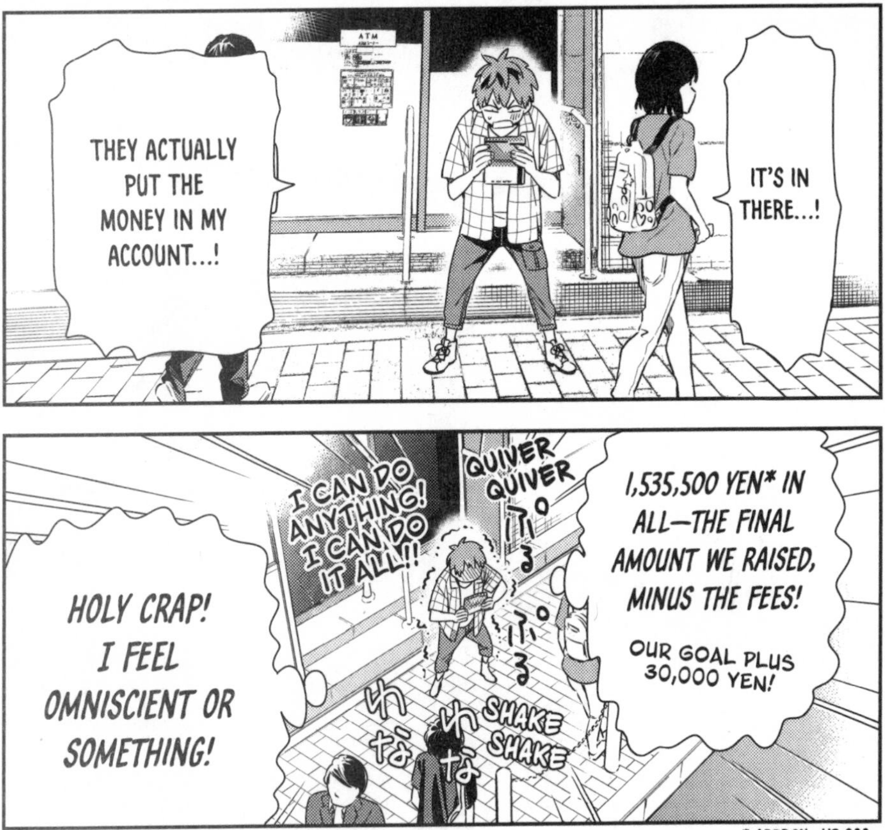
IT'S IN THERE...!
THEY ACTUALLY PUT THE MONEY IN MY ACCOUNT...!
1,535,500 YEN* IN ALL—THE FINAL AMOUNT WE RAISED, MINUS THE FEES!
OUR GOAL PLUS 30,000 YEN!
QUIVER QUIVER
ぷるぷる
I CAN DO ANYTHING! I CAN DO IT ALL!!
HOLY CRAP! I FEEL OMNISCIENT OR SOMETHING!
SHAKE SHAKE
わなわな
ATM

* APPROX. $12,000

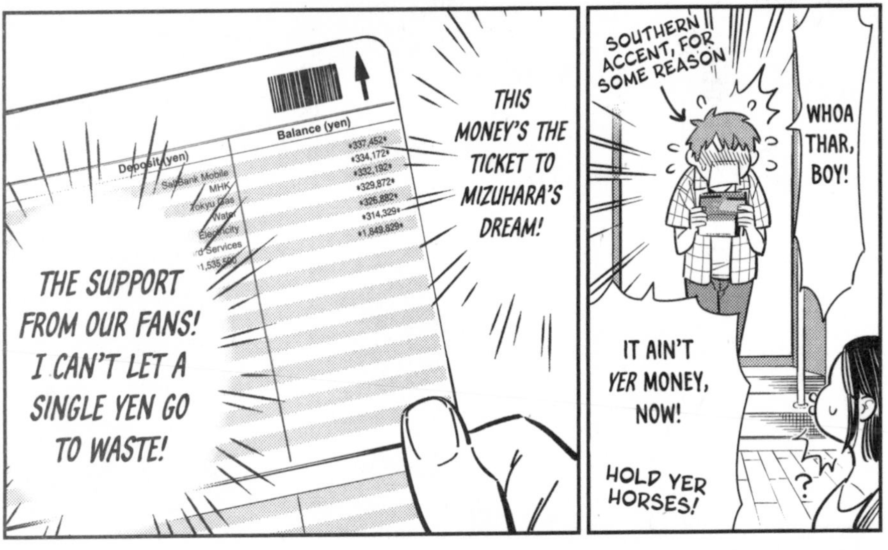
WHOA THAR, BOY!
SOUTHERN ACCENT, FOR SOME REASON
IT AIN'T YER MONEY, NOW!
HOLD YER HORSES!
?
THIS MONEY'S THE TICKET TO MIZUHARA'S DREAM!
THE SUPPORT FROM OUR FANS! I CAN'T LET A SINGLE YEN GO TO WASTE!
Deposit (yen)
Balance (yen)
SabBank Mobile
MHK
Tokyu Gas
Water
Electricity
¥337,452
¥334,172
¥332,192
¥329,872
¥326,882
¥314,329
¥1,849,829

THAT'S RIGHT...! MY MISSION HERE IS TO COMPLETE THAT FILM AND SHOW IT TO SAYURI!

THIS IS JUST A CHECKPOINT ALONG THE WAY...!

THE MONEY MAKES IT SEEM SO REAL...

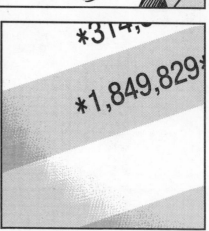

*314,
1,849,829

WOW...

MONEY IS SO HEAVY.

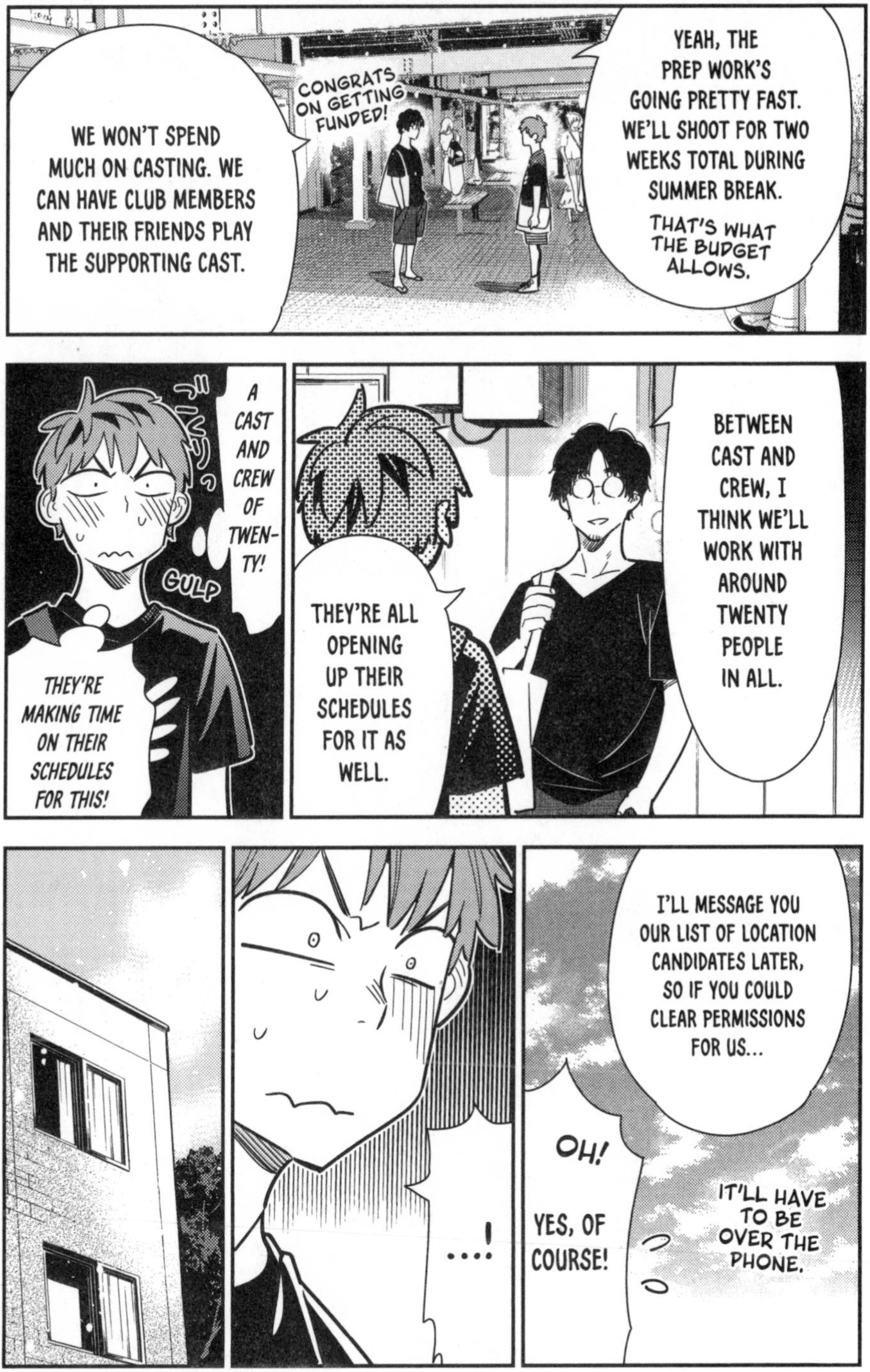
YEAH, THE PREP WORK'S GOING PRETTY FAST. WE'LL SHOOT FOR TWO WEEKS TOTAL DURING SUMMER BREAK.
THAT'S WHAT THE BUDGET ALLOWS.
CONGRATS ON GETTING FUNDED!
WE WON'T SPEND MUCH ON CASTING. WE CAN HAVE CLUB MEMBERS AND THEIR FRIENDS PLAY THE SUPPORTING CAST.
BETWEEN CAST AND CREW, I THINK WE'LL WORK WITH AROUND TWENTY PEOPLE IN ALL.
THEY'RE ALL OPENING UP THEIR SCHEDULES FOR IT AS WELL.
A CAST AND CREW OF TWEN-TY!
GULP
THEY'RE MAKING TIME ON THEIR SCHEDULES FOR THIS!
I'LL MESSAGE YOU OUR LIST OF LOCATION CANDIDATES LATER, SO IF YOU COULD CLEAR PERMISSIONS FOR US...
OH!
YES, OF COURSE!
IT'LL HAVE TO BE OVER THE PHONE.
...!

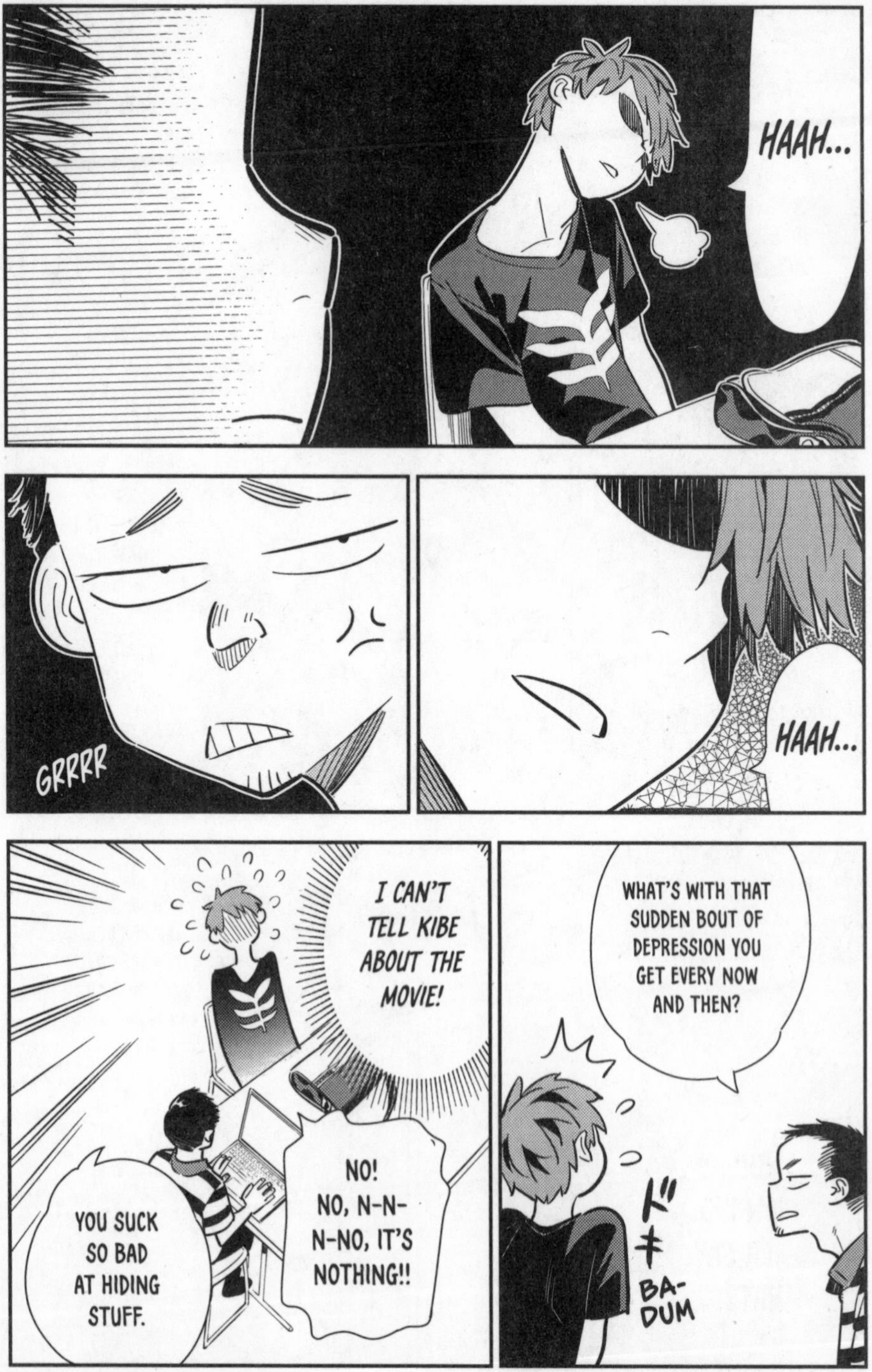
HAAH...
HAAH...
GRRRR
WHAT'S WITH THAT SUDDEN BOUT OF DEPRESSION YOU GET EVERY NOW AND THEN?
ドキ
BA-DUM
I CAN'T TELL KIBE ABOUT THE MOVIE!
NO! NO, N-N-N-NO, IT'S NOTHING!!
YOU SUCK SO BAD AT HIDING STUFF.

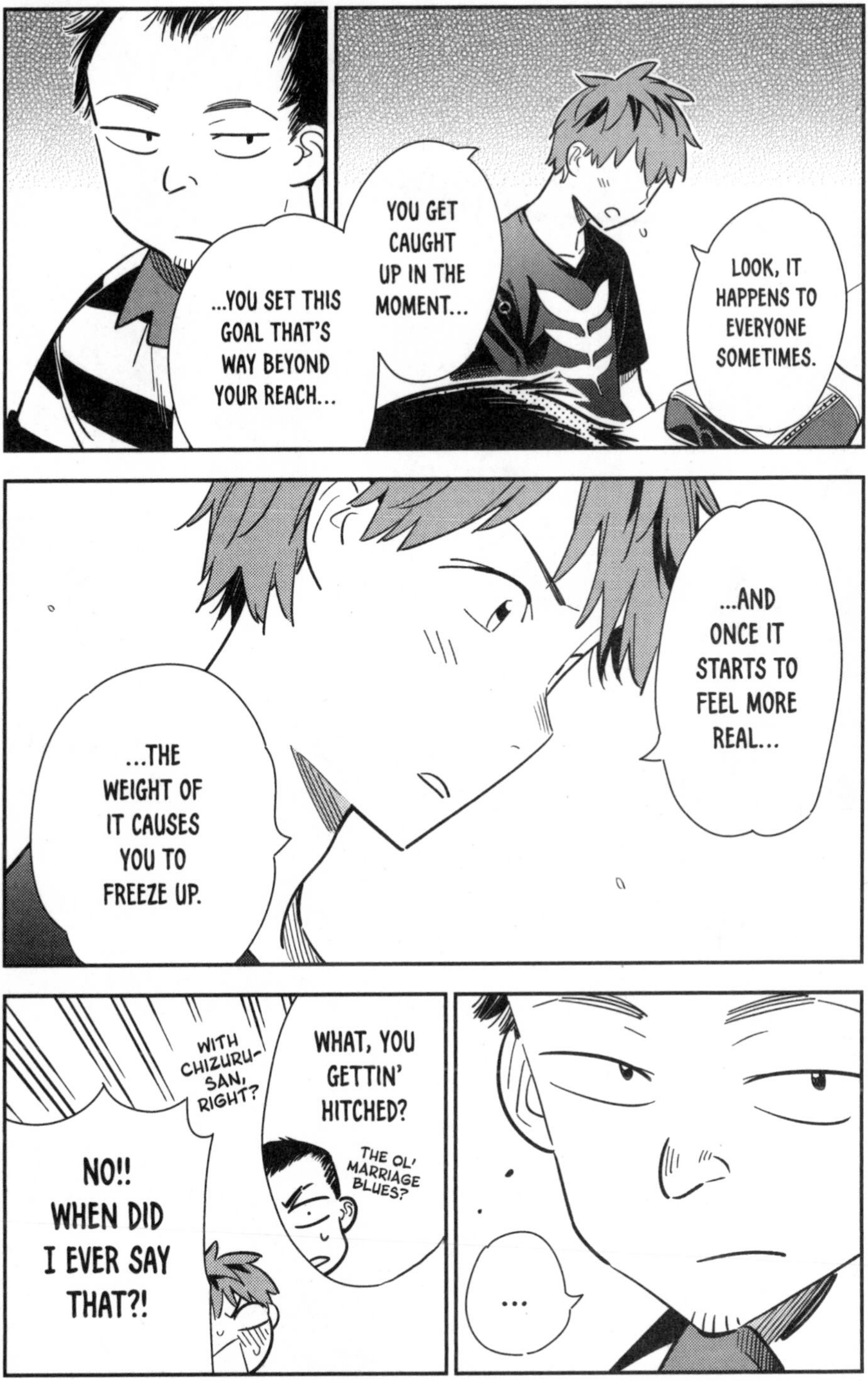
LOOK, IT HAPPENS TO EVERYONE SOMETIMES.
YOU GET CAUGHT UP IN THE MOMENT...
...YOU SET THIS GOAL THAT'S WAY BEYOND YOUR REACH...
...AND ONCE IT STARTS TO FEEL MORE REAL...
...THE WEIGHT OF IT CAUSES YOU TO FREEZE UP.
...
WHAT, YOU GETTIN' HITCHED?
THE OL' MARRIAGE BLUES?
WITH CHIZURU-SAN, RIGHT?
NO!! WHEN DID I EVER SAY THAT?!

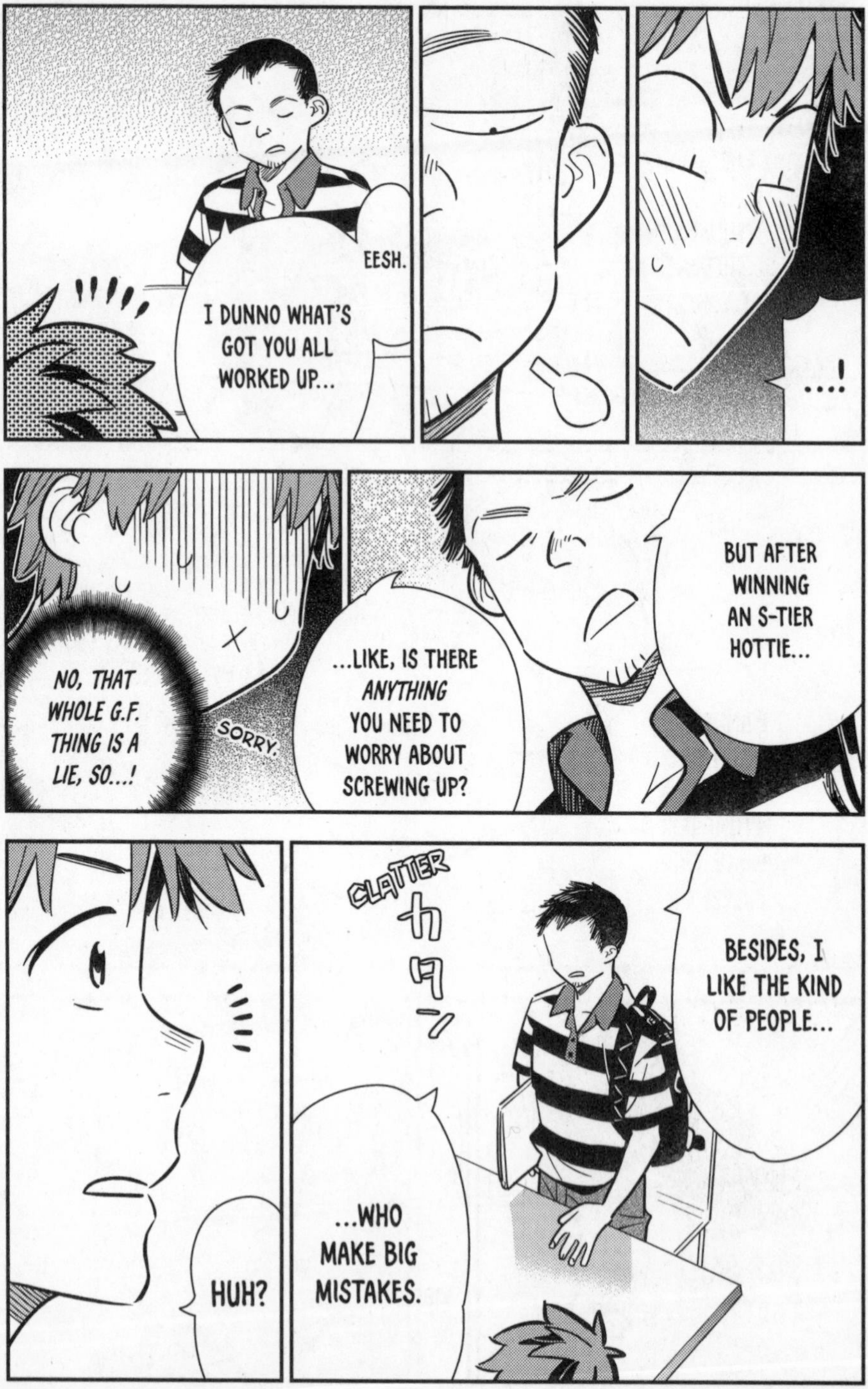
...!
EESH.
I DUNNO WHAT'S GOT YOU ALL WORKED UP...
BUT AFTER WINNING AN S-TIER HOTTIE...
...LIKE, IS THERE *ANYTHING* YOU NEED TO WORRY ABOUT SCREWING UP?
NO, THAT WHOLE G.F. THING IS A LIE, SO...!
SORRY.
CLATTER
カタン
BESIDES, I LIKE THE KIND OF PEOPLE...
...WHO MAKE BIG MISTAKES.
HUH?

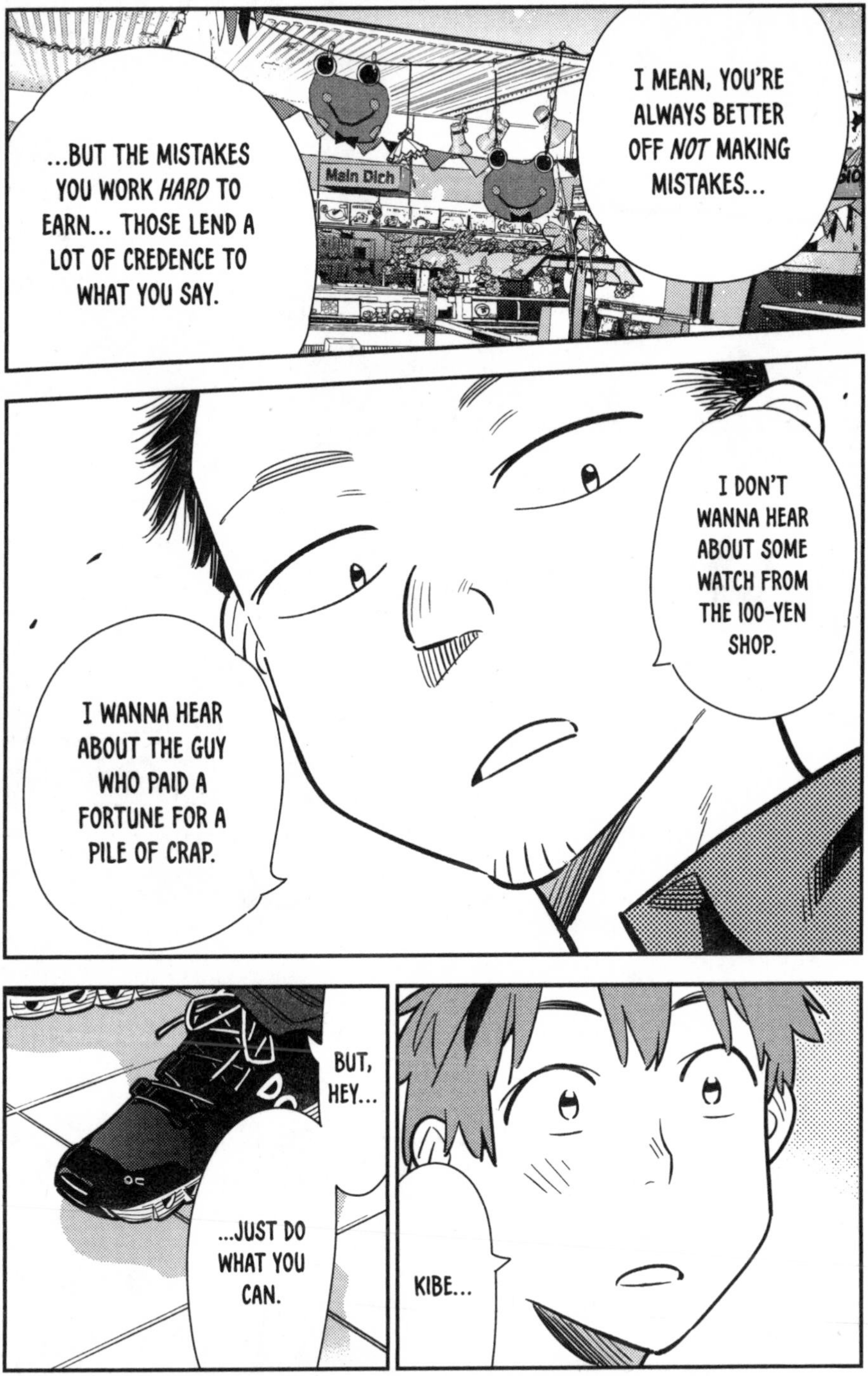
I MEAN, YOU'RE ALWAYS BETTER OFF *NOT* MAKING MISTAKES...
Main Dich
...BUT THE MISTAKES YOU WORK *HARD* TO EARN... THOSE LEND A LOT OF CREDENCE TO WHAT YOU SAY.
I DON'T WANNA HEAR ABOUT SOME WATCH FROM THE 100-YEN SHOP.
I WANNA HEAR ABOUT THE GUY WHO PAID A FORTUNE FOR A PILE OF CRAP.
KIBE...
BUT, HEY...
...JUST DO WHAT YOU CAN.

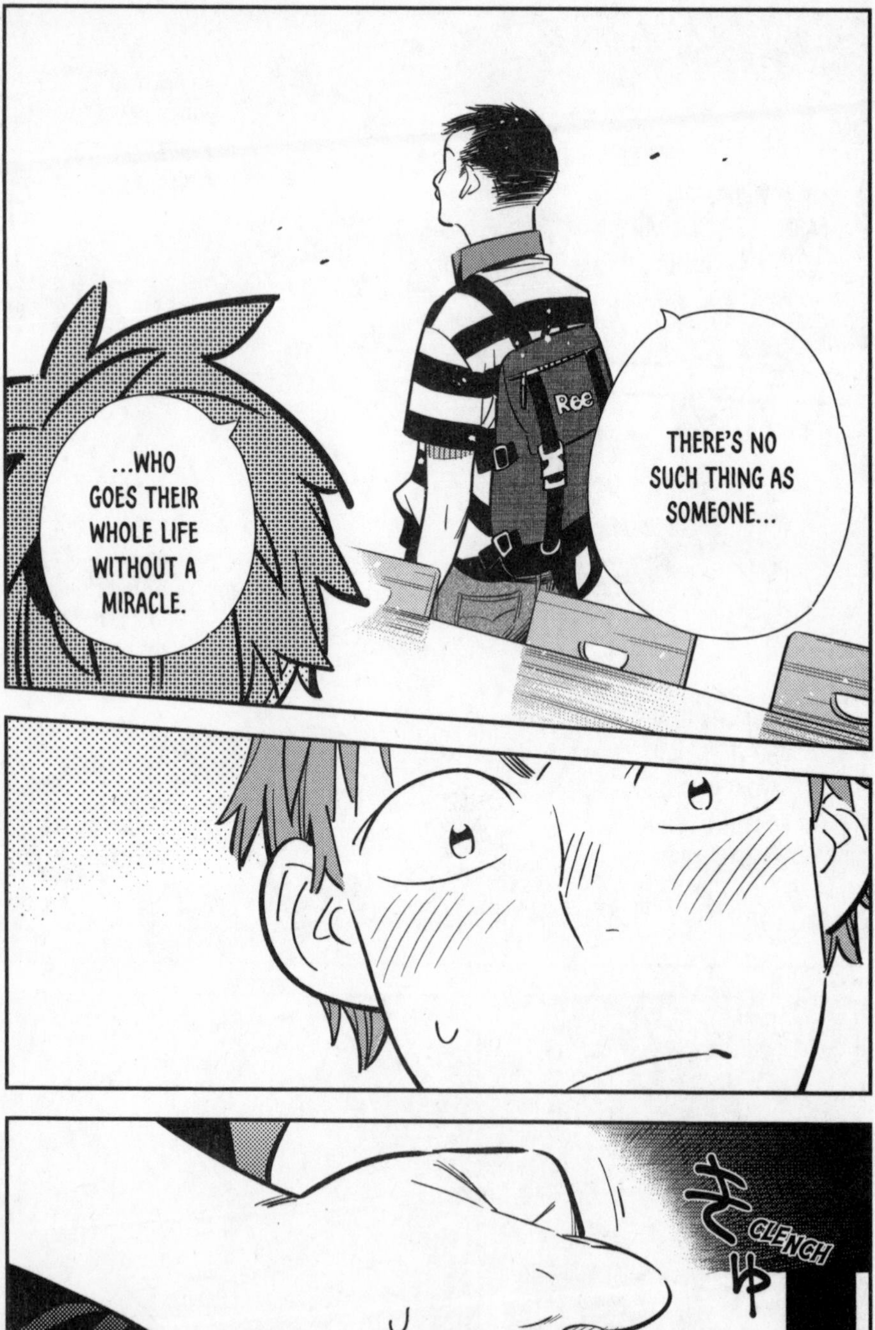
THERE'S NO SUCH THING AS SOMEONE...
...WHO GOES THEIR WHOLE LIFE WITHOUT A MIRACLE.
ぎゅ
CLENCH

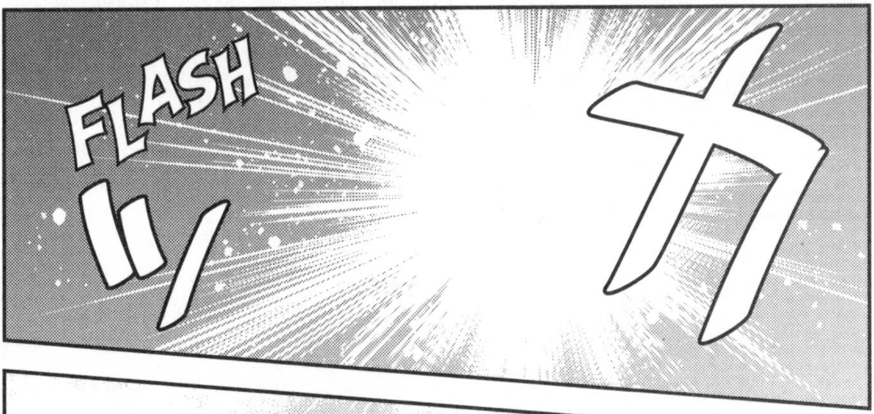
カッ
FLASH

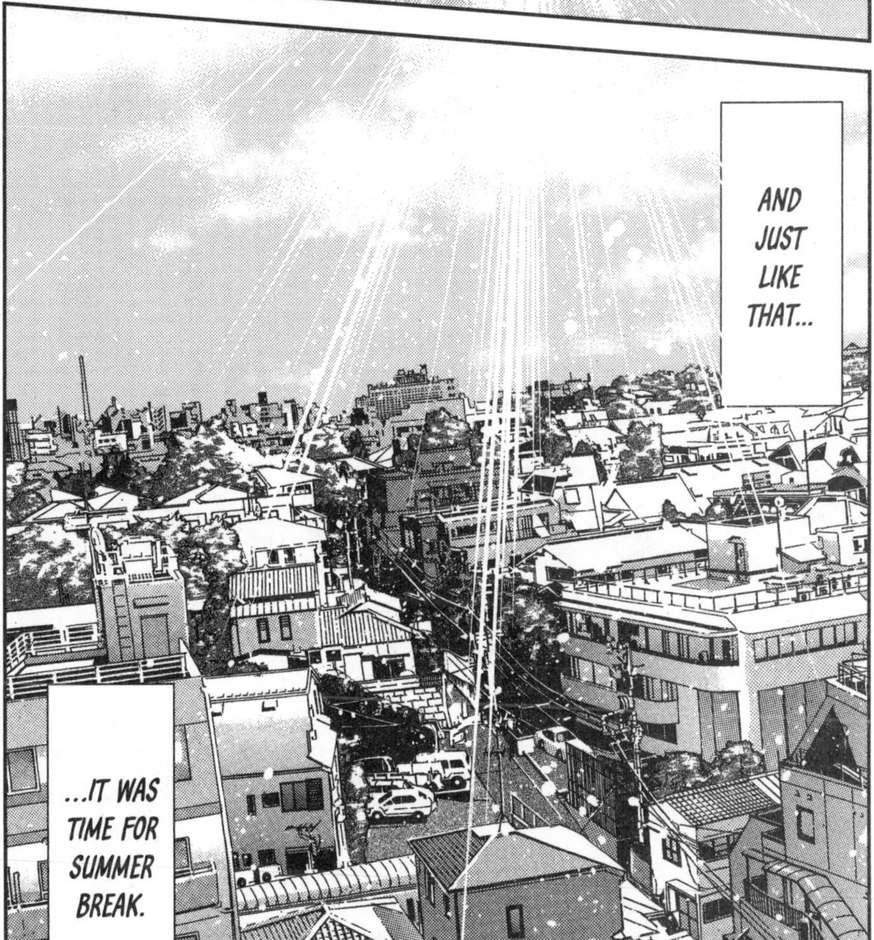
AND JUST LIKE THAT...
...IT WAS TIME FOR SUMMER BREAK.

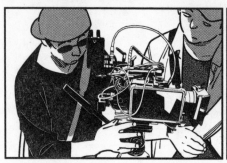

I'M SORRY, CAN YOU USE THAT PATH?

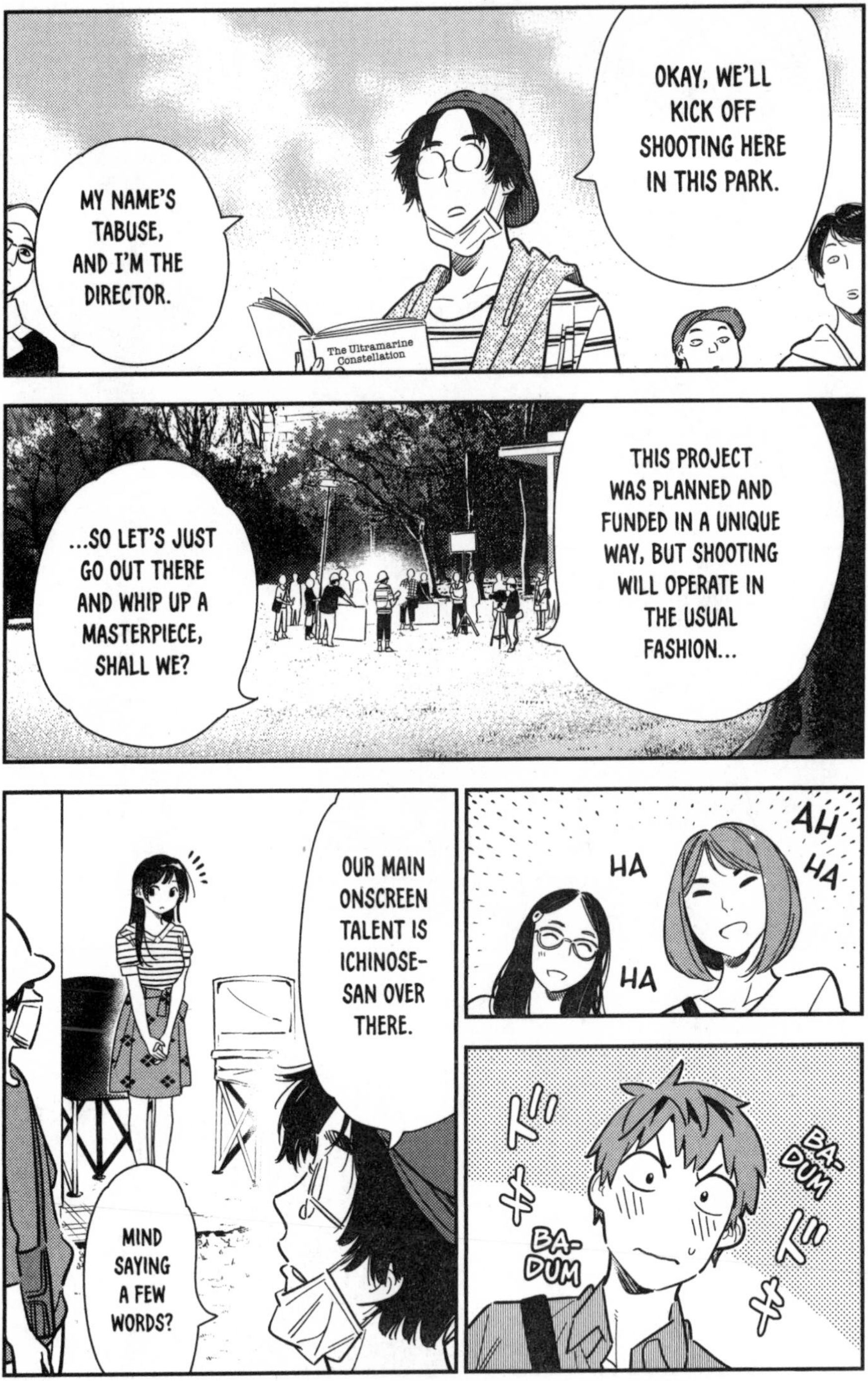
OKAY, WE'LL KICK OFF SHOOTING HERE IN THIS PARK.
MY NAME'S TABUSE, AND I'M THE DIRECTOR.
The Ultramarine Constellation
THIS PROJECT WAS PLANNED AND FUNDED IN A UNIQUE WAY, BUT SHOOTING WILL OPERATE IN THE USUAL FASHION...
...SO LET'S JUST GO OUT THERE AND WHIP UP A MASTERPIECE, SHALL WE?
AH HA HA
HA HA
BA-DUM
BA-DUM
OUR MAIN ONSCREEN TALENT IS ICHINOSE-SAN OVER THERE.
MIND SAYING A FEW WORDS?

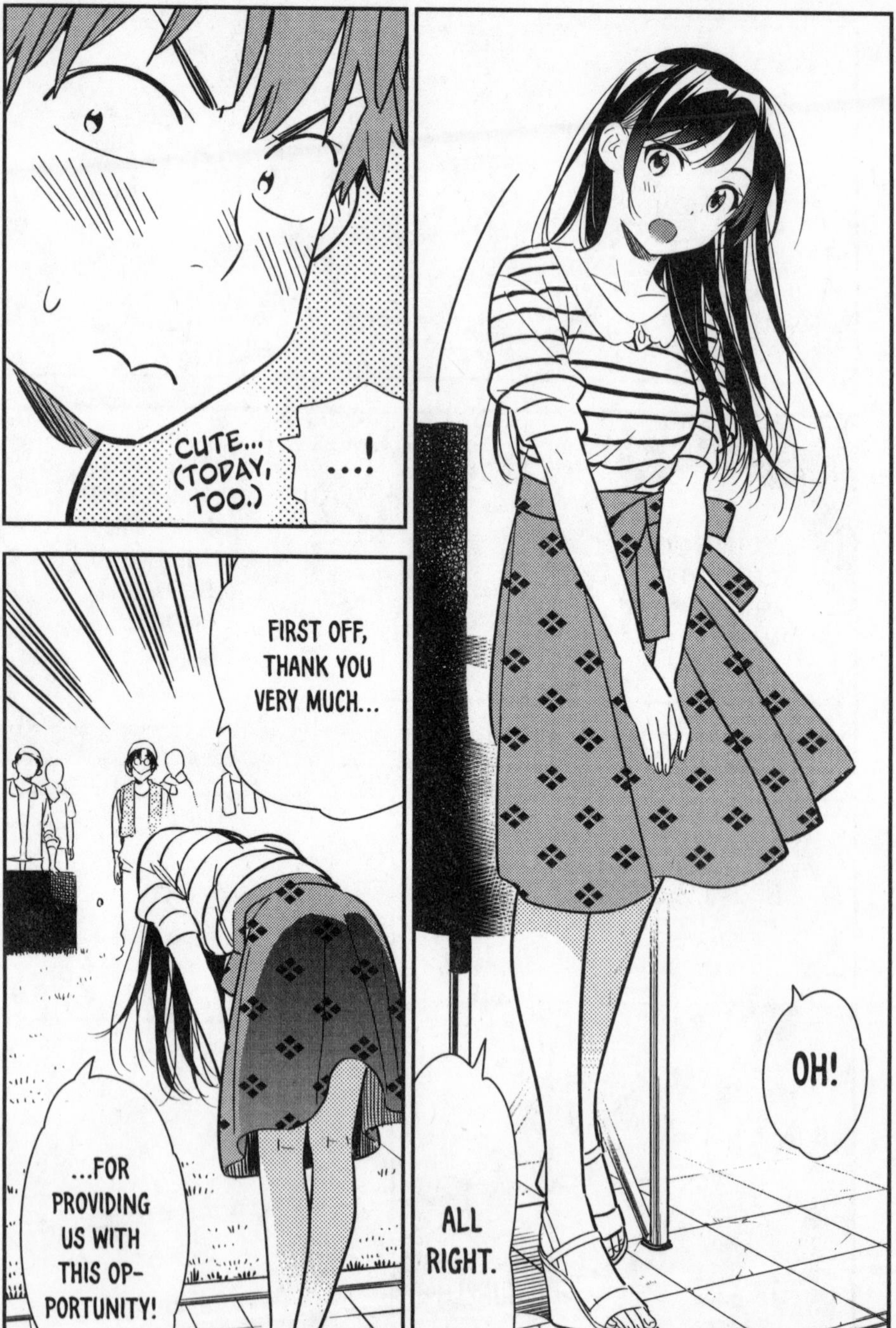
OH!
ALL RIGHT.
...!
CUTE... (TODAY, TOO.)
FIRST OFF, THANK YOU VERY MUCH...
...FOR PROVIDING US WITH THIS OP-PORTUNITY!

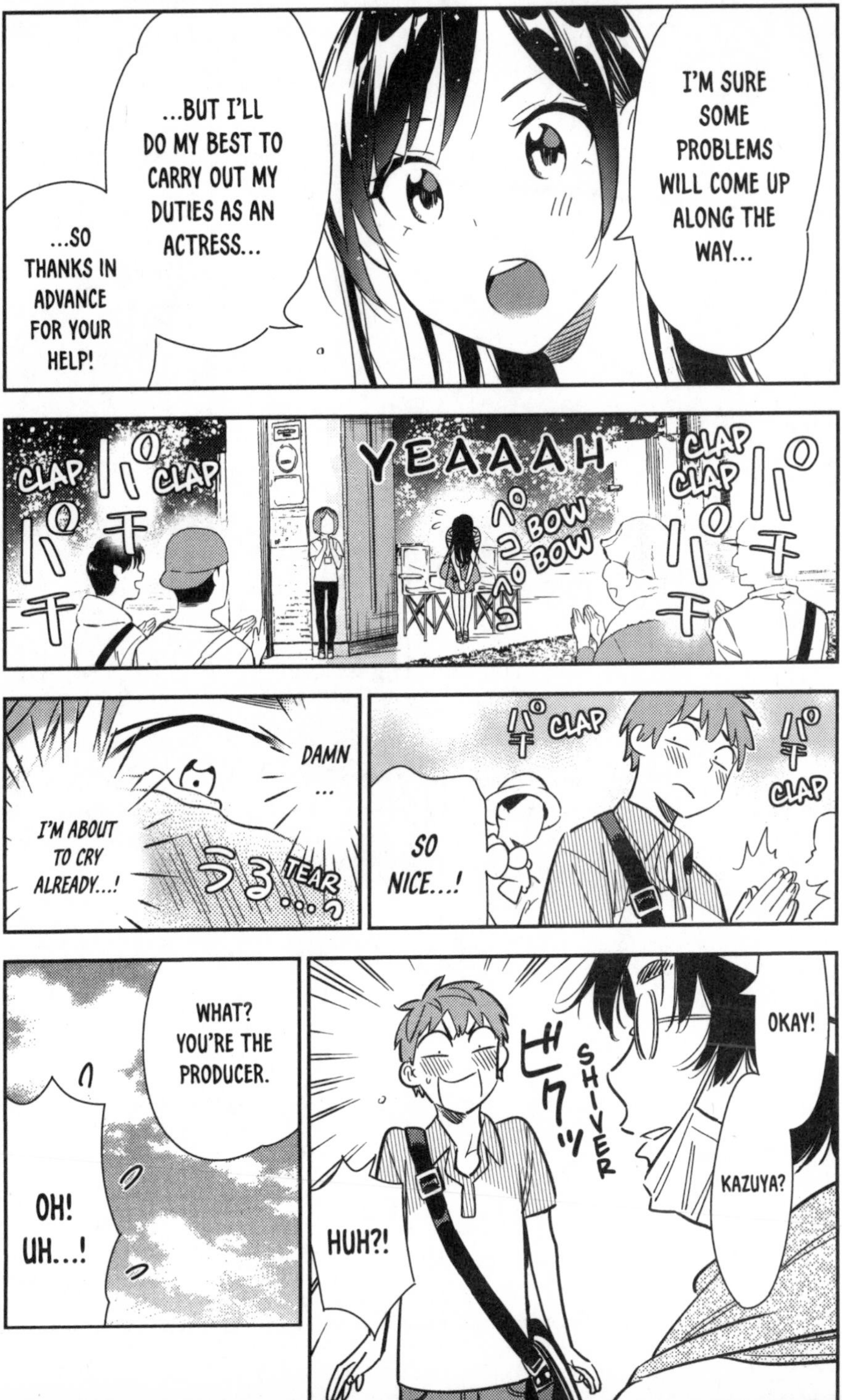
I'M SURE SOME PROBLEMS WILL COME UP ALONG THE WAY...
...BUT I'LL DO MY BEST TO CARRY OUT MY DUTIES AS AN ACTRESS...
...SO THANKS IN ADVANCE FOR YOUR HELP!
パチ パチ
CLAP CLAP
ペコ ペコ
BOW BOW
YEAAAH
CLAP
パチ パチ
CLAP
パチ CLAP
パチ CLAP
SO NICE...!
DAMN...
I'M ABOUT TO CRY ALREADY...!
うる TEAR
OKAY!
KAZUYA?
ビクッ SHIVER
HUH?!
WHAT? YOU'RE THE PRODUCER.
OH! UH...!

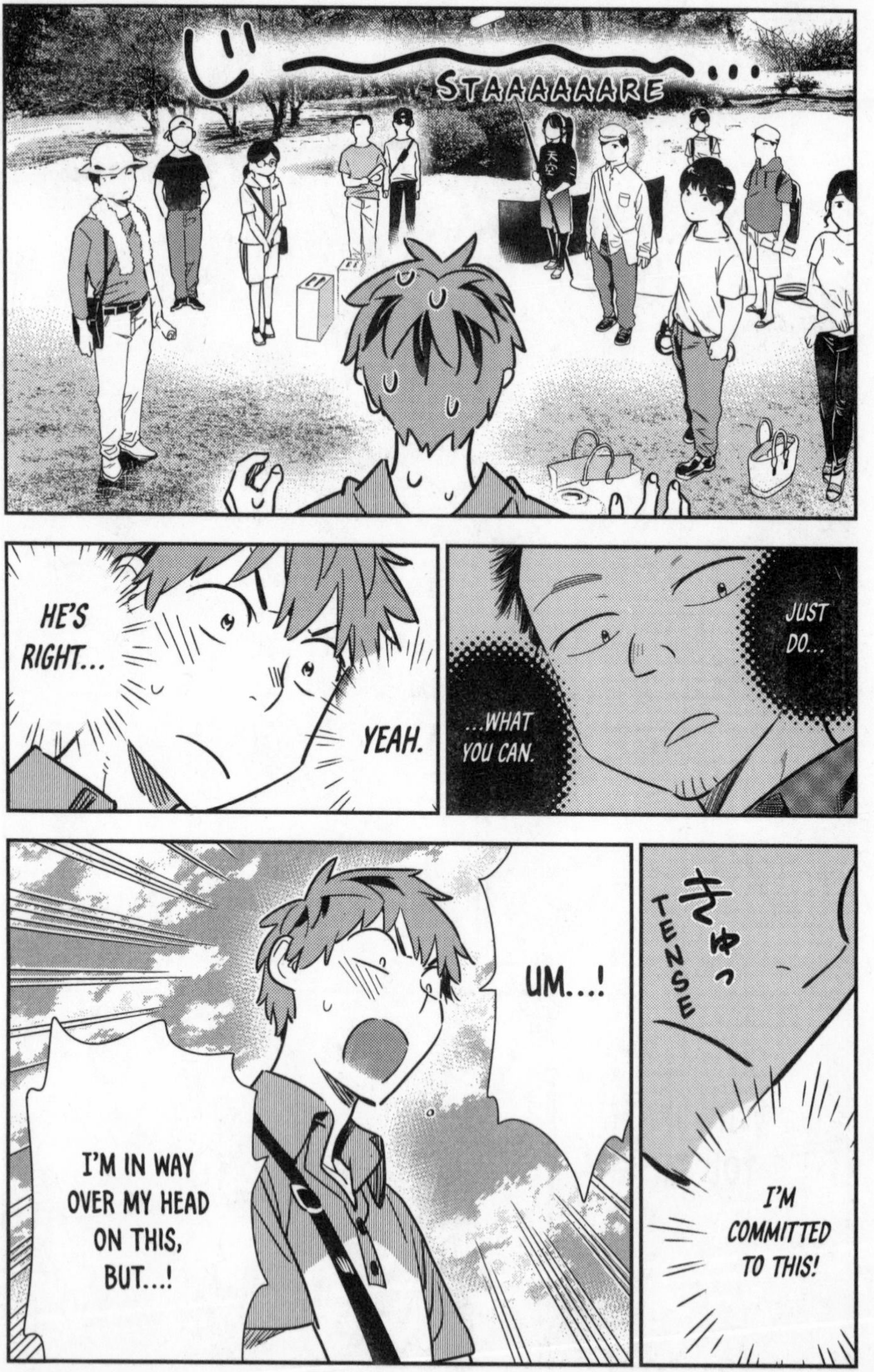
じ———…
STAAAAAARE
JUST DO...
...WHAT YOU CAN.
HE'S RIGHT...
YEAH.
きゅっ
TENSE
I'M COMMITTED TO THIS!
UM...!
I'M IN WAY OVER MY HEAD ON THIS, BUT...!

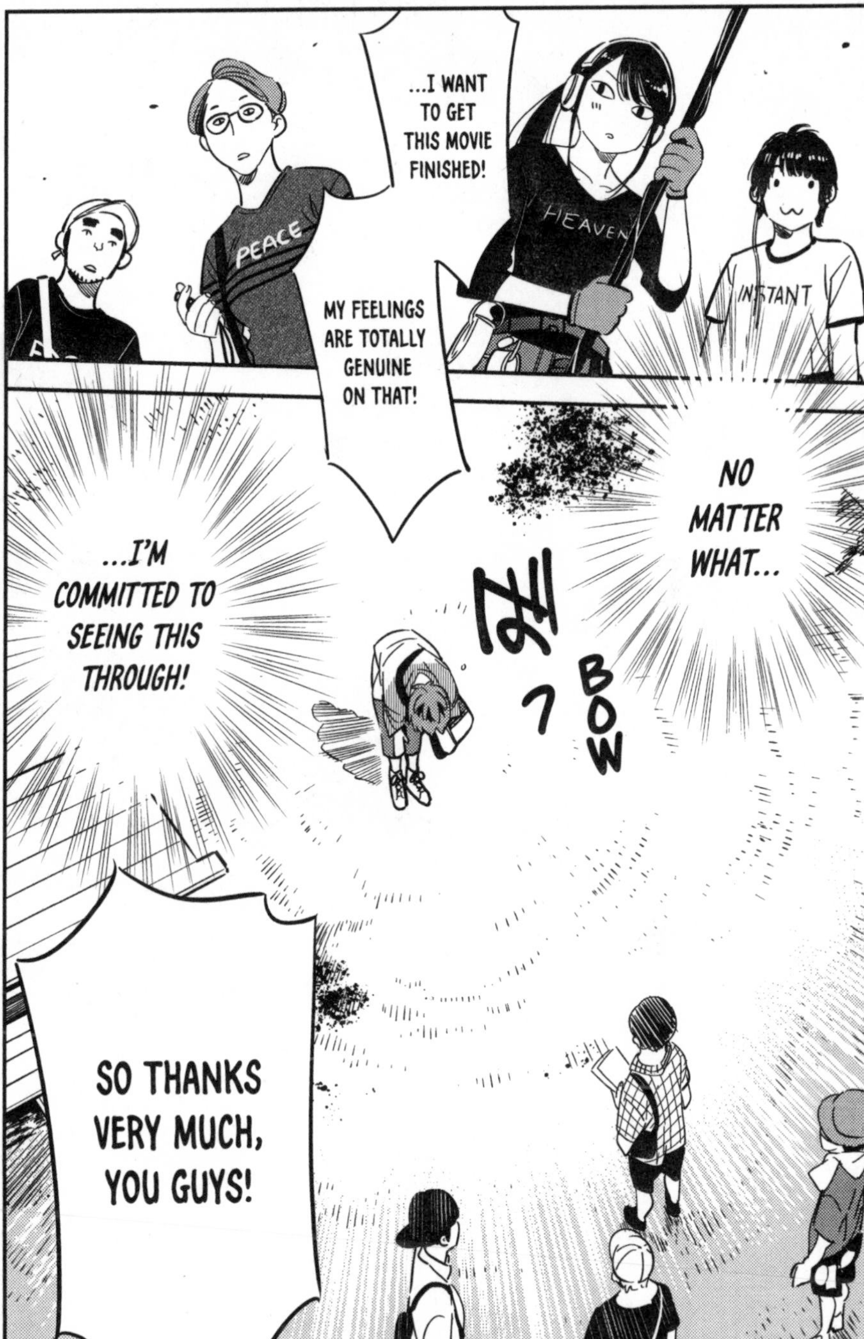
...I WANT TO GET THIS MOVIE FINISHED!
MY FEELINGS ARE TOTALLY GENUINE ON THAT!
INSTANT
HEAVEN
PEACE
NO MATTER WHAT...
BOW
...I'M COMMITTED TO SEEING THIS THROUGH!
SO THANKS VERY MUCH, YOU GUYS!

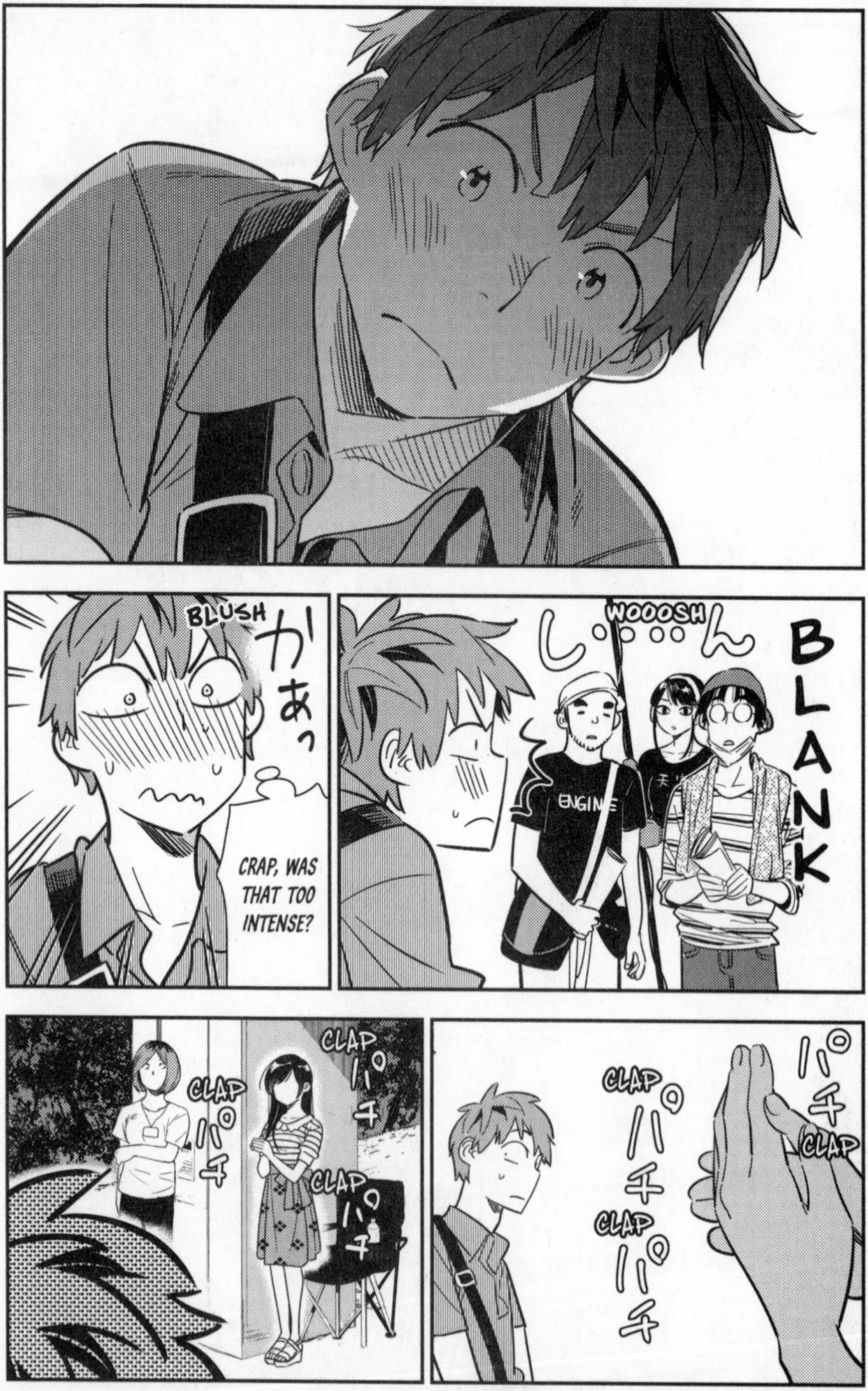
WOOOSH
し…ん
BLANK
BLUSH
かあっ
CRAP, WAS THAT TOO INTENSE?
パチ
CLAP
パチ
CLAP
パチ
CLAP
パチ
CLAP
パチ
CLAP
パチ
CLAP
パチ
CLAP
パチ

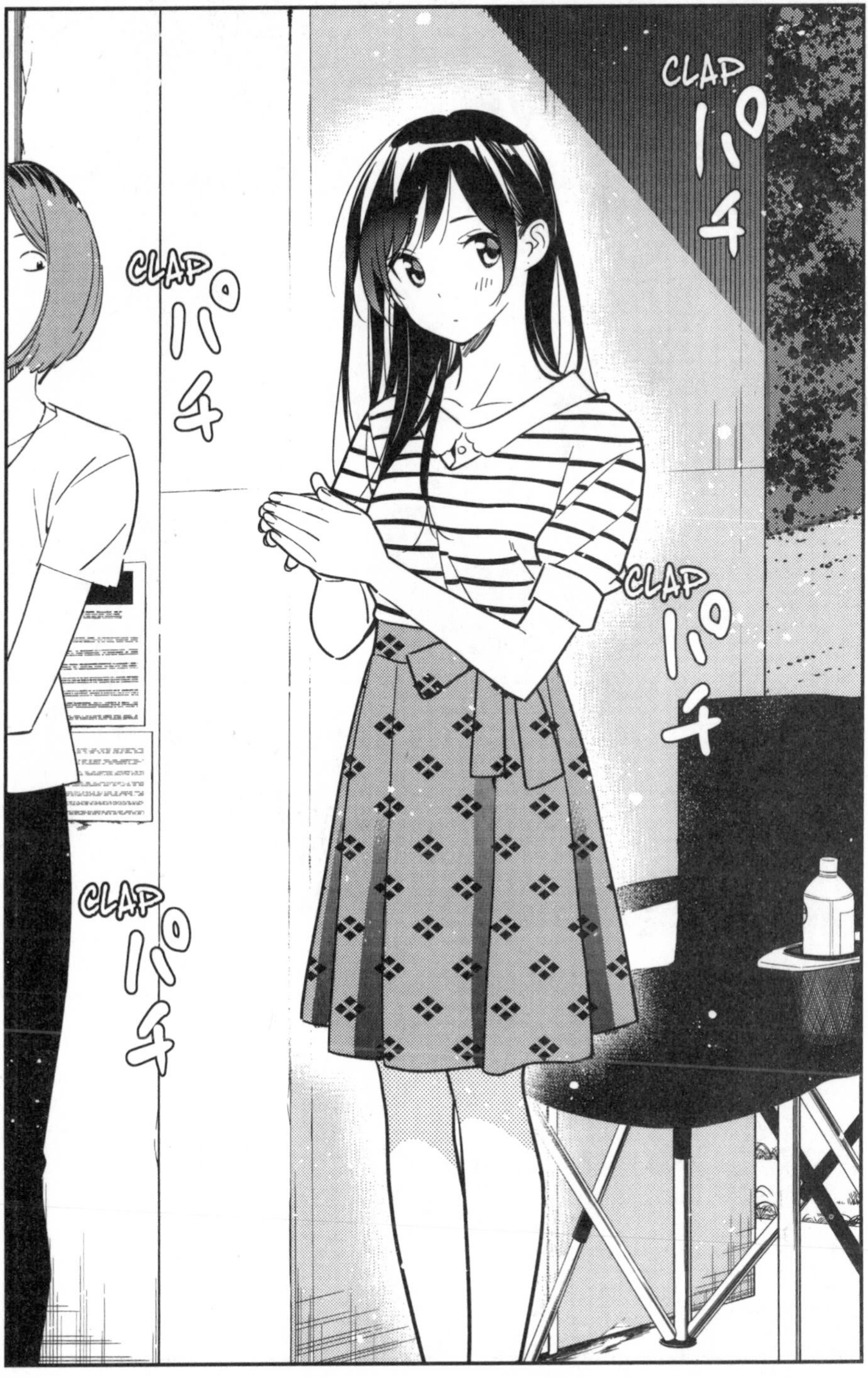

CLAP
パチ
CLAP
パチ
CLAP
パチ
CLAP
パチ

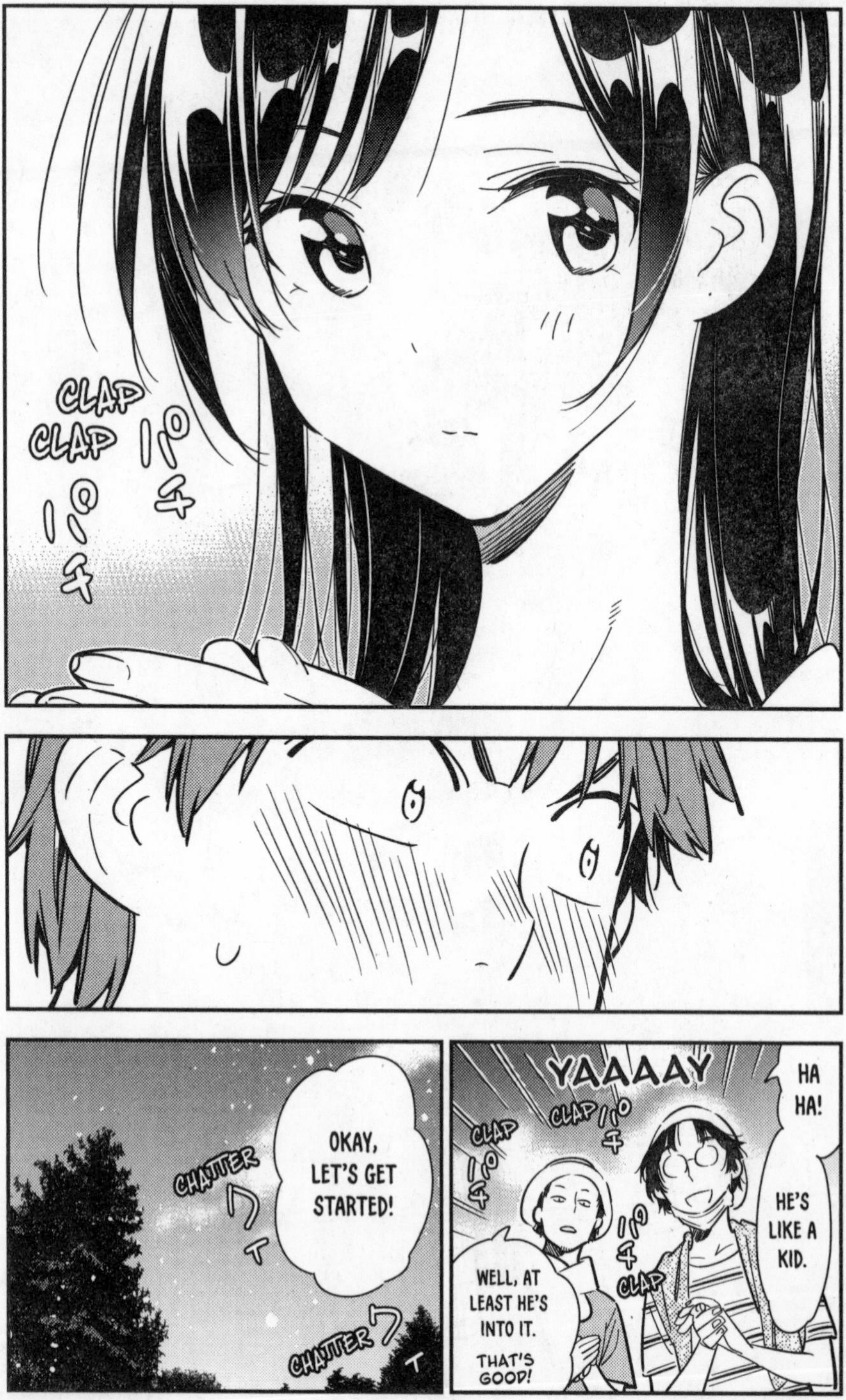
CLAP CLAP
パチ
パチ
HA HA!
HE'S LIKE A KID.
YAAAAY
CLAP パチ
CLAP パチ
パチ CLAP
WELL, AT LEAST HE'S INTO IT.
THAT'S GOOD!
OKAY, LET'S GET STARTED!
CHATTER ワイ
CHATTER ワイ

RATING 129 SHOOTING AND MY GIRLFRIEND 1

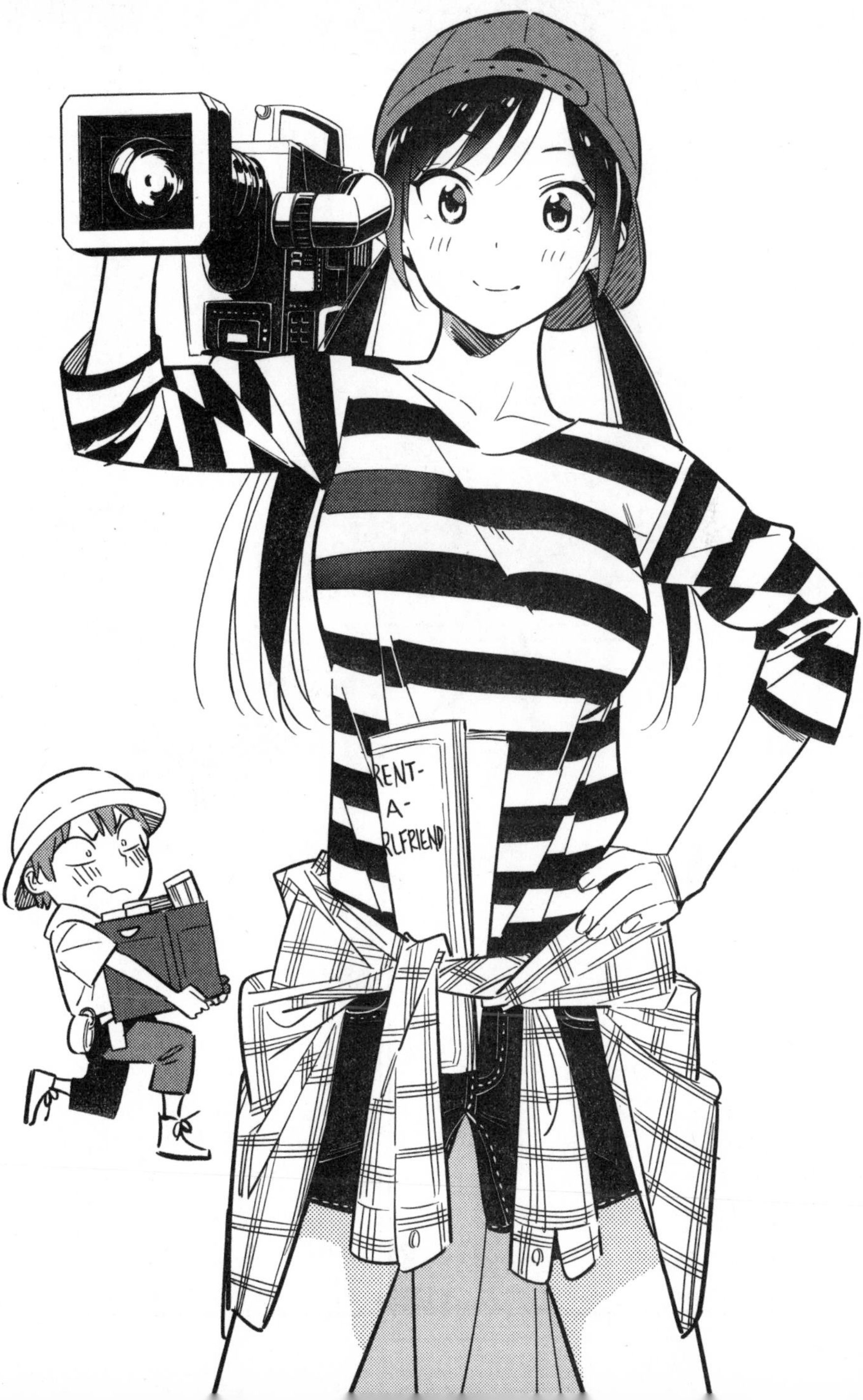
RENT-
A-
RLFRIEND

SCREE
SCREE

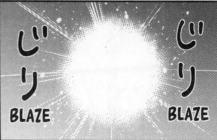

BLAZE
BLAZE

SCRIPT

WHEELCHAIR MADE INTO MOBILE MONITOR

KAZUYA!

WEDNES-DAY.

HEAD-PHONES

AUGUST 17TH.

YEAH?

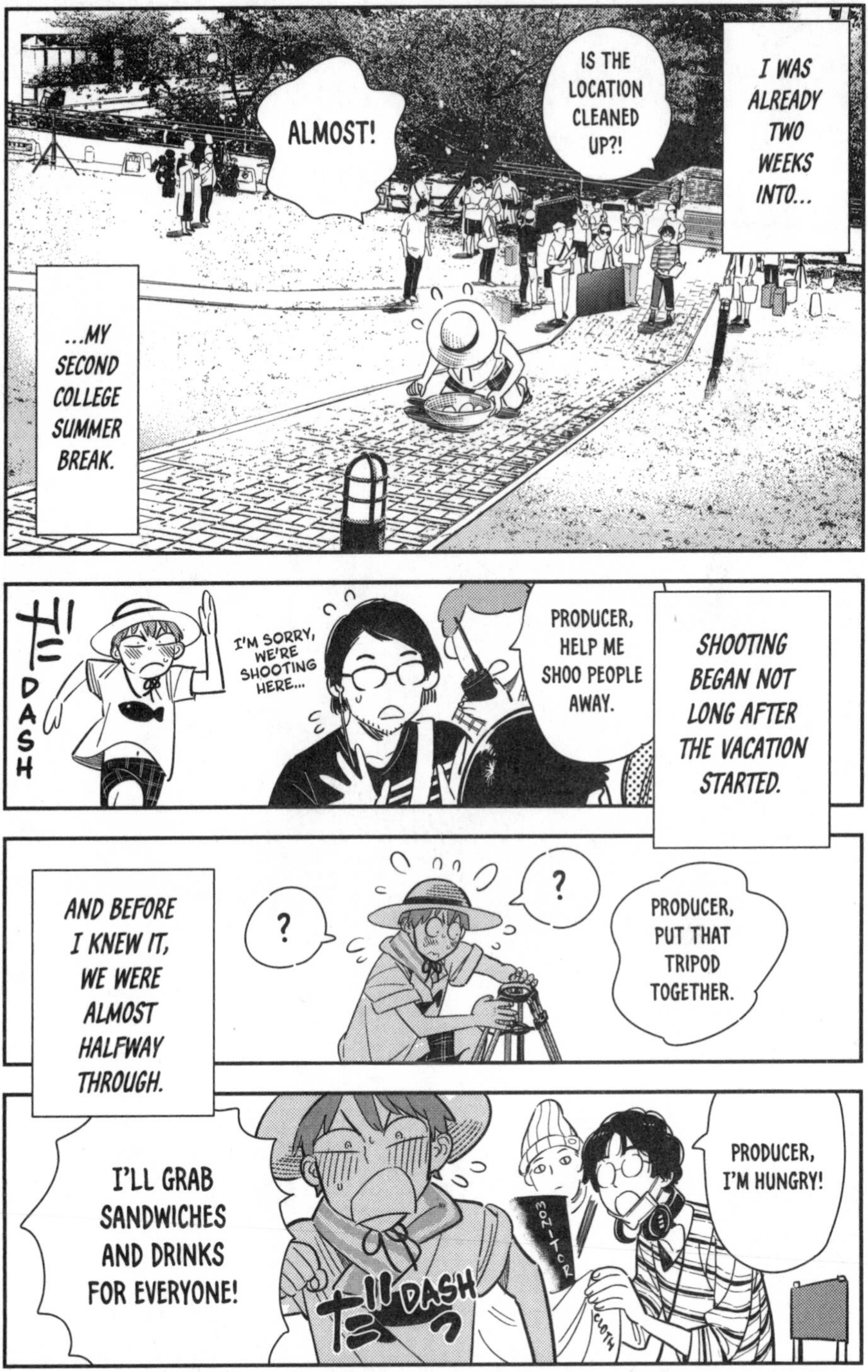
I WAS ALREADY TWO WEEKS INTO...
IS THE LOCATION CLEANED UP?!
ALMOST!
...MY SECOND COLLEGE SUMMER BREAK.
SHOOTING BEGAN NOT LONG AFTER THE VACATION STARTED.
PRODUCER, HELP ME SHOO PEOPLE AWAY.
I'M SORRY, WE'RE SHOOTING HERE...
DASH
PRODUCER, PUT THAT TRIPOD TOGETHER.
?
?
AND BEFORE I KNEW IT, WE WERE ALMOST HALFWAY THROUGH.
PRODUCER, I'M HUNGRY!
MONITOR
CLOTH
DASH
I'LL GRAB SANDWICHES AND DRINKS FOR EVERYONE!

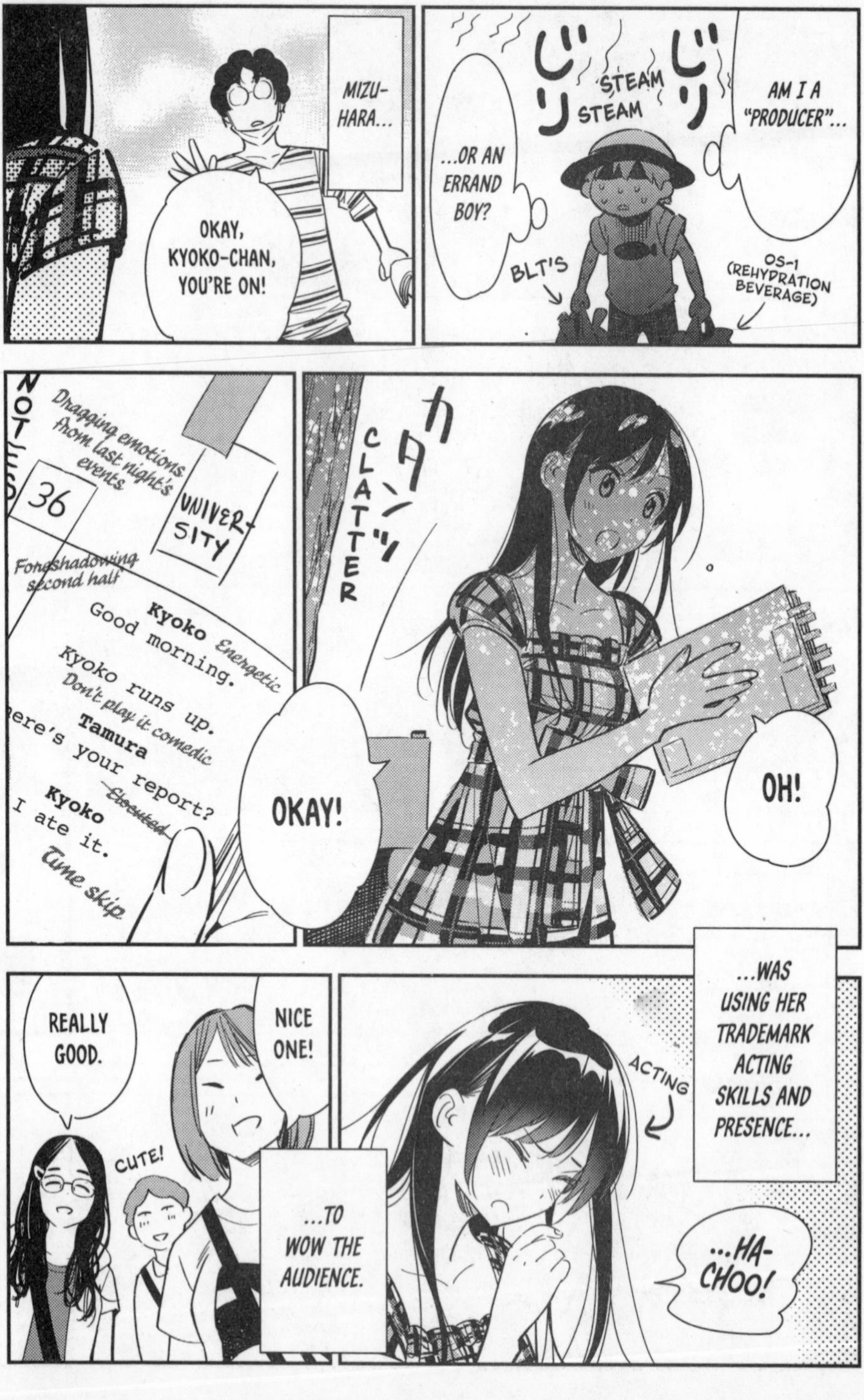
じり
じり
STEAM
STEAM
AM I A "PRODUCER"...
...OR AN ERRAND BOY?
OS-1 (REHYDRATION BEVERAGE)
BLT'S
MIZU-HARA...
OKAY, KYOKO-CHAN, YOU'RE ON!
カタンッ
CLATTER
OH!
OKAY!
NOTES
Dragging emotions from last night's events
36
UNIVERSITY
Foreshadowing second half
Kyoko Energetic
Good morning.
Kyoko runs up.
Don't play it comedic
Tamura
ere's your report?
Shouted
Kyoko
I ate it.
Time skip
...WAS USING HER TRADEMARK ACTING SKILLS AND PRESENCE...
ACTING
...HA-CHOO!
NICE ONE!
REALLY GOOD.
CUTE!
...TO WOW THE AUDIENCE.

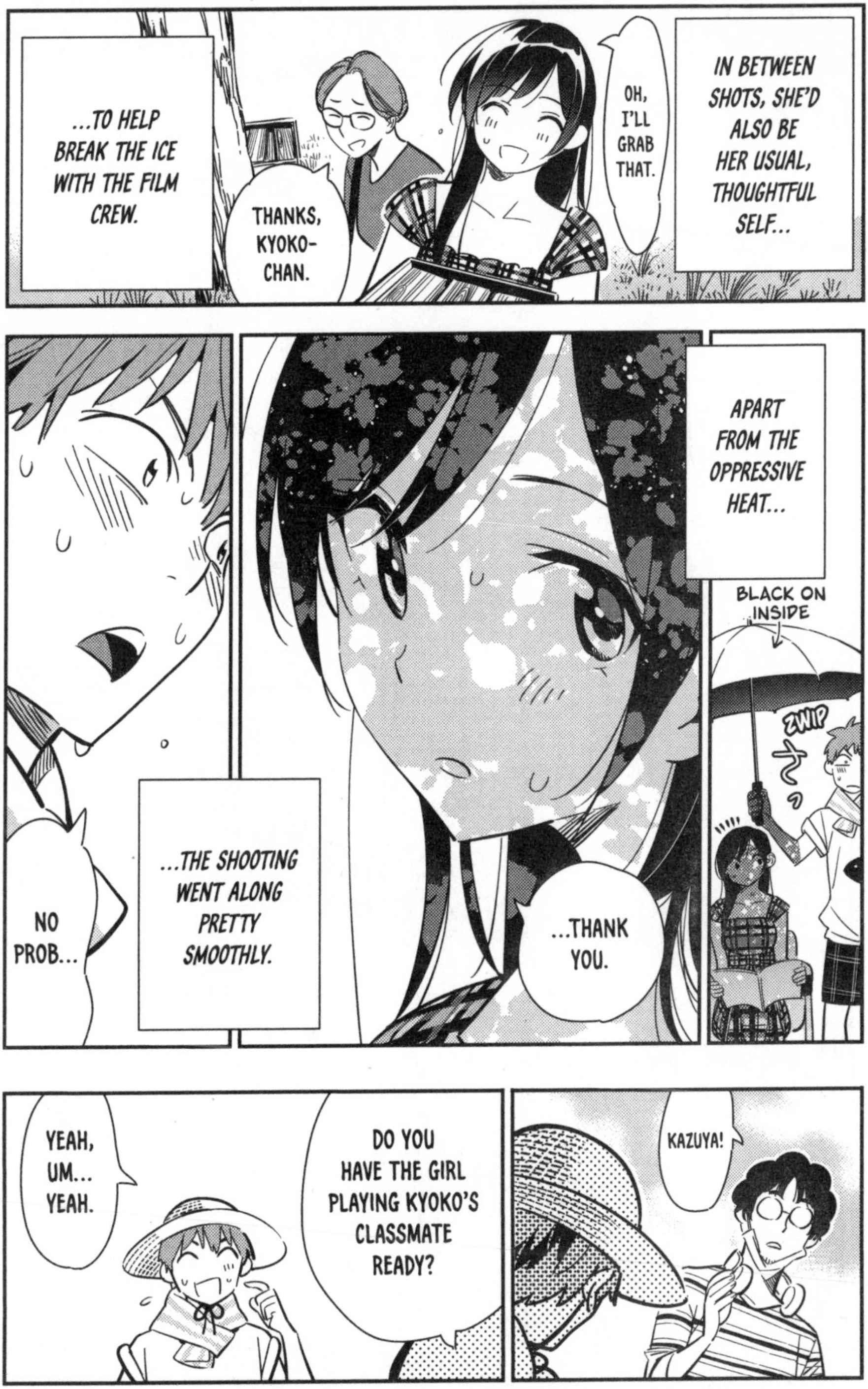
IN BETWEEN SHOTS, SHE'D ALSO BE HER USUAL, THOUGHTFUL SELF...
OH, I'LL GRAB THAT.
THANKS, KYOKO-CHAN.
...TO HELP BREAK THE ICE WITH THE FILM CREW.
APART FROM THE OPPRESSIVE HEAT...
BLACK ON INSIDE
ZWIP
...THANK YOU.
...THE SHOOTING WENT ALONG PRETTY SMOOTHLY.
NO PROB...
KAZUYA!
DO YOU HAVE THE GIRL PLAYING KYOKO'S CLASSMATE READY?
YEAH, UM... YEAH.

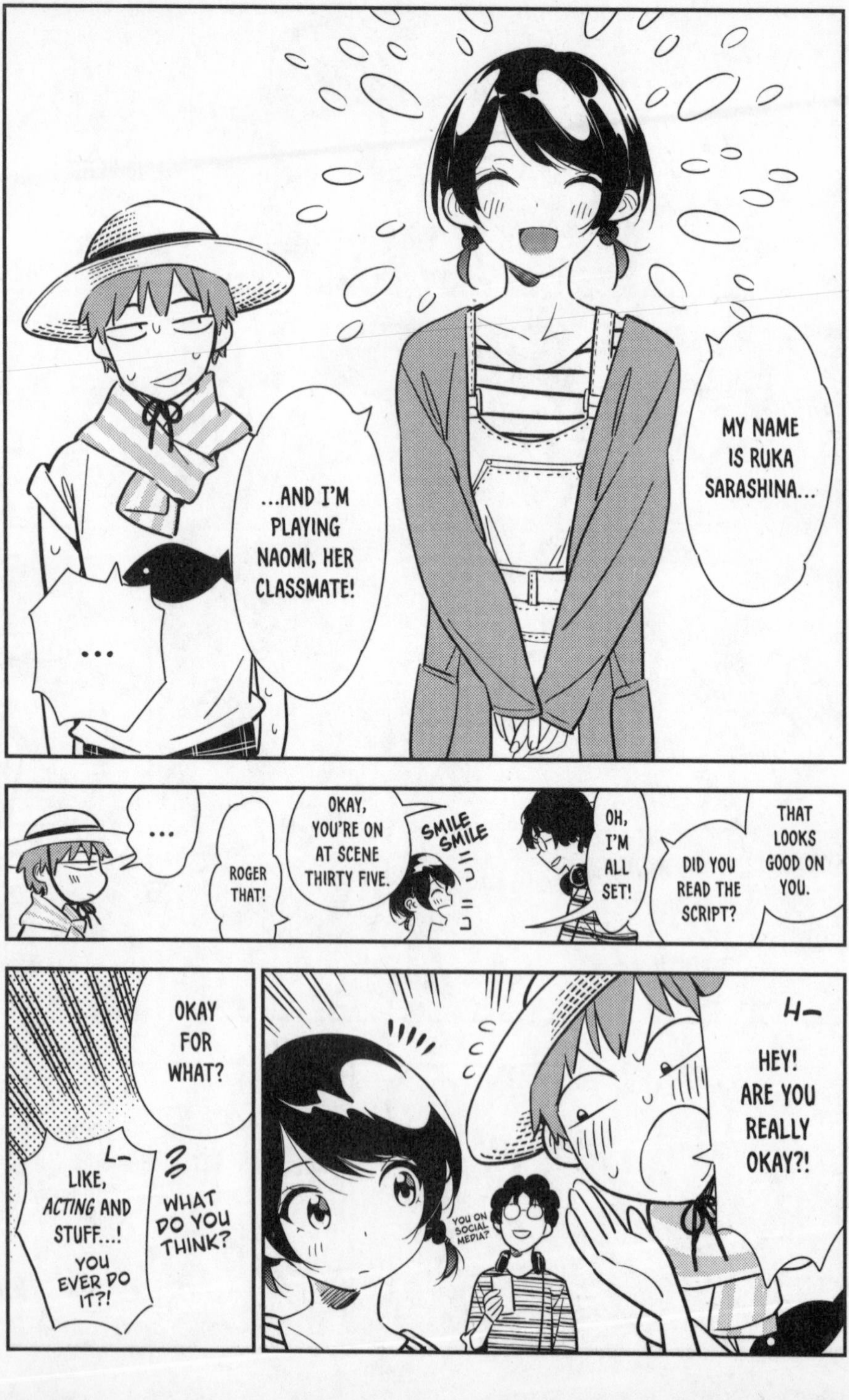
MY NAME IS RUKA SARASHINA...
...AND I'M PLAYING NAOMI, HER CLASSMATE!
...
THAT LOOKS GOOD ON YOU.
DID YOU READ THE SCRIPT?
OH, I'M ALL SET!
SMILE SMILE
OKAY, YOU'RE ON AT SCENE THIRTY FIVE.
ROGER THAT!
...
H-
HEY! ARE YOU REALLY OKAY?!
YOU ON SOCIAL MEDIA?
OKAY FOR WHAT?
WHAT DO YOU THINK?
L- LIKE, *ACTING* AND STUFF...! YOU EVER DO IT?!

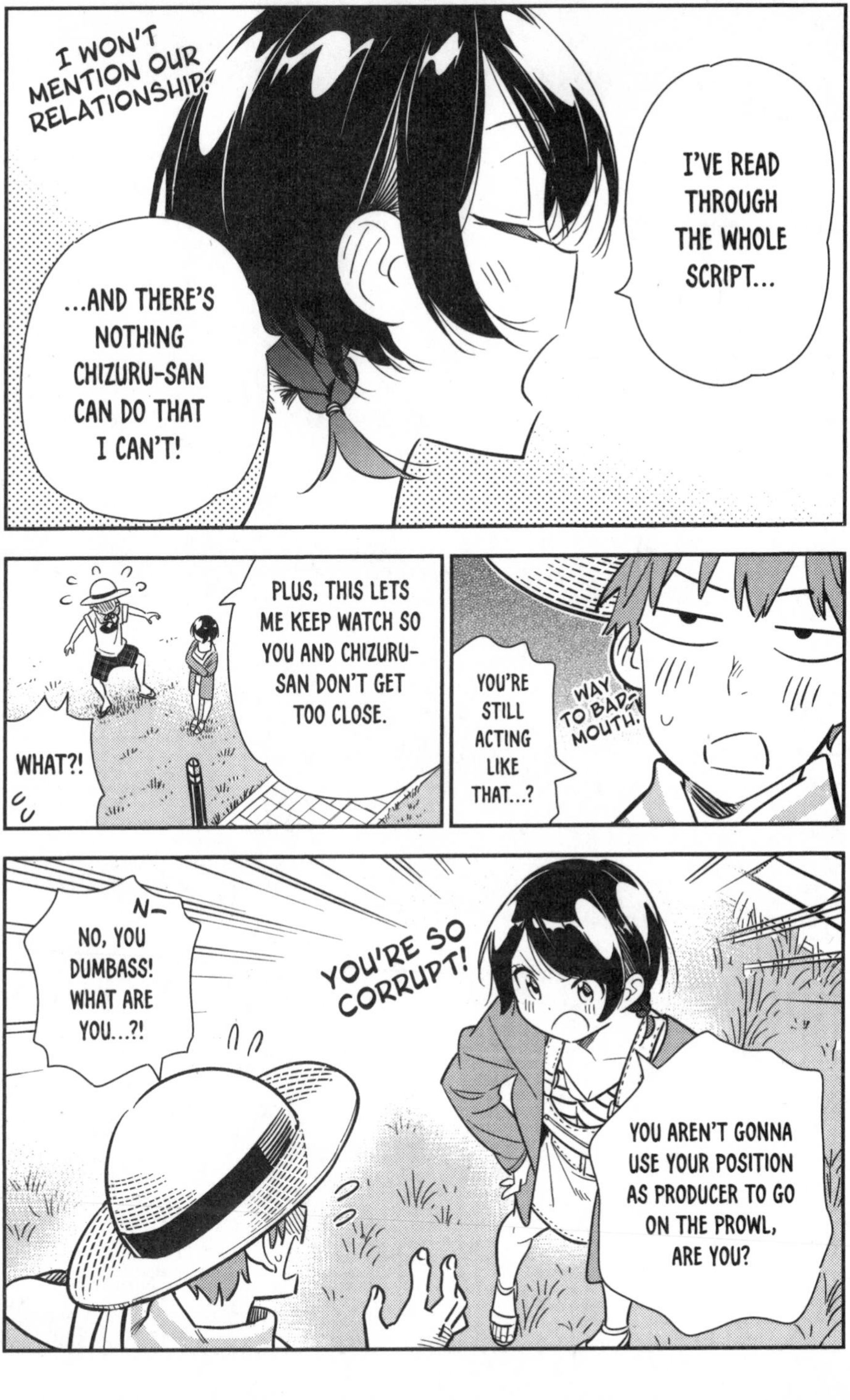
I'VE READ THROUGH THE WHOLE SCRIPT...
I WON'T MENTION OUR RELATIONSHIP!
...AND THERE'S NOTHING CHIZURU-SAN CAN DO THAT I CAN'T!
YOU'RE STILL ACTING LIKE THAT...?
WAY TO BAD-MOUTH.
PLUS, THIS LETS ME KEEP WATCH SO YOU AND CHIZURU-SAN DON'T GET TOO CLOSE.
WHAT?!
YOU AREN'T GONNA USE YOUR POSITION AS PRODUCER TO GO ON THE PROWL, ARE YOU?
YOU'RE SO CORRUPT!
N— NO, YOU DUMBASS! WHAT ARE YOU...?!

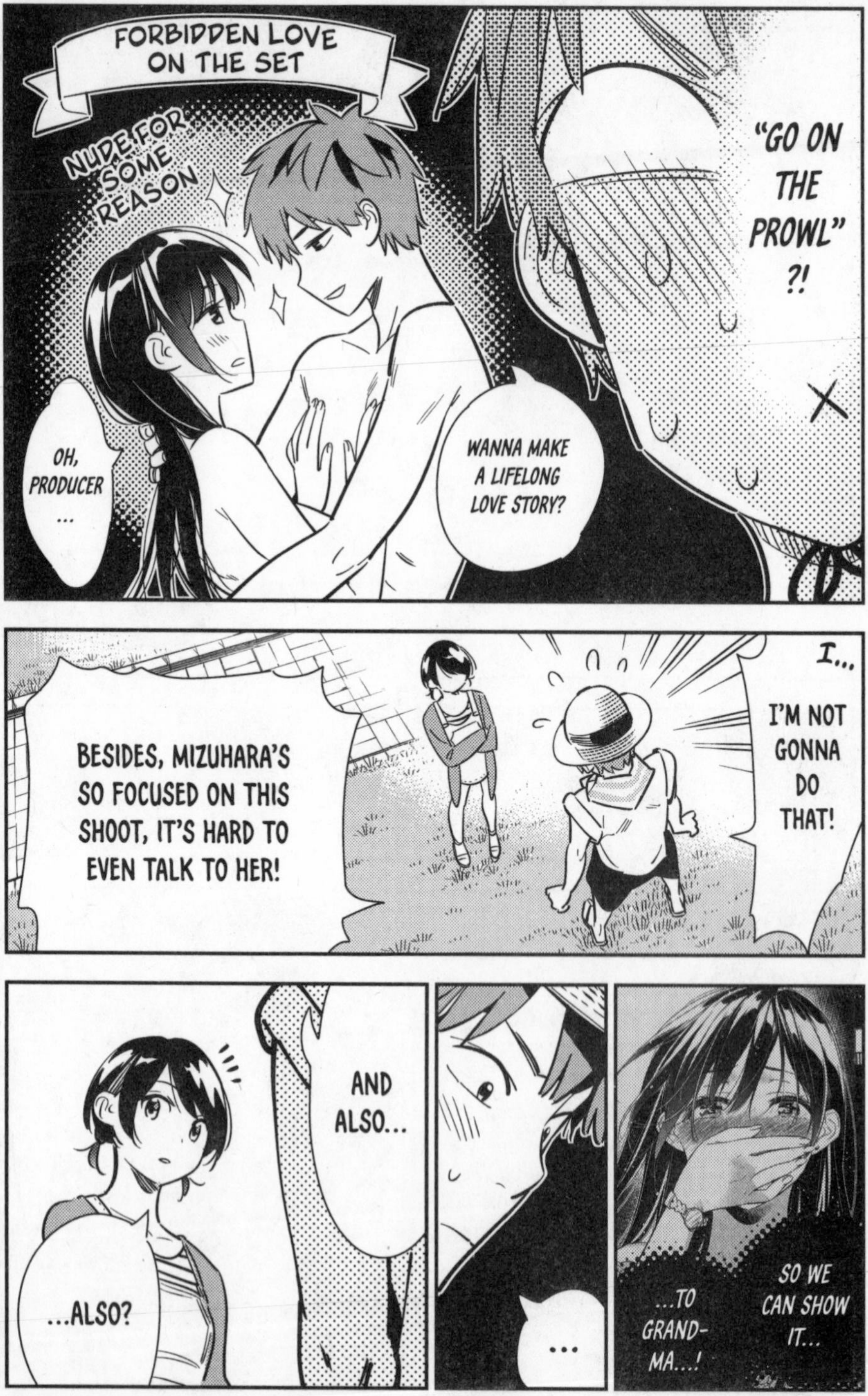
"GO ON THE PROWL" ?!
FORBIDDEN LOVE ON THE SET
NUDE FOR SOME REASON
WANNA MAKE A LIFELONG LOVE STORY?
OH, PRODUCER ...
I...
I'M NOT GONNA DO THAT!
BESIDES, MIZUHARA'S SO FOCUSED ON THIS SHOOT, IT'S HARD TO EVEN TALK TO HER!
SO WE CAN SHOW IT...
...TO GRAND-MA...!
...
AND ALSO...
...ALSO?

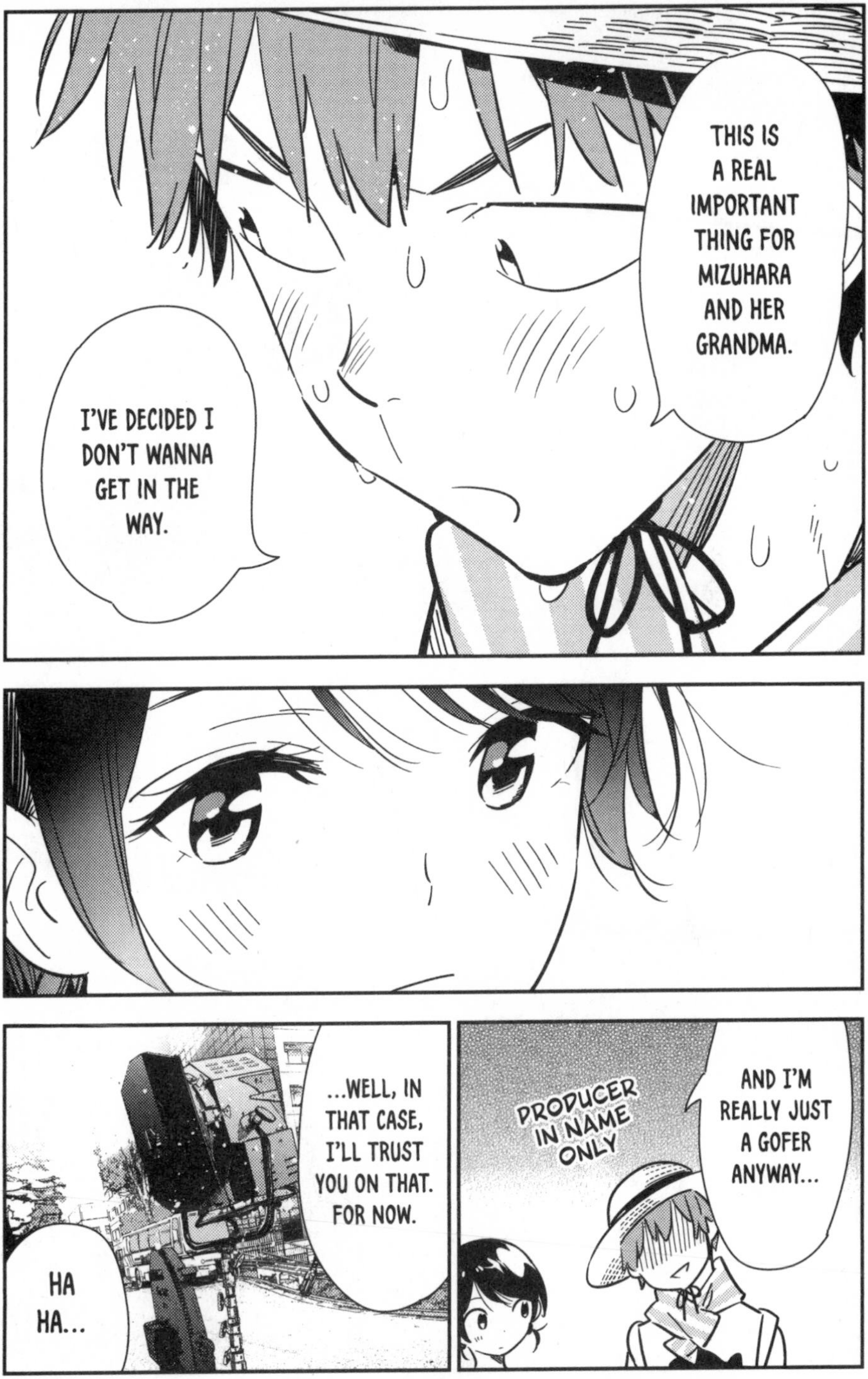
THIS IS A REAL IMPORTANT THING FOR MIZUHARA AND HER GRANDMA.
I'VE DECIDED I DON'T WANNA GET IN THE WAY.
AND I'M REALLY JUST A GOFER ANYWAY...
PRODUCER IN NAME ONLY
...WELL, IN THAT CASE, I'LL TRUST YOU ON THAT. FOR NOW.
HA HA...

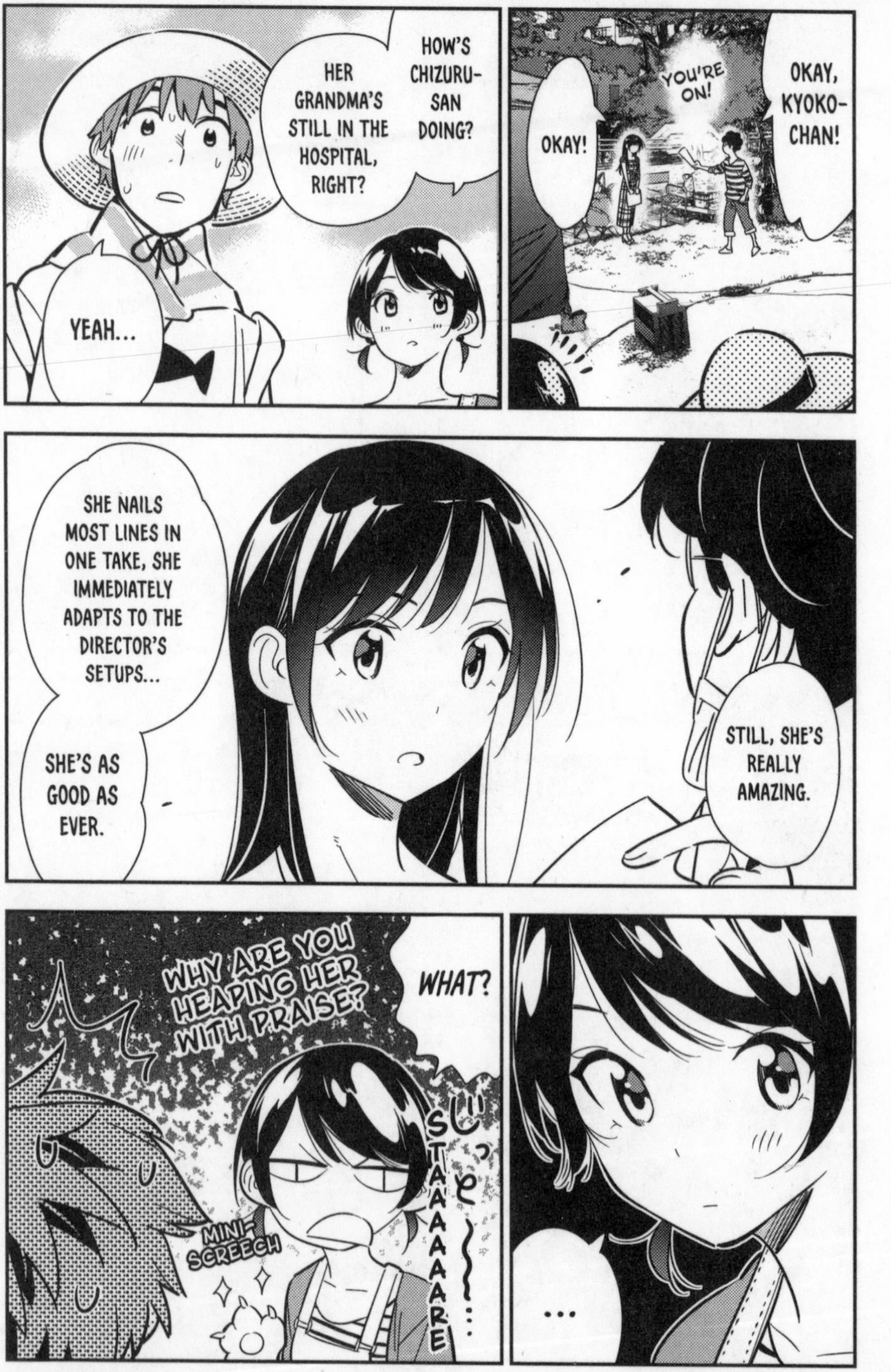
OKAY, KYOKO-CHAN!
YOU'RE ON!
OKAY!
HOW'S CHIZURU-SAN DOING?
HER GRANDMA'S STILL IN THE HOSPITAL, RIGHT?
YEAH...
STILL, SHE'S REALLY AMAZING.
SHE NAILS MOST LINES IN ONE TAKE, SHE IMMEDIATELY ADAPTS TO THE DIRECTOR'S SETUPS...
SHE'S AS GOOD AS EVER.
...
WHAT?
WHY ARE YOU HEAPING HER WITH PRAISE?
じっと~
STAAAAAAARE...
MINI-SCREECH

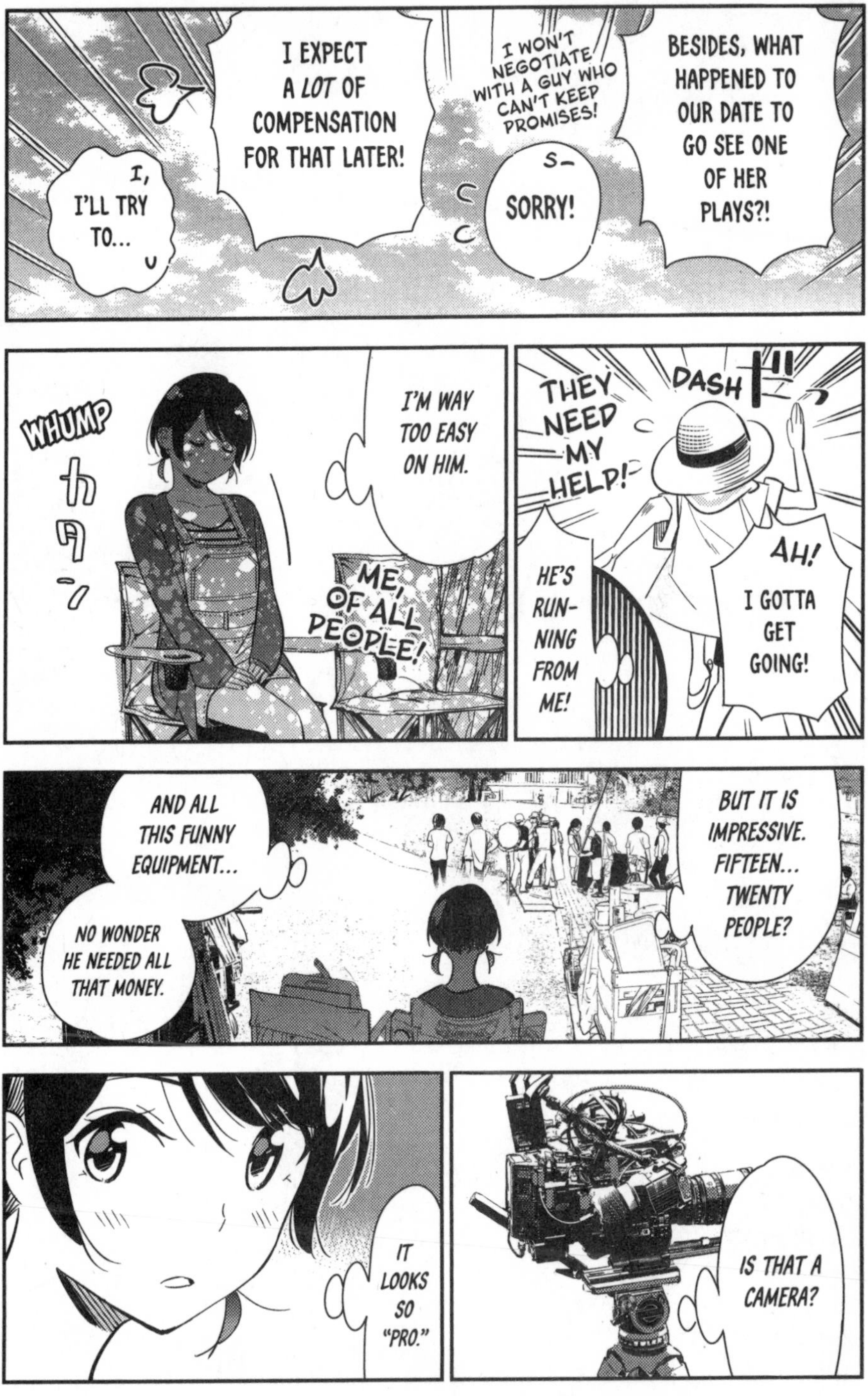
BESIDES, WHAT HAPPENED TO OUR DATE TO GO SEE ONE OF HER PLAYS?!
I WON'T NEGOTIATE WITH A GUY WHO CAN'T KEEP PROMISES!
S— SORRY!
I EXPECT A *LOT* OF COMPENSATION FOR THAT LATER!
I, I'LL TRY TO...
DASH
THEY NEED MY HELP!
AH! I GOTTA GET GOING!
HE'S RUNNING FROM ME!
I'M WAY TOO EASY ON HIM.
ME, OF ALL PEOPLE!
WHUMP
BUT IT IS IMPRESSIVE. FIFTEEN... TWENTY PEOPLE?
AND ALL THIS FUNNY EQUIPMENT...
NO WONDER HE NEEDED ALL THAT MONEY.
IS THAT A CAMERA?
IT LOOKS SO "PRO."

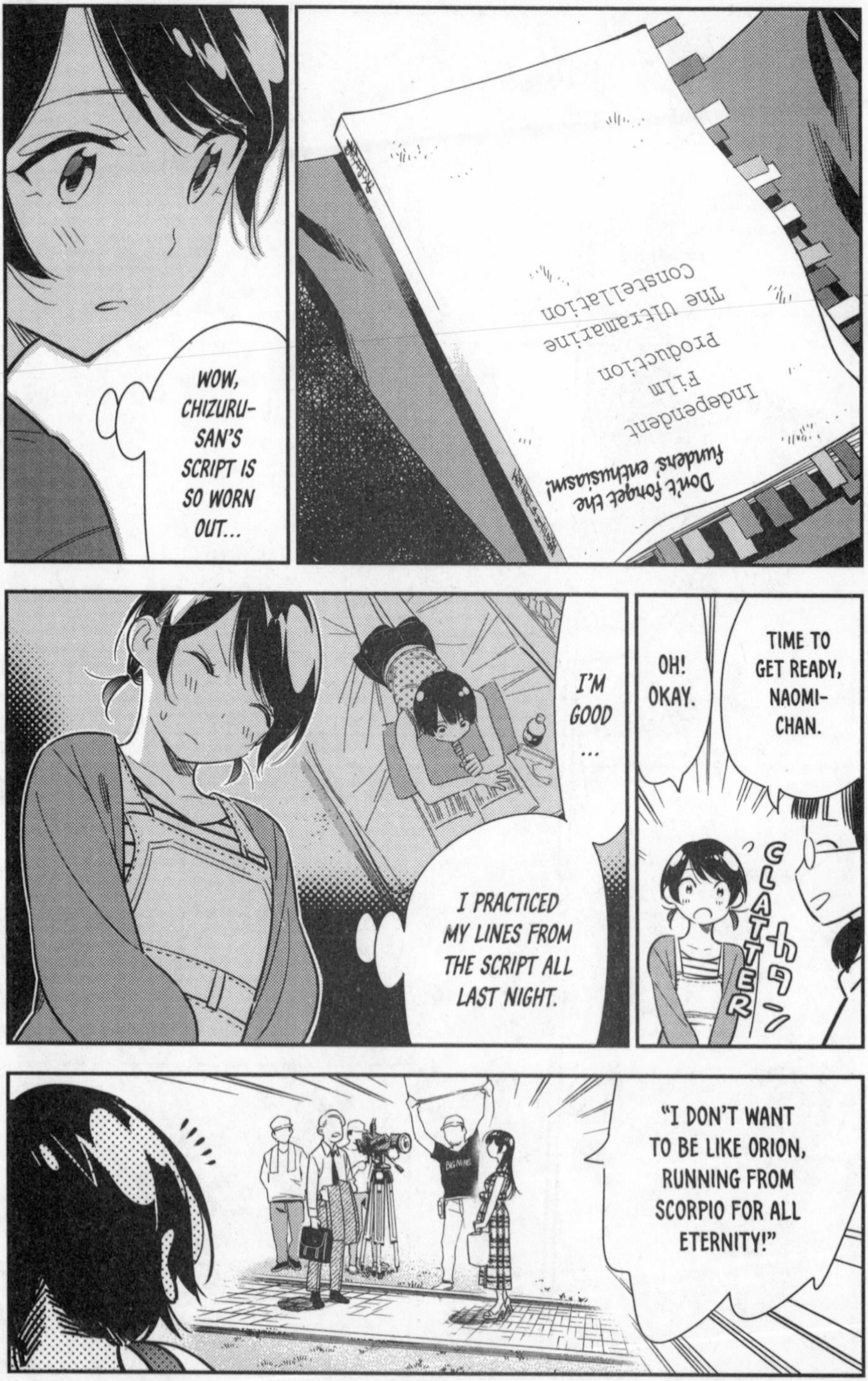
Don't forget the funders' enthusiasm!
Independent Film Production
The Ultramarine Constellation
WOW, CHIZURU-SAN'S SCRIPT IS SO WORN OUT...
TIME TO GET READY, NAOMI-CHAN.
OH! OKAY.
CLATTER
I'M GOOD...
I PRACTICED MY LINES FROM THE SCRIPT ALL LAST NIGHT.
"I DON'T WANT TO BE LIKE ORION, RUNNING FROM SCORPIO FOR ALL ETERNITY!"

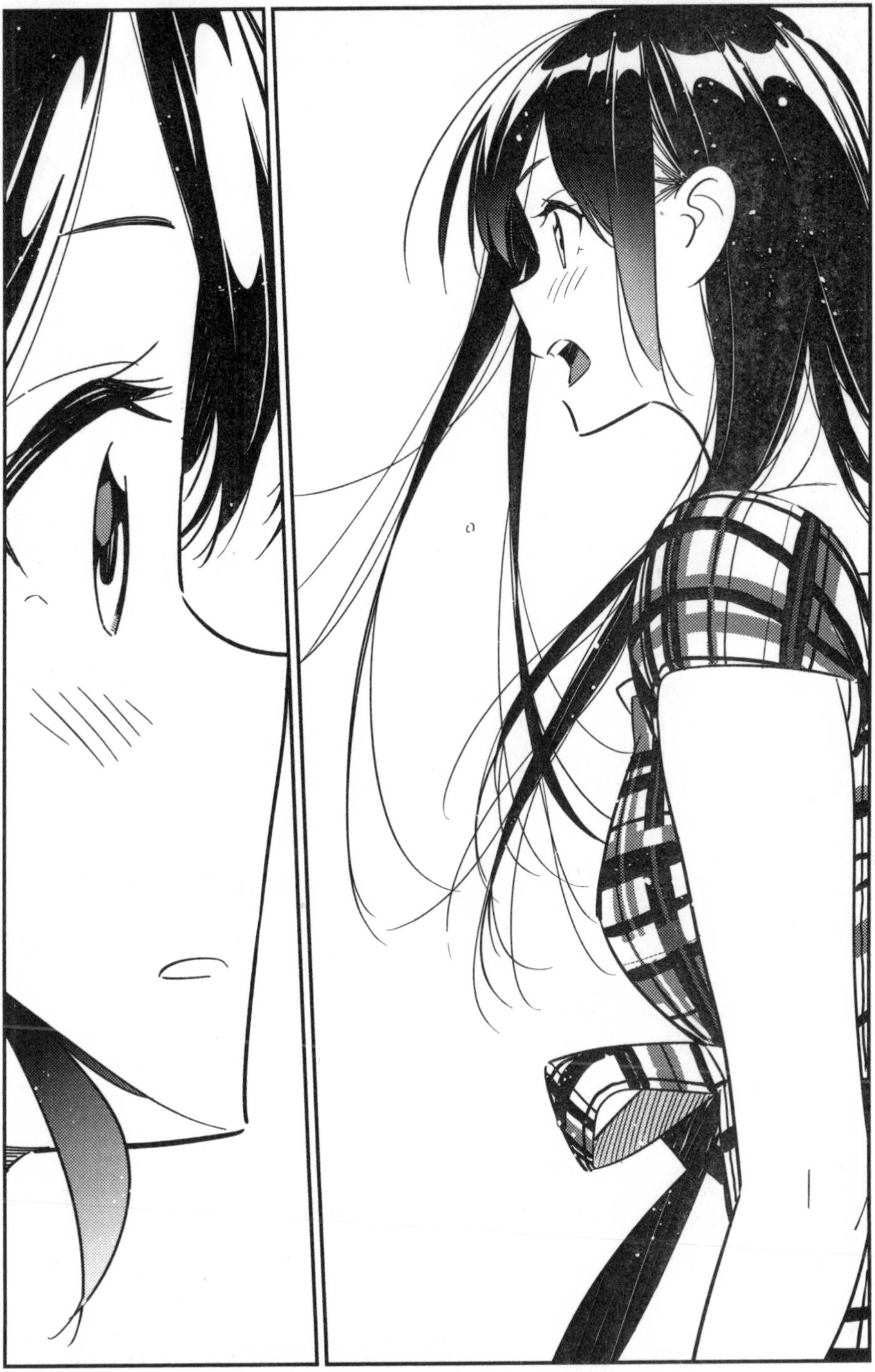

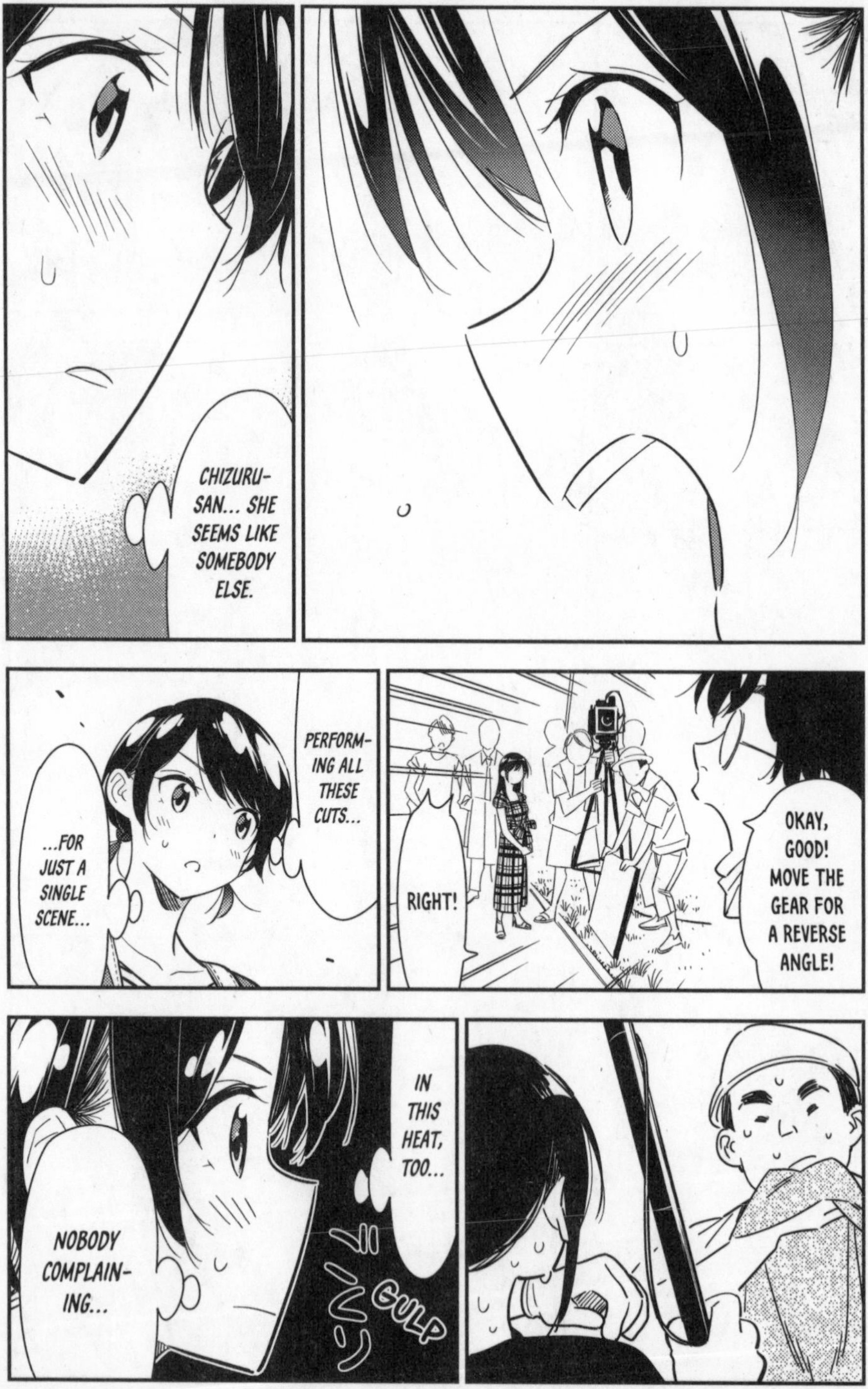
CHIZURU-SAN... SHE SEEMS LIKE SOMEBODY ELSE.
OKAY, GOOD! MOVE THE GEAR FOR A REVERSE ANGLE!
RIGHT!
PERFORMING ALL THESE CUTS...
...FOR JUST A SINGLE SCENE...
IN THIS HEAT, TOO...
GULP
NOBODY COMPLAINING...

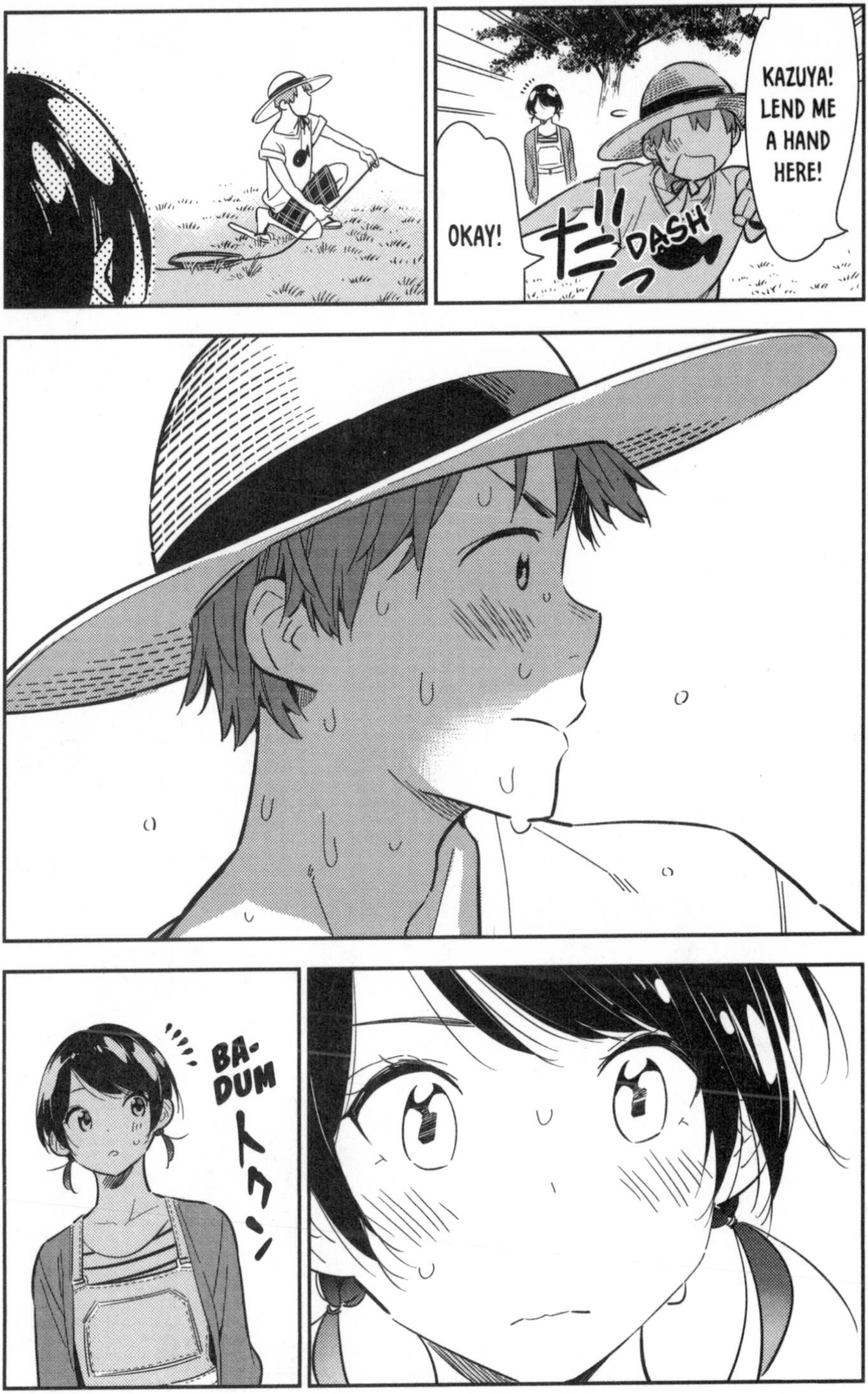
KAZUYA! LEND ME A HAND HERE!
OKAY!
だっ
DASH
BA-DUM
トクン

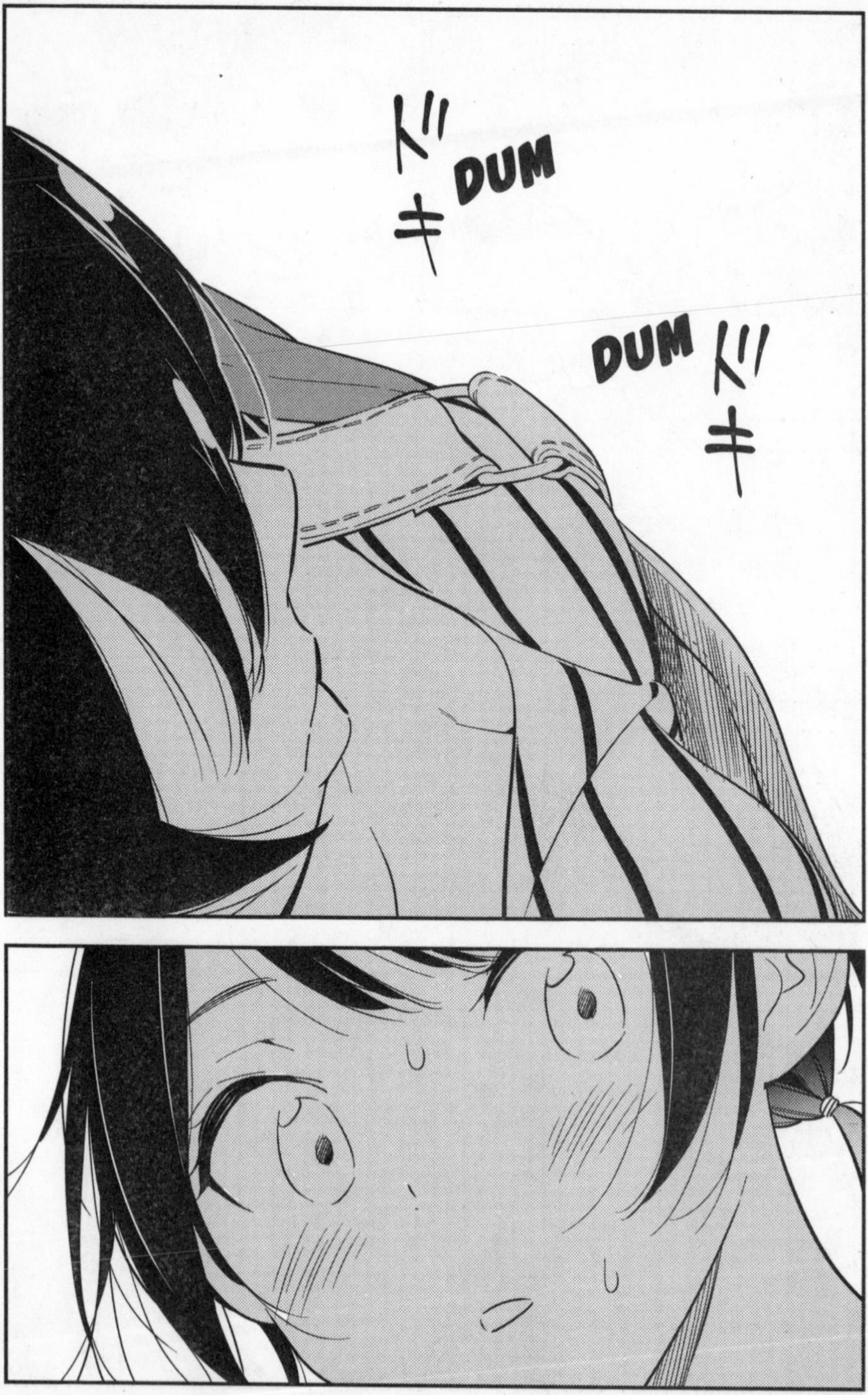
ドキ
DUM
ドキ
DUM

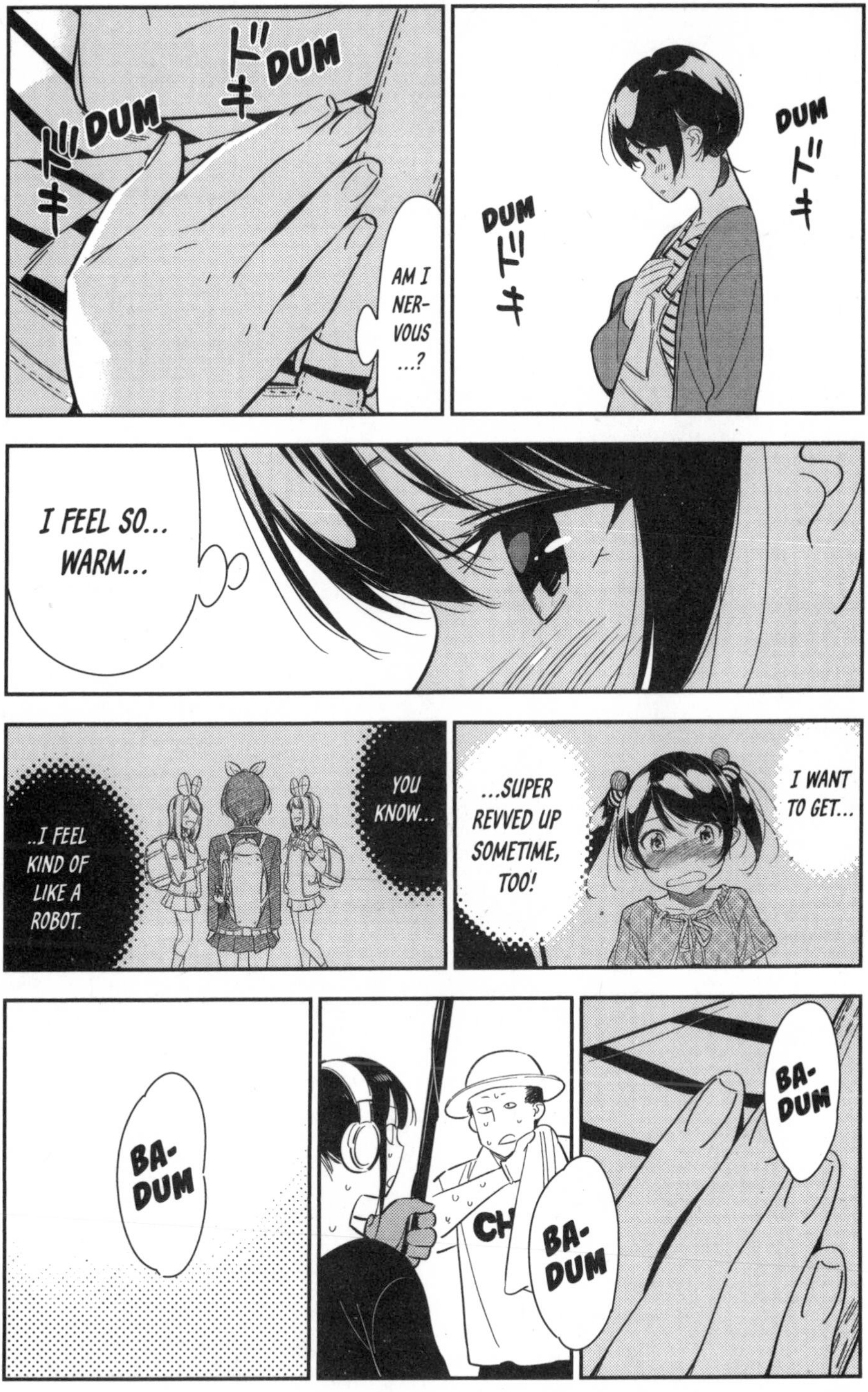
DUM
ドキ
DUM
ドキ
ドキ
DUM
ドキ
DUM
AM I NERVOUS...?
I FEEL SO... WARM...
I WANT TO GET...
...SUPER REVVED UP SOMETIME, TOO!
YOU KNOW...
..I FEEL KIND OF LIKE A ROBOT.
BA-DUM
BA-DUM
CH
BA-DUM

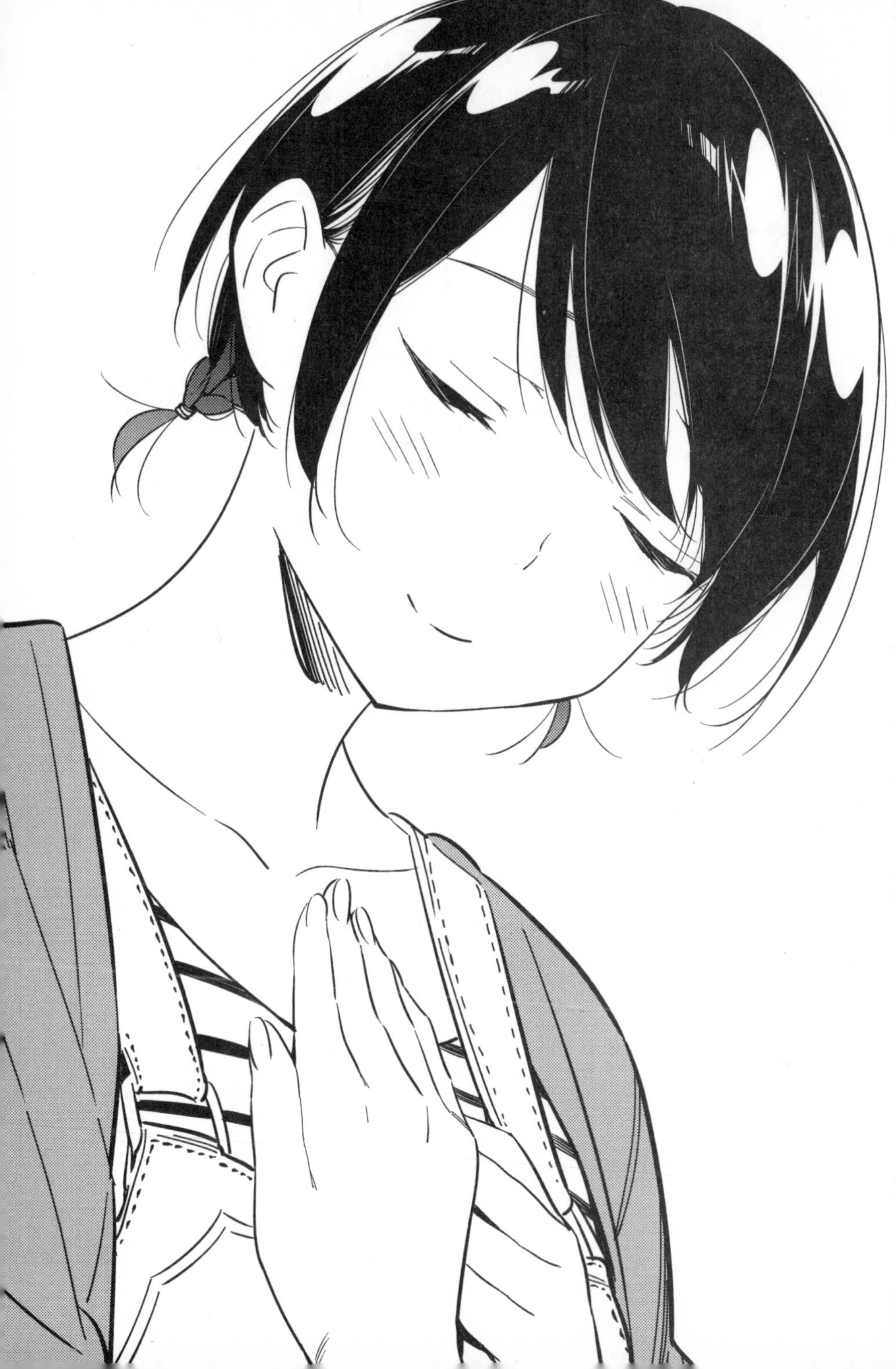

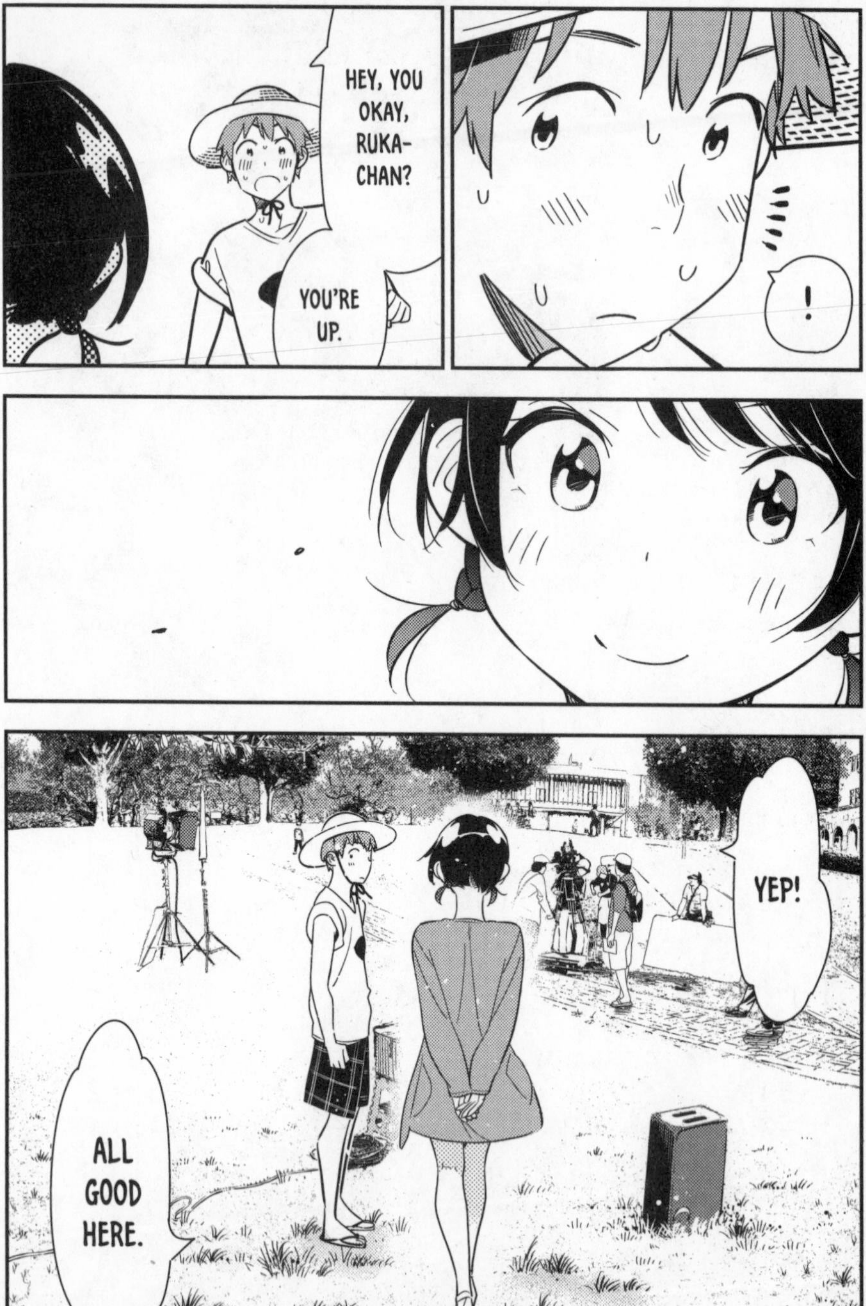
!
HEY, YOU OKAY, RUKA-CHAN?
YOU'RE UP.
YEP!
ALL GOOD HERE.

RATING 130 SHOOTING AND MY GIRLFRIEND 2

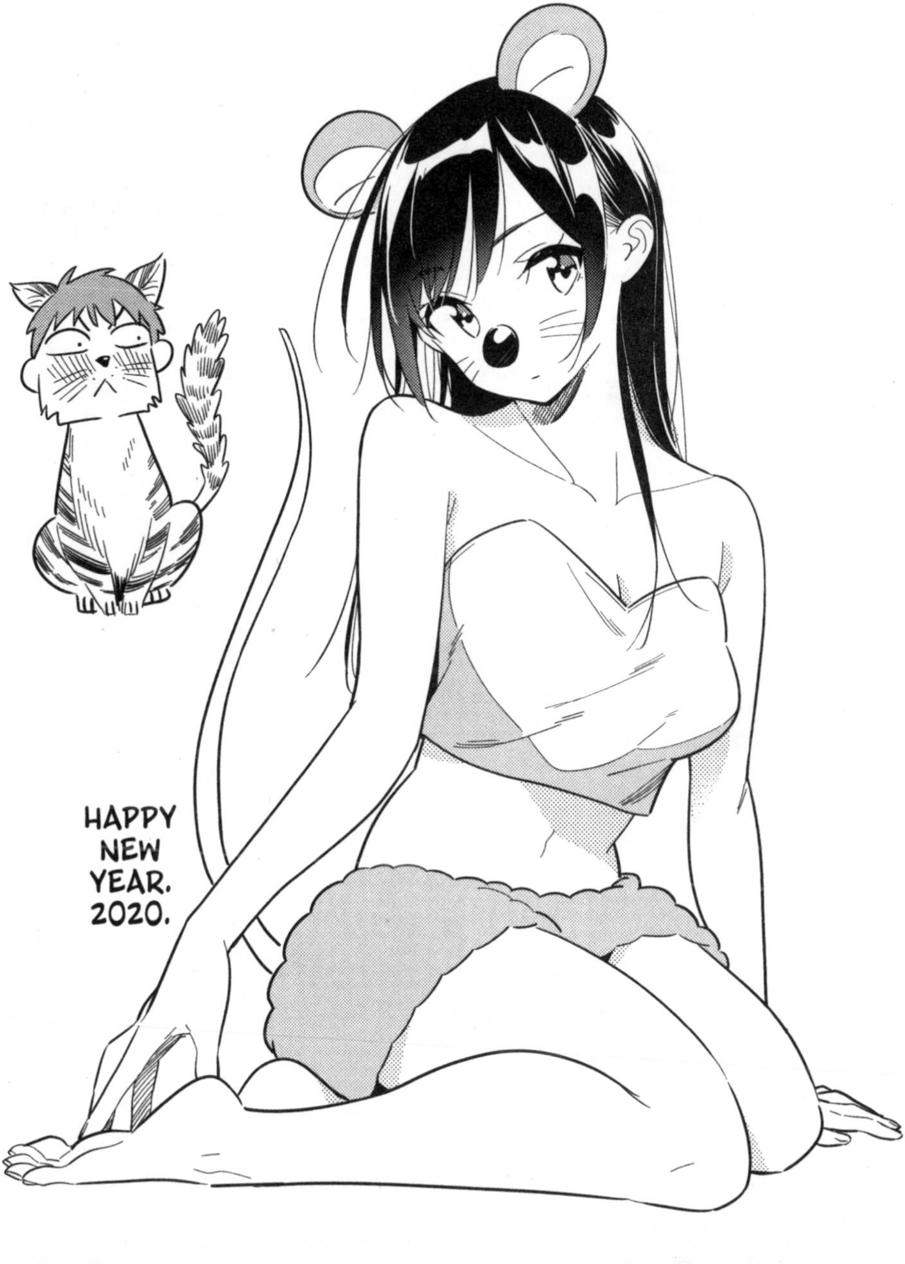
HAPPY NEW YEAR. 2020.

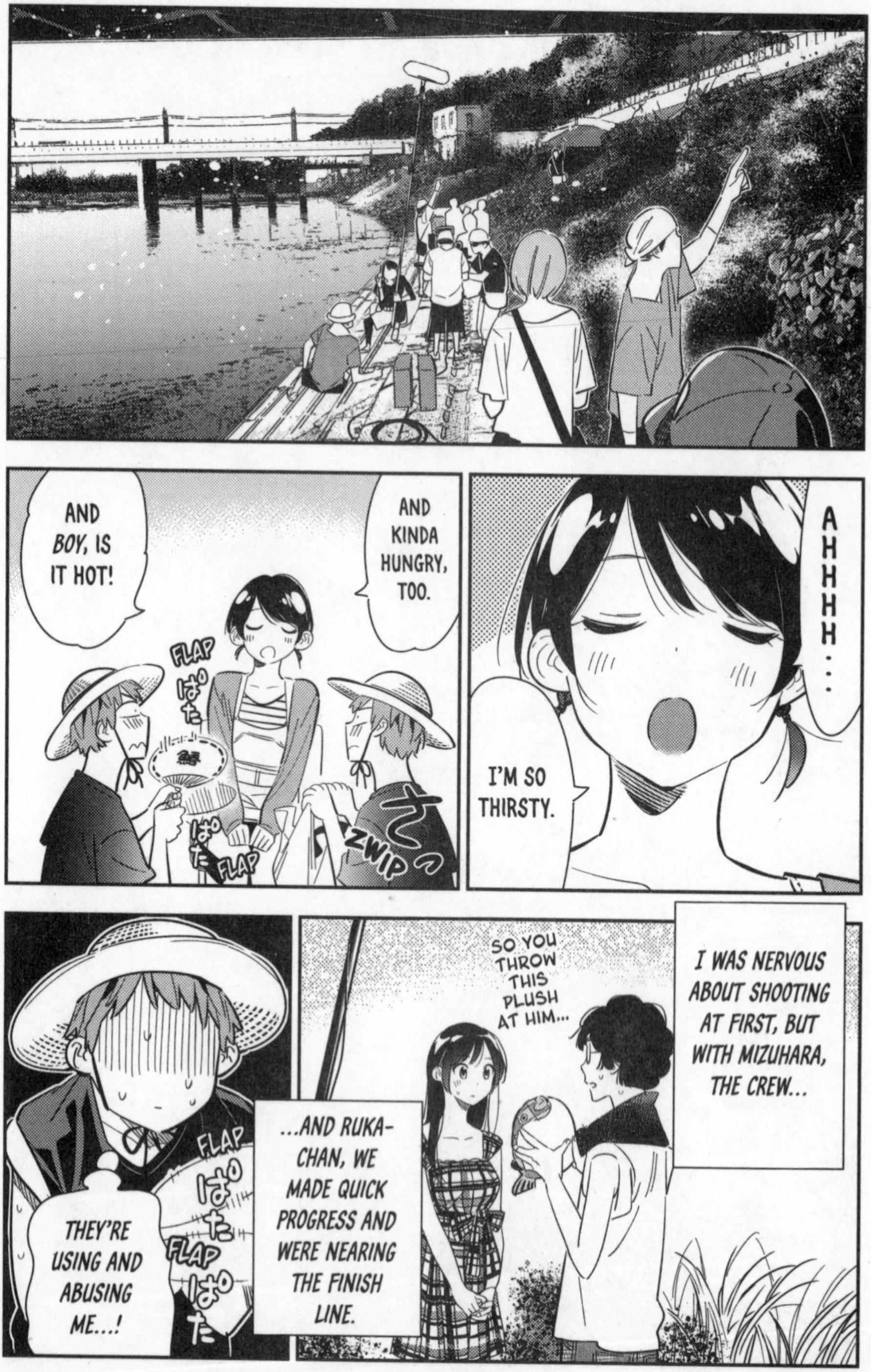
AHHHH...
I'M SO THIRSTY.
AND KINDA HUNGRY, TOO.
AND BOY, IS IT HOT!
FLAP ぱた
ZWIP さっ
ぱた FLAP
I WAS NERVOUS ABOUT SHOOTING AT FIRST, BUT WITH MIZUHARA, THE CREW...
SO YOU THROW THIS PLUSH AT HIM...
...AND RUKA-CHAN, WE MADE QUICK PROGRESS AND WERE NEARING THE FINISH LINE.
FLAP ぱた
FLAP ぱた
THEY'RE USING AND ABUSING ME...!

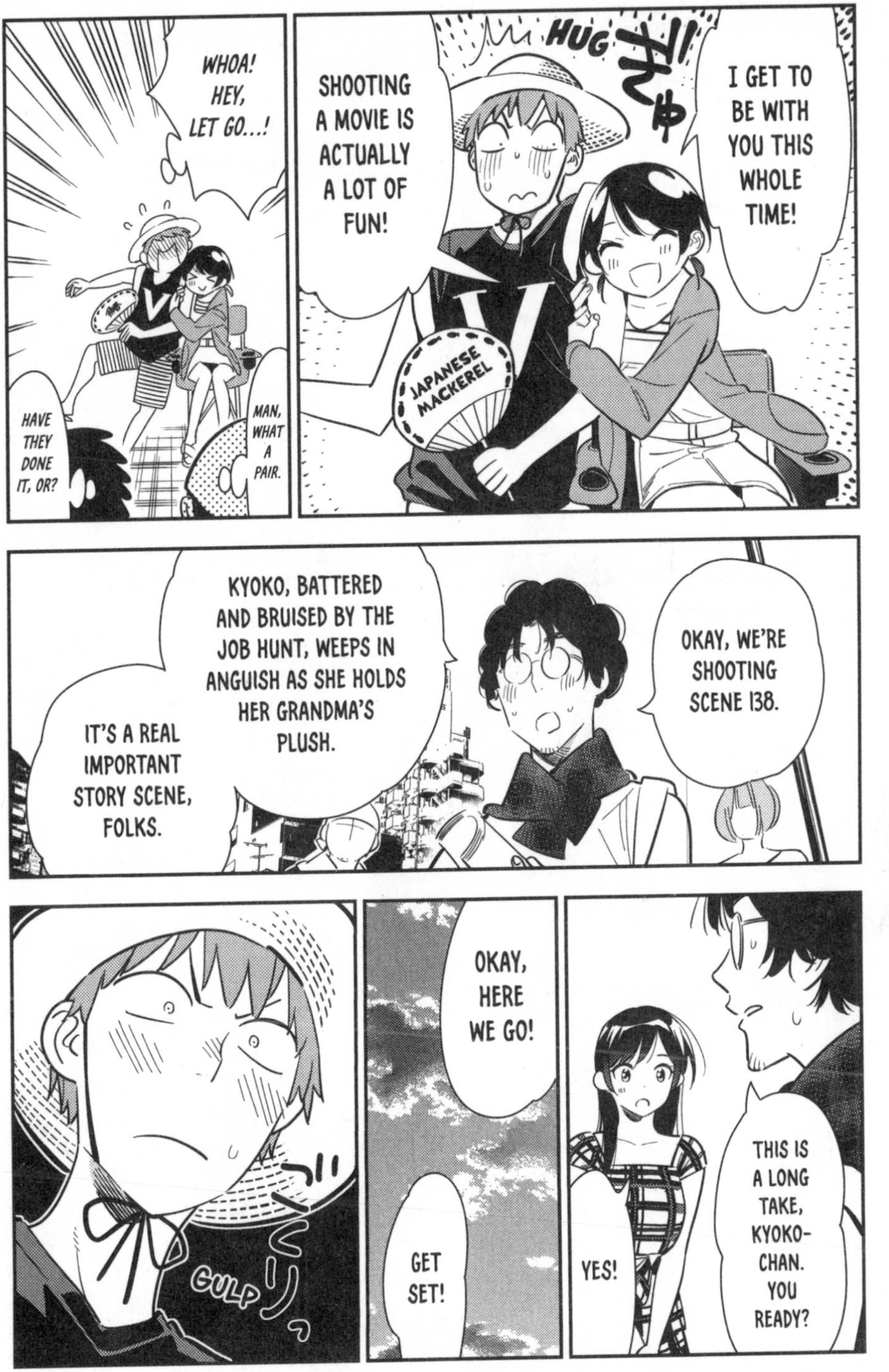
HUG
I GET TO BE WITH YOU THIS WHOLE TIME!
SHOOTING A MOVIE IS ACTUALLY A LOT OF FUN!
JAPANESE MACKEREL
WHOA! HEY, LET GO...!
MAN, WHAT A PAIR.
HAVE THEY DONE IT, OR?
OKAY, WE'RE SHOOTING SCENE 138.
KYOKO, BATTERED AND BRUISED BY THE JOB HUNT, WEEPS IN ANGUISH AS SHE HOLDS HER GRANDMA'S PLUSH.
IT'S A REAL IMPORTANT STORY SCENE, FOLKS.
THIS IS A LONG TAKE, KYOKO-CHAN. YOU READY?
YES!
OKAY, HERE WE GO!
GET SET!
GULP

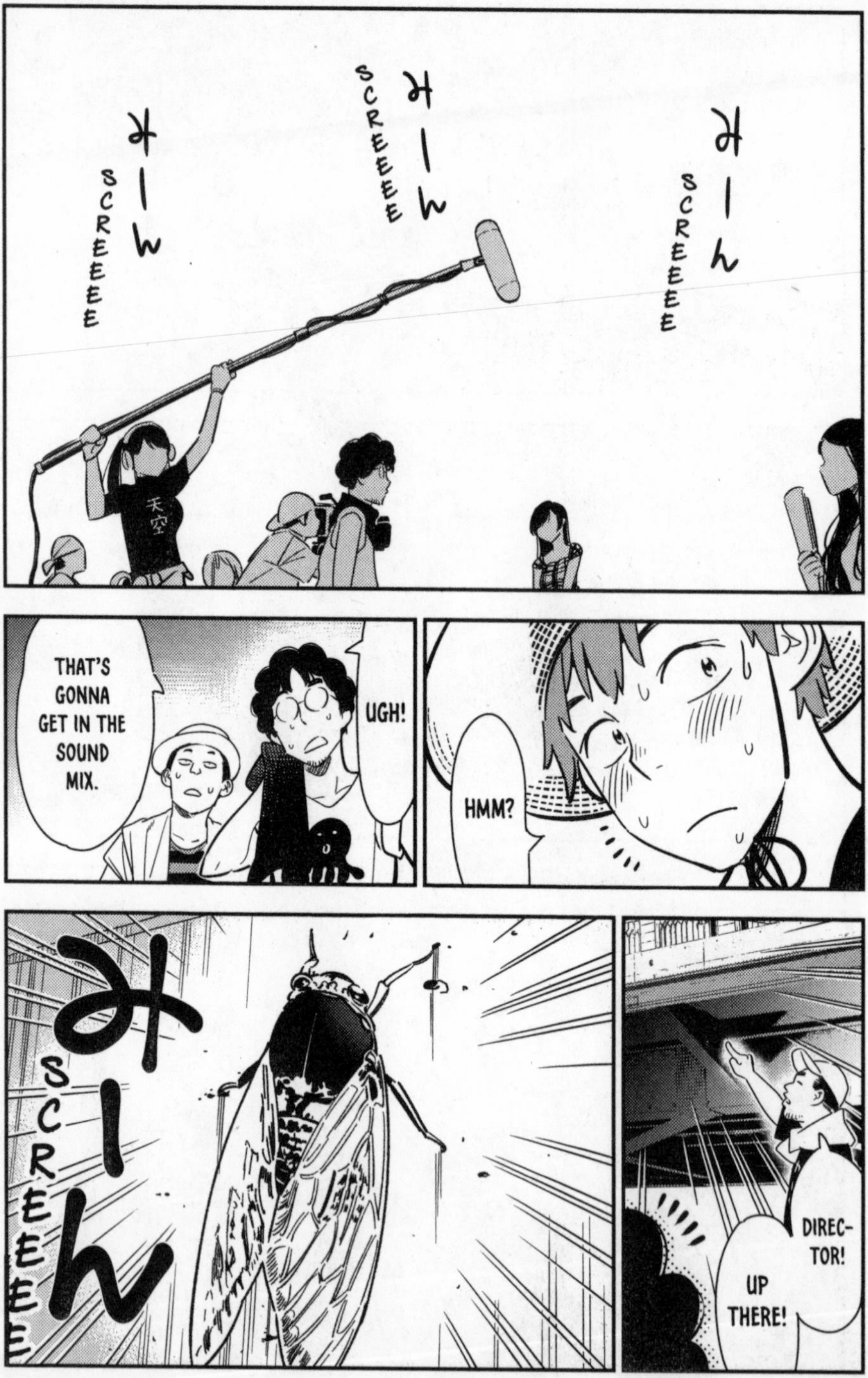
みーん
SCREEEE
みーん
SCREEEEE
みーん
SCREEEE
天空
HMM?
UGH!
THAT'S GONNA GET IN THE SOUND MIX.
DIREC-TOR!
UP THERE!
みーん
SCREEEEE

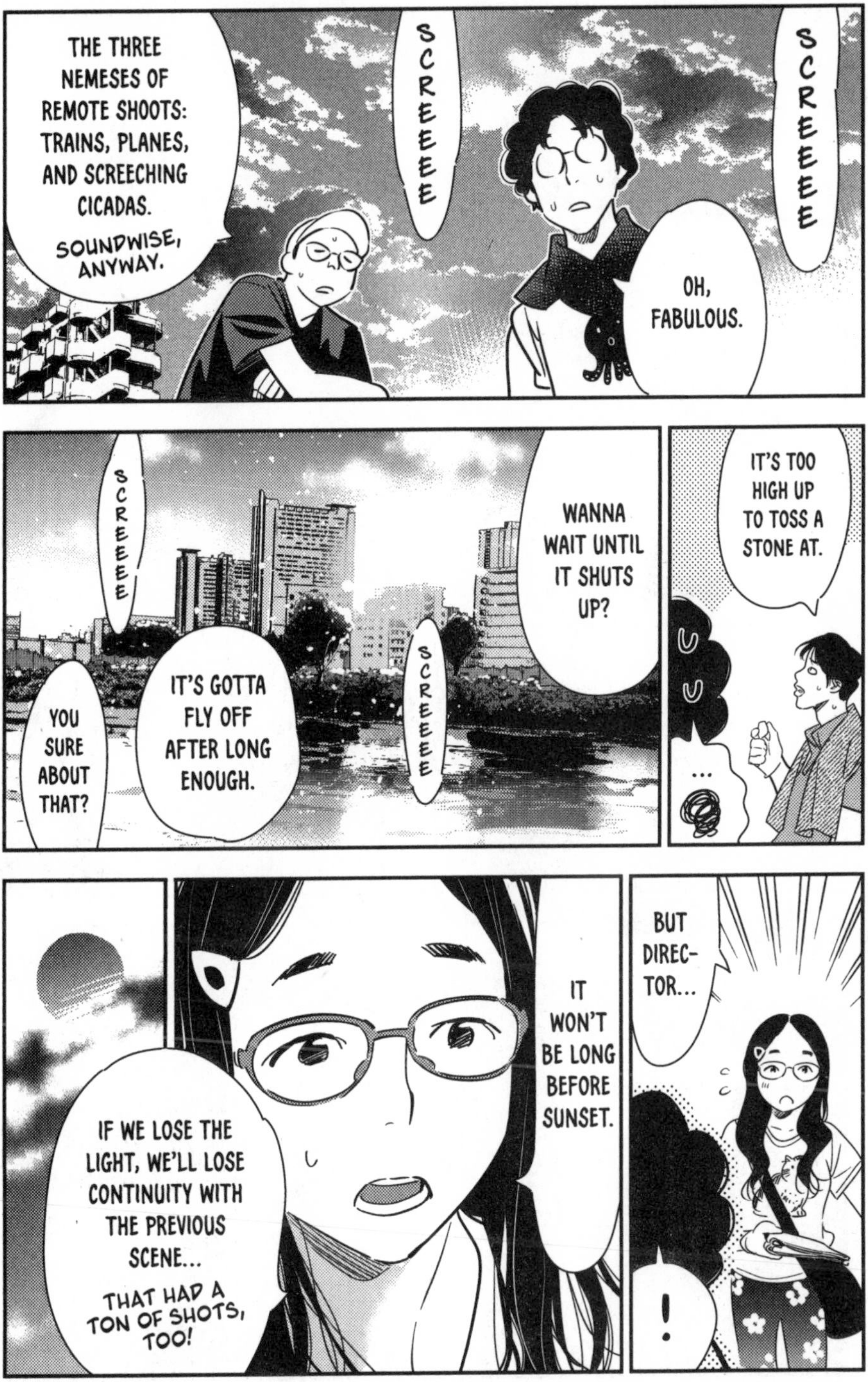
SCREEEE
OH, FABULOUS.
SCREEEE
THE THREE NEMESES OF REMOTE SHOOTS: TRAINS, PLANES, AND SCREECHING CICADAS.
SOUNDWISE, ANYWAY.
IT'S TOO HIGH UP TO TOSS A STONE AT.
...
WANNA WAIT UNTIL IT SHUTS UP?
SCREEEE
IT'S GOTTA FLY OFF AFTER LONG ENOUGH.
SCREEEEE
YOU SURE ABOUT THAT?
BUT DIRECTOR...
!
IT WON'T BE LONG BEFORE SUNSET.
IF WE LOSE THE LIGHT, WE'LL LOSE CONTINUITY WITH THE PREVIOUS SCENE...
THAT HAD A TON OF SHOTS, TOO!

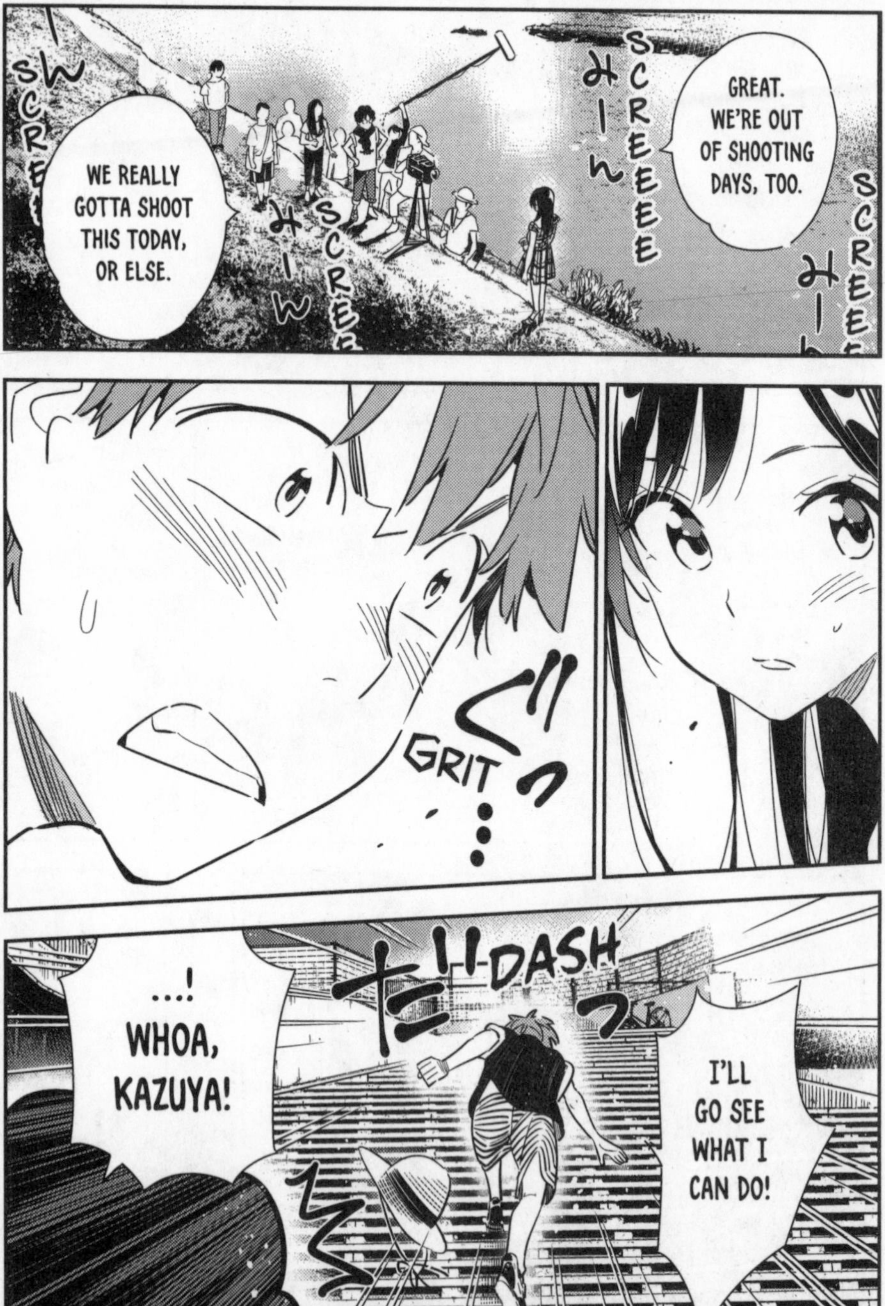
SCREEEE
みーん
GREAT. WE'RE OUT OF SHOOTING DAYS, TOO.
SCREEEE
みーん
WE REALLY GOTTA SHOOT THIS TODAY, OR ELSE.
SCREE
みーん
GRIT
...
DASH
I'LL GO SEE WHAT I CAN DO!
...! WHOA, KAZUYA!

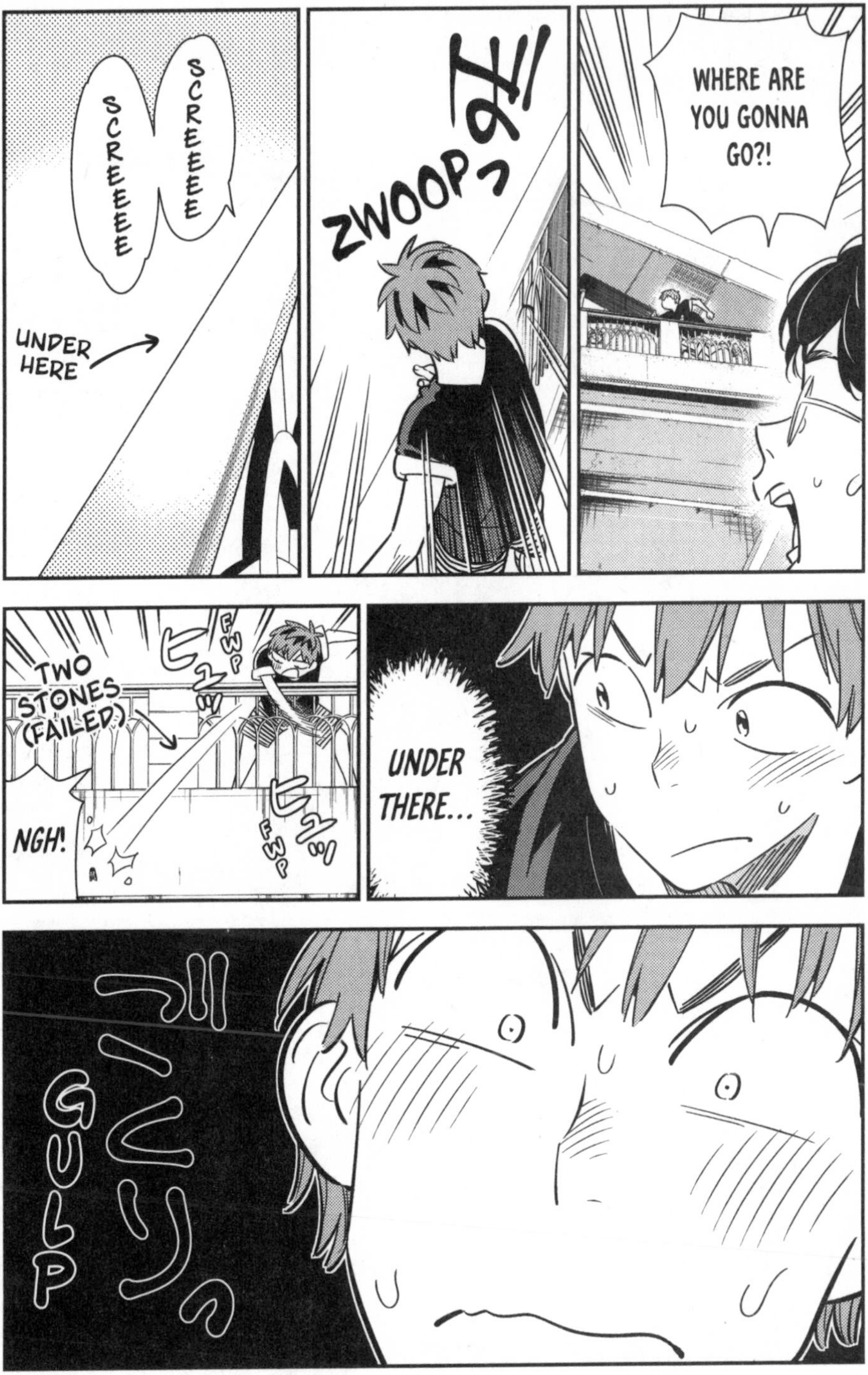
WHERE ARE YOU GONNA GO?!
ZWOOP
SCREEEE
SCREEEE
UNDER HERE
UNDER THERE...
FWP
TWO STONES (FAILED)
FWP
NGH!
GULP

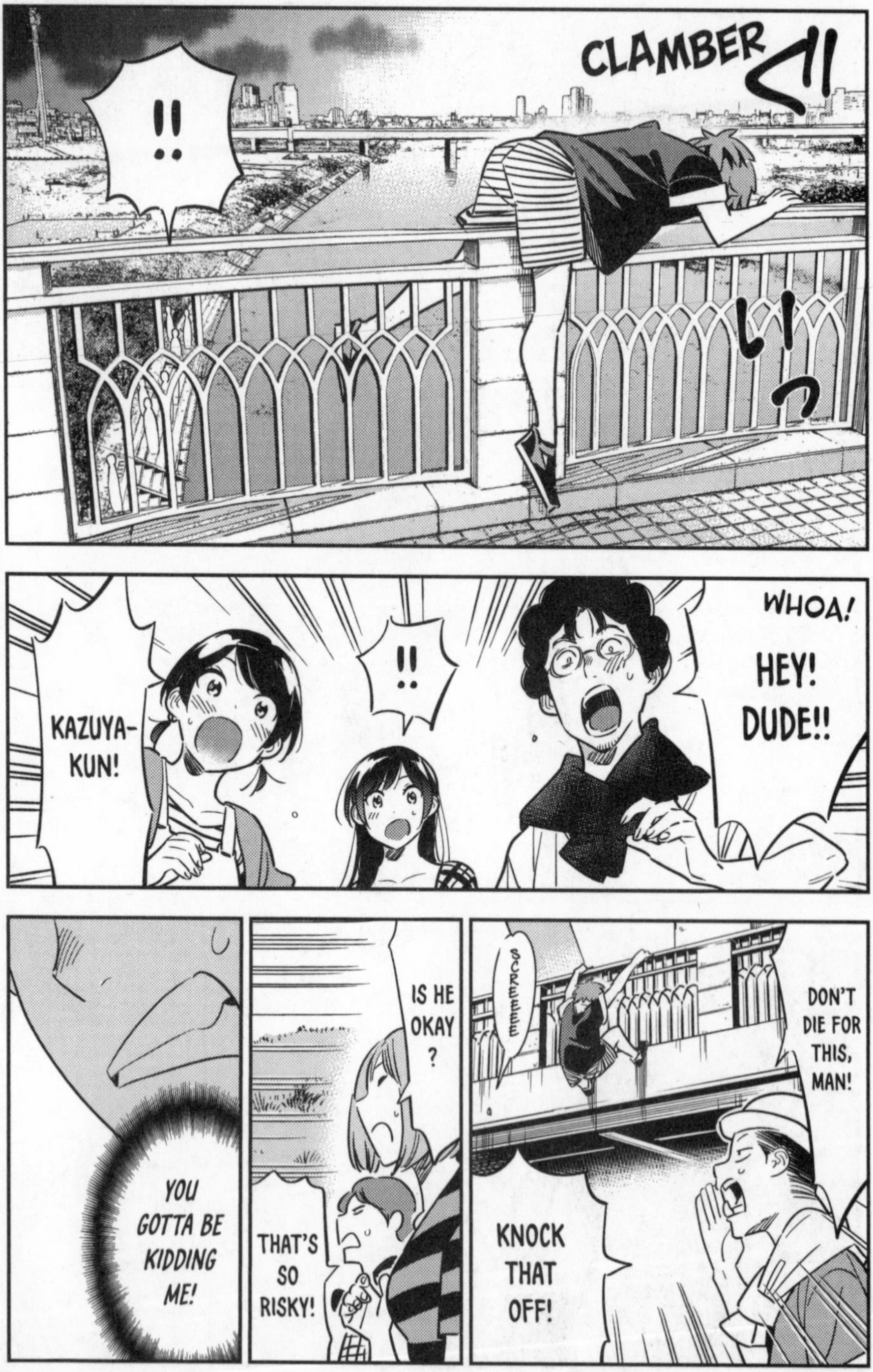
CLAMBER
!!
WHOA!
HEY! DUDE!!
!!
KAZUYA-KUN!
DON'T DIE FOR THIS, MAN!
SCREEEE
KNOCK THAT OFF!
IS HE OKAY?
THAT'S SO RISKY!
YOU GOTTA BE KIDDING ME!

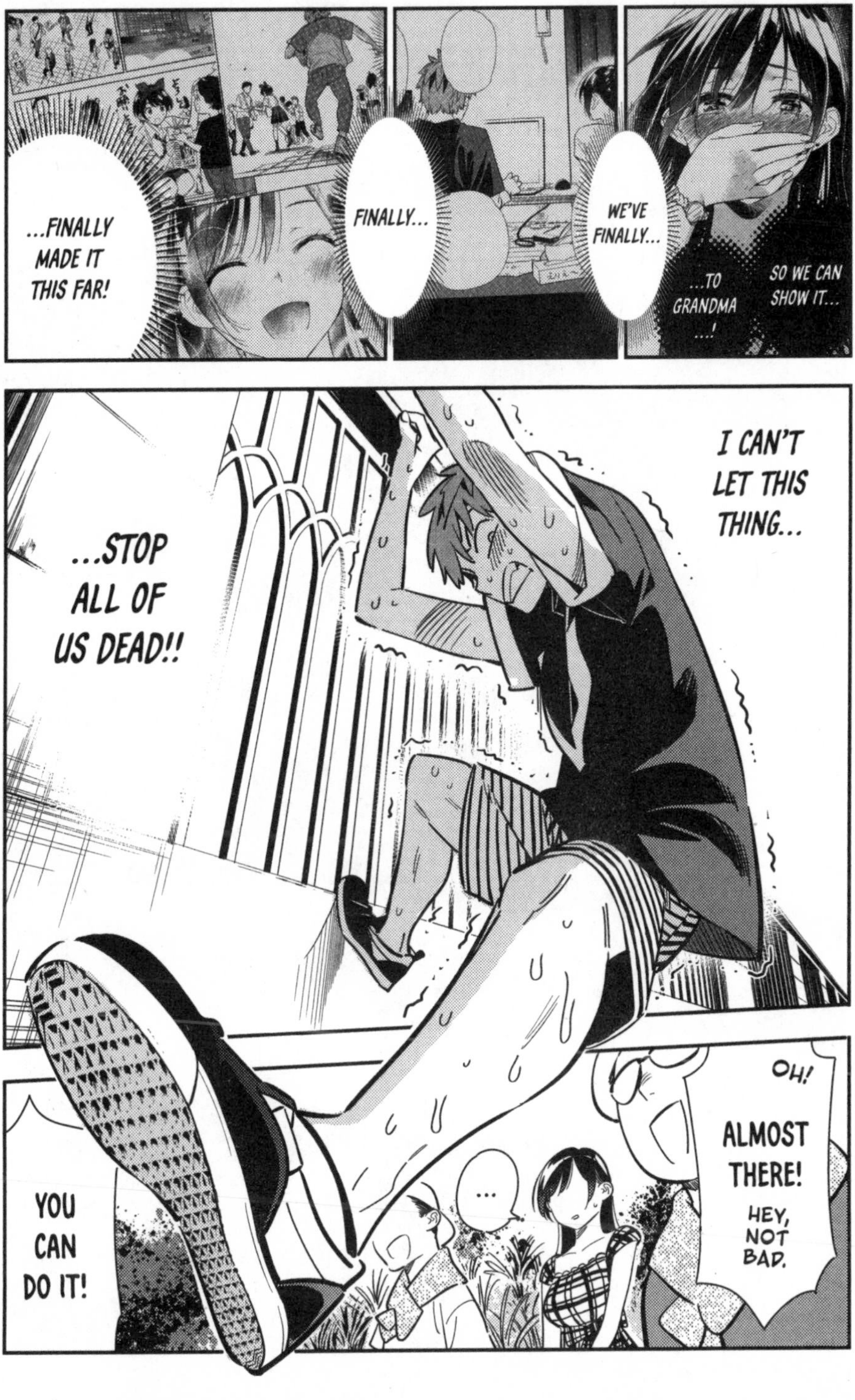
WE'VE FINALLY...
SO WE CAN SHOW IT...
...TO GRANDMA ...!
FINALLY...
...FINALLY MADE IT THIS FAR!
I CAN'T LET THIS THING...
...STOP ALL OF US DEAD!!
OH!
ALMOST THERE!
HEY, NOT BAD.
...
YOU CAN DO IT!

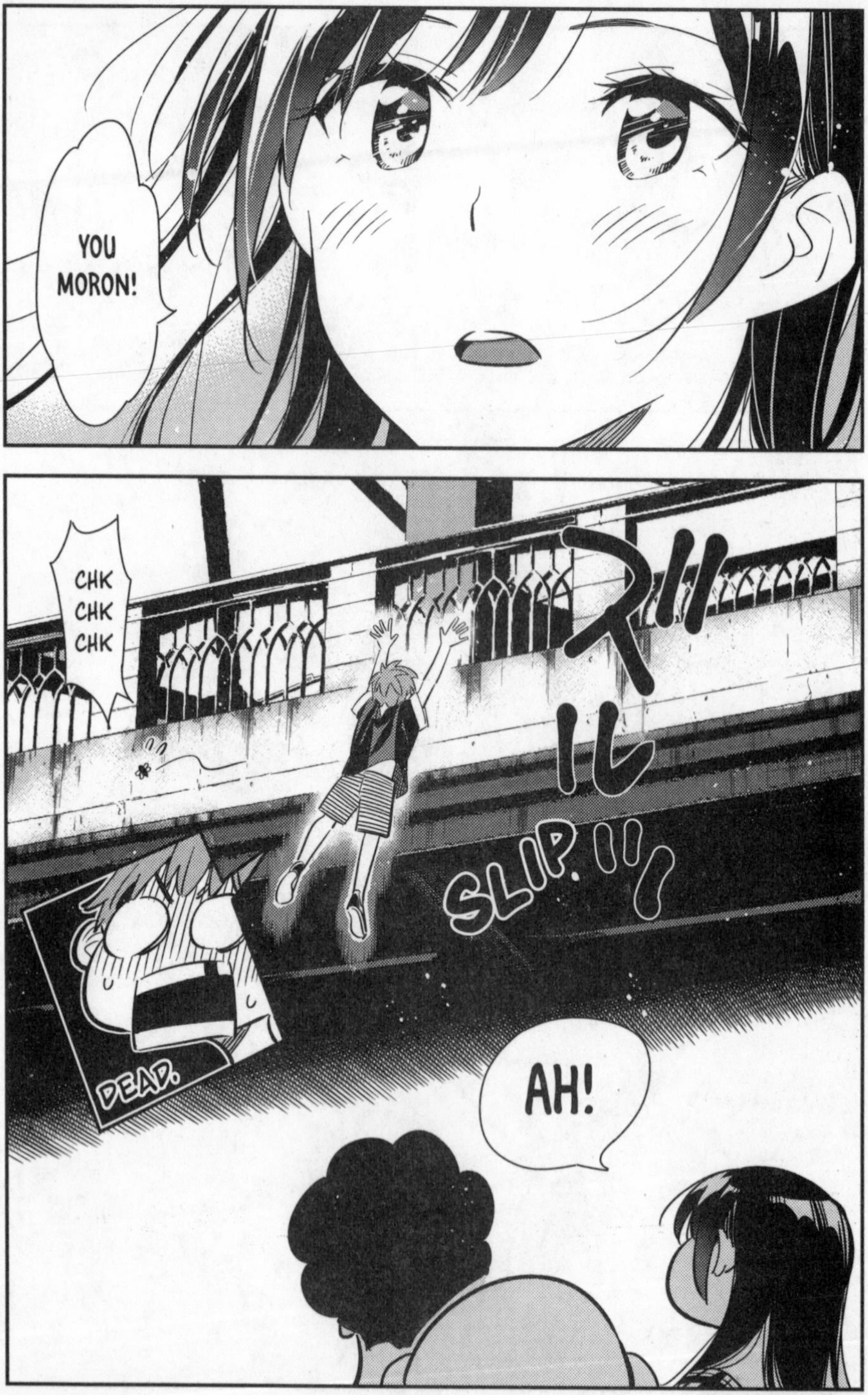
YOU MORON!
ズル
SLIP
CHK CHK CHK
DEAD.
AH!

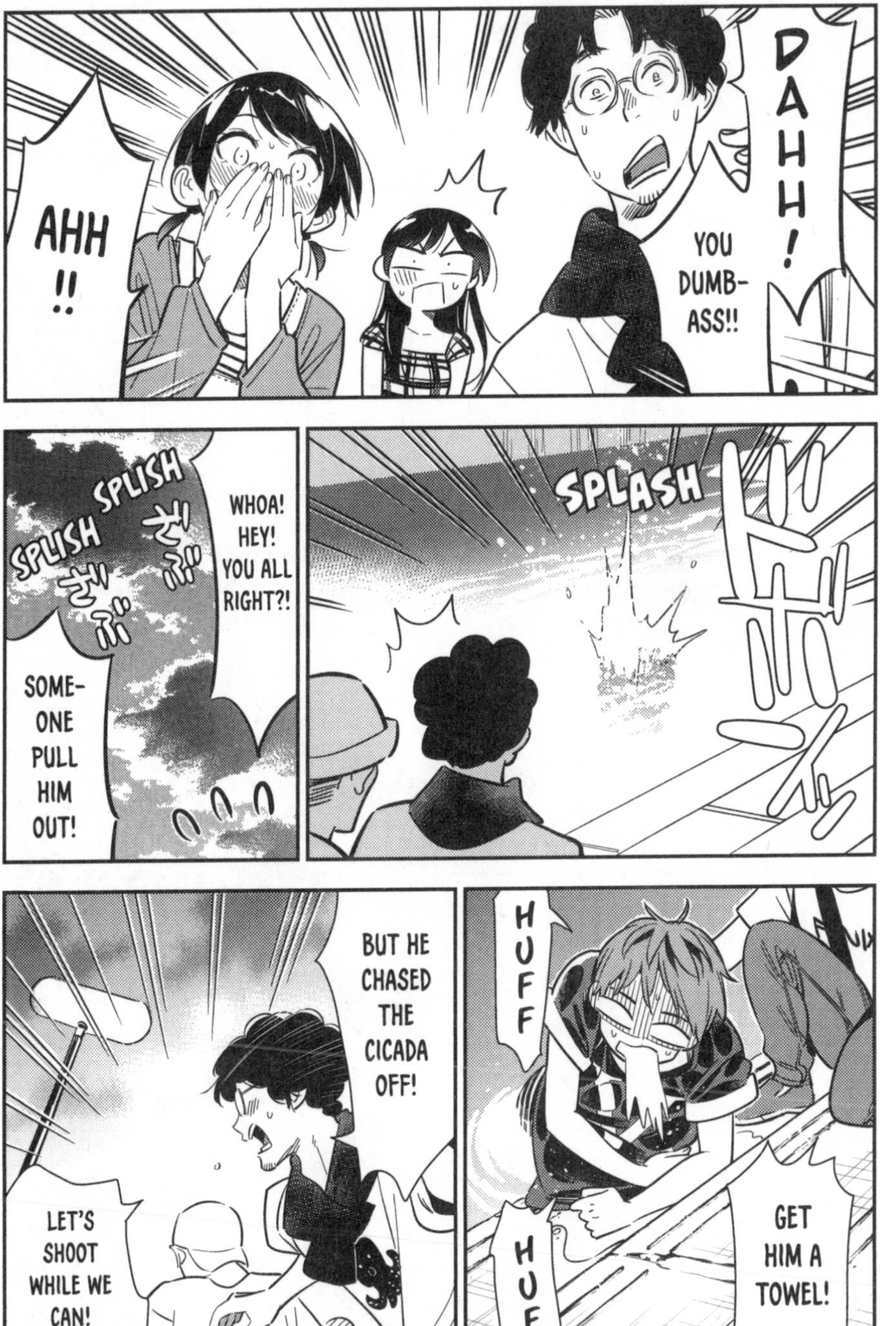
DAHH!
YOU DUMB-ASS!!
AHH !!
SPLASH
ドボーン
WHOA! HEY! YOU ALL RIGHT?!
SPLISH SPLISH
ざぶざぶ
SOME-ONE PULL HIM OUT!
HUFF
HUFF
GET HIM A TOWEL!
BUT HE CHASED THE CICADA OFF!
LET'S SHOOT WHILE WE CAN!
IT MAY COME BACK!

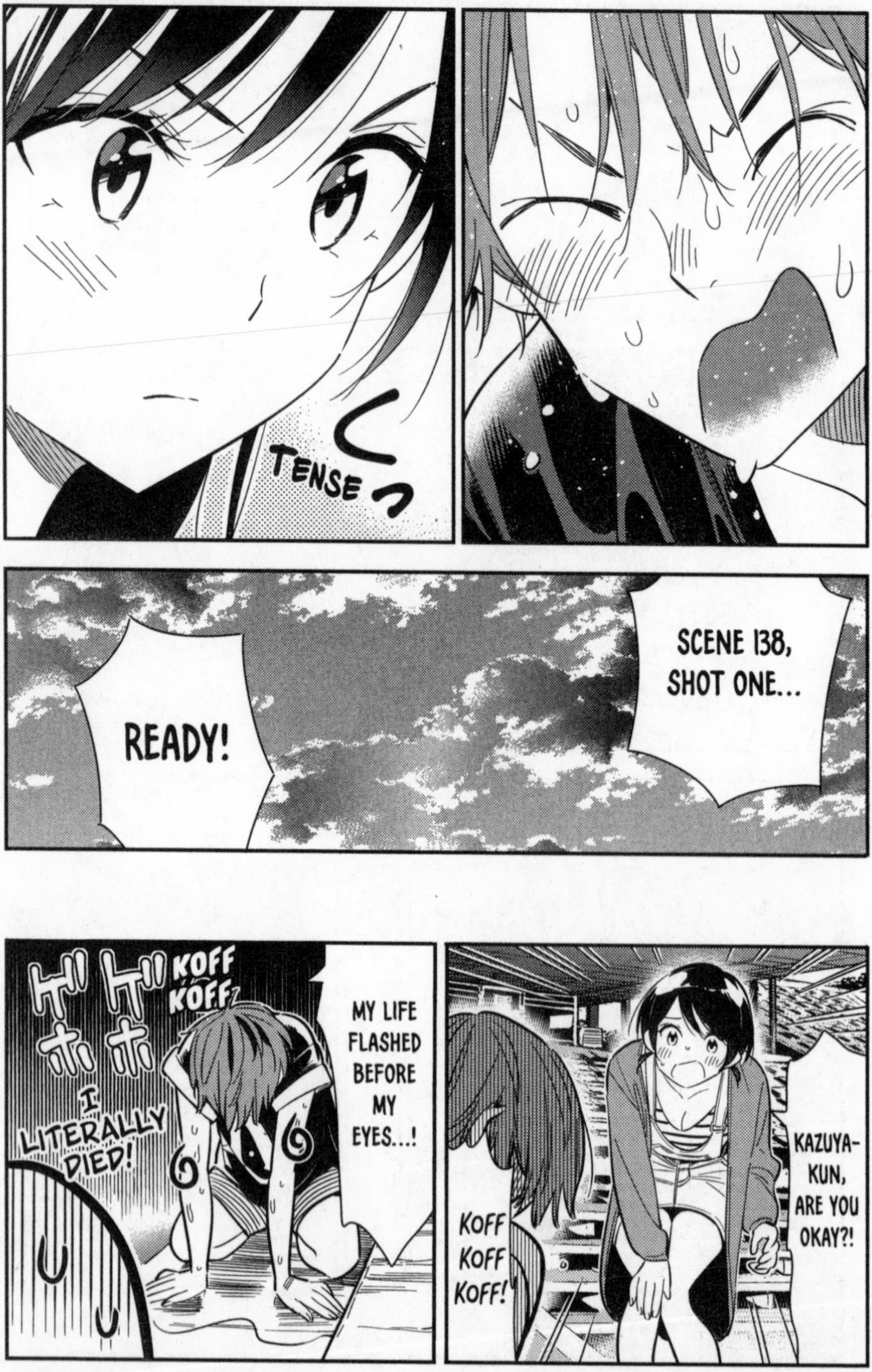
くっ
TENSE
SCENE 138, SHOT ONE...
READY!
KAZUYA-KUN, ARE YOU OKAY?!
KOFF KOFF KOFF!
MY LIFE FLASHED BEFORE MY EYES...!
KOFF KOFF
ゲホ ゲホ
I LITERALLY DIED!

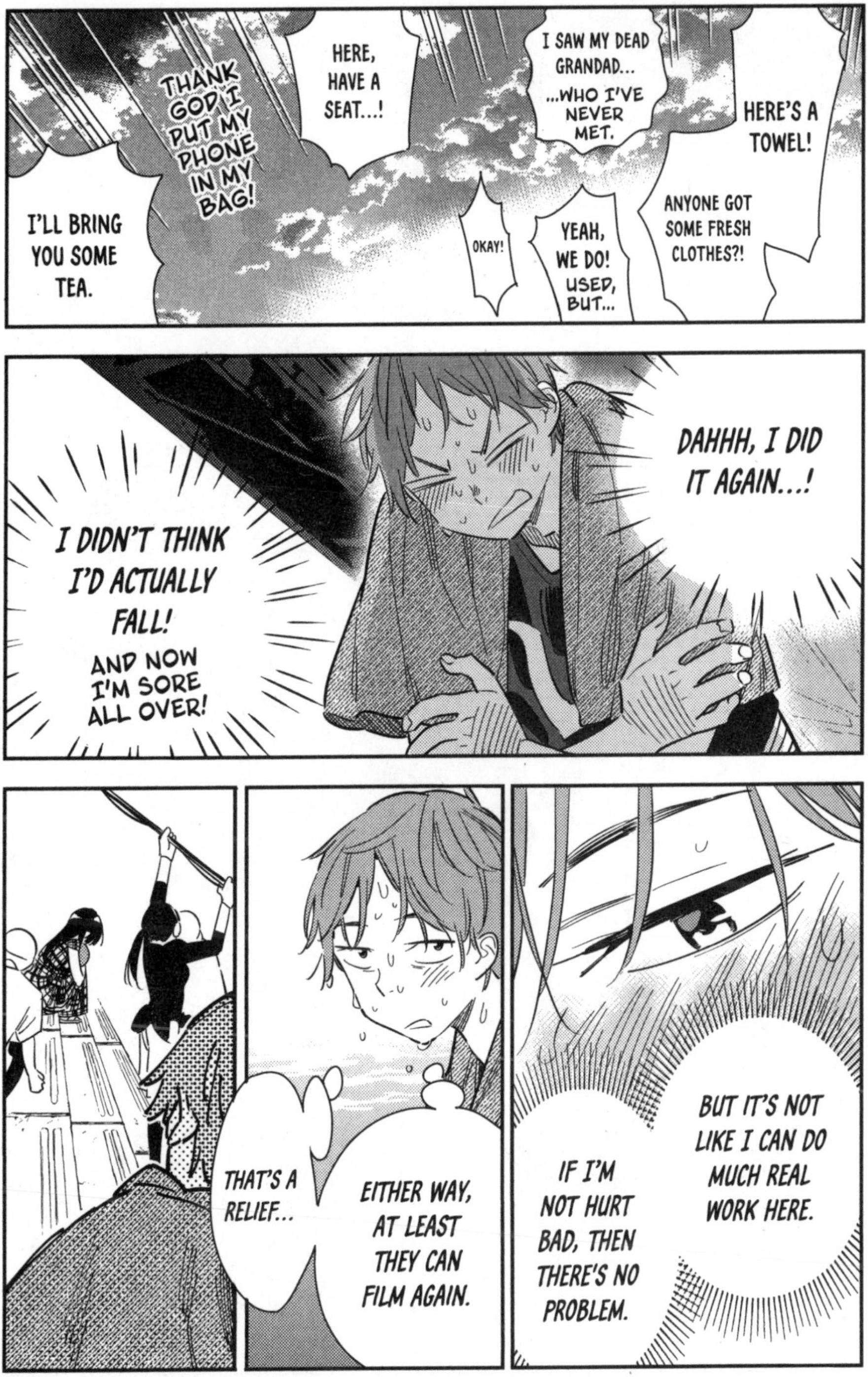
HERE'S A TOWEL!
ANYONE GOT SOME FRESH CLOTHES?!
I SAW MY DEAD GRANDAD...
...WHO I'VE NEVER MET.
YEAH, WE DO!
USED, BUT...
OKAY!
HERE, HAVE A SEAT...!
THANK GOD I PUT MY PHONE IN MY BAG!
I'LL BRING YOU SOME TEA.
DAHHH, I DID IT AGAIN...!
I DIDN'T THINK I'D ACTUALLY FALL!
AND NOW I'M SORE ALL OVER!
BUT IT'S NOT LIKE I CAN DO MUCH REAL WORK HERE.
IF I'M NOT HURT BAD, THEN THERE'S NO PROBLEM.
EITHER WAY, AT LEAST THEY CAN FILM AGAIN.
THAT'S A RELIEF...

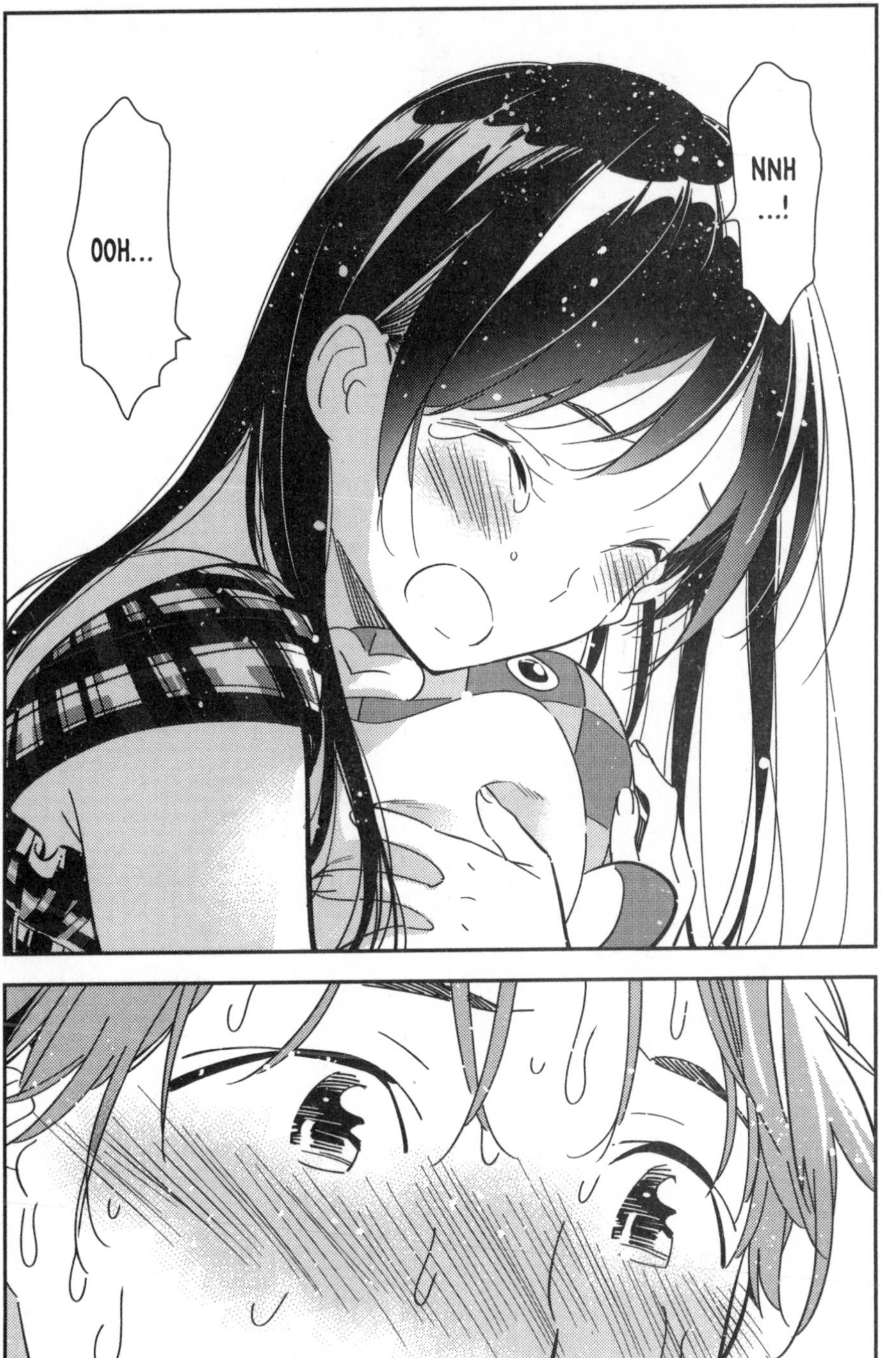
NNH ...!
OOH...

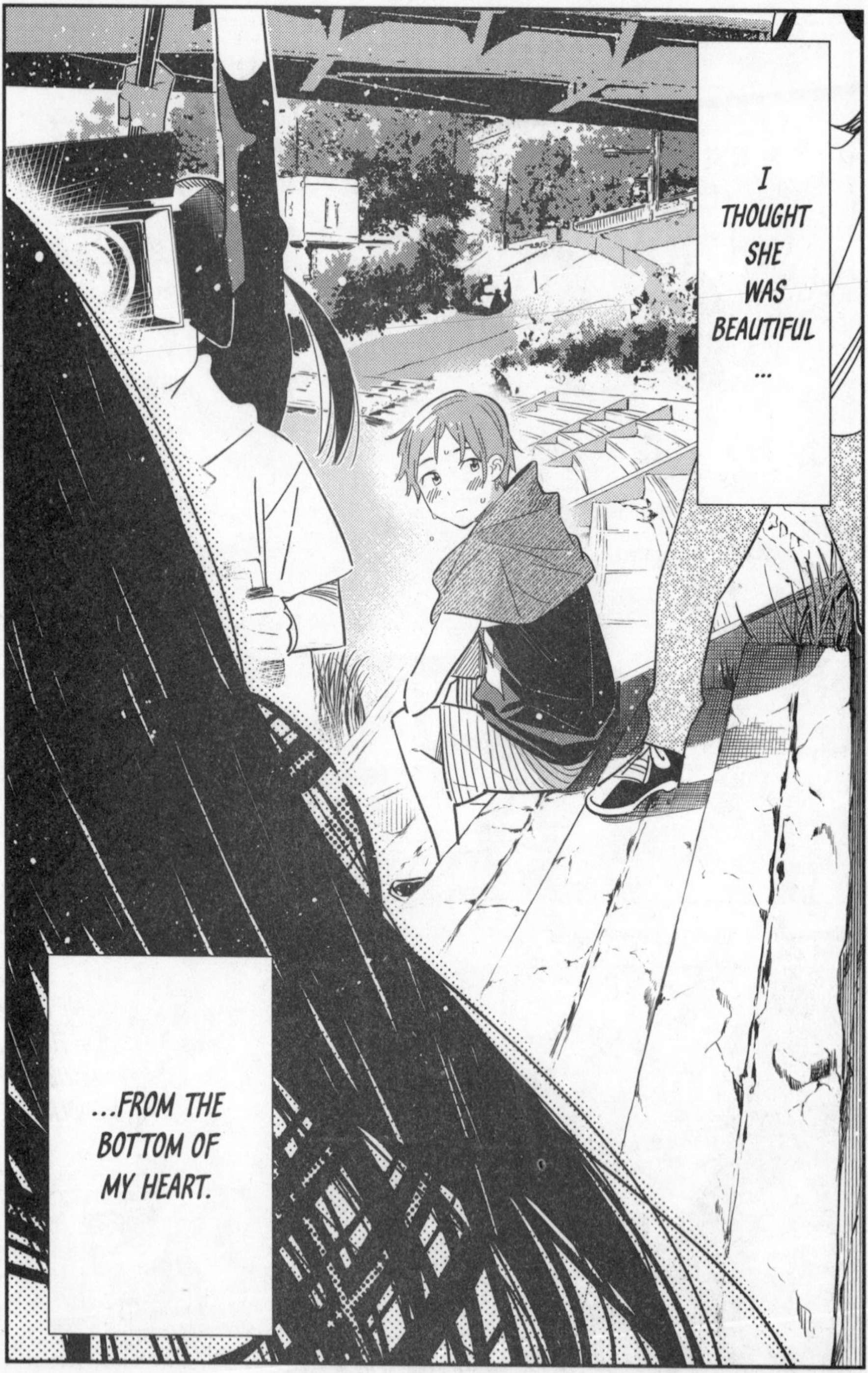
I THOUGHT SHE WAS BEAUTIFUL...
...FROM THE BOTTOM OF MY HEART.

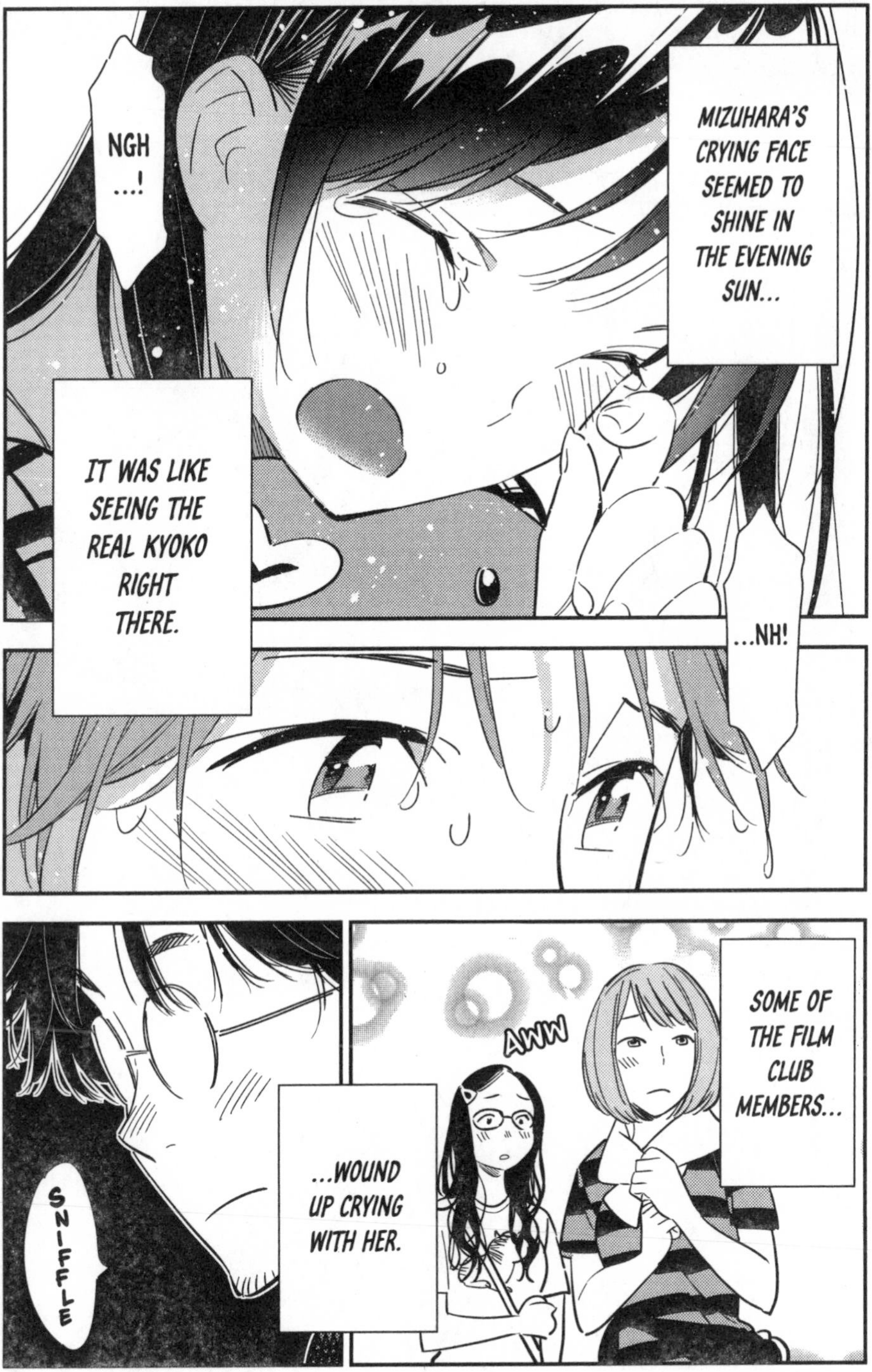
MIZUHARA'S CRYING FACE SEEMED TO SHINE IN THE EVENING SUN...
NGH ...!
IT WAS LIKE SEEING THE REAL KYOKO RIGHT THERE.
...NH!
SOME OF THE FILM CLUB MEMBERS...
AWW
...WOUND UP CRYING WITH HER.
SNIFFLE

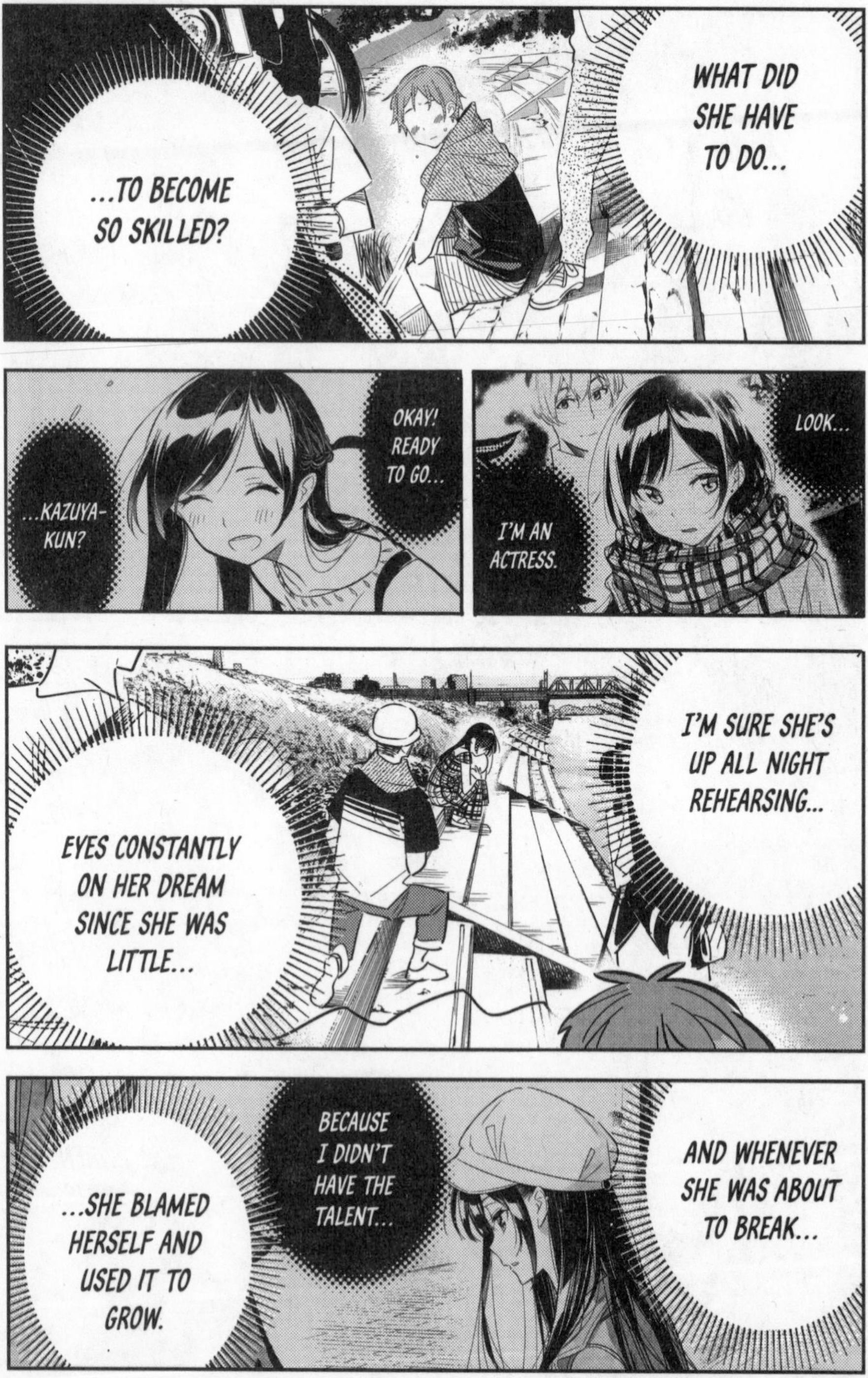
WHAT DID SHE HAVE TO DO...
...TO BECOME SO SKILLED?
LOOK...
I'M AN ACTRESS.
OKAY! READY TO GO...
...KAZUYA-KUN?
I'M SURE SHE'S UP ALL NIGHT REHEARSING...
EYES CONSTANTLY ON HER DREAM SINCE SHE WAS LITTLE...
AND WHENEVER SHE WAS ABOUT TO BREAK...
BECAUSE I DIDN'T HAVE THE TALENT...
...SHE BLAMED HERSELF AND USED IT TO GROW.

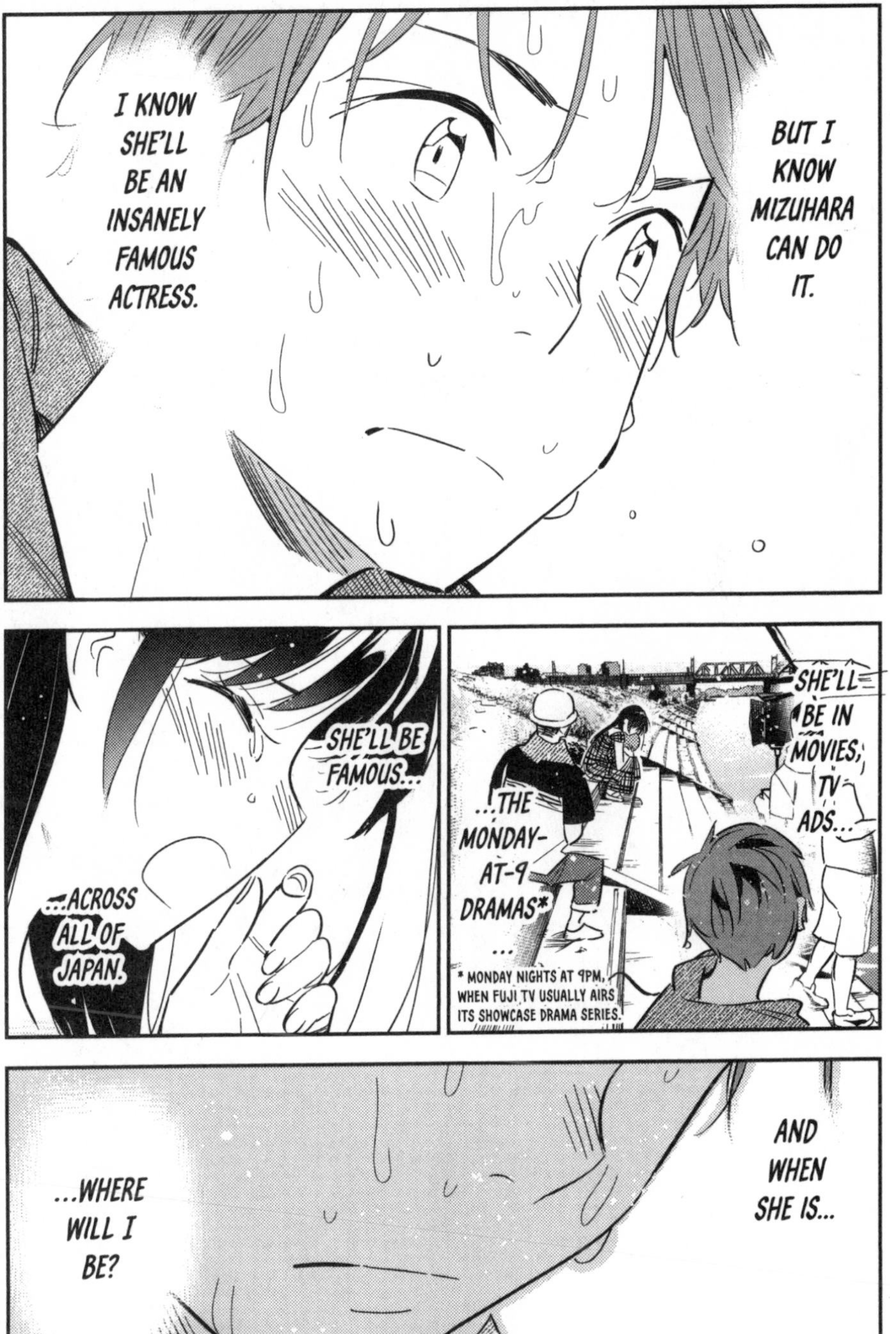
BUT I KNOW MIZUHARA CAN DO IT.
I KNOW SHE'LL BE AN INSANELY FAMOUS ACTRESS.
SHE'LL BE IN MOVIES, TV ADS...
...THE MONDAY-AT-9 DRAMAS* ...
* MONDAY NIGHTS AT 9PM, WHEN FUJI TV USUALLY AIRS ITS SHOWCASE DRAMA SERIES.
SHE'LL BE FAMOUS...
...ACROSS ALL OF JAPAN.
AND WHEN SHE IS...
...WHERE WILL I BE?

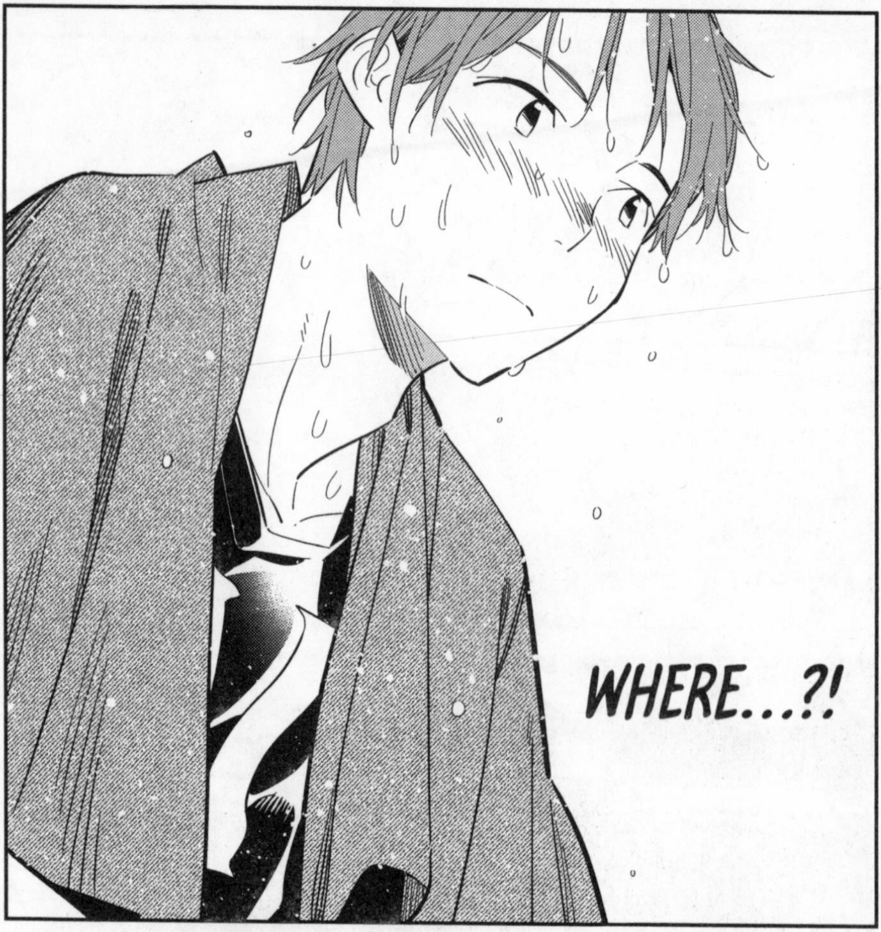
WHERE...?!
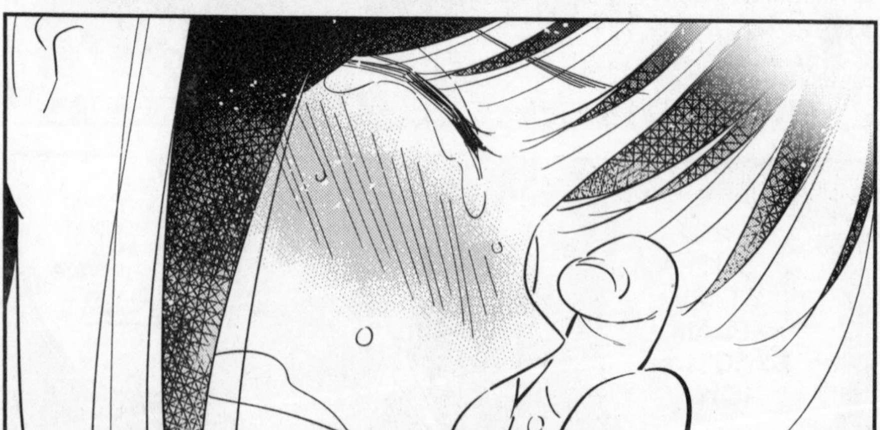
TO BE CONTINUED!

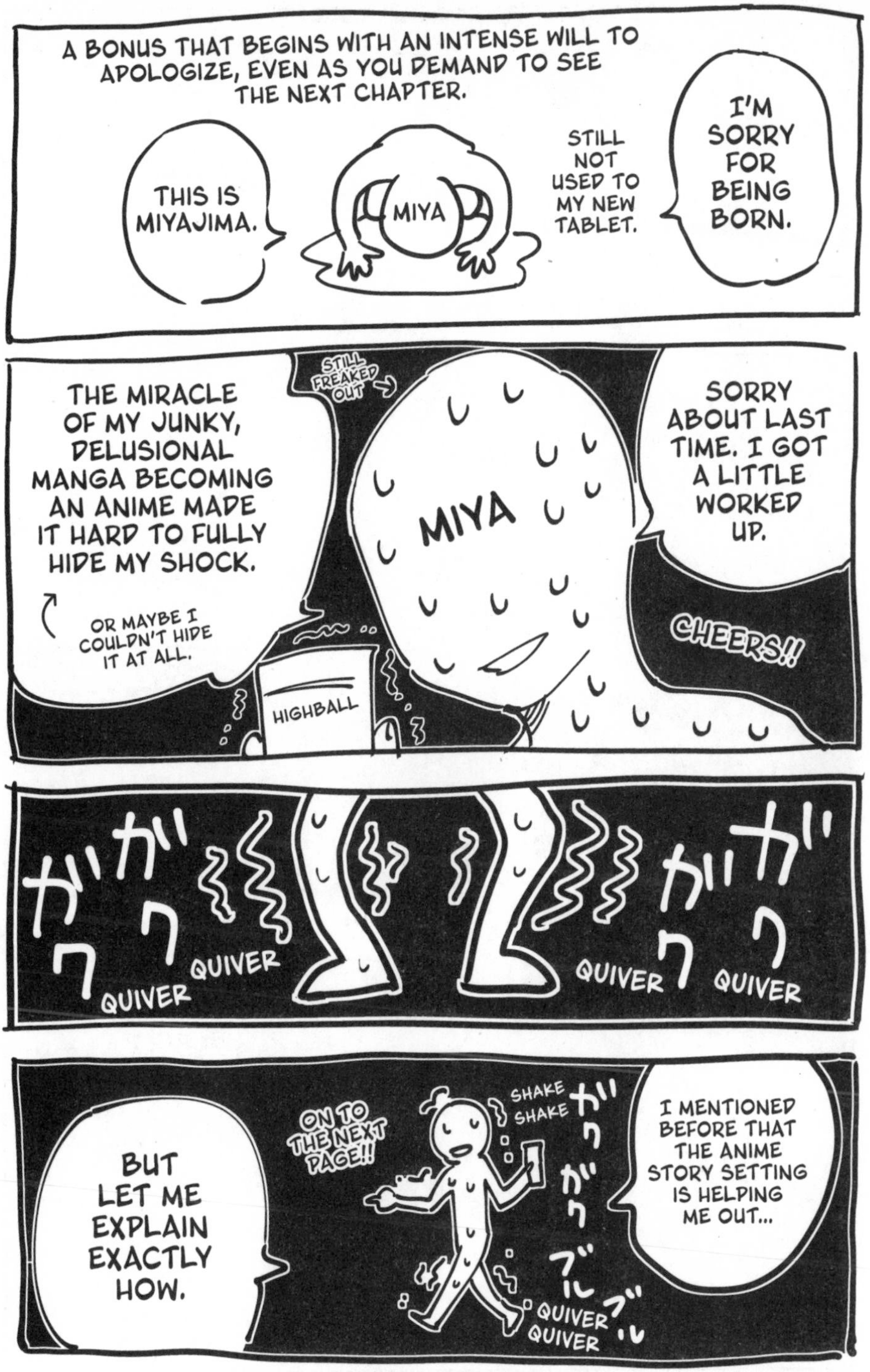
A BONUS THAT BEGINS WITH AN INTENSE WILL TO APOLOGIZE, EVEN AS YOU DEMAND TO SEE THE NEXT CHAPTER.
I'M SORRY FOR BEING BORN.
STILL NOT USED TO MY NEW TABLET.
MIYA
THIS IS MIYAJIMA.
SORRY ABOUT LAST TIME. I GOT A LITTLE WORKED UP.
CHEERS!!
STILL FREAKED OUT
MIYA
THE MIRACLE OF MY JUNKY, DELUSIONAL MANGA BECOMING AN ANIME MADE IT HARD TO FULLY HIDE MY SHOCK.
OR MAYBE I COULDN'T HIDE IT AT ALL.
HIGHBALL
QUIVER
QUIVER
QUIVER
QUIVER
I MENTIONED BEFORE THAT THE ANIME STORY SETTING IS HELPING ME OUT...
SHAKE SHAKE
QUIVER QUIVER
ON TO THE NEXT PAGE!!
BUT LET ME EXPLAIN EXACTLY HOW.

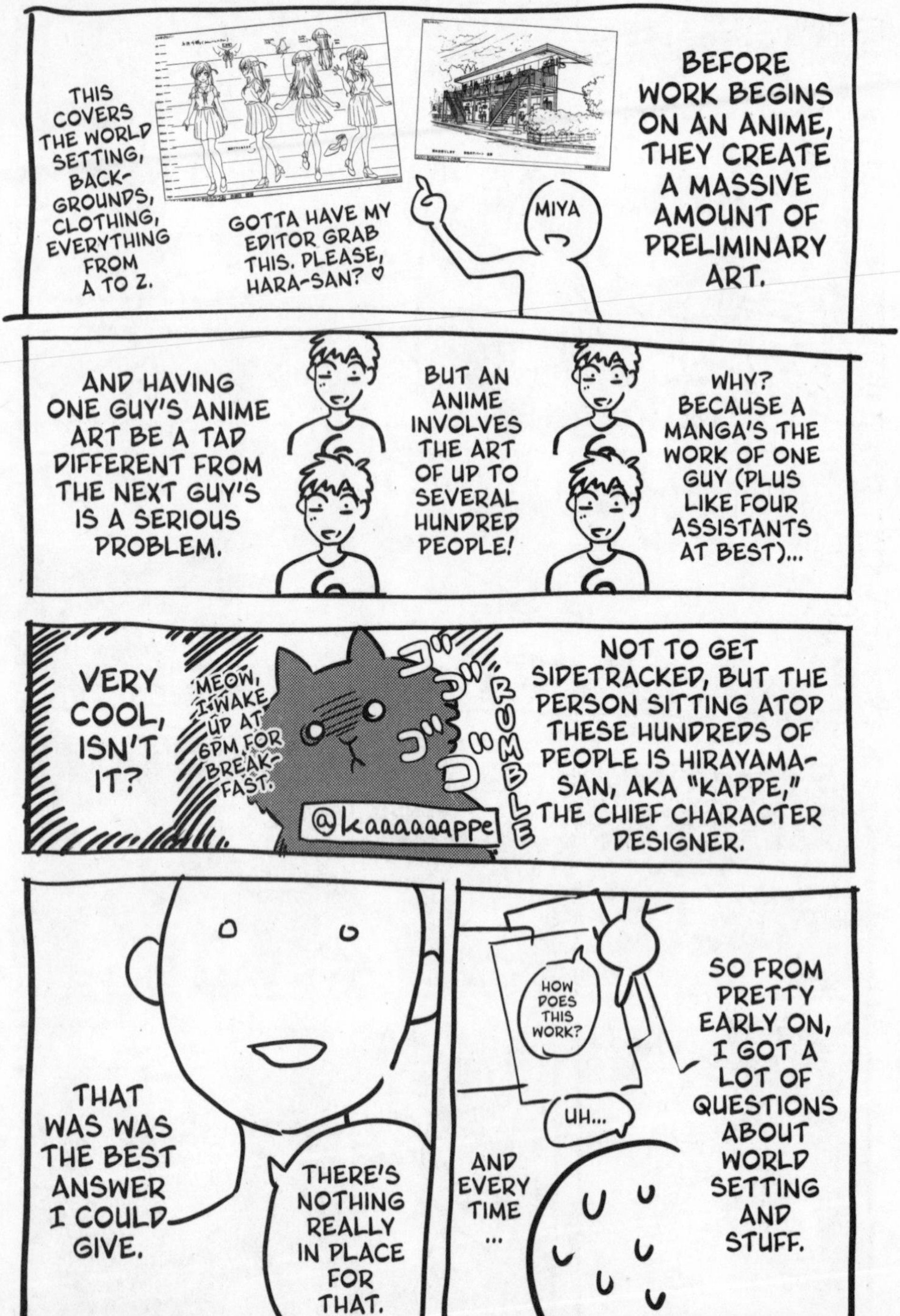
BEFORE WORK BEGINS ON AN ANIME, THEY CREATE A MASSIVE AMOUNT OF PRELIMINARY ART.
MIYA
GOTTA HAVE MY EDITOR GRAB THIS. PLEASE, HARA-SAN? ♡
THIS COVERS THE WORLD SETTING, BACK-GROUNDS, CLOTHING, EVERYTHING FROM A TO Z.
WHY? BECAUSE A MANGA'S THE WORK OF ONE GUY (PLUS LIKE FOUR ASSISTANTS AT BEST)...
BUT AN ANIME INVOLVES THE ART OF UP TO SEVERAL HUNDRED PEOPLE!
AND HAVING ONE GUY'S ANIME ART BE A TAD DIFFERENT FROM THE NEXT GUY'S IS A SERIOUS PROBLEM.
NOT TO GET SIDETRACKED, BUT THE PERSON SITTING ATOP THESE HUNDREDS OF PEOPLE IS HIRAYAMA-SAN, AKA "KAPPE," THE CHIEF CHARACTER DESIGNER.
RUMBLE
@kaaaaaappe
MEOW, I WAKE UP AT 6PM FOR BREAK-FAST.
VERY COOL, ISN'T IT?
SO FROM PRETTY EARLY ON, I GOT A LOT OF QUESTIONS ABOUT WORLD SETTING AND STUFF.
HOW DOES THIS WORK?
UH...
AND EVERY TIME ...
THERE'S NOTHING REALLY IN PLACE FOR THAT.
THAT WAS WAS THE BEST ANSWER I COULD GIVE.

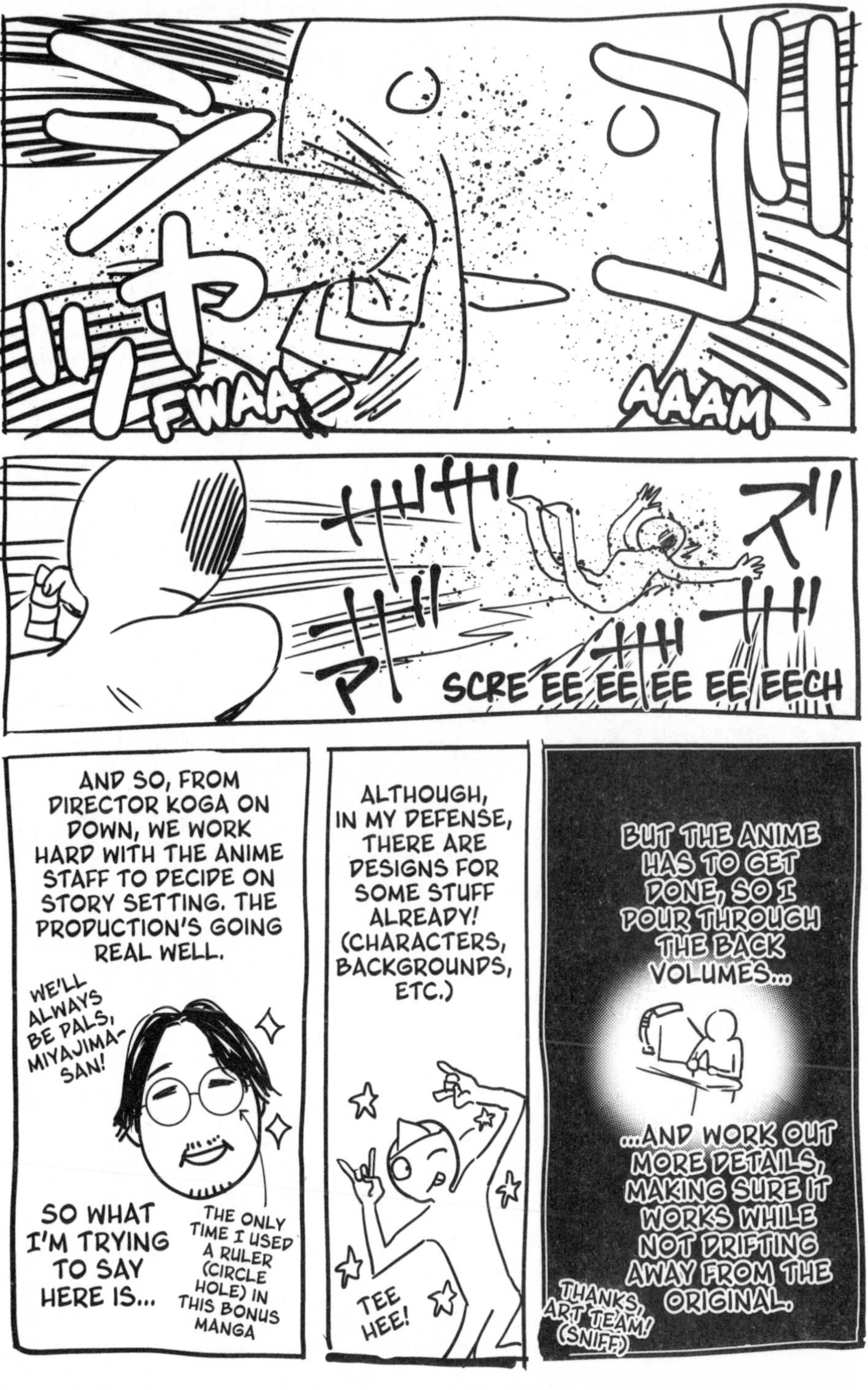
FWAAA
AAAM
SCRE EE EE EE EE EECH
AND SO, FROM DIRECTOR KOGA ON DOWN, WE WORK HARD WITH THE ANIME STAFF TO DECIDE ON STORY SETTING. THE PRODUCTION'S GOING REAL WELL.
WE'LL ALWAYS BE PALS, MIYAJIMA-SAN!
SO WHAT I'M TRYING TO SAY HERE IS...
THE ONLY TIME I USED A RULER (CIRCLE HOLE) IN THIS BONUS MANGA
ALTHOUGH, IN MY DEFENSE, THERE ARE DESIGNS FOR SOME STUFF ALREADY! (CHARACTERS, BACKGROUNDS, ETC.)
TEE HEE!
BUT THE ANIME HAS TO GET DONE, SO I POUR THROUGH THE BACK VOLUMES...
...AND WORK OUT MORE DETAILS, MAKING SURE IT WORKS WHILE NOT DRIFTING AWAY FROM THE ORIGINAL.
THANKS, ART TEAM! (SNIFF)

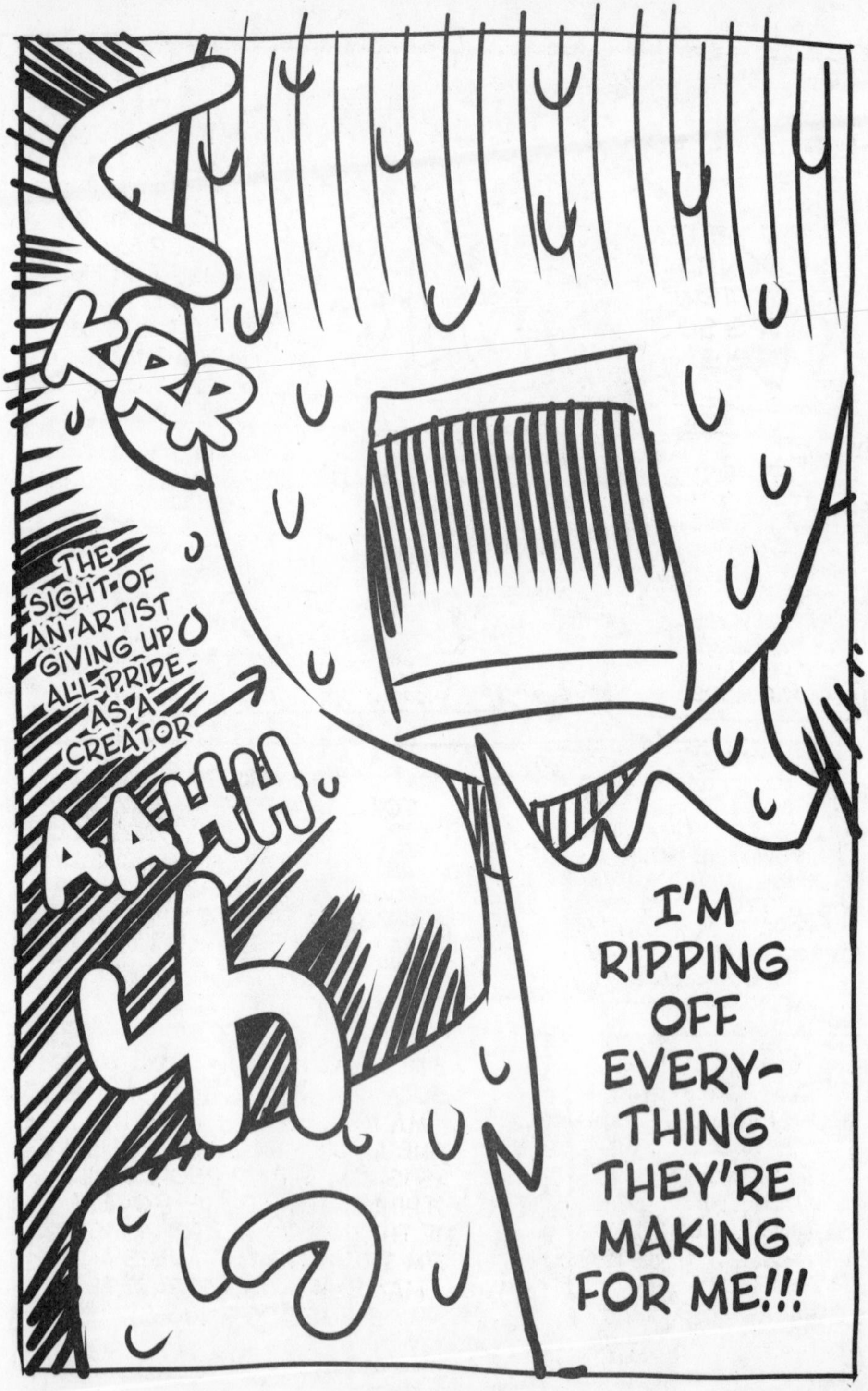
KRR
THE SIGHT OF AN ARTIST GIVING UP ALL PRIDE AS A CREATOR
AAHH
I'M RIPPING OFF EVERY-THING THEY'RE MAKING FOR ME!!!

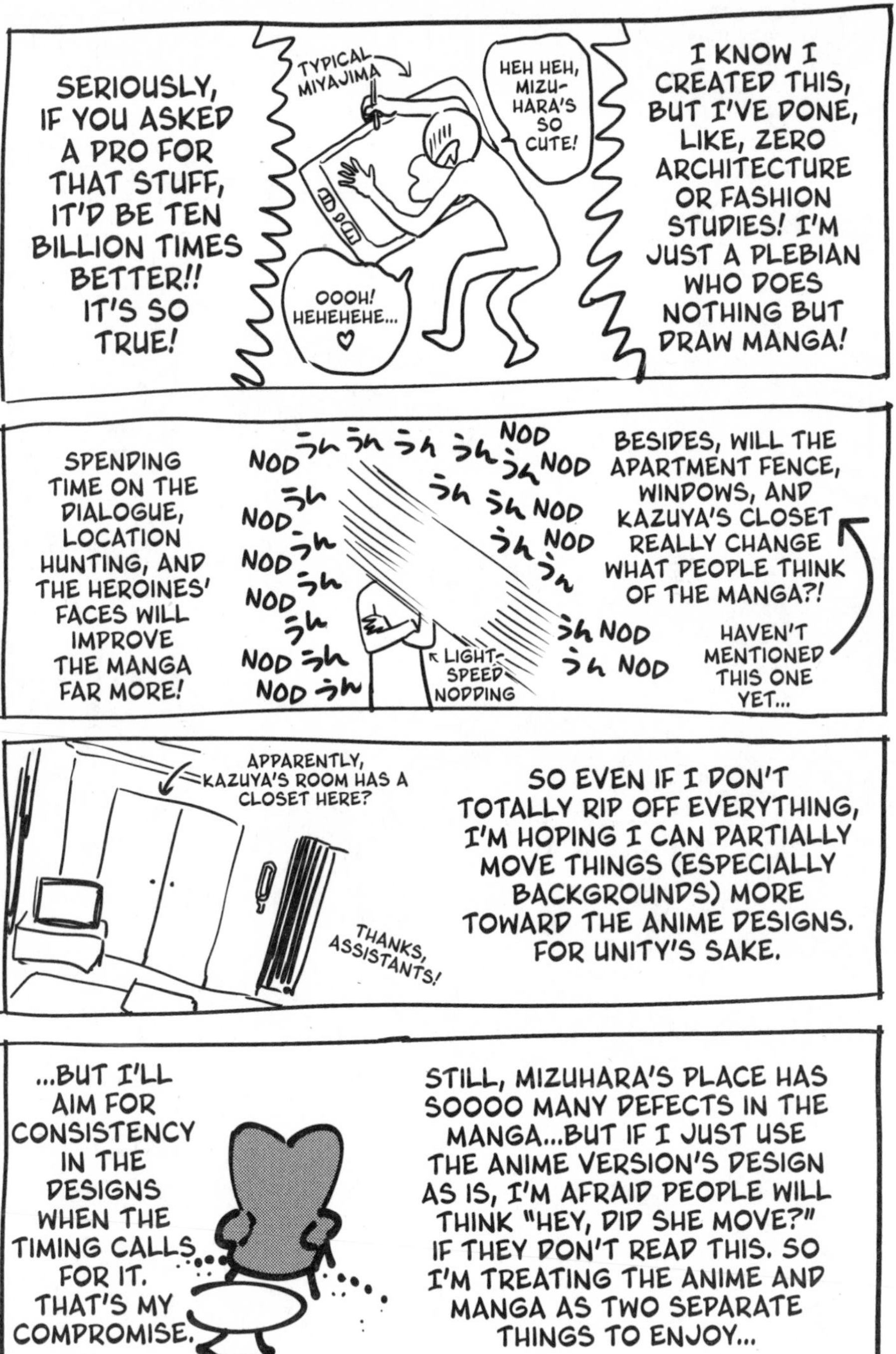
I KNOW I CREATED THIS, BUT I'VE DONE, LIKE, ZERO ARCHITECTURE OR FASHION STUDIES! I'M JUST A PLEBIAN WHO DOES NOTHING BUT DRAW MANGA!
HEH HEH, MIZUHARA'S SO CUTE!
TYPICAL MIYAJIMA
OOOH! HEHEHEHE... ♡
SERIOUSLY, IF YOU ASKED A PRO FOR THAT STUFF, IT'D BE TEN BILLION TIMES BETTER!! IT'S SO TRUE!
BESIDES, WILL THE APARTMENT FENCE, WINDOWS, AND KAZUYA'S CLOSET REALLY CHANGE WHAT PEOPLE THINK OF THE MANGA?!
HAVEN'T MENTIONED THIS ONE YET...
NOD うん NOD うん NOD うん NOD うん
LIGHT-SPEED NODDING
SPENDING TIME ON THE DIALOGUE, LOCATION HUNTING, AND THE HEROINES' FACES WILL IMPROVE THE MANGA FAR MORE!
SO EVEN IF I DON'T TOTALLY RIP OFF EVERYTHING, I'M HOPING I CAN PARTIALLY MOVE THINGS (ESPECIALLY BACKGROUNDS) MORE TOWARD THE ANIME DESIGNS. FOR UNITY'S SAKE.
APPARENTLY, KAZUYA'S ROOM HAS A CLOSET HERE?
THANKS, ASSISTANTS!
STILL, MIZUHARA'S PLACE HAS SOOOO MANY DEFECTS IN THE MANGA...BUT IF I JUST USE THE ANIME VERSION'S DESIGN AS IS, I'M AFRAID PEOPLE WILL THINK "HEY, DID SHE MOVE?" IF THEY DON'T READ THIS. SO I'M TREATING THE ANIME AND MANGA AS TWO SEPARATE THINGS TO ENJOY...
...BUT I'LL AIM FOR CONSISTENCY IN THE DESIGNS WHEN THE TIMING CALLS FOR IT. THAT'S MY COMPROMISE.

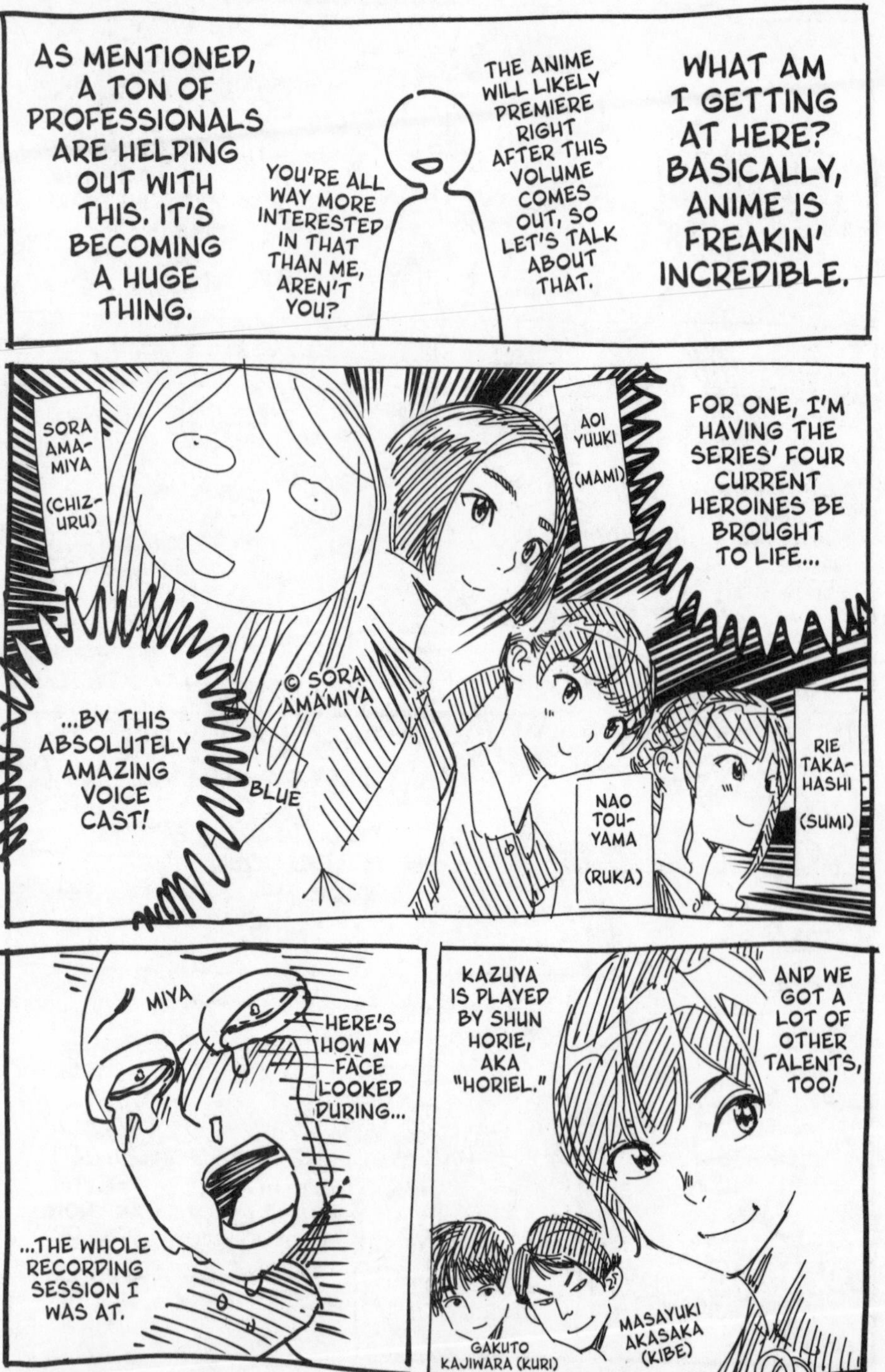
WHAT AM I GETTING AT HERE? BASICALLY, ANIME IS FREAKIN' INCREDIBLE.
THE ANIME WILL LIKELY PREMIERE RIGHT AFTER THIS VOLUME COMES OUT, SO LET'S TALK ABOUT THAT.
YOU'RE ALL WAY MORE INTERESTED IN THAT THAN ME, AREN'T YOU?
AS MENTIONED, A TON OF PROFESSIONALS ARE HELPING OUT WITH THIS. IT'S BECOMING A HUGE THING.
FOR ONE, I'M HAVING THE SERIES' FOUR CURRENT HEROINES BE BROUGHT TO LIFE...
AOI YUUKI (MAMI)
RIE TAKAHASHI (SUMI)
NAO TOUYAMA (RUKA)
SORA AMAMIYA (CHIZURU)
© SORA AMAMIYA
BLUE
...BY THIS ABSOLUTELY AMAZING VOICE CAST!
AND WE GOT A LOT OF OTHER TALENTS, TOO!
KAZUYA IS PLAYED BY SHUN HORIE, AKA "HORIEL."
MASAYUKI AKASAKA (KIBE)
GAKUTO KAJIWARA (KURI)
MIYA
HERE'S HOW MY FACE LOOKED DURING...
...THE WHOLE RECORDING SESSION I WAS AT.

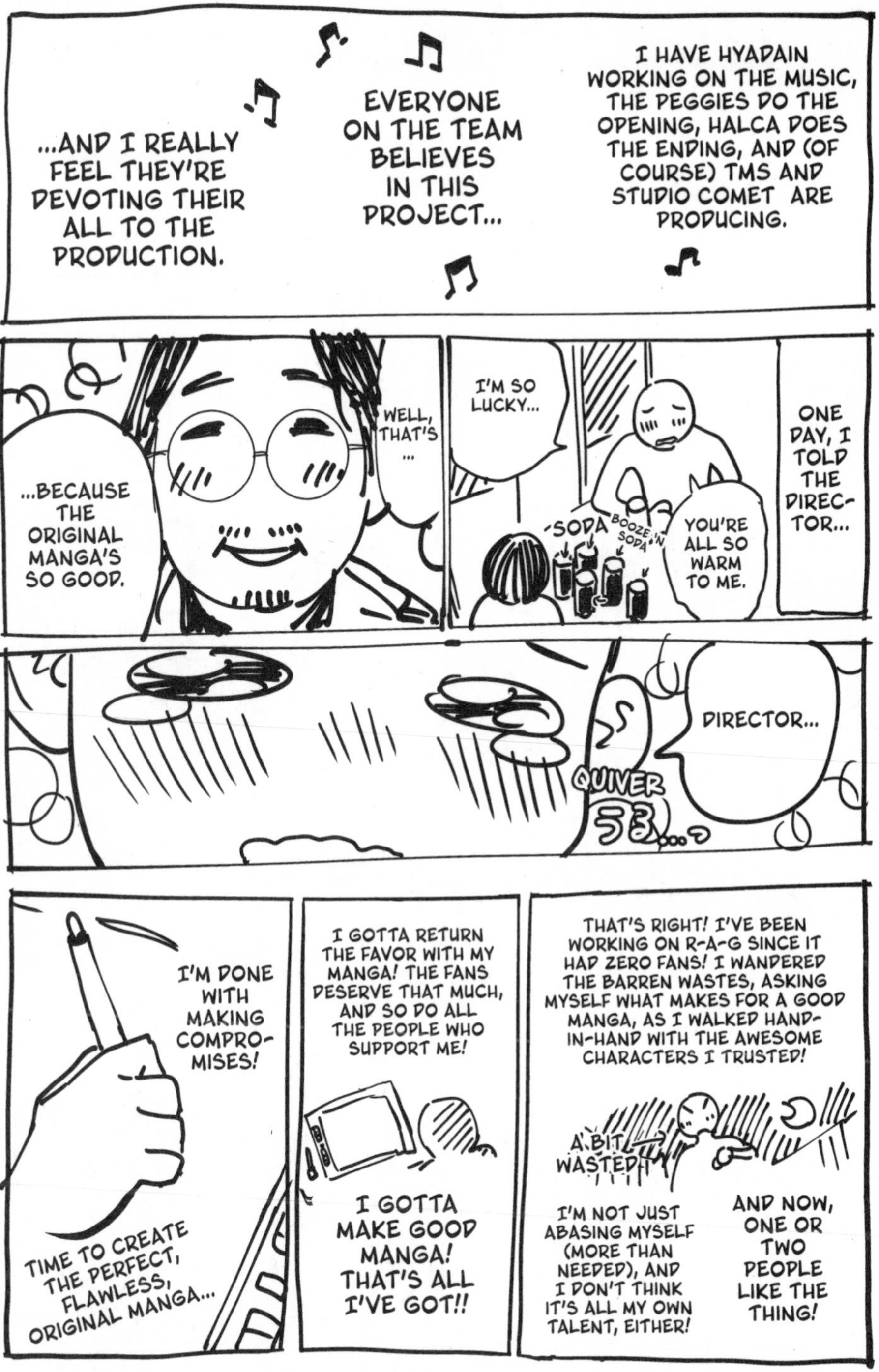
I HAVE HYADAIN WORKING ON THE MUSIC, THE PEGGIES DO THE OPENING, HALCA DOES THE ENDING, AND (OF COURSE) TMS AND STUDIO COMET ARE PRODUCING.
EVERYONE ON THE TEAM BELIEVES IN THIS PROJECT...
...AND I REALLY FEEL THEY'RE DEVOTING THEIR ALL TO THE PRODUCTION.
ONE DAY, I TOLD THE DIREC-TOR...
YOU'RE ALL SO WARM TO ME.
BOOZE IN SODA
SODA
I'M SO LUCKY...
WELL, THAT'S ...
...BECAUSE THE ORIGINAL MANGA'S SO GOOD.
DIRECTOR...
QUIVER
THAT'S RIGHT! I'VE BEEN WORKING ON R-A-G SINCE IT HAD ZERO FANS! I WANDERED THE BARREN WASTES, ASKING MYSELF WHAT MAKES FOR A GOOD MANGA, AS I WALKED HAND-IN-HAND WITH THE AWESOME CHARACTERS I TRUSTED!
A BIT WASTED
AND NOW, ONE OR TWO PEOPLE LIKE THE THING!
I'M NOT JUST ABASING MYSELF (MORE THAN NEEDED), AND I DON'T THINK IT'S ALL MY OWN TALENT, EITHER!
I GOTTA RETURN THE FAVOR WITH MY MANGA! THE FANS DESERVE THAT MUCH, AND SO DO ALL THE PEOPLE WHO SUPPORT ME!
I GOTTA MAKE GOOD MANGA! THAT'S ALL I'VE GOT!!
I'M DONE WITH MAKING COMPRO-MISES!
TIME TO CREATE THE PERFECT, FLAWLESS, ORIGINAL MANGA...

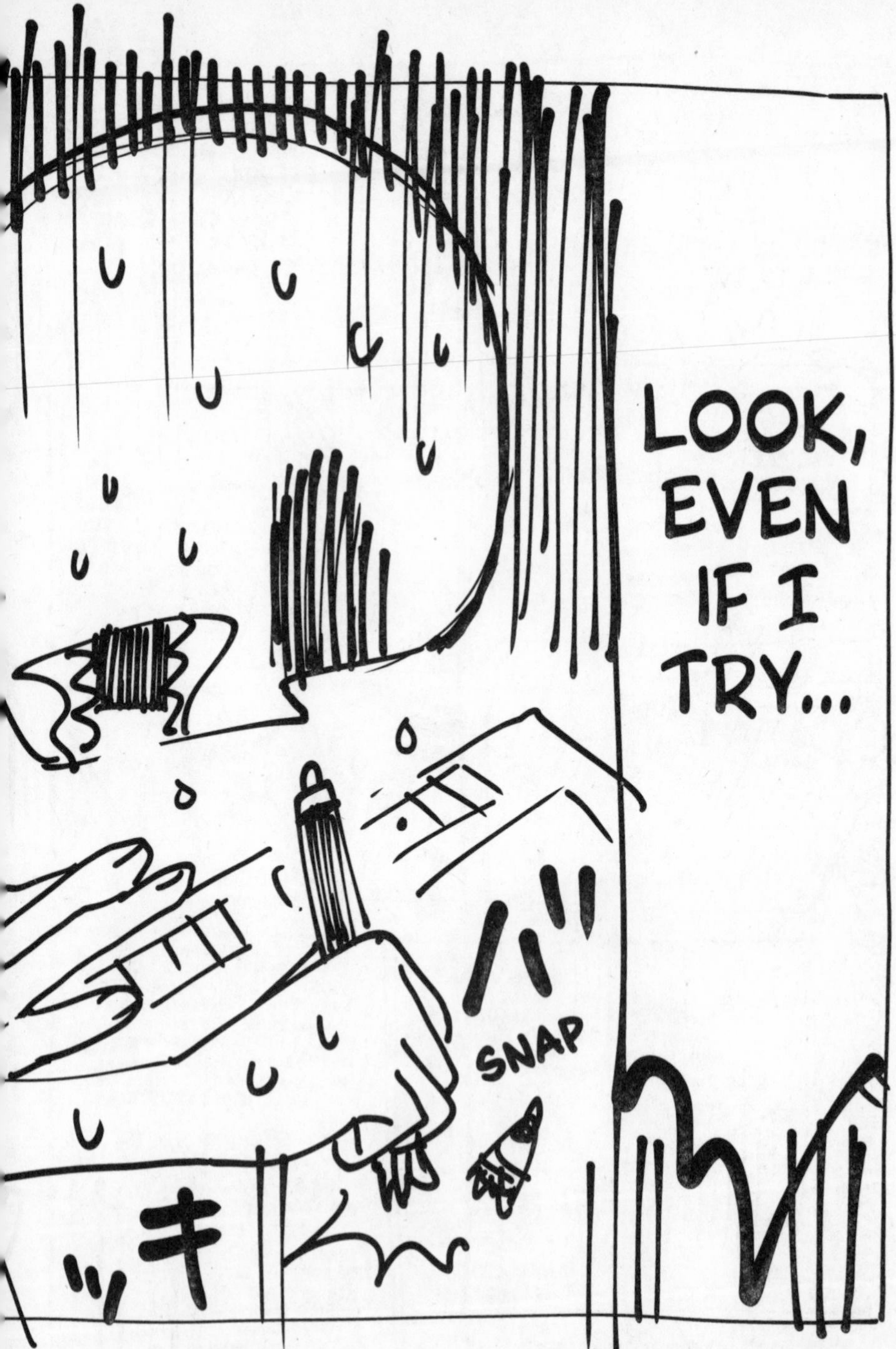
LOOK, EVEN IF I TRY...
SNAP

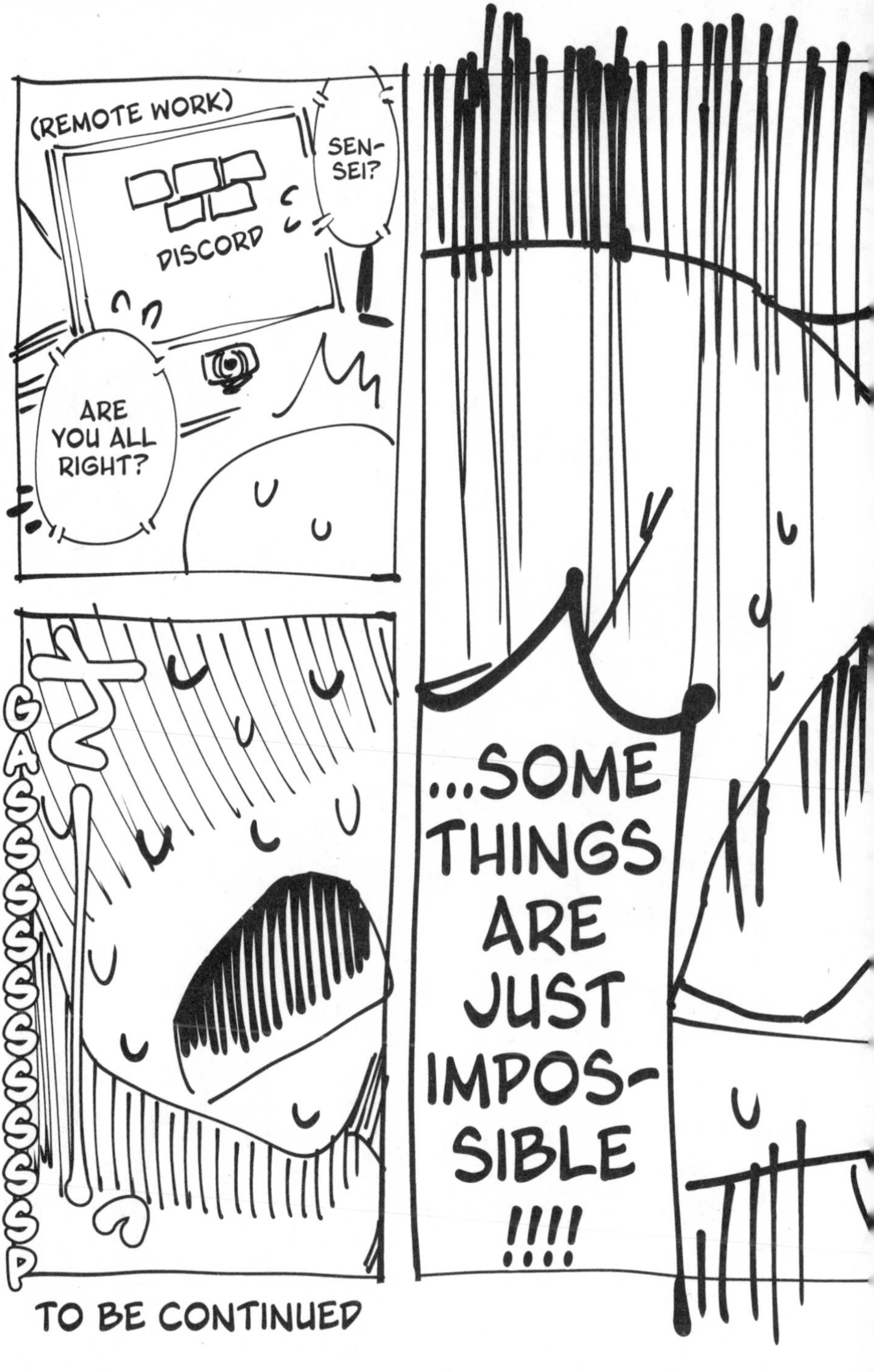
...SOME THINGS ARE JUST IMPOSSIBLE!!!!
(REMOTE WORK)
SENSEI?
DISCORD
ARE YOU ALL RIGHT?
GASSSSSSSSSSSP

TO BE CONTINUED

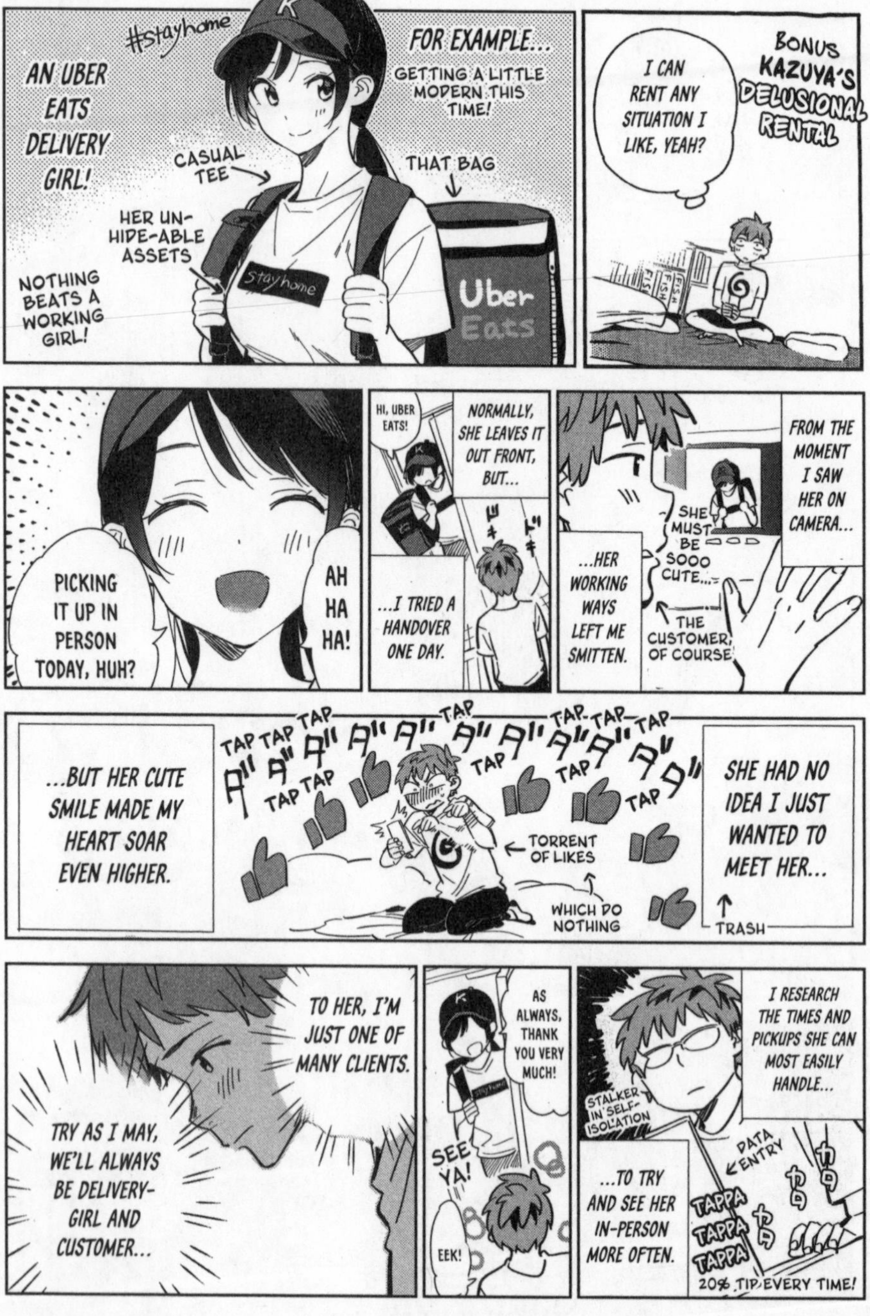
BONUS KAZUYA'S DELUSIONAL RENTAL
I CAN RENT ANY SITUATION I LIKE, YEAH?
FISH
FOR EXAMPLE...
GETTING A LITTLE MODERN THIS TIME!
#stayhome
AN UBER EATS DELIVERY GIRL!
THAT BAG
CASUAL TEE
HER UN-HIDE-ABLE ASSETS
stayhome
NOTHING BEATS A WORKING GIRL!
Uber Eats
FROM THE MOMENT I SAW HER ON CAMERA...
SHE MUST BE SOOO CUTE...
...HER WORKING WAYS LEFT ME SMITTEN.
THE CUSTOMER, OF COURSE
NORMALLY, SHE LEAVES IT OUT FRONT, BUT...
HI, UBER EATS!
...I TRIED A HANDOVER ONE DAY.
AH HA HA!
PICKING IT UP IN PERSON TODAY, HUH?
SHE HAD NO IDEA I JUST WANTED TO MEET HER...
TRASH
TAP TAP TAP TAP TAP TAP TAP TAP TAP TAP TAP TAP
TORRENT OF LIKES
WHICH DO NOTHING
...BUT HER CUTE SMILE MADE MY HEART SOAR EVEN HIGHER.
I RESEARCH THE TIMES AND PICKUPS SHE CAN MOST EASILY HANDLE...
DATA ENTRY
TAPPA TAPPA TAPPA
STALKER IN SELF-ISOLATION
...TO TRY AND SEE HER IN-PERSON MORE OFTEN.
20% TIP EVERY TIME!
AS ALWAYS, THANK YOU VERY MUCH!
SEE YA!
EEK!
TO HER, I'M JUST ONE OF MANY CLIENTS.
TRY AS I MAY, WE'LL ALWAYS BE DELIVERY-GIRL AND CUSTOMER...

RENT-A-GIRLFRIEND STAFF: A, MIIKE, MIKURA, TEMAENO, MINATO.

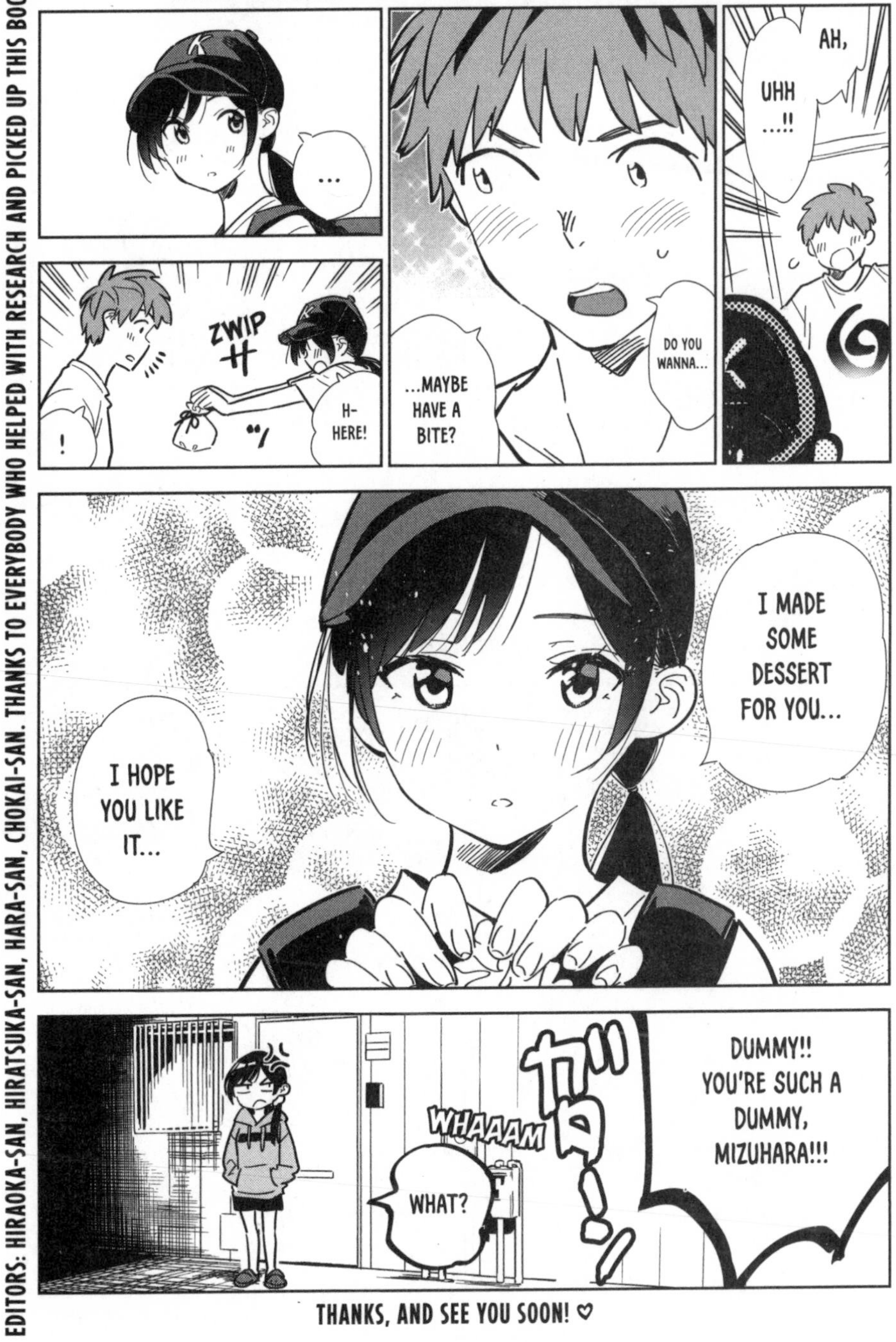
AH,
UHH ...!!
DO YOU WANNA...
...MAYBE HAVE A BITE?
...
ZWIP
H-HERE!
!
I MADE SOME DESSERT FOR YOU...
I HOPE YOU LIKE IT...
DUMMY!! YOU'RE SUCH A DUMMY, MIZUHARA!!!
WHAAAM
WHAT?

THANKS, AND SEE YOU SOON! ♡

EDITORS: HIRAOKA-SAN, HIRATSUKA-SAN, HARA-SAN, CHOKAI-SAN. THANKS TO EVERYBODY WHO HELPED WITH RESEARCH AND PICKED UP THIS BOOK!!

Young characters and steampunk setting, like *Howl's Moving Castle* and *Battle Angel Alita*

Beyond the Clouds
The Girl Who Fell From the Sky
BY
Nicke
VOLUME
01
KC
KODANSHA
COMICS

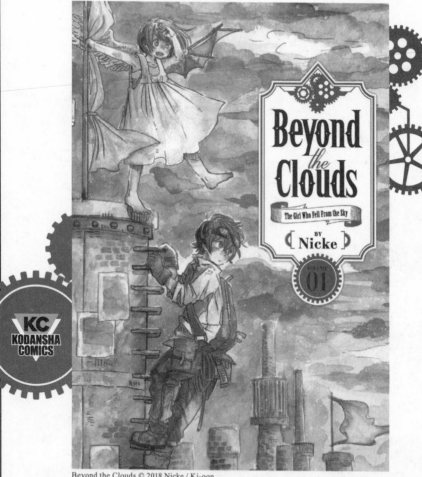

Beyond the Clouds © 2018 Nicke / Ki-oon

A boy with a talent for machines and a mysterious girl whose wings he's fixed will take you beyond the clouds! In the tradition of the high-flying, resonant adventure stories of Studio Ghibli comes a gorgeous tale about the longing of young hearts for adventure and friendship!

A SMART, NEW ROMANTIC COMEDY FOR FANS OF *SHORTCAKE CAKE* AND *TERRACE HOUSE!*

A romance manga starring high school girl Meeko, who learns to live on her own in a boarding house whose living room is home to the odd (but handsome) Matsunaga-san. She begins to adjust to her new life away from her parents, but Meeko soon learns that no matter how far away from home she is, she's still a young girl at heart — especially when she finds herself falling for Matsunaga-san.

PERFECT WORLD

Rie Aruga

> A TOUCHING NEW SERIES ABOUT LOVE AND COPING WITH DISABILITY

An office party reunites Tsugumi with her high school crush Itsuki. He's realized his dream of becoming an architect, but along the way, he experienced a spinal injury that put him in a wheelchair. Now Tsugumi's rekindled feelings will butt up against prejudices she never considered — and Itsuki will have to decide if he's ready to let someone into his heart...

"Depicts with great delicacy and courage the difficulties some with disabilities experience getting involved in romantic relationships... Rie Aruga refuses to romanticize, pushing her heroine to face the reality of disability. She invites her readers to the same tasks of empathy, knowledge and recognition."
—Slate.fr

"An important entry [in manga romance]... The emotional core of both plot and characters indicates thoughtfulness... [Aruga's] research is readily apparent in the text and artwork, making this feel like a real story."
—Anime News Network

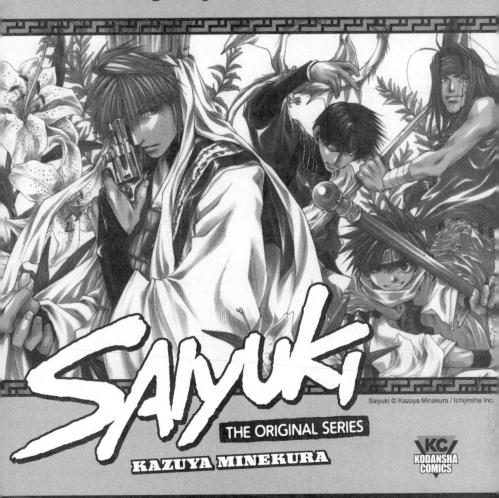

The beloved characters from *Cardcaptor Sakura* return in a brand new, reimagined fantasy adventure!

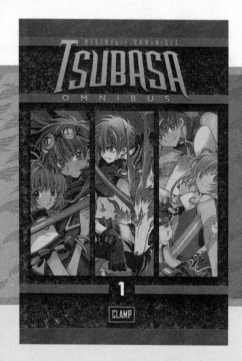

"[*Tsubasa*] takes readers on a fantastic ride that only gets more exhilarating with each successive chapter." —Anime News Network

In the Kingdom of Clow, an archaeological dig unleashes an incredible power, causing Princess Sakura to lose her memories. To save her, her childhood friend Syaoran must follow the orders of the Dimension Witch and travel alongside Kurogane, an unrivaled warrior; Fai, a powerful magician; and Mokona, a curiously strange creature, to retrieve Sakura's dispersed memories!

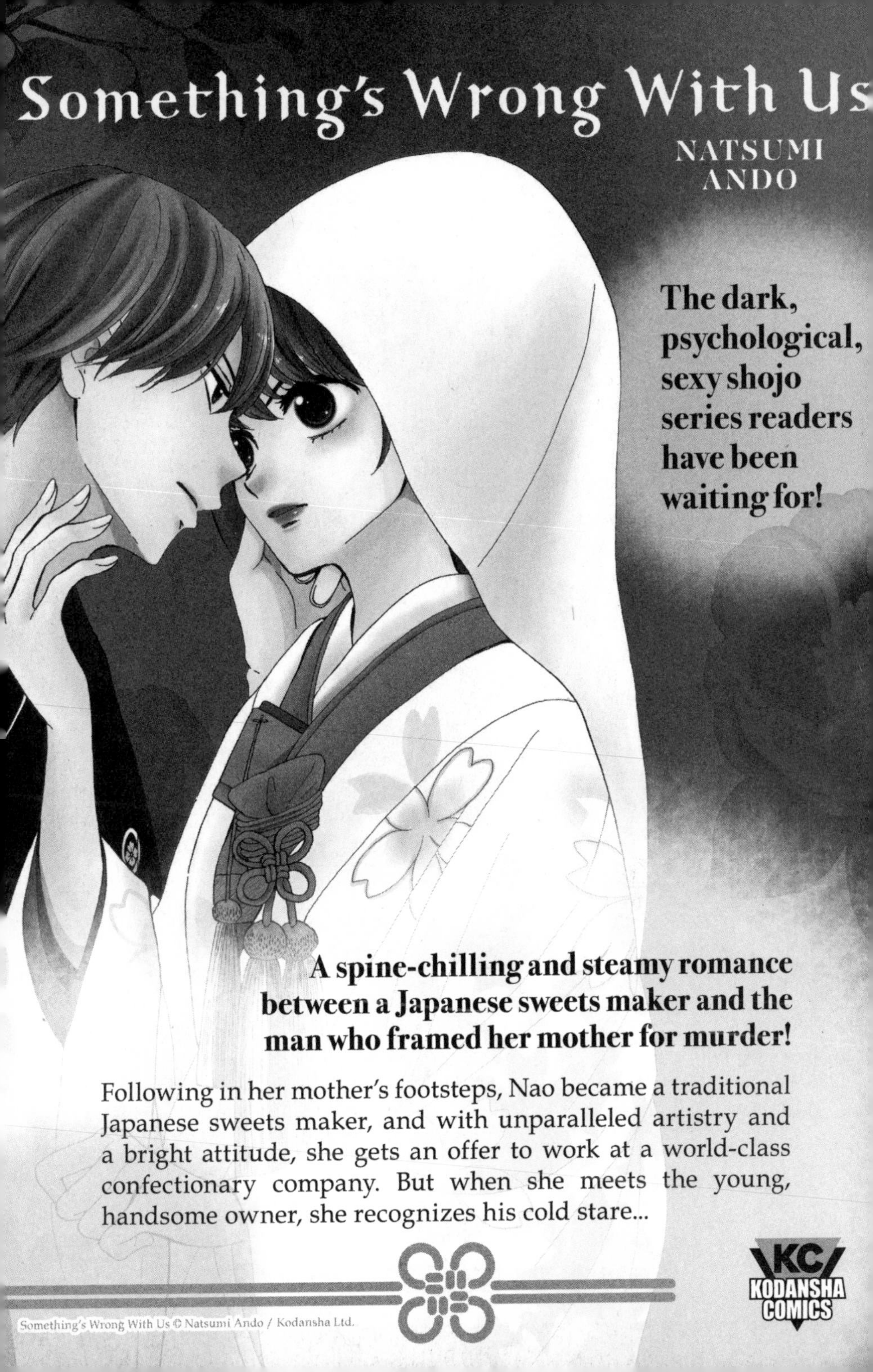
Something's Wrong With Us
NATSUMI ANDO
The dark, psychological, sexy shojo series readers have been waiting for!
A spine-chilling and steamy romance between a Japanese sweets maker and the man who framed her mother for murder!
Following in her mother's footsteps, Nao became a traditional Japanese sweets maker, and with unparalleled artistry and a bright attitude, she gets an offer to work at a world-class confectionary company. But when she meets the young, handsome owner, she recognizes his cold stare...
KC KODANSHA COMICS
Something's Wrong With Us © Natsumi Ando / Kodansha Ltd.

"Clever, sassy, and original....*xxxHOLiC* has the inherent hallmarks of a runaway hit."
—NewType magazine

Beautifully seductive artwork and uniquely Japanese depictions of the supernatural will hypnotize CLAMP fans!

Kimihiro Watanuki is haunted by visions of ghosts and spirits. He seeks help from a mysterious woman named Yuko, who claims she can help. However, Watanuki must work for Yuko in order to pay for her aid. Soon Watanuki finds himself employed in Yuko's shop, where he sees things and meets customers that are stranger than anything he could have ever imagined.

The adorable new odd-couple cat comedy manga from the creator of the beloved *Chi's Sweet Home*, in full color!

Praise for Chi's Sweet Home

"Nearly impossible to turn away... a true all-ages title that anyone, young or old, cat lover or not, will enjoy. The stories will bring a smile to your face and warm your heart."

—School Library Journal

Sue & Tai-chan

Konami Kanata

Sue is an aging housecat who's looking forward to living out her life in peace... but her plans change when the mischievous black tomcat Tai-chan enters the picture! Hey! Sue never signed up to be a catsitter! *Sue & Tai-chan* is the latest from the reigning meow-narch of cute kitty comics, Konami Kanata.

KC
KODANSHA
COMICS

The art-deco cyberpunk classic from the creators of *xxxHOLiC* and *Cardcaptor Sakura*!

"Starred Review.
This experimental
sci-fi work from
CLAMP reads like a
romantic version of
AKIRA."
—Publishers Weekly

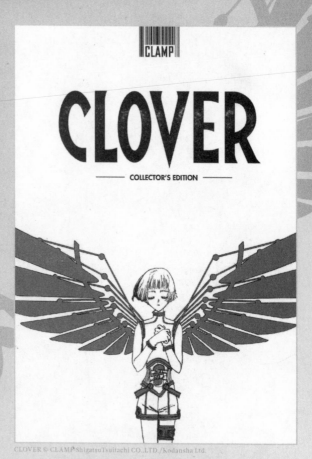

CLOVER © CLAMP ShigatsuTsuitachi CO.,LTD./Kodansha Ltd.

Su was born into a bleak future, where the government keeps tight control over children with magical powers—codenamed "Clovers." With Su being the only "four-leaf" Clover in the world, she has been kept isolated nearly her whole life. Can ex-military agent Kazuhiko deliver her to the happiness she seeks? Experience the complete series in this hardcover edition, which also includes over twenty pages of ravishing color art!

KC
KODANSHA
COMICS

THE SWEET SCENT OF LOVE IS IN THE AIR! FOR FANS OF OFFBEAT ROMANCES LIKE *WOTAKOI*

Sweat and Soap © Kintetsu Yamada / Kodansha Ltd.

In an office romance, there's a fine line between sexy and awkward... and that line is where Asako — a woman who sweats copiously — meets Koutarou — a perfume developer who can't get enough of Asako's, er, scent. Don't miss a romcom manga like no other!

KC
KODANSHA
COMICS

THE WORLD OF CLAMP!

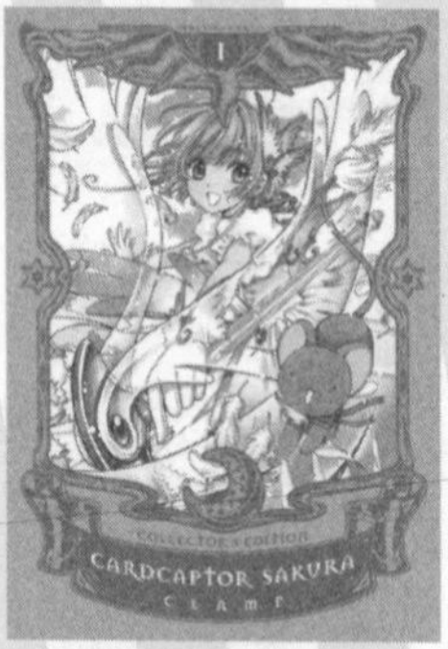
1
COLLECTOR'S EDITION
CARDCAPTOR SAKURA
CLAMP

Cardcaptor Sakura
Collector's Edition

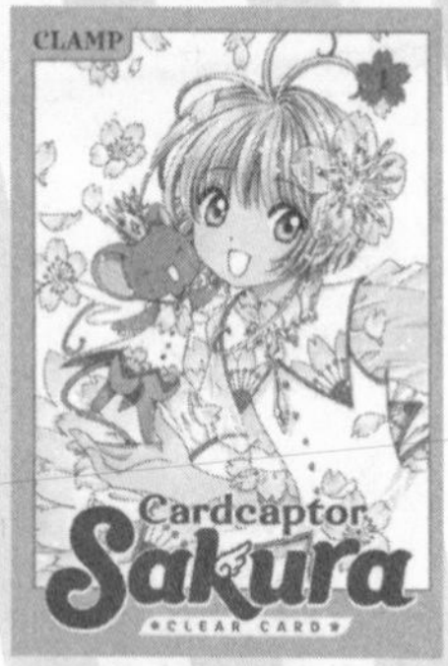
CLAMP
Cardcaptor
Sakura
CLEAR CARD

Cardcaptor Sakura:
Clear Card

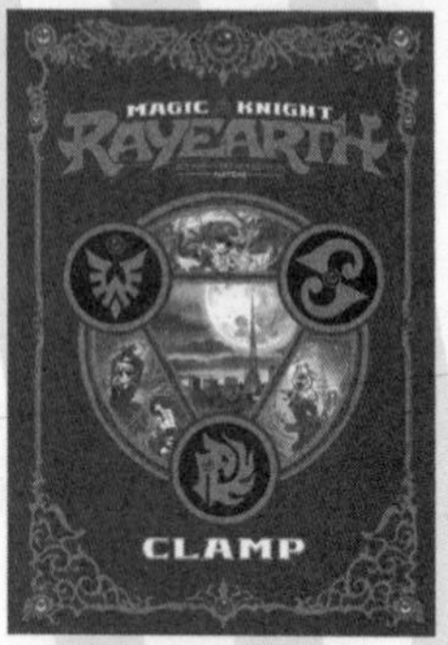
MAGIC KNIGHT
RAYEARTH
CLAMP

Magic Knight Rayearth
25th Anniversary Box Set

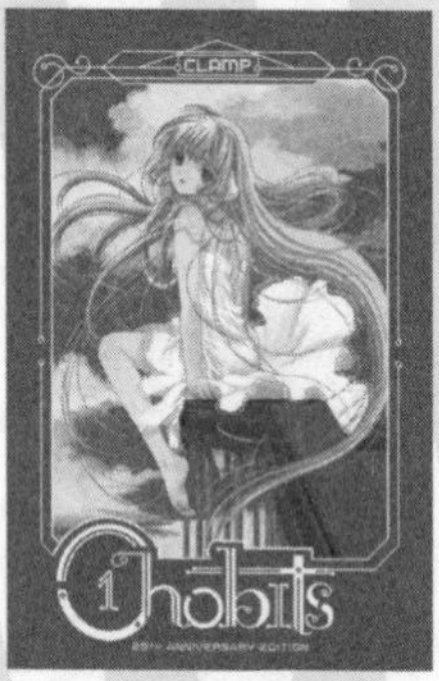
CLAMP
1 Chobits

Chobits

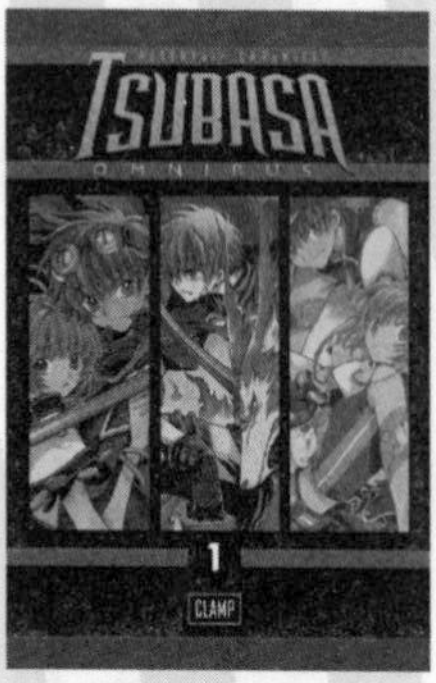
TSUBASA
OMNIBUS
1
CLAMP

TSUBASA Omnibus

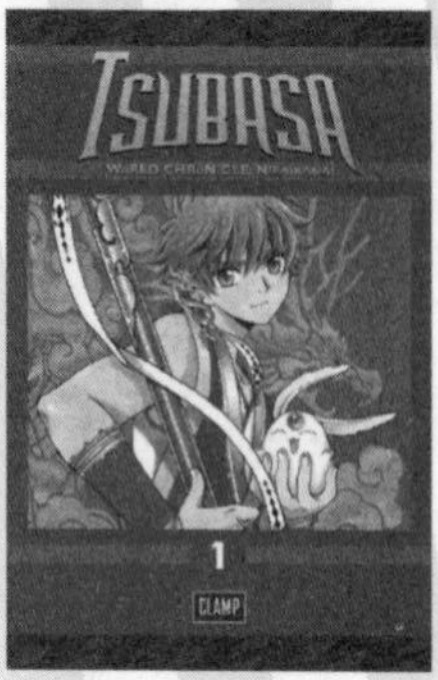
TSUBASA
1
CLAMP

TSUBASA WoRLD CHRoNiCLE

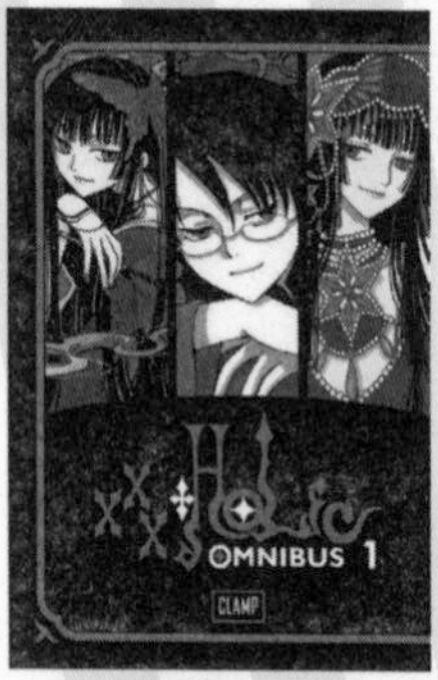
xxxHOLiC
OMNIBUS 1
CLAMP

xxxHOLiC Omnibus

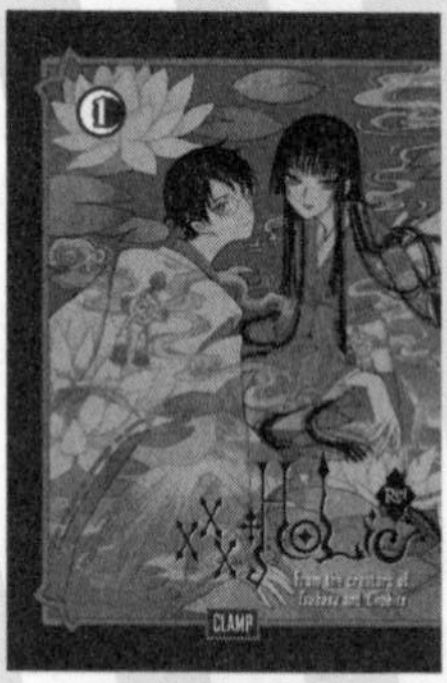
xxxHOLiC
CLAMP

xxxHOLiC Rei

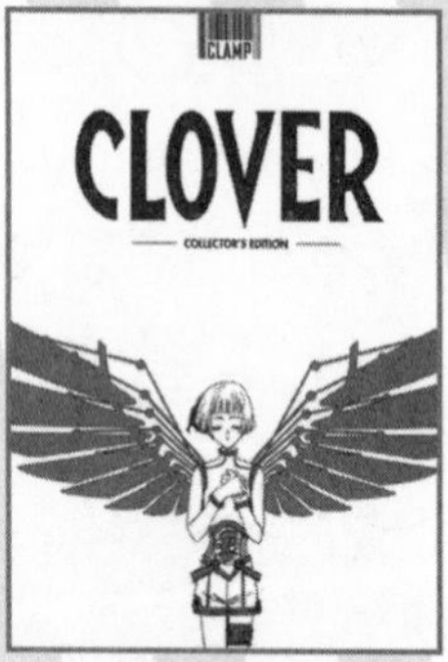
CLAMP
CLOVER
COLLECTOR'S EDITION

CLOVER Collector's Edition

KC KODANSHA COMICS

Kodansha Comics welcomes you to explore the expansive world of CLAMP, the all-female artist collective that has produced some of the most acclaimed manga of the century. Our growing catalog includes icons like *Cardcaptor Sakura* and *Magic Knight Rayearth*, each crafted with CLAMP's one-of-a-kind style and characters!

A Kodansha Comics Trade Paperback Original
Rent-A-Girlfriend 15 copyright © 2020 Reiji Miyajima
English translation copyright © 2022 Reiji Miyajima

Published in the United States by Kodansha Comics, an imprint of Kodansha USA Publishing, LLC, New York.

Publication rights for this English edition arranged through Kodansha Ltd., Tokyo.

First published in Japan in 2020 by Kodansha Ltd., Tokyo as *Kanojo, okarishimasu*, volume 15.

ISBN 978-1-64651-534-9

Printed in the United States of America.

www.kodansha.us

1st Printing
Translation: Kevin Gifford
Lettering: Paige Pumphrey
Editing: Jordan Blanco
Kodansha Comics edition cover design by Phil Balsman

Publisher: Kiichiro Sugawara

Director of publishing services: Ben Applegate
Director of publishing operations: Dave Barrett
Associate director of publishing operations: Stephen Pakula
Publishing services managing editors: Madison Salters, Alanna Ruse, with Grace Chen
Production manager: Jocelyn O'Dowd
Logo and character art ©Kodansha USA Publishing, LLC